Religion and Media in America

Religion and Media in America

Anthony Hatcher

LEXINGTON BOOKS
Lanham • Boulder • New York • London

Published by Lexington Books
An imprint of The Rowman & Littlefield Publishing Group, Inc.
4501 Forbes Boulevard, Suite 200, Lanham, Maryland 20706
www.rowman.com

Unit A, Whitacre Mews, 26-34 Stannary Street, London SE11 4AB

British Library Cataloguing in Publication Information Available

Library of Congress Cataloging-in-Publication Data

Names: Hatcher, Anthony Earl, author.
Title: Religion and Media in America / Anthony Hatcher.
Description: Lanham : Lexington Books, 2018. | Includes bibliographical references and index.
Identifiers: LCCN 2018009121 (print) | LCCN 2018011809 (ebook) | ISBN 9781498514453 (Electronic) | ISBN 9781498514446 (cloth : alk. paper) | ISBN 9781498514460 (pbk. : alk. paper)
Subjects: LCSH: Christianity and culture--United States. | Mass media and culture--United States. | Mass media in religion--United States. | Mass media--Religious aspects.
Classification: LCC BR517 (ebook) | LCC BR517 .H385 2018 (print) | DDC 261.5/2--dc23
LC record available at https://lccn.loc.gov/2018009121

Printed in the United States of America

Contents

Acknowledgements

When I joined the faculty of Elon University in the fall of 2002, Brad Hamm, then-associate dean of the School of Communications, asked me if I could design a Religion and Media class that would be ready for the spring semester. Brad knew of my scholarly interest in religion, media, and culture, and I am grateful for his support leading to the creation of an academic course that has defined my professional life. I also owe much to the students I have taught in the class over the years. The questions they raised, and their continued engagement with me on the topic post-graduation, sparked my own learning and exploration. The ever-evolving class has led to many papers and presentations, and now this volume. Thanks to the encouragement of Communications Dean Paul Parsons and Elon's generous research sabbatical and course release policy, I was able to complete the book.

I am indebted to my Elon colleagues in the School of Communications, as well as those in Religious Studies, who helped shape this manuscript in one way or another. At the risk of overlooking a name or two, my sincere thanks to David Copeland; Harlen Makemson; Rich Landesberg; Don Grady; Thomas Nelson; Jeffrey Pugh; Geoffrey Claussen; Brian Pennington; Lynn Huber; and Jan Fuller.

Jordan Lockhart was an eager first year Communications student when she asked if she could serve as my research assistant. I gave her the task of searching for articles on Moral Mondays, and she exceeded all expectations. Many of the early news stories that made up the basis for reconstructing a history of the movement came from Jordan's digging.

I wish to extend gratitude to the people featured in this book who consented to interviews: Ole Anthony; Carey Lewis Arban; John W. Baer; Robert Darden; Jenn Gotzon; Harry Guetzlaff; Simon Jenkins; William Leonard; Sister Rose Pacatte; Adam She; and Jonathan Wilson-Hartgrove. Thanks especially to Actors, Models, & Talent for Christ for allowing me to observe their audition process.

Nicolette Amstutz, my editor at Lexington Books, kept me on track throughout the months of writing, editing, and rewriting. This book would not have been completed without her guidance, professionalism, wisdom, and kindness. Many thanks to assistant editor Jessica Thwaite, who always responded cheerfully and knowledgeably to my endless questions. In addition, I am grateful to the anonymous external reviewers of my early drafts for the excellent feedback. From pointing out research I had overlooked to offering solid editorial suggestions, the reviewers were instrumental in making this a better book. If there are errors, they are mine.

On a personal note, I am indebted to my family and friends for unending love and motivation when I needed it most. My daughter Katie, my mother Geraldine, and my brother Dana were among my biggest cheerleaders for this project. Dana passed away in the middle of the writing, but always asked about my progress up until the end.

Last on this page but first in my heart is my wife Tricia who, with unflagging love and bottomless patience, serves as inspiration on good days and bad.

Introduction

America is a nation with the soul of a church.
—G. K. Chesterton[1] (1874–1936)

THE PURPOSE OF THIS BOOK

Religion and Media in the Digital Age is a qualitative study of six distinct ways religion, especially Christianity, has been woven into American popular and civic culture. Under the broad headings of *civil religion, religion and entertainment,* and *sacred and profane media,* this book explores the methods by which Christianity both adapts to and is affected by new media forms. From the Catholic mass order of service featuring ads for local businesses, to the praise band at a megachurch, to the flag pin-wearing politician praising God from the pulpit and selling his latest book in the narthex, media saturate religion, and vice versa.

Christian leaders and communities have long created subcultures for transmitting their values. Christian phone directories for finding like-minded service providers have been distributed in many cities. At Washington, D.C.'s Museum of the Bible and Kentucky's Creation Museum, the Christian founders of each institution provide safe spaces to educate the family about faith, as well as offer alternative religious histories of the world. Catholic schools have a long educational tradition, and recent trends have seen an uptick in conservative Protestant private schools, charter schools, and homeschooling, although homeschooling is gradually becoming more diverse.[2]

The United States at times seems overrun with Christian influencers, many of whom have attempted to "Christianize" public secular culture, disregarding America's increasingly pluralistic composition. The role is occasionally handed down to an influencer's progeny. Franklin Graham, son of prom-

ix

inent evangelist Billy Graham, and Jerry Falwell Jr., son of Moral Majority founder Jerry Falwell, to give two examples, are not only carrying on their fathers' traditions of mingling politics with religion, but have staked out cultural positions that in many cases are more rigid and extreme in their evangelical and conservative fervor. Falwell, president of conservative Christian Liberty University, which was founded by his father, encouraged students of legal age to exercise their Second Amendment right to purchase a handgun to keep on campus to protect themselves. Graham, commenting on the decision by the Boy Scouts to allow gay members and troop leaders, has said, "It's not an organization that's fit to exist."[3]

Religious progressives have historically staked out positions supporting abolition, labor reform, and civil rights. In each of these political and social movements, clergy and other religious leaders played major roles. Those on the Religious Left often find themselves in a posture of protest. As religion reporter Jack Jenkins wrote, "Recent years have seen their public influence eclipsed by the rising influence of the Religious Right, however, even as they continued to fight for immigrants, gun violence prevention, and LGBTQ rights—often as a crucial component of larger progressive campaigns."[4] Fusion movements of unlikely allies, such as Muslim and Jewish groups as well as Christian churches, frequently work together against bigotry and violence.

Despite lamentations from the faithful that religious influence, particularly Christian influence, is waning in the United States, religion remains prominent in everyday cultural life. "Religion" in this book will be considered applicable to many forms of public expression, but will be viewed through a primarily Christian effect lens. When exploring interactions among Christianity, spirituality, media, and popular culture, questions arise such as: What do we mean by religion? What strain of Christianity is under discussion? What tensions have historically existed between Catholics and Protestants? What do people mean by spirituality? What is the definition of popular culture? Why does this matter to Christians, non-Christians, and the nonreligious?

RELIGION IN THE EVERYDAY

Religion permeates American daily life, such as politics, news, and entertainment, and sometimes all three at the same time. There was such a moment in a December 2015 NBC television special featuring British outdoor adventurer and *Running Wild* reality TV star Bear Grylls. Grylls's guest for the episode, set in the Alaskan wilderness, was then-president Barack Obama. After sharing a meal of found salmon that had been partially chewed by an animal, hiking through the wilderness (with camera crew and Secret Service in tow, but out of sight), and pointedly discussing the ravages of climate change, the one-hour show was about to come to a close when Grylls asked President Obama a question:

"Can I pray for you before you go?"

"Absolutely," the president responded.

Heads bowed, Grylls said a prayer for Obama. "Lord I thank you for the president's strength of courage and character. Bless and protect his work and his family. Forgive us when we fall short, and help us to be strong in you. Amen."[5]

In a personal essay following the episode published in the London *Sunday Times*, Grylls, who is open about his Christian faith, wrote, "We discussed the challenges of juggling being a parent with work, our hopes and fears, and at one point we even prayed together. That moment was special."[6]

"The prayer that Bear prayed was a very simple, gentle prayer, which probably did only last 10 seconds," observed John McKenna of the National Service Committee for the Charismatic Renewal in England. "But to see one man lay his hand on another's shoulder (never mind the fact that this man is president of the United States), is something that you never see on mainstream TV in a primetime slot."[7]

Earlier that year, Grylls told the British website *Christian Today*,

I really, desperately have learnt in my life that I need my faith, and I'm just not strong enough on my own. I try to start every day by kneeling down and saying, "Lord Jesus, I ain't got it all right, and I'm nervous about today. I will give it my all, but will you help me?" It's never more complicated than that. I probably don't go to church enough, but my faith is a quiet, strong backbone in my life, and the glue to our family.[8]

Bear Grylls's public prayer moment with Barack Obama, also a professed Christian, was all the more noteworthy in light of detractors who criticized the president for his ties to controversial United Church of Christ minister the Reverend Jeremiah Wright, and/or spread rumors that Obama is a "secret Muslim."[9]

Other presidents have been forced to deal publicly with criticism on religious grounds. Senator John F. Kennedy faced religious battles as the Democratic candidate a half century earlier, primarily from Protestant ministers, going on to become the first president who was a practicing Catholic. Kennedy cited press descriptions of his candidacy in defending himself from spurious charges. "For contrary to common newspaper usage, I am not the Catholic candidate for president. I am the Democratic Party's candidate for president, who happens also to be a Catholic. I do not speak for my church on public matters, and the church does not speak for me."[10]

The accusation that Kennedy would follow papal dictates over the U.S. Constitution was merely another chapter in a long line of tensions between Protestant and Catholic Christians. As American Studies scholar Thomas J. Carty wrote in his book *A Catholic in the White House? Religion, Politics, and John F. Kennedy's Presidential Campaign,*

> Although Catholic Americans assimilated easily during the new nation's first forty years, some native-born Protestants created anti-Catholic conspiracy theories and organizations from the 1830s through the 1850s. In response to an influx of Catholic immigrants in the nineteenth century, the Native American Party and the American Protective Association alleged clerical conspiracies to seduce and violate women and undermine American liberty. Portraying Catholicism as a menacing, alien threat to U.S. ideals, these groups sought to ban Catholics from political office. The Ku Klux Klan revived this message in the 1920s, and evangelicals within various Protestant denominations, such as the Southern Baptists, echoed these arguments. Al Smith's appeal to religious and racial minorities, however, revealed the potential for unity among non-Protestant, nonwhite Americans.[11]

In President Kennedy's inaugural address, delivered January 20, 1961, he said, "We observe today not a victory of party but a celebration of freedom—symbolizing an end as well as a beginning—signifying renewal as well as change. For I have sworn before you and Almighty God the same solemn oath our forbears prescribed nearly a century and three-quarters ago."[12] Reflecting on Kennedy's inaugural in a now familiar essay some six years later, sociologist Robert N. Bellah pondered Kennedy's reference to "Almighty God":

> Considering the separation of church and state, how is a president justified in using the word "God" at all? The answer is that the separation of church and state has not denied the political realm a religious dimension. Although matters of personal religious belief, worship, and association are considered to be strictly private affairs, there are, at the same time, certain common elements of religious orientation that the great majority of Americans share. These have played a crucial role in the development of American institutions and still provide a religious dimension for the whole fabric of American life, including the political sphere. This public religious dimension is expressed in a set of beliefs, symbols, and rituals that I am calling *American civil religion* [emphasis added]. The inauguration of a president is an important ceremonial event in this religion. It reaffirms, among other things, the religious legitimation of the highest political authority.[13]

Bellah notes that "certain common elements of religious orientation" are shared by "the great majority of Americans." This common civil religion, as he called it, is not a religion confined by Christianity, Judaism, Islam, Buddhism, or other specific tradition or denomination. "This religion—there seems no other word for it—while not antithetical to and indeed sharing much in common with Christianity," Bellah concludes, "was neither sectarian nor in any specific sense Christian. At a time when the society was overwhelmingly Christian, it seems unlikely that this lack of Christian reference was meant to spare the feelings of the tiny non-Christian minority. Rather, the civil religion expressed what those who set the precedents felt was appropriate under the circumstances."[14]

Writing in the mid-1960s, sociologist Peter L. Berger observed, "Since the socially significant 'relevance' of religion is primarily in the private sphere, consumer preference reflects the 'needs' of this sphere. This means that religion can more easily be marketed if it can be shown to be 'relevant' to private life than if it is advertised as entailing specific applications to the large public institutions."[15]

In his book, *The Sacred Canopy: Elements of a Sociological Theory of Religion* (1969), Berger examined the historical meaning of secularization in society, leading up to a contemporary definition: "By secularization we mean the process by which sectors of society and culture are removed from the domination of religious institutions and symbols." In the West, Berger wrote, secularization manifested itself by the removal of education from ecclesiastical authority, and the separation of church and state in public life. As religion is further removed from science, the arts, and other cultural areas, "there is a secularization of consciousness," and "an increasing number of individuals who look upon the world and their own lives without the benefit of religious interpretations."[16]

A half century later in their study, "Is the United States a Counterexample to the Secularization Thesis?," sociologists David Voas and Mark Chaves concluded that America is no longer a counterexample to the Western secularization evidenced across Europe and Canada. Voas and Chaves define the *secularization thesis* as "the idea that modernization tends to undermine religious belief and activity." Citing trends rather than current levels of religiosity, the researchers "argue that the United States should not be considered a counterexample for two straightforward empirical reasons. First, American religiosity has in fact been declining for decades, and second, that decline has been produced by the same generational patterns that lie behind religious decline elsewhere in the West: each successive cohort is less religious than the preceding one."[17]

Research has shown that American Millennials, for example, are less religious than their elders. The Pew Research Center's Religious Landscape Study defines Millennials as those born between 1981 and 1996. According to Pew, "Just 27 percent of Millennials say they attend religious services on a weekly basis, a substantially lower share than Baby Boomers (38 percent) and members of the Silent and Greatest generations (51 percent each). Similarly, a smaller share of Millennials say they pray every day compared with those in older generations."[18]

In addition to less religiosity, some research indicates that atheists in the United States may be undercounted. Psychologists Will M. Gervais and Maxine B. Najle write that telephone surveys conducted by established polling organizations such as Pew Research and Gallup place the number of atheists in the United States between 3 percent and 11 percent of the population. "In contrast," Gervais notes, "our most credible indirect estimate is 26 percent (albeit with considerable estimate and method uncertainty)."[19]

Despite increasing secularization and a growing diversity of religions due in part to immigration, American society is still—for now—"overwhelmingly Christian" as Bellah put it.[20] Much of this Christian cultural influence comes from governmental trends. Presidents still swear oaths on Bibles. The U.S. Congress skews heavily Christian and male, and thus is not reflective of national demographics. Ninety-one percent of all members of Congress identified as Christian in 2017.[21] By contrast, 71 percent of Americans identified as Christian, which is still more than two-thirds of the total population.[22]

RELIGION AND MEDIA

In the United States, even non-religious people come at religious understanding through Christianity. Scholar Lynn Schofield Clark has written of the "Protestantization" of the nation. Citing "the paradox of cultural victory and organizational decline" described by sociologist Jay Demerath III, she writes, "Most of us are familiar with the statistics regarding the atrophy of membership in the liberal Protestant church, but, as Demerath points out, we must not overlook the fact that a set of culturally dominant values—a set that includes individualism, freedom, pluralism, tolerance, democracy, and intellectual inquiry—has its roots in the Protestant Reformation and its challenges to the authority of religious institutions."[23]

This *Christian effect* is magnified and perpetuated by digital media use and political realities. With ubiquitous mobile device ownership and an ever-expanding universe of social sharing applications, religious messages can spread as quickly as any other kind of message, and are often more politically controversial and divisive. Bible and Quran apps; denominational websites; pastors, rabbis, and imams on Twitter; and numerous other means of sharing can move religious information around the globe faster than previous generations could ever imagine.

Religions of many stripes use media to spread their gospels, but mainline and evangelical Christians have a tradition of being early adopters of new technologies, from steam printing presses, newspapers, magazines, books, films, and broadcasting, to the internet and mobile media. As communication scholar Quentin J. Schultze has written, "In the 1830s the penny press offered readers an additional source of fairly inexpensive news and human-interest stories in some large American cities. During the same era religious groups created many alternative media. By 1850 there were 181 religious periodicals in the United States, at least half of which were newspapers."[24] As early as the 1920s, "Christian organizations began using radio to preach the Gospel to the nation."[25]

Televangelists, who populated the airwaves from the earliest days of broadcast television through the twentieth century, are still found in large numbers on cable and satellite, as well as on podcasts and live streaming services. CBN's *The 700 Club*, a religious news and talk show hosted by controversial televangelist pioneer Pat Robertson, has been on the air since 1966 and on cable since 1977.[26]

Mediatization theory lays out an argument for considering religion and media as inextricably linked in the digital age. In his seminal study, "The Mediatization of Society: A Theory of Media as Agents of Social and Cultural Change," Stig Hjarvard wrote, "Contemporary society is permeated by the media, to an extent that the media may no longer be conceived of as being separate from cultural and other social institutions."[27] Building on research by others on mediatization's impact on politics and other cultural processes, Hjarvard arrives at a clarifying definition:

> By the mediatization of society, we understand the process whereby society to an increasing degree is submitted to, or becomes dependent on, the media and their logic. This process is characterized by a duality in that the media have become *integrated* into the operations of other social institutions, while they also have acquired the status of social institutions *in their own right*. As a consequence, social interaction—within the respective institutions, between institutions, and in society at large—take place via the media.[28]

Just as Hjarvard asserts that social interactions take place via media, mediatization of religion has made "religion and media" a redundant phrase in the twenty-first century. This is especially true for Christianity.

DEFINING RELIGION

In his book *Spirits Rejoice! Jazz and American Religion*, religion scholar and jazz guitarist Jason C. Bivins writes that, "Religion is not always where we think to look; it moves between and beyond those spaces."[29] While religion may appear in unexpected places, defining it can be an elusive task. As religion and communication scholar Jeffrey Mahan writes,

> *Religion* at first seems simple to describe and then quickly becomes complicated. There are many competing definitions to be found in the discussion of

religion. People often begin with the assumptions of their own religion or those of the dominant religion in their society and then expand their definitions as they become aware of expressions of "religion" that do not quite fit their definition.

Many people see religion as a matter of belief, focusing on one or more central deities, such as the God of Judaism, Islam, or Christianity, or the gods in Hinduism or Greek mythology . . .

Another approach in defining religion is to describe it in the terms of practice and ask what adherents of religion do with their bodies. You can see that they go to particular places that they regard as sacred, they carry out rituals at particular times, and they observe rules about how they should and should not behave.[30]

In 1961, sociologist Gerhard Lenski offered what he labeled as "a moderately inclusive definition of religion." Religion, he wrote, could "be defined as a *system of beliefs about the nature of the force(s) ultimately shaping man's destiny, and the practices associated therewith, shared by the members of a group*"[31] (italics in original).

Anthropologist Clifford Geertz, writing a dozen years after Lenski, offered a two part definition: "(1) a religion is a system of symbols which acts to (2) establish powerful, pervasive, and long-lasting moods and motivations in men [people]. . . ."[32] In his book *Between Heaven and Earth*, religious studies scholar Robert A. Orsi writes, "Religion is the practice of making the invisible visible, of concretizing the order of the universe, the nature of human life and its destiny, and the various dimensions and possibilities of human interiority itself. . ."[33] Mahan observes that "Geertz thinks of religion as a 'system of symbols' that establish particular ways to act in society, while Orsi thinks of religion as a 'practice' related to the interior life and how we understand the meaning of the universe."[34]

In *Religion in the News: Faith and Journalism in American Public Discourse* (1998), Stewart Hoover writes, "Scholars of religion have long held that there are two major ways of defining and understanding it." One focuses on the *essential* or *substantive*, and centers on meaning and practice. The other is *functionalist* and "focuses on the purposes, meanings, and practices that surround those areas of culture we think of as religious."[35] Hoover maintains that this distinction is an "overgeneralization" debated within religious studies, but the functionalist approach to "contemporary religious evolution" is the one that is useful to journalists who often write about practice, symbolism, and ritual.[36]

Widespread use of digital media, including various social networks, has changed the way religious people consume religion, interact with culture, and practice their faith. "To understand the digital culture that is emerging, students of religion, media, and culture look for places where new media, with their capacities for sampling and hybridity, become part of religious practice and ask what religion looks like in these new media spaces," according to Mahan.[37] "Religion is constructed and performed, often with elements sampled from different traditions, even when . . . those traditions reflect religious worldviews that seem to be at odds with one another."[38] *Constructivism theory* shifts the realm of reality from realism to relativism. Constructivists reject "standards by which truth can be universally known," forming their own truth from assorted religions.[39]

Religious syncretism is the blending of multiple belief systems, as when one adopts the consumerist posture of selecting tenets of various religions that he or she finds appealing. The Pew Research Center's Religion & Public Life survey noted in 2009 that,

> Three-in-ten Protestants say they attend multiple types of religious services, including those who attend services at Protestant denominations different than their own; 18 percent of Protestants indicate that they attend non-Protestant services . . .
>
> Roughly one-in-five Catholics say they attend services of at least one faith other than Catholicism, with most of these (18 percent of Catholics overall and 16 percent of white Catholics) saying they attend Protestant services. About one-in-twenty Catholics report attending services at Jewish synagogues (5 percent) and 1 percent say they attend Muslim mosques.[40]

How Americans practice a single faith can also reflect this selective approach. According to Pew, "Roughly half or more of U.S. Catholics say that using contraceptives, living with a romantic partner outside of marriage and remarrying after a divorce without an annulment are *not* sins. And about four-in-ten (39 percent) say homosexual behavior is not a sin."[41] Religion is constructed and adapted by many to fit a particular and preferred lifestyle. Some beliefs are accepted, others ignored. Colloquially, this may be referred to as "cafeteria Christianity." Cafeteria Christians choose a bit of this, and a bit of that, constructing the religion they wish to practice. While other religions may have adherents who do this, such as Reform Jews, Christians vary widely in diversity of practice and belief.

Coinciding with the rise of digital media is the rise of "*nones*," people who do not identify with any faith tradition or denomination. This group consists of atheists, agnostics, and believers who simply do not follow or practice a particular faith. A 2015 Pew demographic survey noted that "the number of religiously unaffiliated adults has increased by roughly 19 million since 2007. There are now approximately 56 million religiously unaffiliated adults in the U.S., and this group—sometimes called religious 'nones'—is more numerous than either Catholics or mainline Protestants. . . . Indeed, the unaffiliated are now second in size only to evangelical Protestants among major religious groups in the U.S."[42]

Although the number of Christians in the United States is declining, particularly among mainline denominations, roughly 7 in 10 Americans still identify with some branch of Christianity.[43] Many Americans consider the United States to be a "Christian country," but as indicated above, the number is shrinking. In a survey by the Public Religion Research Institute (PRRI) conducted in partnership with the Brookings Institution, and released a few months prior to the outcome of the 2016 presidential election, 59 percent of white evangelical Protestants said the United States is no longer a Christian country. That number jumped 11 points from just 48 percent in 2012. A Religion News Service (RNS) story on the survey noted that, "While a strong majority of white evangelical Protestants agree that the U.S. has lost its Christian identity, Americans overall are split on the question—41 percent say it was Christian and remains so, and 42 percent say it was in the past but is no longer. Relatively few (15 percent) say America never has been a Christian nation."[44]

Republican Senator John McCain of Arizona, Barack Obama's challenger in the 2008 presidential race, told an interviewer during that campaign, "I would probably have to say yes, that the Constitution established the United States of America as a Christian nation."[45] In an op-ed published the following week, historian Jon Meacham wrote, "The founders were not anti-religion. Many of them were faithful in their personal lives, and in their public language they evoked God. They grounded the founding principle of the nation—that all men are created equal—in the divine. But they wanted faith to be one thread in the country's tapestry, not the whole tapestry."[46]

Robert P. Jones, founding chief executive officer of PRRI, noted that "seven in 10 white evangelical Protestants say the country has changed for the worse since the 1950s."[47] That 70 percent figure concerning white evangelical views parallels Pew's findings about overall Christian identification. In his book, *The End of White Christian America* (2016), Jones opens with "An Obituary for White Christian America":

> After a long life spanning nearly two hundred and forty years, White Christian America—a prominent cultural force in the nation's history—has died. WCA first began to exhibit troubling symptoms in the 1960s when white mainline Protestant denominations began to shrink, but showed no signs of rallying with the rise of the Christian Right in the 1980s.[48]

The mock obit lists White Christian America's accomplishments, including hospitals, the Boy Scouts, and the YMCA, and noted that, "Virtually every American president has drawn from WCA's well, particularly during moments of strife."[49] The obit ends with a list of survivors:

> WCA is survived by two principal branches of descendants: a mainline Protestant family residing primarily in the Northeast and upper Midwest and an

evangelical Protestant family living mostly in the South. Plans for a public memorial service have not been announced.[50]

DEFINING EVANGELICALS

Like religion, defining who is an "evangelical" is tricky. The word has become as much of a political label as a spiritual one. As British scholar David W. Bebbington and other religious historians have written, an evangelical is not associated with a particular Christian religion, but commonly refers to someone who is "of the gospel."[51] Someone who evangelizes is spreading the gospel of Christ. With roots in the Protestant Reformation, Bebbington writes, the evangelical movement has existed in Britain since at least 1730.

There are the four qualities that have been the special marks of Evangelical religion:

> *conversionism*, the belief that lives need to be changed; *activism*, the expression of the gospel in effort; *biblicism*, a particular regard for the Bible; and what may be called *crucicentrism*, a stress on the sacrifice of Christ on the cross. Together they form a quadrilateral of priorities that is the basis of Evangelicalism.[52]

Historian Thomas A. Kidd summarized Bebbington's evangelical quadrilateral, as it is known, this way:

1. *Conversion*, or the need to be born again.
2. *Biblicism*, or the need to base one's faith fundamentally on the Bible.
3. The *theological priority of the cross*, where Jesus died and won forgiveness for sinners.
4. *Activism*, or acting on the mandates of one's faith, through supporting your church, sharing the gospel, and engaging in charitable endeavors.[53]

"When proposed thirty years ago, Bebbington's definition was a valuable steppingstone," wrote Timothy Gloege, a historian of evangelicalism.

> It pushed historians to ask new questions and research new groups. But the findings of that research also revealed the definition's flaws. Its characteristics simply do not translate into identifiable patterns of belief and practice. . . . It's not a definition, but a prospectus for a theological agenda.

> Consider the definition at work. To be evangelical, we are told, is to believe in "conversion." But is conversion a uniquely evangelical idea? It's not even uniquely Christian; Muslims convert too.[54]

Gloege said he finds "it troubling that a group of media-savvy evangelicals is poised to dictate the terms of our national conversation. Insiders, not scholars, now determine who 'counts' as an evangelical. . . . Respectable evangelicals have been defining away their embarrassing spiritual kin for a century, at least. . . . Whether televangelist scandals, or hurricanes-are-God's-judgment-jeremiads, or homophobic protests at military funerals: it's not us."[55]

In 2005, *TIME* magazine named American scholar Mark A. Noll one of the top 25 most influential evangelicals.[56] Noll is the author of *The Scandal of the Evangelical Mind*, a landmark book whose first sentence reads: "The scandal of the evangelical mind is that there is not much of an evangelical mind."[57] He decries the anti-intellectualism streak among many evangelicals, and maintains that believing in the Bible and thinking on a higher plane are not incompatible. "The things that David Bebbington identified, that others have used and I've used—cross, Bible, conversion, activity in the world—these all characterize broadly speaking 'evangelical' people," Noll told an interviewer for the Wheaton College newspaper upon his retirement from teaching in 2016.[58]

"I don't actually think 'evangelicalism' exists," Noll said. "There are evangelical institutions, evangelical movements, evangelical people, evangelical emphases. But you say, what's the institutional or organizational continuity? And there just isn't any. So does the word mean anything? If when people hear 'evangelical' they think of something political first, then the serious meaning of the word is gone."[59]

In the 2016 presidential election, older white evangelical Protestants voted overwhelmingly for Republican Donald Trump over Democrat Hillary Clinton. Evangelicals who are younger, African American, Hispanic American, or Asian American heavily favored Clinton over Trump. "This group of Christians shares the same core beliefs, but they don't vote the same way," according to Scott McConnell of LifeWay Research. "There are significant cultural and political divides among evangelicals that will remain long after the election is over."[60]

"I think what's called 'evangelical support for Trump' had to do with the pro-life position of the Republican party, it had to do with a lot of antagonism against some of the cultural steps taken by the Obama administration," Noll said. "It certainly had to do with the memory of Bill Clinton's immorality in the White House, and a lot of white evangelicals were concerned about economics. . . . I do think we have increasing numbers of Christian academics who would have a much more sophisticated approach to political life than, 'I'm angry at Hillary so I'm voting for Trump.' But I'm worried about the Christian populace at large listening all the time to their media go-to and never being concerned about folks who are trying to see things more broadly."[61]

In her major work *The Evangelicals: The Struggle to Shape America* (2017), historian Frances FitzGerald lays out a history of the fundamentalist movement, including its activism in the twentieth century. "During the 1950s fundamentalists divided into two camps, corresponding to the two conflicting impulses present in fundamentalism since its inception: one to guard doctrinal purity without compromise; the other to reclaim America and to gain the world for Christ through revivals."[62]

One camp, FitzGerald writes, was separatist, leaning toward outsider status as politically extremist. The other, preferring the evangelical label, was "inclusivist, bent on regaining respectability and cultural influence."[63] The National Association of Evangelicals (NAE) was comprised of Pentecostals and other conservative denominations, but many liberal believers considered themselves evangelicals as well. While fundamentalists used the terms interchangeably, less militant NAE leaders preferred to be called evangelicals to distinguish themselves from perceptions of narrowness.[64] Today, "evangelical" is often used as media shorthand, without nuance, to describe those who publicly declare belief in Jesus Christ and attend church regularly. The word is prominent in news stories every election year.

DEFINING SPIRITUALITY

"I'm spiritual, but not religious" is a common phrase among the religiously unaffiliated nones, especially Millennials and those who have left the churches they were raised in. "But while Millennials are not as religious as older Americans by some measures of religious observance, they are as likely to engage in many spiritual practices," according to Pew Research Center.[65] The notion of "spiritual, but not religious," while not a new concept, is becoming a widespread American philosophy.

The Pew Religion & Public Life survey found in 2012 that "the unaffiliated are not wholly secular. Substantial portions of the unaffiliated—particularly among those who describe their religion as 'nothing in particular'—say they believe in God or a universal spirit. And while 42 percent of the unaffiliated describe themselves as neither a religious nor a spiritual person, 18 percent say they are a religious person, and 37 percent say they are spiritual but not religious."[66]

"With the phrase generally comes the presumption that religion has to do with doctrines, dogmas, and ritual practices, whereas spirituality has to do with the heart, feeling, and experience," writes Christian Studies Professor Amy Hollywood in the *Harvard Divinity Bulletin* in a discussion of monasticism, commitment, ritual, and belief. "For the spiritual, religion is inert, arid, and dead; the practitioner of religion, whether consciously or not, is at best without feeling, at worst insincere."[67] Hollywood says this criticism is coming from both within religious traditions and those who simply call themselves spiritual.

"The catchphrase 'spiritual but not religious' is among the most glib and insipid pieties of our times," according to *National Catholic Register* film critic Steven D. Greydanus. "'Spirituality' has no traditions or rituals, makes no demands, gives us nothing to *do* in times of crisis."[68]

Christian Smith, a sociologist at the University of Notre Dame, coined the term "Moralistic Therapeutic Deist" (MTD) to describe Millennial teens. MTDs view religion as something that should make you happy, feel good, and be nice to others. Smith writes that the "creed" of this de facto Millennial religion can be summarized this way:

1. A God exists who created and orders the world and watches over human life on earth.
2. God wants people to be good, nice, and fair to each other, as taught in the Bible and by most world religions.
3. The central goal of life is to be happy and to feel good about oneself.
4. God does not need to be particularly involved in one's life except when he is needed to resolve a problem.
5. Good people go to heaven when they die.[69]

This checklist is hardly reflective of traditional Christian orthodoxy. Smith's research argues that Moralistic Therapeutic Deism is displacing traditional Christianity in the United States. "This is not a religion of repentance from sin, of keeping the Sabbath, of living as a servant of a sovereign divine, of steadfastly saying one's prayers, of faithfully observing high holy days, of building character through suffering, of basking in God's love and grace, of spending oneself in gratitude and love for the cause of social justice, etc.," Smith writes.[70] "America has lived a long time off its thin Christian veneer," he says. "That is all finally being stripped away by the combination of mass consumer capitalism and liberal individualism."[71]

A 2005 *Newsweek* cover feature, "Spirituality in America," reported on the findings of a poll the magazine conducted in August of that year, as well as highlighting the individual stories of a Christian environmentalist; a Muslim community youth outreach in Southern California; a Pentecostal preacher in Memphis; an Alabama Baptist turned Buddhist; conservative Catholics influenced by Pope John Paul II; and a rabbi extolling Kabbalah meditation. *Newsweek* defines "spirituality" in this compilation of stories as "the impulse to seek communion with the Divine."[72] In doing so, the publication appears to conflate spirituality with religion, even though its poll questions divided the two. This further complicates the search for a concrete, summative definition of either spirituality or religion.

Browsing the "Spirituality" section in a retail or online bookstore is an enlightening experience. In fact, enlightenment is the topic of many spiritual self-help books. Some discuss spirituality in Buddhism, particularly as part of yoga practice. *Outrageous Openness: Letting the Divine Take the Lead* (2011) is by Tosha Silver, who says on her website (ToshaSilver.com) that she "graduated from Yale with a degree in English Literature but along the way fell madly in love with yogic philosophy." She refers to letting "God" or the "Divine" lead the way. "Because our culture is about chasing and grasping, this is for people ready to let the inner Divine lead. Learning to invite this Force is a muscle that grows stronger over time," Silver writes. "Sometimes answers are immediate, sometimes you wait. But one way or another, you come to trust that you will always be shown the Way."[73]

The essence of spirituality for some is transcending the stresses of everyday life. German born and Cambridge educated, Eckhart Tolle is a spiritual teacher and bestselling author of *The Power of Now: A Guide to Spiritual Enlightenment* (2004). Tolle's book seeks to help people live without pain and anxiety, and has sold more than 2 million copies in 30 languages.[74] His idea centers on freeing oneself of the analytical mind and being present in the world.

Sometimes, spiritual awareness comes after a life-threatening ordeal. Mexican physician Don Miguel Ruiz nearly died in an auto accident and abandoned medicine to research Toltec mythology. He became a shaman, and in 1997 published *The Four Agreements: A Practical Guide to Personal Freedom: A Toltec Wisdom Book*. The four agreements referred to in the book's title are:

1. Be impeccable with your word.
2. Don't take anything personally.
3. Don't make assumptions.
4. Always do your best.

Publisher's Weekly said in its review of *The Four Agreements:*

> Ruiz's explanations of Toltec-based cosmography got a major boost when publishing pooh-bah Oprah Winfrey mentioned his work on her TV show. Ruiz, whose workshop teachings are distilled here, was born into a Mexican family of traditional healers, became a surgeon in adulthood, then underwent a near-death experience that made him reexamine his life, his beliefs. Like the popular works of the late Carlos Castaneda, Ruiz's teachings focus on dreams and visions.[75]

Oprah Winfrey, the media titan who was an iconic cultural force when she hosted her television show for 25 years (1986–2011) and remains so, lends credence and popularity to nearly anything she favors, including spirituality movements. Winfrey endorsed *The Secret*, a 2006 documentary film by Rhonda Byrne that Byrne later turned into a bestselling book. Byrne based *The Secret* on Wallace D. Wattles's *The Science of Getting Rich* (1910) and New Thought, which has its origins in the nineteenth century. New Thought operates on the "law of attraction," holding that positive or negative thoughts affect not only behavior, but outcomes.

In her book *Oprah: The Gospel of an Icon* (2011), Religious Studies and American Studies scholar Kathryn Lofton explains that rather than a movement, "New Thought is probably better understood as a potent combinatory trope," involving Christian Science, the Unity School of Christianity, the United Church of Religious Science, and Church of Christ Scientist, among other religious bodies, organizations, and alliances.[76] "Committed to philosophical idealism and mind cure, New Thought proponents were identifiable by a devotion to the possibility of physical healing through spiritual healing. Coming into consciousness with God produces health; likewise, coming into consciousness with God produces abundance."[77] Positive thinking breeds positive results, and those results can include material wealth. Many critics of New Thought, *The Secret*, and Winfrey see parallels with the prosperity gospel, a message preached by some televangelists and megachurch pastors, loosely based on the book of Matthew: "Ask, and it shall be given you."[78] If you think that you *can* achieve wealth, you *will* achieve wealth. (See chapter 6, "Jesus Laughed: The Uses and Abuses of Religious Satire," for an in-depth discussion of prosperity preachers.)

Winfrey has a catchphrase she shares frequently with followers: "Live your best life." She often illustrated how to do just that by the topics she explored on her show, a theme that continues in her magazine *O*, and in various productions she oversees. When Byrne and other discussants appeared on her show, Winfrey declared, "I realized I've always lived by the secret. . . . And for years on this show, this is what I have been trying to do, is to get people to see [the secret] through different ways manifested through the lives of other people."[79] Winfrey's enthusiasm for *The Secret* was potent enough to warrant a follow-up episode.

United Church of Christ minister Lillian Daniel has little patience for people who overshare their spirituality. "On airplanes, I dread the conversation with the person who finds out I am a minister and wants to use the flight time to explain to me that he is 'spiritual but not religious,'" she said. "Such a person will always share this as if it is some kind of daring insight, unique to him, bold in its rebellion against the religious status quo."[80] The Reverend Daniel, who pastors the First Congregational Church of Glen Ellyn near Chicago, wrote a widely shared *Huffington Post* column in 2011 that mocked the lack of depth in the "spiritual."

Next thing you know, he's telling me that he finds God in the sunsets. These people always find God in the sunsets. And in walks on the beach. Sometimes I think these people never leave the beach or the mountains, what with all the communing with God they do on hilltops, hiking trails and . . . did I mention the beach at sunset yet?

Like people who go to church don't see God in the sunset! Like we are these monastic little hermits who never leave the church building. How lucky we are to have these geniuses inform us that God is in nature. As if we don't hear that in the psalms, the creation stories and throughout our deep tradition.

Being privately spiritual but not religious just doesn't interest me. There is nothing challenging about having deep thoughts all by oneself. What is interesting is doing this work in community, where other people might call you on stuff, or heaven forbid, disagree with you. Where life with God gets rich and provocative is when you dig deeply into a tradition that you did not invent all for yourself.[81]

Daniel expanded on her essay in a book two years later, titled *When "Spiritual But Not Religious" Is Not Enough: Seeing God in Surprising Places, Even the Church.* For those who seek spirituality in sunsets, who say communing with nature is their "church," Daniel responds, "So you find God in the sunset? Great, so do I. But how about in the face of cancer? Cancer is nature too. Do you worship that as well?"[82]

In an interview with the "faith, culture, and intentional living" magazine *Relevant*, comedian and recovered drug addict Marc Maron discussed the 12-step program that helped him get clean as "slightly gutted Christianity."[83] Maron, whose popular podcast titled *WTF* means what you think it means, typically consists of obscenities as well as deep, often moving, conversations with famous people—including Barack Obama. Just as he ate partially chewed salmon with Bear Grylls on television, Obama sat for an audio interview with Maron in his garage studio, though their talk was less spiritual than topical.[84] Maron, who is culturally Jewish, describes himself as someone who is "not willing to commit to believing—so I live in that place."[85]

A growing number of people live in that place, between secularism and religious commitment, between believing and almost believing, between nonbelief and spirituality. Three religious studies scholars at Elon University were asked to offer their definitions of "Spirituality." Despite their varied backgrounds, traditions, and areas of research, the responses were similar in that they each found the word amorphous.

- Brian Pennington is a scholar of Hindu-Christian encounters and religion in India, and director of Elon's Center for the Study of Religion, Culture & Society. "I would say that spirituality is a contemporary form of religiosity that aims to achieve a sense of belonging and wholeness outside the structures and authority of traditional religions."

- Geoffrey Claussen is the Lori and Eric Sklut Emerging Scholar in Jewish Studies and Jewish Studies Program Coordinator, and is an ordained rabbi. "The word 'spirituality' (or 'spiritual') may have certain clear meanings in certain cultural contexts, but I often try to avoid using the word because I think that it seldom makes matters clearer. The same is true, though, of the word 'religion' (or 'religious'), which I also try to avoid using. In fact, the attempt to create a cultural category called 'religion' that's distinct from the 'secular' is even more troubling to me than creating a cultural category called 'spirituality.' And one possible benefit of the term 'spirituality' is that it can have the effect of helping to break down that false dichotomy between what's 'religious' and what's 'secular.'"

- Jeffrey C. Pugh is the Maude Sharpe Powell Professor of Religious Studies and an ordained Christian (Methodist) minister. "Spirituality can be a vague and protean term, reflecting nothing more a projection of our own desires. In this way the term is meaningless to denote anything other than humankind's wish-fulfillment for a 'happy ending.' When the idea of spirituality centers itself around traditions and communities of lived practice, it can take on a more textured meaning, something akin to the intuition that the way we order our world may fall well short of divine intention for how we are to live and treat one another and the planet. Tradition and discipline shaped expressions of spirituality can be powerful forms of resistance (in my tradition I think of Oscar Romero, the Berrigan brothers, Dietrich Bonhoeffer) to the political and economic powers that presently shape and dominate the world."

Wade Clark Roof and Robert Wuthnow have noted that since the 1950s, "spirituality" has taken on the meaning of a search for self and purpose. In 1993, Roof published *A Generation of Seekers: The Spiritual Journeys of the Baby Boom Generation*, which explored spirituality among Baby Boomers as a distinct trend.[86] The book was based on hundreds of interviews conducted with this cohort in the late 1980s. His follow-up book, *Spiritual Marketplace: Baby Boomers and the Remaking of American Religion* (1999), revisited many of the Boomers interviewed previously to see where they were on their spiritual journeys.

Roof identified the quest for meaning among many Boomers as more spiritual rather than religious. "Today's spiritual quest culture," Roof wrote, "can be analyzed in terms of four interrelated components: *the social world, producers, the audience*, and *cultural objects*."[87] Many Boomers respond to the fragmenting social world, the various producers of religion, and cultural objects, such as "symbols and spiritual themes . . . in relation to this social world and audience," by being spiritual seekers.

Leonard Norman Primiano has written of the "plurality of perspectives" in "television talk shows and newsmagazines in the 1980s and 1990s [that] became forums for the views of institutional religious representatives and a variety of belief systems described as contemporary spiritualities."

> "Religion" presented on such programs can be perceived as organized, established forms of religious belief and practice: that is, religious traditions that have taken institutional form. "Spirituality," however, can be understood as more multilayered belief and practice, representing the core truths of one or several religious traditions, contributing to the creation and nurturing of private (and sometimes communal) belief systems.[88]

"This spirituality of seeking," according to Primiano, "is characterized by a deeply personal but transient religiosity with roots in traditional religious beliefs and practices; an interest in noninstitutionalized religious contexts; and an eclectic, idiosyncratic, and at times isolated spirituality fascinated with the supernatural."[89]

There is unpredictability, fluidity, disagreement, and vagueness among the spiritual but not religious, but the distinctness and endurance of the mode is real for its many practitioners.

DEFINING POPULAR CULTURE

Ray B. Browne, father of the academic study of popular culture, wrote in 1970 that, "'Popular Culture' is an indistinct term whose edges blur into imprecision."[90] Popular culture, wrote scholar Gordon Lynch, is "the shared environment, practices, and resources of everyday life."[91] According to writer Will Rockett, "Popular culture refers to the art, entertainment, and cultural objects 'which have proved most successful in garnering a significant audience.'"[92] Religion and media scholar Daniel A. Stout has observed that, "Genres of popular culture range widely from TV soap operas to country western music; in print media it might include romance novels and comic books. The term *culture war* was popularized in the 1980s and 1990s by writers seeking a descriptive label for what they perceived to be religious reaction to popular forms of communication."[93]

If "cultures are simply systems of conflict, tension, and contradictory approaches to certain values," asks religion and popular culture scholar John C. Lyden, "then what would *popular* culture be?" Culture can be seen as high or low, but that perception changes over time. As Lyden notes, "jazz might have begun as a popular art form, but it soon became so sophisticated that the majority of the population lost interest in it, and now it is primarily played and studied more in academic settings than in nightclubs."[94]

Lyden suggests that we shouldn't worry about distinctions in culture vs. popular culture, but offers this definition: "'Popular culture' indicates some sort of shared cultural values of a populace, or at least a set of issues around which negotiations and conflicts over meaning occur in a populace . . . and this may involve some elements of elite, avant-garde, or folk culture, so called; all of these may be popular with certain groups, and this is worth studying."[95]

In his 1994 book, *Selling God: American Religion in the Marketplace of Culture*, R. Laurence Moore says of the wide array of items spotted for sale in a Christian bookstore, "It is, in fact, difficult to wander through these bookstores and imagine any aspect of popular culture that has been left uncloned."[96] Moore further notes that religion is not subsumed by consumerism, but has become another product:

> [M]uch of what we usually mean by speaking of secularization has to do not with the disappearance of religion but its commodification, the ways in which churches have grown by participation in the market, or more specifically how religious influences established themselves in the forms of commercial culture that emerged in the nineteenth century, turning the United States into a flowering Eden of leisure industries by the middle of the twentieth . . . It is a study of religious influence in determining the taste of people who were learning to purchase "culture" as a means of self-improvement and relaxation.[97]

In a 1954 Guggenheim Fellowship essay that later became the preface for a posthumous book collection titled *The Immediate Experience: Movies, Comics, Theatre and Other Aspects of Popular Culture*, mid-twentieth century critic Robert Warshow argued that movies and other such topics were legitimate subjects for serious cultural study. Warshow, an editor for *Commentary*, the neoconservative Jewish magazine, wrote, "In the long run, I hope that my work may even make some contribution to the 'legitimization' of the movies; but I do not think one can make such a contribution by pretending that 'legitimization' has already taken place." Of his intention to use the fellowship to write a book of essays on films, Warshow stated,

> The movies—and American movies in particular—stand at the center of that unresolved problem of "popular culture" which has come to be a kind of nagging embarrassment to criticism, intruding itself on all our efforts to understand the special qualities of our culture and to define our own relation to it . . .
>
> My own ambition, in the present work, is only to produce a body of criticism dealing with specific films and types of films, with certain actors, certain themes, and with two or three of the general problems which may point towards a theory. If it is successful, the book should bring its readers pleasure and illumination in connection with one of the leading elements in modern culture, and perhaps go some way towards resolving the curious tension that surrounds the problem of "popular culture."[98]

Warshow's intellectually informed essays range from novels of the 1930s to Clifford Odets to fellow essayist E. B. White to the *Krazy Kat* comic to "The Gangster as Tragic Hero" of American film. Lyden compares the study of such a wide array of cultural phenomena to the work of the anthropologist who examines the "everyday life of a people in order to understand what they value and how they make meaning. . . . Should we do less for the study of our own culture (or cultures)?"[99]

"Religious groups have always expressed a love-hate relationship with American popular culture" observes Quentin Schultze, who has studied Christian evangelicals' interactions with media. "Protestants hoped they could use mass media to evangelize the unsaved. But they found that popular culture also sparks culture wars."[100] One problem Schultze points out concerning religious popular culture is that, while unifying Christians, such fare "can polarize groups within society by antagonizing people who do not share the same beliefs. Religious popular culture often politicizes religion for the purposes of quickly mobilizing audiences and raising funds. It sometimes even demonizes others for the benefit of its own religious cause." In addition, multiple moral media crusades and campaigns "whips religious consumers from one current agenda to another," eroding established religious traditions.[101]

"The rituals of both popular culture and of religious tribes invite people to share the meanings of narratives," Schultze writes. "Over the centuries Jews gathered around the Passover table and Protestants met in homes and churches to celebrate Communion. Today television audiences meet in front of the tube for a ritualistic enactment of a community's shared hopes and fears. Like religious rituals, mass media rituals can dramatize communal belief."[102]

THE SYSTEMATIC STUDY OF RELIGION, MEDIA, AND CULTURE

The academic study of religion, media, and culture is still a relatively new field, but a significant body of work precedes the present volume. Religion and communication scholars have produced research that explores the intersection of religion with journalism, politics, digital media, materialism, modernity, and all manner of popular culture. Some researchers have examined how audiences *use* religious media, while others have studied the *effects* of media on religious audiences. In addition, there is a growing list of colleges and universities that offer courses with some variation of religion, culture, and media in the title.

"The study of religion and popular culture . . . has not established a solid foothold in the halls of academia, perhaps because it is too recent in origin, or because it appears to lack the coherence and discernment required for inclusion," according to Lyden. "There is something we call religion, and there is something we call popular culture, however contested and slippery the definitions of these terms remain."[103] Writing in the mid-1980s before the digital revolution, William F. Fore noted that Christian fundamentalists embrace technology for purposes of conversion. "It also explains why fundamentalist religion has been quick to grasp every new communication technique—from radio to motion pictures to television and satellite TV and videocassettes. For them, the only question is how to build a bigger and better pipe to deliver the simple gospel message to the recipient."[104] In the digital present, the internet has become that bigger and better pipe.

In 1996, the *Journal of the American Academy of Religion* published a thematic issue on "Religion and American Popular Culture."[105] In an introductory essay, Religious Studies scholar Catherine L. Albanese wrote, "[T]he expressers and purveyors of personal experience—the print and electronic media that 'semioticize' it—achieve a special cogency as religious agents and spaces. . . . Students of religion need to pay strenuous attention to them."[106] Albanese would have had no way of knowing the semiotic forms digital media would take in the decades hence, but she was prescient in her assessment of mediated religious messaging and practice.

Communication scholar Heidi Campbell has published widely on the topic of digital media's relationship to religion, including two books that explore how religions interact with what was once commonly referred to as "new media." Published in 2010, *When Religion Meets New Media* focuses on how Jewish, Christian, and Muslim communities engage with technology. "At the heart of this book is the argument that religious people are not anti-technology," Campbell writes in her introduction, "rather they are constrained by a number of social and faith-based factors which inform and guide their responses to the possibilities and challenges offered by new forms of media."[107]

The social shaping of technology (SST) theory Campbell employs in her approach to the study of religion holds that technology is shaped by social interaction, possibly leading to new and different forms of technology. Campbell suggests a specific framework for fellow researchers studying how religious people and communities respond to technology. "What is needed is a framework that also acknowledges how a religious community's historical life practice, interpretive tradition, and the contemporary outworking of their values inform their choices about the adoption and adaptation of technology," she writes.[108] "These include highlighting: 1) history and tradition; 2) core beliefs and patterns; 3) negotiation processes; and 4) communal framing and discourses. Together these form the basis of the religious-social shaping of technology approach to the study of religious communities uses of media."[109]

Campbell's book *Digital Religion: Understanding Religious Practice in New Media Worlds* (2013) is an edited volume that casts a wider net, encompassing Buddhism and Hinduism, as well as Christianity, Islam, and Judaism.[110] This expansive book builds upon previous research that looked at "cyber religion," including religious communities that formed online. (See, e.g., Brenda E. Brasher, *Give Me That Online Religion*, 2001; Lorne L. Dawson and Douglas E. Cowan, *Religion Online: Finding Faith on the Internet*, 2004; and Elizabeth Drescher, *Tweet If You Love Jesus: Practicing Church in the Digital Reformation*, 2011, a book that offers a Christian perspective on media use.)

The three sections of Campbell's *Digital Religion* focus on six themes: *Ritual, Identity, Community, Authority, Authenticity, Religion.* Assorted chapters detail case studies of faith communities explored through these themes. The final third of the book offers reflections on theoretical frameworks, ethical issues, and theology, plus concluding thoughts by media studies scholar Stewart M. Hoover, director of the Center for Media, Religion, and Culture (CMRC) at the University of Colorado at Boulder. Part of the CMRC's work is the *Public Religion Project*, which explores the public's understanding of religion. "Religion is more and more at the center of contemporary political and social life," Hoover says in a statement on the Public Religion Project website. "[T]his project begins with the fact that religion's role is increasingly a role defined by modern media."[111]

In his brief coda to Campbell's book, Hoover outlines three broad "lessons that come out of reflections on religion and the internet":

> The first concerns the ways we think about the digital and its locus of generation as a new space, as a "third space." . . . It is important to understand that constitution of the third space does not grow out of the logic of the technology, but out of the logic of digital practice.
>
> Second is the issue of how these third spaces act and are understood . . . third spaces are in a way small sphericals of focused interactions.
>
> Finally. . . . Attention and discussion given to digital religion is usually focused on what it produces in the digital space. Yet we have to keep in mind that at some fundamental level digital religion is essentially about religion and spirituality.[112]

Religion is intimately connected to media, even though individual digital devices have led to a more fragmented media audience. In a nod to mediatization theory, Hoover argues in his own book *Religion in the Media Age* (2006) that religion and media "occupy the same spaces, serve many of the same purposes, and invigorate the same practices in late modernity. Today, it is probably better to think of them as related than to think of them as separate."[113] Of media in particular, Hoover writes, "Their cultural location is derived from their capacity—described in a range of ways—to be both *shap-*

ers of culture and *products* of that same culture. This 'double articulation' of the media makes their role and impact particularly difficult to pin down, and is one of the reasons that, today, we are still unsure of the nature and extent of their significance."[114]

Hoover's earlier works include a 1982 book titled *The Electronic Giant: A Critique of the Telecommunications Revolution from a Christian Perspective*, published when videocassette recorders made home taping possible, VHS tapes were available for rental, and just as cable television was expanding viewer choices beyond broadcast channels. Hoover and Robert Abelman also published an edited volume called *Religious Television: Controversies and Conclusions* (1990), a history and data-driven social analysis of religious television content, including the influence of televangelists.

Hoover and Lynn Schofield Clark have collaborated on many works, including *Practicing Religion in the Age of the Media: Explorations in Media, Religion, and Culture* (2002). Hoover's introduction touches on the reasoning behind the selection of topics:

> The realms of both "religion" and "the media" are themselves transforming and being transformed. Religion today is much more a public, commodified, therapeutic, and personalized set of practices than it has been in the past. At the same time, the media . . . are collectively coming to constitute a realm where important projects of "the self" take place—projects that include spiritual, transcendent, and deeply meaningful "work." This means that . . . religion and media are increasingly converging. They are meeting on a common turf: the everyday world of lived experience.[115]

In a book mentioned earlier, *Religion in the News: Faith and Journalism in American Public Discourse* (1998), Hoover noted that religious audiences consume news as much as the general public, yet observed that coverage of religion remains controversial. At the time *Religion in the News* was published, he observed that "significant segments of the various religious communities, the public, and the press, have no expectation that religion will be covered at all."[116] Religion coverage has increased significantly since then, but perhaps is no less controversial.

Other scholars have explored religion and journalism, including Mark Silk, a former newspaper reporter, now director of the Leonard E. Greenberg Center for the Study of Religion in Public Life at Trinity College. Silk's 1995 book, *Unsecular Media: Making News of Religion in America*, examines the "topoi" of news coverage of religion. These topoi are general concepts that are assumed, used, and reused in news stories over and over. Topoi in religion news are reflections of the public, Silk, writes. "[T]he topoi will mirror public attitudes, if only because it is in the nature of the media to need to be comprehensible to the undifferentiated audience it seeks—that is, morally comprehensible, for the media trade largely in tales of good and evil."[117]

In his book, *From Yahweh to Yahoo! The Religious Roots of the Secular Press*, former *Seattle Times* reporter and media historian Doug Underwood notes that, "It is almost forgotten in our more secular times that many of the early advocates of freedom of the press were preachers and proselytizers whose religious zeal—and the writings that poured forth from their pens—placed them solidly in the tradition of the world's first 'journalists.'"

> While the values of free expression put forth by these religious reformers have been transformed into secular principles that we now identify as constitutional (as in the protections of free speech and press freedom in the U.S. Constitution) or professional in nature (as in journalists' defense of the "public's right to know"), the origins of these bedrock principles of a free press can be found in the passionate religious disputes of a time when religion was interwoven with virtually all controversies of public life.[118]

Judith M. Buddenbaum and Debra L. Mason in their book *Readings on Religion as News* (2000) offer a detailed history of religion news, as well as discussions of contemporary issues such as abortion, pluralism, and separation of church and state.[119] Buddenbaum has also partnered with Daniel Stout on a number of projects, including the founding of the *Journal of Media and Religion* in 2002. Books Buddenbaum and Stout have produced include *Religion and Mass Media: Audiences and Adaptations* (1996) and *Religion and Popular Culture: Studies on the Interaction of Worldviews* (2001). The former offers a thorough review of previous literature in religion and media, as well as theoretical perspectives of the uses of media by religious communities. Agenda-setting theory plays a role in the latter book. As Buddenbaum noted, "[I]t seems obvious that both mass media and religion shape public opinion."[120]

Accommodations to the diversity and multiplicity of religious lifestyles have brought commercial religious media into the mainstream. In a study titled "Interpretive Community: An Approach to Media and Religion," media studies scholar Thomas R. Lindlof wrote of the rapid growth of this media sector.

> Religiously inflected cultural products valued in the billions of dollars are now produced and distributed by publishers, bookstores, recorded music divisions, video companies, television networks, and other media companies. Many of these products are targeted solely for the evangelical Christian market, but a growing number of them—for example, contemporary Christian music; novels such as the hugely successful *Left Behind* series; movies made by Christian film companies . . . demonstrate crossover appeal to a broader consumer base. Even the mainstream entertainment industry is taking the "faith market" more seriously than ever before, with overtly religious characters and themes featured in movies and primetime television series.[121]

Lindlof's article was published in 2002, and in the intervening years, the faith market's crossover appeal has expanded considerably. One of the most successful books of 2007 was *The Shack* by William Paul Young, who spent part of his childhood in New Guinea with his missionary parents. Young's novel revolves around a man who was abused as a child, grows up to have a loving family, but has a daughter go missing on a camping trip. A trio of strangers, representing God, Jesus, and the Holy Ghost, reveal meaning in the man's life by appearing to him in a shack in the woods. A film version released a decade later grossed $57 million domestically and $89 million worldwide.[122]

As media scholar David Sloan has written, "One of the most common misconceptions about the history of mass communication is that the media and religion have always been natural enemies."[123] As religion adapts to a more secular culture, it is, in effect, doing what it has always done—evolving to reach people where they are. As noted earlier, religious communities have historically been at the forefront of communication technology and media use, from the hand operated printing press to wireless internet.

In introductory media history courses, students learn that the first book assembled on the first printing press in the West was a Christian Bible, printed by Johannes Gutenberg in Mainz, Germany in the 1450s. The first book printed on the first press in the American colonies was *The Whole Booke of Psalmes*, a hymnal produced in 1640 by printer Stephen Daye of the Massachusetts Bay Colony. David Paul Nord reminds us that, "Between 1815 and 1835, centralized, systematic mass publication had become part of the American way of doing things. The origin . . . was religious and evangelical."[124]

Through discussion of religion and its intersection with all manner of media, we learn about diverse cultures, rituals, and societies. Pairing the study of various religious traditions with nonreligious perspectives serves both scholarly and social purposes of teaching diversity. Societal issues presented in news and entertainment media concerning minorities, women, and the lesbian, gay, bisexual and transgender (LGBT) community, have religious connections.

The Reverend Jerry Falwell Sr. (1933–2007) used values-based tactics to politicize religion when his Moral Majority organization helped Ronald Reagan become the 40th president of the United States. Falwell, a Southern Baptist pastor in Lynchburg, Virginia, became a major force through his television ministry and conservative activism. The Gilder Lehrman Institute of American History website provides a succinct overview of the Moral Majority:

> The Moral Majority was a fundamentalist Christian organization founded by televangelist Jerry Falwell in 1979. The Moral Majority was established to

preserve "traditional" American values and to combat increasing acceptance of social movements and culture changes. The organization became a major political influence in its opposition to gay rights, abortion, feminism, and other liberal movements during the 1980s.[125]

President Jimmy Carter, a Democrat and devout Southern Baptist from Georgia, won many evangelical votes when he was elected in 1976. But as a result of his pro-choice views and progressive stands on other issues, highlighted during his second campaign by the Moral Majority as well as the rival GOP, he lost to the more secular Reagan in 1980.

As noted earlier, Southern Baptists comprise the second largest denominational body in the United States after Catholicism, making their influence worthy of study.[126] In the 1980s when the Moral Majority was at its height, Southern Baptist seminaries began purging the more liberal members of their faculties, and focusing on traditional gender roles in ministry. At Southeastern Baptist Theological Seminary in Wake Forest, North Carolina, for example, only men are ordained for preaching, church leadership, and pulpit duties, while women who attend the seminary are trained in supplementary ministries for children or in music.[127]

As a more literalist view of the Bible was adopted by the Southern Baptist Convention, they began to slip in membership, as did other mainline denominations. Southern Baptists lost 1 million members between 2006–2016. "Since 1980, the first year into a 10-year controversy over biblical inerrancy that led to splintering into new groups like the Alliance of Baptists and Cooperative Baptist Fellowship, baptism numbers have dropped by more than a third," Baptist News Global reported in 2017.[128]

As evidenced by FitzGerald's description of fundamentalists of varying extremes, clashes occur between factions within denominational bodies as well as between the religious and the non-religious or anti-religious. Just as Jimmy Carter divided Southern Baptist loyalties in the 1970s, controversial Republican candidate Donald Trump did so in the 2016 election. "Barack Obama [2008–2016] didn't divide us," Nathan A. Finn, dean of the School of Theology and Missions at Union University, a Southern Baptist college in Jackson, Tennessee, told *USA Today.* "Donald Trump divided us. His personal behavior, his policy views, his temperament and character, his religious values, all were highly questionable."[129] As noted earlier, Trump won the presidency thanks in large part to white evangelical voters, many of them Southern Baptists.[130]

THE CHAPTERS OF THIS BOOK

We encounter religion in our daily lives, whether we want to or not. Some seek out religious and spiritual experiences, while others endure, tolerate, resist, or are indifferent to them. Many Christians, particularly evangelicals, have expressed dismay at the rise of the religiously unaffiliated, the nones, in the United States. Some maintain that the faith is under assault from liberals, the politically correct, leftist academic elites, and "the media," not to mention "terrorists," a coded word that often refers to immigrants who practice Islam.[131] Despite some Christians' fears of Christianity being marginalized by such factors, the faith remains the dominant religion in the United States, and a formidable cultural force.

Utilizing primary and secondary sources, public records, and interviews, this book provides historical and contemporary perspectives on six unique ways religion influences American culture, and vice versa. The chapters are arranged in pairs under the following three categories:

* *Civil Religion*

  * Moral Mondays in the South: God-Talk, Christian Activism, and Civil Disobedience in the Digital Age
  * So Blessed by God: Adding the Almighty to the Pledge of Allegiance to the Flag

* *Religion and Entertainment*

  * God Wants His Stars Everywhere: The Media Mission of Actors, Models, & Talent for Christ
  * Sacramental Pilgrimage: Catholicism, Humanism, Spirituality, and Community Along *The Way*

* *Sacred and Profane Media*

  * Copyrighting God: Translating, Publishing, Marketing, and Selling the Bible
  * Jesus Laughed: The Uses and Abuses of Religious Satire

Chapter 1, "Moral Mondays in the South: God-Talk, Christian Activism, and Civil Disobedience in the Digital Age," is a history of a modern civil rights protest movement in the South, characterized by its use of religious language and moral justification. The Moral Monday movement, which began in 2013 in North Carolina, was partially about income inequality and economic injustice, but also aimed at legislation curbing voting rights, gay rights, and other issues proposed by a conservative Republican majority in the state General Assembly. More than 25,000 Moral Monday protestors of various ages, races, and professions such as healthcare workers, teachers, and clergy, traveled to the state capital of Raleigh that year (80,000 gathered in a follow-up rally in early 2014) to protest what they saw as "immoral" laws. Moral Mondays were led by a dynamic preacher and leader of the state chapter of the NAACP, the Reverend William J. Barber II, who cited the Reverend Martin Luther King Jr., the Bible, and the U.S. Constitution in equal measure in his fiery rally speeches. Barber built upon King's rhetoric and initiatives, such as the Poor People's Campaign, to launch a new civil rights struggle with a religious revivalist undertone.

Chapter 2 on the addition of "under God" to the Pledge of Allegiance details the Cold War origins of this phrase, as well as the media support behind it. Many court and political battles are detailed in "So Blessed by God: Adding the Almighty to the Pledge of Allegiance to the Flag," as well as the role the press played in getting the phrase inserted into what was a secular flag pledge written for a magazine as a promotional scheme by a Christian Socialist minister.

Chapter 3, "God Wants His Stars Everywhere: The Media Mission of Actors, Models, & Talent for Christ," combines interviews with ethnographic research to detail the evolution of a secular modeling agency into a ministry for training models, actors, comedians, and singers, with an emphasis on making ethical choices and developing a personal relationship with Jesus Christ. Coaching talented performers as a method of evangelistic outreach is at the heart of this Georgia-based nonprofit.

Chapter 4, "Sacramental Pilgrimage: Catholicism, Humanism, Spirituality, and Community Along *The Way*," discusses the 2010 film *The Way* starring Martin Sheen and written and directed by his son, Emilio Estevez. The chapter argues that this little-seen, low budget film more genuinely reflects the lived human experiences of redemption and forgiveness than those of more didactic, melodramatic, Christian-based movies, as well as tangentially Biblically-based, CGI-laden Hollywood blockbusters such as *Noah*. The ways in which faith has been depicted onscreen, the growth of the Christian film industry, and the motivations of various creators of religiously-themed films and television shows are explored as well.

Chapter 5, "Copyrighting God: Translating, Publishing, Marketing, and Selling the Bible," answers the question, How can you copyright the Bible? Doesn't the Word of God belong to everyone who seeks it? Perhaps, but royalties are generated if you include supplements to the Word. Add illustrations, a concordance, or unique packaging, publish a new translation, or remake the Bible into a teen magazine, and you have a new creation. This chapter discusses Bible societies, sources of various translations, histories of religious publishers, and details a highly successful Kickstarter project that produced a newly packaged Bible in an old translation. The Bible is not only a bestseller, it's big business.

Chapter 6, "Jesus Laughed: The Uses and Abuses of Religious Satire," examines religious humor from both religious and nonreligious sources. Can biting satire reveal religious truth, even if it comes from a hostile source? How does a Christian satirize his peers, and what is the motivation for doing so? This chapter explores historical and contemporary instances of Christians and non-Christians utilizing humor in an attempt to effect positive change, as they see it, among God's people. Multiple examples will be discussed, but two religious satire magazines, one American and one British (*The Wittenburg Door* and *Ship of Fools*); and two television comedians who practice religious satire, one American and one British (Stephen Colbert and John Oliver), will be examined in detail.

Christians are not a monolithic group. By exploring in-depth the six disparate yet related topic areas that make up this book, *Religion and Media in America* offers a critical assessment of Christian engagement with American media and popular culture.

NOTES

1. Chesterton wrote this phrase in his 1922 book, *What I Saw in America.*
2. See, for example: Kyle Greenwalt, "Here's How Homeschooling is Changing America," *The Conversation*, September 11, 2016, http://theconversation.com/heres-how-homeschooling-is-changing-in-america-63175; "1.5 Million Homeschooled Students in the United States in 2007," U.S. Department of Education, December 2008, https://nces.ed.gov/pubs2009/2009030.pdf.
3. See, for example: Andy Thomason, "3 Things You Should Know About Jerry Falwell Jr.," *The Chronicle of Higher Education*, January 31, 2017, http://www.chronicle.com/article/3-Things-You-Should-Know-About/239065; Ed Mazza, "Jerry Falwell Jr. Calls Donald Trump The 'Dream President' For Evangelicals," *Huffington Post*, April 30, 2017, http://www.huffingtonpost.com/entry/jerry-falwell-jr-dream-president-trump_us_5906950fe4b05c3976807a08; Emma Green, "Franklin Graham Is the Evangelical Id," *The Atlantic*, May 21, 2017, https://www.theatlantic.com/politics/archive/2017/05/franklin-graham/527013/; Sarah Pulliam Bailey, "How Donald Trump is Bringing Billy Graham's Complicated Family Back into White House Circles," *Washington Post*, January 12, 2017, https://www.washingtonpost.com/news/acts-of-faith/wp/2017/01/12/how-donald-trump-is-bringing-billy-grahams-complicated-family-back-into-white-house-circles/?utm_term=.0485709baed8.
4. Jack Jenkins, "Nobody is Laughing at the Religious Left in 2017," *Think Progress*, December 13, 2017, https://thinkprogress.org/2017-is-the-year-trump-and-the-religious-right-made-the-religious-left-unavoidable-3e89528104b6/.
5. John McKenna, "Bear Grylls Prayed with Barack Obama . . . and Gave Me My New Year's Resolution," *Catholic Charismatic Renewal*, n.d., http://www.ccr.org.uk/articles/bear-grylls-prayed-with-barack-obamaand-gave-me-my-new-years-resolution/#sthash.7bqJXhWO.dpuf. See also, David Barrett, "Barack Obama Prayed with Bear Grylls in Alaskan Wilderness," *The Telegraph*, December 13, 2015, http://www.telegraph.co.uk/news/worldnews/barackobama/12048108/Barack-Obama-prayed-with-Bear-Grylls-in-Alaskan-wilderness.html.
6. Edward Michael, "Bear" Grylls, "Glad This Was the Only Bear I Met in the Park," *The Sunday Times*, December 13, 2015, Accessed May 3, 2016, http://www.thesundaytimes.co.uk/sto/Magazine/article1640800.ece.
7. McKenna, "Bear Grylls Prayed with Barack Obama."
8. Ruth Gledhill, "Bear Grylls: My Christian Faith is My Backbone," *Christian Today* website, September 8, 2015, https://www.christiantoday.com/article/bear.grylls.my.christian.faith.is.my.backbone/64197.htm.

9. Among other contemporaneous news sources, see: Asawin Suebsaeng and Dave Gilson, "Chart: Almost Every Obama conspiracy Theory Ever," *Mother Jones*, November 2, 2012, http://www.motherjones.com/politics/2012/10/chart-obama-conspiracy-theories. The Reverend Wright, who performed Barack and Michelle Obama's marriage ceremony, was assailed by conservatives for his incendiary sermons indicting the United States for racism and other social ills. A number of Republicans and conservative commentators accused Obama of being a Muslim who was sympathetic to "Islamic terrorists." Donald Trump, who succeeded President Obama in office, leveled the charge of being a Muslim who was not born in America at Obama before, during, and after his own campaign for the presidency.

10. See: Colleen Carroll Campbell, "The Enduring Costs of John F. Kennedy's Compromise," *The Catholic Word Report* (San Francisco: Ignatius Press, February 2007), 32–37; "John F. Kennedy and Religion," John F. Kennedy Presidential Library and Museum, https://www.jfklibrary.org/JFK/JFK-in-History/JFK-and-Religion.aspx. As described by NPR, "On Sept. 12, 1960, presidential candidate John F. Kennedy gave a major speech to the Greater Houston Ministerial Association, a group of Protestant ministers, on the issue of his religion. At the time, many Protestants questioned whether Kennedy's Roman Catholic faith would allow him to make important national decisions as president independent of the church." The speech was recorded, and a transcript is available. See: "Transcript: JFK's Speech on His Religion," NPR, December 5, 2007, http://www.npr.org/templates/story/story.php?storyId=16920600. A video of the speech is available on the John F. Kennedy Presidential Library and Museum website: jfklibrary.org, https://www.jfklibrary.org/Asset-Viewer/ALL6YEBJMEKYGMCntnSCvg.aspx.

11. Thomas J. Carty, *A Catholic in the White House? Religion, Politics, and John F. Kennedy's Presidential Campaign* (New York: Palgrave Macmillan, 2004), 6. Southern Baptist opposition to Catholicism is significant because Catholics comprise the largest denomination in the United States, followed by Southern Baptists. Former Democratic New York governor Al Smith, who was Irish Catholic, ran for president in 1928. He was defeated by Herbert Hoover, in part due to anti-Catholic sentiment among many voters. See William E. Leuchtenburg, *The Perils of Prosperity, 1914–1932* (Chicago: University of Chicago Press, 1958), 225–240. Leuchtenburg wrote, "A man of ability, Al Smith arrived too early on the political scene to be accepted as a national symbol. His rejection, particularly the manner in which he was denied, not only embittered Smith, but also left a wound that would not heal until the 1960 election admitted to the White House a much more urbane Irish Catholic, John Fitzgerald Kennedy."

12. John F. Kennedy Inaugural Address, January 20, 1961, John F. Kennedy Presidential Library and Museum, https://www.jfklibrary.org/Asset-Viewer/BqXIEM9F4024ntFl7SVAjA.aspx.

13. Robert Bellah, "Civil Religion in America," *Daedalus* 96, no. 1 (Winter 1967): 1–21. Reprinted with commentary and rejoinder in Donald R. Cutler, ed., *The Religious Situation 1968* (Boston: Beacon, 1968), 388–393.

14. Ibid.

15. Peter L. Berger, *The Sacred Canopy: Elements of a Sociological Theory of Religion* (Garden City: Anchor, 1969), 147.

16. Ibid., 106–108.

17. David Voas and Mark Chaves, "Is the United States a Counterexample to the Secularization Thesis?," *American Journal of Sociology* 121, no. 5 (March 2016): 1517–1556.

18. Becka A. Alper, "Millennials Are Less Religious Than Older Americans, But Just As Spiritual," Pew Research Center, November 23, 2015, http://www.pewresearch.org/fact-tank/2015/11/23/millennials-are-less-religious-than-older-americans-but-just-as-spiritual/.

19. Will M. Gervais and Maxine B. Najle, "How Many Atheists Are There?" University of Kentucky Psychology, PsyArXiv, May 31, 2017, https://psyarxiv.com/edzda/ DOI 10.17605/OSF.IO/EDZDA.

20. "The Religious Affiliation of U.S. Immigrants: Majority Christian, Rising Share of Other Faiths," Pew Research Center, May 17, 2013, http://www.pewforum.org/2013/05/17/the-religious-affiliation-of-us-immigrants/.

21. Aleksandra Sandstrom, "Faith on the Hill," Pew Research Center, January 3, 2017. http://www.pewforum.org/2017/01/03/faith-on-the-hill-115/. Females comprise about 20 percent of

the 535 members of both houses of Congress. Half the population of the United States is female.

22. Religious Landscape Study, Pew Forum, 2017. http://www.pewforum.org/religious-landscape-study/.

23. Lynn Schofield Clark, "Overview: The 'Protestantization' of Research into Media, Religion, and Culture," in *Practicing Religion in the Age of Media*, eds. Stewart M. Hoover and Lynn Schofield Clark (New York: Columbia University Press, 2002), 7. See also, N. Jay Demerath III, "Cultural Victory and Organizational Defeat in the Paradoxical Decline of Liberal Protestantism," *Journal for the Scientific Study of Religion* 34, no. 4 (1995), 458–469.

24. Quentin J. Schultze, *Christianity and the Mass Media in America: Toward a Democratic Accommodation* (East Lansing: Michigan State University Press, 2003, 95. Religious periodical total quoted in Dennis N. Voskuil, "Reaching Out: Mainline Protestantism and the Media," in *Between the Times: The Travail of the Protestant Establishment in America 1900–1960*, ed. William R. Hutchinson (Cambridge: Cambridge University Press, 1989), 73.

25. Schultze, *Christianity and the Mass Media in America*, 142.

26. See the CBN website, http://www1.cbn.com. CBN was originally called the Christian Broadcast Network before shortening its moniker. Pat Robertson was also a one-time Republican presidential candidate. For information on Robertson's career, see, for example, Leslie Bentz, "Facebook 'Vomit' Button for Gays and Other Pat Robertson Quotes," CNN, July 9, 2013, http://www.cnn.com/2013/07/09/us/pat-robertson-facebook-remark/index.html.

27. Stig Hjarvard, "The Mediatization of Society: A Theory of Media as Agents of Social and Cultural Change," *Nordicom Review* 29, no. 2, (2008), 105.

28. Ibid., 113. For earlier work concerning mediatization, see, for example: Winfried Schulz, "Reconstructing Mediatization as an Analytical Concept," *European Journal of Communication* 19, no. 1 (2004), 87–101.

29. Jason C. Bivins, *Spirits Rejoice! Jazz and American Religion* (New York: Oxford University Press, 2015), 21.

30. Jeffrey H. Mahan, *Media, Religion, and Culture: An Introduction* (New York: Routledge, 2014), 6–7.

31. Gerhard Lenski, *The Religious Factor: A Sociologist's Inquiry* Rev. ed. (New York: Anchor Books, 1963), 331. Lenski's definition was informed by the work of French sociologist and philosopher Émile Durkheim and his 1912 work, *The Elementary Forms of the Religious Life*.

32. Clifford Geertz, *The Interpretation of Cultures* (New York: Basic Books, 1977), 90.

33. Robert A. Orsi, *Between Heaven and Earth: The Religious Worlds People Make and the Scholars Who Study Them* (Princeton: Princeton University Press, 2006), 73.

34. Mahan, *Media, Religion, and Culture* 7.

35. Stewart M. Hoover, *Religion in the News: Faith and Journalism in American Public Discourse* (Thousand Oaks, CA: Sage, 1998), 14–15.

36. Ibid., 15.

37. Mahan, *Media, Religion, and Culture* 36.

38. Ibid., 27.

39. Egon G. Guba and Yvonna S. Lincoln, "Paradigmatic Controversies, Contradictions, and Emerging Confluences. In Norman K. Denzin and Yvonna S. Lincoln (Eds.), *The Landscape of Qualitative Research: Theories and Issues* 2nd ed. (Thousand Oaks, CA: Sage, 2003), 273.

40. "Many Americans Mix Multiple Faiths," Pew Research Center, December 9, 2009, http://www.pewforum.org/2009/12/09/many-americans-mix-multiple-faiths/

41. Michael Lipka, "Key Findings About American Catholics," Pew Research Center, September 2, 2015, http://www.pewresearch.org/fact-tank/2015/09/02/key-findings-about-american-catholics/.

42. "America's Changing Religious Landscape," Pew Research Center, May 12, 2015, http://www.pewforum.org/2015/05/12/americas-changing-religious-landscape/.

43. Ibid.

44. Emily McFarlan Miller, "Survey: White Evangelicals Say US No Longer a Christian Nation," *Religion News Service*, June 23, 2016, accessed January 18, 2017, http://religion-

news.com/2016/06/23/survey-evangelicals-say-us-no-longer-a-christian-nation/. The 2016 presidential contest between Hillary Clinton and Donald Trump was a contentious, divisive, and expensive race. Clinton garnered nearly 3 million more votes in the popular vote count, but Trump won the Electoral College, defeating Clinton 306–232.

45. Stephen Labaton, "Constitution Based in Christian Principles, McCain Says," *New York Times*, September 29, 2007, http://www.nytimes.com/2007/09/29/us/politics/29cnd-mccain.html.

46. John Meacham, "A Nation of Christians Is Not a Christian Nation," *New York Times*, October 7, 2007, http://www.nytimes.com/2007/10/07/opinion/07meacham.html.

47. Robert P. Jones, "The Great Trump Hope," *New York Times*, July 11, 2016, A23.

48. Robert P. Jones, *The End of White Christian America* (New York: Simon & Schuster, 2016), 1.

49. Ibid., 2.

50. Ibid., 3.

51. David W. Bebbington, *Evangelicalism in Modern Britain: A History from the 1730s to the 1980s* (New York: Taylor & Francis, 1989), 1.

52. Ibid., 2–3. This definition has been called the "Bebbington quadrilateral."

53. Timothy Gloege, "#Itsnotus: Being Evangelical Means Never Having To Say You're Sorry," Religion Dispatches, January 3, 2018, http://religiondispatches.org/itsnotus-being-evangelical-means-never-having-to-say-youre-sorry/.

54. Ibid.

55. Ibid.

56. "Influential Evangelicals: Mark Noll," *TIME*, February 7, 2005, http://content.time.com/time/specials/packages/article/0,28804,1993235_1993243_1993309,00.html.

57. Mark A. Knoll, *The Scandal of the Evangelical Mind* (Grand Rapids: Eerdmans, 1994), 3.

58. Ciera Horton, "*The Record* Meets with Acclaimed Academic Mark Noll," *The Wheaton Record*, December 28, 2017, http://www.wheatonrecord.com/news/record-meets-acclaimed-academic-mark-noll/.

59. Ibid.

60. Bob Smietana, "Latest Survey: Most Evangelicals Are Not Voting Trump," *Christianity Today*, October 14, 2016, http://www.christianitytoday.com/news/2016/october/most-evangelicals-not-voting-trump-beliefs-identity-lifeway.html. There is confusion about how many evangelicals there are in the United States, and just who qualifies as an evangelical. Many evangelicals are labeled as such because they self-identify. "'Fewer than half of those who identify as evangelicals (45 percent) strongly agree with core evangelical beliefs. . . . There's a gap between who evangelicals say they are and what they believe,' said Scott McConnell, executive director of LifeWay Research. And a significant number of evangelical believers reject the term 'evangelical.' Only two-thirds (69 percent) of evangelicals by belief self-identify as evangelicals." See Bob Smietana, "Many Who Call Themselves Evangelical Don't Actually Hold Evangelical Beliefs," LifeWay Research, December 6, 2017, http://lifewayresearch.com/2017/12/06/many-evangelicals-dont-hold-evangelical-beliefs/.

61. Horton, President Bill Clinton had a sexual affair with intern Monica Lewinsky that went public in 1998.

62. Frances FitzGerald, *The Evangelicals: The Struggle to Shape America* (New York: Simon & Schuster, 2017), 147.

63. Ibid., 147–148.

64. Ibid., 163–164.

65. Becka A. Alper, "Millennials Are Less Religious Than Older Americans, But Just As Spiritual," Pew Research Center, November 23, 2015, http://www.pewresearch.org/fact-tank/2015/11/23/millennials-are-less-religious-than-older-americans-but-just-as-spiritual/.

66. "Religion and the Unaffiliated," Pew Research Center, October 9, 2012, accessed August 3, 2015, http://www.pewforum.org/2012/10/09/nones-on-the-rise-religion/.

67. Amy Hollywood, "Spiritual but Not Religious," *Harvard Divinity Bulletin*, Winter/Spring 2010, 19–20.

68. Steven D. Greydanus, "Martin Sheen and Emilio Estevez Travel the Ancient Pilgrimage Route Together and Finish their Journey of Faith with a Flourish," *National Catholic Register*, October 7, 2011, accessed August 9, 2015, http://www.ncregister.com/daily-news/sdg-reviews-the-way.

69. Christian Smith, "On 'Moralistic Therapeutic Deism' as U.S. Teenagers' Actual, Tacit, De Facto Religious Faith," *Religion and Youth* (2010), 41–46. This essay was adapted from "Summary Interpretation: Moralistic Therapeutic Deism," in *Soul Searching: The Religious and Spiritual Lives of American Teenagers* by Christian Smith with Melinda Lundquist Denton (Oxford, OUP, 2005).

70. Smith, "On 'Moralistic Therapeutic Deism.'"

71. Christian Smith, quoted in Rod Dreher, "Trump Can't Save American Christianity," *New York Times*, August 3, 2017, A19.

72. Jerry Adler, "In Search of the Spiritual," *Newsweek*, August 29/September 5, 2005, pp. 46–65.

73. ToshaSilver.com, accessed December 20, 2017, https://toshasilver.com.

74. *The Power of Now* Facebook site, https://www.facebook.com/The-Power-of-Now-A-Guide-to-Spiritual-Enlightenment-352603881600892/.

75. "The Four Agreements: A Practical Guide to Personal Freedom Audio Book," *Publishers Weekly*, accessed August 3, 2015, http://www.publishersweekly.com/978-1-878424-43-3.

76. Kathryn Lofton, *Oprah: The Gospel of an Icon* (Berkeley: University of California Press, 2011), 42.

77. Ibid.

78. Matthew 7:7, KJV. Practitioners of the Prosperity Gospel include Robert Tilton and Joel Osteen.

79. Lofton, *Oprah* 43.

80. Lillian Daniel, "Spiritual But Not Religious? Please Stop Boring Me," *The Huffington Post*, September 13, 2011, http://www.huffingtonpost.com/lillian-daniel/spiritual-but-not-religio_b_959216.html.

81. Ibid.

82. Lillian Daniel, *When "Spiritual But Not Religious" Is Not Enough: Seeing God in Surprising Places, Even the Church* (New York: Jericho Books, 2013), 6.

83. Eric Vanvalin, "Marc Maron: Peeling Back the Layers of Comedy's Most Spiritually Minded Skeptic," *Relevant*, May–June 2015, 62.

84. *WTF* Podcast 613–President Barack Obama, June 22, 2015. See also, "Obama Visits Marc Maron's Garage; Cats Annoyed They Were Shut In Bedroom," *Fresh Air*, NPR, June 22, 2015, accessed January 18, 2017, http://www.npr.org/sections/itsallpolitics/2015/06/22/416481081/obama-visits-marc-marons-garage-cats-annoyed-they-were-shut-in-bedroom.

85. Vanvalin, "Marc Maron," 63.

86. Wade Clark Roof, *A Generation of Seekers: The Spiritual Journeys of the Baby Boom Generation* (San Francisco: Harper San Francisco, 1993). Demographically, Baby Boomers are defined as the post-world War II generation born between 1945–1962.

87. Wade Clark Roof, *Spiritual Marketplace: Baby Boomers and the Remaking of American Religion* (Princeton: Princeton University Press, 1999), 80.

88. Leonard Norman Primiano, "Oprah, Geraldo, Barbara, and Things That Go Bump in the Night: Negotiating the Supernatural on American Television," in *God in the Details: American Religion in Popular Culture,* eds. Eric Michael Mazur and Kate McCarthy (New York: Routledge, 2001), 57.

89. Primianio, 58. For more on spirituality as a melding of traditions, see Robert Wuthnow, *After Heaven: Spirituality in America Since the 1950s* (Berkeley: University of California Press, 1998), 72–74; 114–41.

90. Ray B. Browne, "Popular Culture: Notes Toward a Definition," *Popular Culture and Curricula* (Bowling Green, OH: Bowling Green University Popular Press, 1970), pp. 3–11; reprinted in *Popular Culture and the Expanding Consciousness*, ed. Ray B. Browne (New York: John Wiley & Sons, 1973), 14.

91. Gordon Lynch, *Understanding Theology and Popular Culture* (Oxford: Blackwell, 2005), 14, quoted in Lyden and Mazur, 14.

92. Will Rockett, "Crossing Wire Borders: Concepts of Popular Culture in film & Television Studies," in *Continuities in Popular Culture: The Present in the Past & The Past in the Present and Future*, eds. Ray B. Browne and Ronald J. Ambrosetti (Bowling Green: Bowling Green State University Popular Press, 1993), 150; quoted in *Religion and Popular Culture*, eds. Daniel A. Stout and Judith M. Buddenbaum (Ames, IA: Iowa State University Press, 2001), 5.

93. *Religion and Popular Culture*, eds. Daniel A. Stout and Judith M. Buddenbaum (Ames, IA: Iowa State University Press, 2001), 5.

94. John C. Lyden, "Definitions," *The Routledge Companion to Religion and Popular Culture*, eds. John C. Lyden and Eric Michael Mazur (London: Routledge, 2015), 12–13.

95. Ibid., 14.

96. R. Laurence Moore, *Selling God: American Religion in the Marketplace of Culture* (New York: Oxford UP, 1994), 254.

97. Ibid., 5.

98. Robert Warshow, "Author's Preface," *The Immediate Experience: Movies, Comics, Theatre and Other Aspects of Popular Culture* (Garden City, NY: Anchor Books, 1964), xxiii, xxviii.

99. Lyden, "Definitions," 14.

100. Quentin J. Schultze, "Touched by Angels and Demons: Religion's Love-Hate Relationship with Popular Culture," in *Religion and Popular Culture*, eds. Daniel A. Stout and Judith M. Buddenbaum (Ames, IA: Iowa State University Press, 2001), 46.

101. Ibid., 42.

102. Schultze, *Christianity and the Mass Media in America*, 187.

103. John C. Lyden, "Definitions," in *The Routledge Companion to Religion and Popular Culture*, eds. John C. Lyden and Eric Michael Mazur (New York: Routledge, 2015), 7.

104. William F. Fore, "The Church and Communication in the Technological Era," *The Christian Century*, September 24, 1986, 811.

105. *Journal of the American Academy of Religion* 59, no. 4 (Fall 1996).

106. Catherine L. Albanese, "Religion and American Popular Culture: An Introductory Essay," *Journal of the American Academy of Religion* 59, no. 4 (Fall 1996), 736. See also, Charles H. Long, "Popular Religion," *The Encyclopedia of Religion* ed. Mircea Eliade, et al. (New York: Macmillan, 1987).

107. Heidi Campbell, *When Religion Meets New Media* (London: Routledge, 2010), 6.

108. Ibid., 41.

109. Campbell, *When Religion Meets New Media*, 60. For more on the theory of social shaping of technology, or SST, see, for example: Donald MacKenzie and Judy Wajcman, eds., *The Social Shaping of Technology: How the Refrigerator Got Its Hum* (Milton Keynes, UK: Open University Press, 1985); Robin Williams and David Edge, "The Social Shaping of Technology," *Research Policy* 25 (1996), 865–899.

110. Heidi Campbell, *Digital Religion: Understanding Religious Practice in New Media Worlds* (London: Routledge, 2013).

111. Stewart M. Hoover, Public Religion Project, Center for Media, Religion and Culture, University of Colorado, Boulder, accessed December 15, 2017, https://www.colorado.edu/cmrc/public-religion-project.

112. Stewart M. Hoover, "Concluding Thoughts: Imagining the Religious in and Through the Digital," in Heidi Campbell, *Digital Religion: Understanding Religious Practice in New Media Worlds*, 267–268.

113. Stewart M. Hoover, *Religion in the Media Age* (London: Routledge, 2006), 9.

114. Ibid., 8.

115. Stewart M. Hoover and Lynn Schofield Clark, *Practicing Religion in the Age of the Media: Explorations in Media, Religion, and Culture* (New York: Columbia University Press, 2002), 2.

116. Stewart M. Hoover, *Religion in the News: Faith and Journalism in American Public Discourse* (Thousand Oaks, CA: Sage, 1998), 1.

117. Mark Silk, *Unsecular Media: Making News of Religion in America* (Urbana: University of Illinois Press, 1995), 53.

xliv *Introduction*

118. Doug Underwood, *From Yahweh to Yahoo! The Religious Roots of the Secular Press* (Urbana: University of Illinois Press, 2002), 19–20.

119. Judith M. Buddenbaum and Debra L. Mason, *Readings on Religion as News* (Ames, IA: Iowa State University Press, 2000).

120. Judith M. Buddenbaum and Daniel A. Stout, *Religion and Popular Culture: Studies on the Interaction of Worldviews* (Ames, IA: Iowa State University Press, 2001), 30; Judith M. Buddenbaum and Daniel A. Stout, *Religion and Mass Media: Audiences and Adaptations* (Thousand Oaks, CA: Sage, 1996). For the seminal article on agenda-setting theory, see Maxwell E. McCombs and Donald L. Shaw, "The Agenda-Setting Function of Mass Media," *Public Opinion Quarterly* 36, no. 2, January 1972, 176–187. Agenda-setting theory holds that media do not tell audiences what to think, but through salience, selection, and placement of stories, can influence what audiences think *about.*

121. Thomas R. Lindlof, "Interpretive Community: An Approach to Media and Religion," *Journal of Media and Religion* 1, no. 1 (2002), 62.

122. *The Shack*, Box Office Mojo, accessed May 24, 2017, http://www.boxofficemojo.com/movies/?id=theshack.htm. The film is discussed in more detail in this book.

123. David Sloan, *Media and Religion in American History* (Northport, AL: Vision Press, 2000), vii.

124. David Paul Nord, "The Evangelical Origins Of Mass Media in America, 1815–1835." *Journalism Monographs* 88 (1984): 1–30.

125. "Moral Majority," Gilder Lehrman Institute of American History, accessed June 13, 2017, https://www.gilderlehrman.org/history-by-era/age-reagan/timeline-terms/moral-majority.

126. Religious Landscape Study, Pew Forum, 2017.

127. From the Southeastern Seminary website: "At the heart of Southeastern's mission is to provide trained, passionate and humble men of God to serve as pastors in Southern Baptist and other evangelical churches." Southeastern Baptist Theological Seminary, "MDiv in Preaching and Pastoral Ministry," https://www.sebts.edu/academics/masters/MDiv/mdiv-preaching-and-pastoral.aspx.

128. Bob Allen, "Southern Baptists Have Lost A Million Members in 10 Years," *Baptist News Global*, June 9, 2017, https://baptistnews.com/article/southern-baptists-lost-million-members-10-years/#.WT__7MbllDX. See the LifeWay Christian Resources Annual Church Profile Statistical Summary at: Carol Pipe, "ACP: Churches Up in 2016; Baptisms, Membership Decline," June 8, 2017, http://www.bpnews.net/49005/acp--churches-up-in-2016-baptisms-membership-decline.

129. David Waters, Holly Meyer, and Amy McRary, "How Trump is Highlighting Divisions Among Southern Baptists," *USA Today Network*, June 10, 2017, https://www.usatoday.com/story/news/nation-now/2017/06/10/how-trump-highlighting-divisions-among-southern-baptists/386329001/?utm_source=Pew+Research+Center&utm_campaign=2b3cd8e83b-EMAIL_CAMPAIGN_2017_06_13&utm_medium=email&utm_term=0_3e953b9b70–2b3cd8e83b-399903629.

130. Gregory A. Smith and Jessica Martinez, "How the Faithful Voted: A Preliminary 2016 Analysis," Pew Research Center, November 9, 2016, http://www.pewresearch.org/fact-tank/2016/11/09/how-the-faithful-voted-a-preliminary-2016-analysis/. According to Pew, "eight-in-ten self-identified white, born-again/evangelical Christians say they voted for Trump, while just 16 percent voted for [Democrat Hillary] Clinton."

131. Julie Zauzmer and Michelle Boorstein, "Evangelicals Fear Muslims; Atheists Fear Christians: New Poll Show[s] How Americans Mistrust One Another," the *Washington Post*, September 7, 2017, https://www.washingtonpost.com/news/acts-of-faith/wp/2017/09/07/evangelicals-fear-muslims-atheists-fear-christians-how-americans-mistrust-each-other/?utm_term=.c3e632c6408c. For original poll data, see Baylor Religion Survey, September 2017, https://www.baylor.edu/baylorreligionsurvey/doc.php/292546.pdf.

I

Civil Religion

Chapter One

Moral Mondays in the South

God-Talk, Christian Activism, and Civil Disobedience in the Digital Age

And the King shall answer and say unto them, Verily I say unto you, Inasmuch as ye have done it unto one of the least of these my brethren, ye have done it unto me.

—Matthew 25:40, KJV

INTRODUCTION

God is never mentioned in the U.S. Constitution. It is legal (though unlikely) for an atheist to be elected president, and there is no religious litmus test for holding any public office or judgeship. Yet, Congress opens its sessions with a prayer, and it employs a chaplain; both Congressional Democrats and Republicans attend National Prayer Breakfasts and speak in houses of worship; presidents routinely end addresses with the closing words, "God bless the United States of America"; the U.S. Supreme Court convenes with the words, "God save the United States and this Honorable Court!"[1]

Nearly 91 percent of members of the 115th Congress sworn in after the 2016 elections identified as Christian, according to Pew Research. That figure is far higher than the general population, which is made up of 75 percent self-professed Christians.[2] Those in conservative and progressive religious camps often reject the right/left terminology associated with their respective causes. Many argue that these designations are too narrow to describe nuanced positions that can vary from issue to issue, and they would be correct.

3

"Religious Right" and "Religious Left" are media and journalistic terms of descriptive convenience.

Issues typically associated with the Protestant Religious Right and conservative Catholicism include policies seen as intrusions upon personal belief and practice. Abortion is viewed as murder, and anti-abortion rallies are staged in front of the U.S. Supreme Court each January on the anniversary of the 1973 Roe v. Wade decision legalizing abortion.[3] Some employers object to the use of contraceptives on religious grounds and seek to opt out of healthcare mandates. Homosexuality is regarded as sinful. County magistrates invoke Bible verses when refusing to issue marriage licenses to same-sex couples, as do bakers and florists who decline to serve gay weddings.[4]

Politically active Christian figures closely associated with these and similar causes are Franklin Graham, president of the Billy Graham Evangelistic Association (BGEA) and Samaritan's Purse, a Christian relief organization; Timothy Busch, founder and funder of the conservative Catholic Napa Institute; Pat Robertson, founder of Regent University and *The 700 Club* television program; Liberty University president Jerry Falwell, Jr.; and Bob Jones III, president of Bob Jones University.[5]

The Religious Left is historically enmeshed with issues of poverty and social justice. Suffragette, pacifist, socialist, and homeless advocate Dorothy Day spawned the Catholic Worker Movement in the early twentieth century. Day's charity work and writings, including in her newspaper *The Catholic Worker*, were grounded in her faith. During civil rights battles of the 1950s and 1960s, Dr. Martin Luther King Jr., a Baptist minister, quoted the Bible regularly in his fight for racial equality. King marched and preached in Montgomery and Selma, Alabama and other Southern cities alongside progressive rabbis, priests, Protestant pastors of all races, as well as lay members of various faiths. In the present age, income imbalance, access to healthcare, and marriage equality are rallying cries of the Religious Left, though some progressive congregations have split over same-sex unions.[6]

Christian conservatives have been largely successful in seeking public office. Scholar Albert J. Raboteau framed the current political and religious environment this way in his book *American Prophets: Seven Religious Radicals & Their Struggle for Social and Political Justice:*

> Current distrust of the role of religion in politics is focused on the divisive force of hot-button issues, such as abortion, gay and lesbian rights, school prayer, "family values," the putative "secularization" of American society, and the role of the religious right in electoral politics, augmented by the intemperate and emotional, if not vitriolic language of print, radio, television, and Internet commentators, who increase and arouse their audiences by frequently belittling, ridiculing, and demonizing those with whom they disagree.[7]

Elements of Raboteau's analysis were present in critiques of the progressive Moral Monday movement, including criticism "augmented by the intemperate and emotional, if not vitriolic language of print, radio, television, and Internet commentators." Moral Monday organizers resisted left/right labels, however, arguing that they were fighting for equality and justice for all, as King did. Media portrayals, however, hewed more closely to a storyline of liberal social justice warriors pitted against right-wing extremists.

MORAL MONDAYS

The influence, and in some cases corruption, of corporations and banks was the driving force behind the 2011 global protests known collectively as the Occupy Movement, a largely secular populist campaign that stretched from New York to London and beyond.[8] The religiously tinged Moral Monday movement two years later in the previously moderate Southern state of North Carolina was partially about income inequality, but was also aimed at a plethora of legislation concerning voting rights, gay rights, and other issues regulated by a conservative Republican majority in the state General Assembly.

The Moral Monday movement was spearheaded by a Protestant pastor, the Reverend Dr. William J. Barber II, then-head of the state chapter of the National Association for the Advancement of Colored People (NAACP). "William Barber is the closest person we have to Martin Luther King, Jr. in our midst," declared Cornel West, the outspoken Professor of Philosophy and Christian Practice at Union Theological Seminary.[9]

More than 25,000 Moral Monday protestors of various ages, races, and professions such as healthcare workers, teachers, and clergy, traveled from around the state to the capital of Raleigh during the summer of 2013 (80,000 gathered in a follow-up rally in early 2014) to protest what they saw as "immoral" laws.[10] No blood was shed, and the stakes were arguably lower than those of King's lifetime, but the months-long Moral Monday protests were filled with high drama—preaching, prayer, politics, nearly 1,000 arrests, international news coverage, a smattering of show business, and social media retaliation. This was a political and religious social movement for the Digital Age.

This chapter is a case study of the 2013 Moral Monday movement in North Carolina, and the use of progressive Christianity and religious rhetoric as tactics for social justice protest in the modern media era. Moral Mondays and related movements led by Barber continued beyond 2013, but the focus here will be on the initial burst of protests that first formative year.

Themes explored include: 1) the role religious rhetoric played in this twenty-first century protest movement; 2) the tone of news coverage of Moral Mondays; 3) how social media was used by both the protestors and their critics; and 4) the political effectiveness of the protests, including:

- Outcomes of the 2014 midterm elections in North Carolina.
- Protestors' legal challenges to Republican-passed bills, including Voter ID, gerrymandered political redistricting, and other laws.
- Public awareness and perception of the Moral Monday movement.
- The rising public profile and national influence of William Barber.

EVANGELICALS AND POLITICAL MOVEMENTS

Religion is ever-present in American politics and civic culture, especially among Protestant Christian evangelicals. According to historian and journalist Frances FitzGerald, "Evangelicals are a product of the two Great Awakenings in the eighteenth and nineteenth centuries that turned virtually all American Protestants into evangelicals—people who believe in a high view of the Bible, salvation coming from Christ's sacrifice on the cross, and the need to be born again in Christ. They also believed in spreading the good news of the gospel."[11]

Spreading the gospel is not only about outreach for evangelicals, but also about public demonstrations of piety. Evangelical piety takes many forms, and has outsized influence in the realm of American politics, particularly when race is a factor. White conservative, born-again, evangelical Christians have long been identified with the Republican Party.[12] In the 1960s, the GOP courted white Southern voters with what was called the "Southern Strategy." Up through the mid-twentieth century, most Southerners had been Democrats since the election of Franklin D. Roosevelt, but disenchantment set in for many whites when the party began supporting civil rights and integration.

As Robert P. Jones, CEO of the Public Religion Research Institute (PRRI), noted, "[W]ith the passage of landmark civil rights legislation like the Civil Rights Act of 1964 and the Voting Rights Act of 1965, Republican Party Strategists saw an opportunity to coax disgruntled white southern voters into their camp."[13]

"Beginning in 1960," writes scholar and journalist Kenneth L. Woodward, "no Democratic candidate for president had won a majority of the white Evangelical vote." That changed in 1976 when Georgia's Democratic Governor, Jimmy Carter, ran for president. In response to a question, Carter said he was "born again," a statement that confused the press, but "sent a linguistic signal to Southern Baptists in particular and Evangelicals in general that he was one of them."[14]

Carter defeated Republican incumbent Gerald Ford, despite Ford's declaration that he, too, was an Evangelical Christian.[15] Two weeks before the election, Woodward published a cover story in *Newsweek* "proclaiming 1976 'The Year of the Evangelicals.'" This article, coming out in the nation's bicentennial year, was seen as a "media milestone" by many Evangelicals, Woodward notes. "[F]or the first time, Evangelical Americans were recognized as a distinct and numerous movement in American religion, right up there with Catholics and mainline Protestants."[16]

Carter served only one term as president, but white Evangelicals were just getting started. "Carter's election in 1976 was only a temporary stay in what would ultimately be a decisive judgment against the Democratic Party by white, mostly Christian voters in the South," according to Jones.[17] He refers to this shift as the "White Christian Strategy." By 1980, the Jerry Falwell-led Moral Majority had formed, consolidating power into a new Christian Right—not a *Religious* Right, but a uniquely *Christian* one. There were three presidential candidates that year: Carter, Republican contender Ronald Reagan, and independent John Anderson. All three claimed to be born-again Christians. Falwell and other Christian Right leaders threw their weight behind the conservative Reagan, who, as Woodward put it, "rarely saw the inside of a church."[18]

But Reagan was a former actor who knew how to work a crowd and deliver a line. Speaking to 17,000 Evangelicals at a right wing Religious Roundtable rally, Reagan said, "I know you cannot endorse me, but I want you to know that I endorse you."[19] Reagan trounced Carter in the 1980 election, going on to win by an even larger margin in 1984 over Walter Mondale, Carter's former vice president.[20] Thomas Jefferson's wall of separation between church and state had been punched full of holes.[21]

In his book, *The End of White Christian America*, Jones follows the trail of the White Christian Strategy beyond the Reagan era. In the 1990s, "Pat Robertson and Ralph Reed of the Christian Coalition of America, James Dobson of Focus on the Family, and Gary Bauer and Tony Perkins of the Family Research Council spoke for White Christian America through a proliferation of statewide and local chapters of their organizations."[22] It's worth noting that Pat Robertson and Gary Bauer each ran for president on the GOP ticket in 1988 and 2000, respectively.

By pounding away at expanding secularism and pluralism, white Christian numbers and influence continued to grow. Dobson emerged as a power broker and political activist for a time, using his broadcasting and publishing media concerns to reach millions of listeners and readers well into the George W. Bush administration. "Dobson was one of the engineers of the 2004 'Value Voters' campaign, which buoyed Bush's re-election and the passage of more than a dozen state-level bans on same-sex marriage," Jones writes.[23]

The Christian Right was aided in its mission of amassing political and cultural power by the coverage it received, and still receives, from the press, says media scholar Diane Winston. Winston, who holds the Knight Chair in Media and Religion at the USC Annenberg School for Communication and Journalism, draws a straight line from Ronald Reagan in the 1980s to the election of President Donald Trump in 2016. "How did a lying, philandering blowhard convince millions of Americans—including white evangelicals and the working poor—that he should be their president? I blame Ronald Reagan and the news media," Winston wrote in an essay published in the *Los Angeles Review of Books*.

According to the Tyndall Report, a news monitoring site, Trump's unorthodox candidacy received more than twice as much broadcast news coverage than Democrat Hillary Clinton during the 2016 campaign.[24] Cable networks often covered his rallies live. Trump also received more coverage than his fellow GOP presidential candidates, and was given more airtime during Republican debates.[25] "News coverage mainstreamed Reagan's worldview to elite and middle America, at the same time that televangelists like Jerry Falwell and Pat Robertson preached it to millions of countercultural Christian viewers," according to Winston. "Broadcast through both secular and religious media, a conservative perspective on the relationships between God and government, individual freedom and civic responsibility shifted the American religious imaginary—a shared notion of what matters and why—and legitimated the economic policies and political practices that gave rise both to Donald Trump and to the citizenry that supports his candidacy."[26]

The Christian effect in American politics remains active, with help from the news media megaphone. This chapter examines how Moral Monday organizers, many of them Christian progressives, used that megaphone for political protest.

SCHOLARSHIP OF RELIGION-INFUSED SOCIAL MOVEMENTS

Michael P. Young has explored major nineteenth-century protest movements "combining the evangelical schemas of *public confession* and *the special sins of the nation* . . . within a national infrastructure of Protestant institutions" [italics in original]. Young points out that, "The movements for temperance and the immediate abolition of slavery were the first national social movements in the United States, but they emerged in interaction with religious and civil institutions, not the state."[27] Amending previous perspectives, such as "contentious politics" and "life politics," as the motivations behind sustained and interregional protest movements, Young makes the case for a religious perspective:

> I argue that what is needed to explain the first U.S. national social movements
> is an appreciation that struggles very much like the life politics of today
> emerged in the 1830s within civil society. A cultural mechanism combining

intensive and extensive religious schemas launched and sustained these popular movements. This mechanism produced a modular form of protest with special and national purposes, and it mobilized actors and resources by fusing personal desires for reformation with goals for national change.[28]

"Evangelical Protestantism constituted a national infrastructure of resources independent of political and economic institutions," Young writes. "These resources conveyed the schemas of confession and sin. The first national social movements emerged as particular variants of the schemas of sin and confession combined."[29]

Religion can be an important resource for protest movements. Religious social networks can be used to mobilize a critical mass of participants, as in the case of Moral Mondays. Religion, even for the nonreligious, can also offer inspiration when addressing right and wrong and championing social justice. As researchers Kraig Beyerlein, Sarah A. Soule, and Nancy Martin noted, "religion supplies *moral resources* to social movements" [italics in original].[30] Beyerlein, Soule, and Martin have also shown that religion even tends to dictate the policing of protest movements. If there is a chance of threatening tactics, increased oversight by authorities occurs:

> We find that police were, in fact, less likely to show up at protest events when general religious actors, actions, or organizations were present, relative to events with secular activists. However, we find that these differences are due to the different ways protesters behave at events. That is, with the introduction of threatening tactics, the significant protective effect of general religion goes away.
>
> We complicate this finding, however, in several ways. First, when disaggregating our broad religion category into different religious traditions, only mainline and black Protestant groups are less likely than secular groups to be policed. As with the general religion finding, both of these traditions' buffering effects are a function of promoting less threatening tactics at events. In addition, we find that, controlling for tactics known from past research to incite police response, law enforcement agents show up to events featuring fundamentalist Christians at *higher* rates than they do events involving secular groups. Further evidence against the theory of religion as privileged legitimacy is observed in that non-Christian religious groups using extremely confrontational tactics are *more* likely to be policed than are similarly behaving secular groups.[31]

Police presence that tends to be heavier for protests by fundamentalist Christians may result from this group being seen as less respected and more of a deviation from mainstream religion.[32] As will be discussed in the sections to come, there was a heavy police presence at Moral Monday events staged inside the North Carolina State Capitol and the General Assembly legislative building.

BACKGROUND OF THE MORAL MONDAY MOVEMENT

Unlike the mostly leaderless and secular Occupy Movement, where dominant voices came and went, Moral Mondays were led by the charismatic African American Disciples of Christ minister William Barber. The weekly protests were an offshoot of Barber's progressive, social justice-focused Forward Together Moral Movement. Moral Mondays initially consisted of rallies concentrated in the state capital of Raleigh against assorted legislation proposed by a Republican supermajority in the legislature, but eventually expanded to other cities around the state. Policies proposed by GOP lawmakers were deemed by the activists to be immoral and hurtful, especially to the poor.

The Reverend Barber had long been involved in social justice causes, including voting rights, health care reform, labor and immigration rights, and funding for disadvantaged students. Barber was born in Indianapolis on August 30, 1963, two days after Martin Luther King Jr. delivered his "I Have a Dream" address at the 1963 March on Washington for Jobs and Freedom. Like King, Barber's father was a preacher, and he planted the seeds of activism in young William when he moved the family to Washington County in rural eastern North Carolina from Indiana in the 1960s to help desegregate local schools. "I grew up under that tutelage of not understanding how to be a Christian without being concerned about justice and the larger community," he said in a 2013 interview with the liberal *Indy Week* alternative newspaper.[33]

Barber later graduated cum laude from historically black North Carolina Central University with a bachelor's degree in political science.[34] He received a Master of Divinity degree from Duke University and his doctorate from Drew University in public policy and pastoral care. Since 1993, Barber has served as pastor of Greenleaf Christian Church in Goldsboro, North Carolina (population 36,400), a majority African-American town. Knowledgeable about politics and history as well as theology, he was elected head of the state NAACP in 2005, stepping down in 2017.[35]

In addition to the Forward Together movement, Moral Mondays also sprang from an earlier fusion protest effort by Barber and the Reverend Dr. Nancy Petty, a white activist and the openly gay pastor of Raleigh's Pullen Memorial Baptist Church. That movement, called the Historic Thousands on Jones Street (HKonJ), named for the location of the legislative building, began in 2006 with 14 assorted and previously unrelated organizations in a display of fusion politics.

As Barber told *The American Prospect* magazine in 2013,

We recognized that many of the same political forces that are against, say, gender rights, are often also against education equality, environmental justice, and policies that help the poor. And so we said that we needed in North Carolina—and we said this is when Democrats were in office—to have a new form of fusion politics if we were going to really address the South . . .

We've been pushing this moral agenda, this positive agenda rooted in constitutional values, even before the Republicans took over. We've talked about the need to have an anti-racism, anti-poverty, anti-war agenda. An anti-discrimination and pro-human rights agenda. And we were successful. That's why North Carolina got same-day registration and early voting and Sunday voting and opened up the most progressive [voting] laws in the South that actually produced [President Barack] Obama. [36]

The 2013 Moral Monday protests coincided with the 50th anniversary of King's "I Have a Dream" speech. At that earlier historic demonstration of fusion politics, King joined with labor and civil rights activists to protest the unequal and harsh treatment of black Americans. The Washington march gave momentum to a movement that eventually led to passage of the Civil Rights Act in 1964.

In early 1965, after being turned back twice by authorities, including a bloody clash on the Edmund Pettus Bridge in Selma, Alabama, a federal court judge permitted King and his fellow protestors to participate in a nonviolent march from Selma to the state capital of Montgomery. On Sunday, March 21, some 3,000 marchers started the trek on foot. The gathering swelled to more than 25,000 by the time they reached the capitol building on Thursday. Less than five months later, President Lyndon Johnson signed the Voting Rights Act of 1965. Raboteau writes that King saw the civil rights movement "as a moral struggle, a 'God-given cause,' that moved citizens of different ethnic, racial, and religious distinctions to act together." [37]

In addition to basic civil rights and the right of citizens to cast a vote, King was also keenly interested in economic justice. Accordingly, he "announced the Poor People's Campaign at a staff retreat for the Southern Christian Leadership Conference (SCLC) in November 1967. Seeking a 'middle ground between riots on the one hand and timid supplications for justice on the other,' King planned for an initial group of 2,000 poor people to descend on Washington, D.C., southern states and northern cities to meet with government officials to demand jobs, unemployment insurance, a fair minimum wage, and education for poor adults and children designed to improve their self-image and self-esteem." [38]

The idea for the Poor People's Campaign came from Marion Wright, director of the NAACP Legal Defense and Education Fund. "Desegregation and the right to vote were essential, but King believed that African Americans and other minorities would never enter full citizenship until they had economic security. Through nonviolent direct action, King and SCLC hoped to focus the nation's attention on economic inequality and poverty."

Pledging support were members of the Native American, Mexican American, Puerto Rican, and poorer white communities.[39]

King would not live to realize the potential of the Poor People's Campaign. He abruptly changed his plans to fly to North Carolina in April 1968 to campaign for the state's first black gubernatorial candidate, Reginald Hawkins. Instead, King traveled to Memphis, Tennessee to support black garbage workers who were on strike. He was assassinated there on the balcony of the Lorraine Motel on April 4. As Raleigh *News & Observer* political columnist Rob Christensen recounted the story,

> Hawkins was a 44-year-old minister, dentist, and civil rights leader from Charlotte. He decided to run for governor after studying the fusionist movement of the 1890s which encouraged him to attempt a coalition of "Negroes, poor people of all races and liberals." In the 1950's and 1960's he was a civil rights activist. He founded the Mecklenburg [County] Organization for Political Affairs (MOPA) and led Charlotte's black community in pickets and boycotts against numerous segregated institutions.[40]

Hawkins came in third behind two white sons of former governors, but garnered 129,808 votes, 18.5 percent of the total.[41]

"In the last years of Dr. King's life," writes poet Drew Dellinger, "his holistic vision led him to emphasize the connections between racism, militarism and economic injustice, and to see continuities across social movements. . . . Dr. King was not, as some charged, calling for what he termed a 'mechanical fusion' of the peace and civil rights movements. Still, he maintained, the issues were connected . . . in a 'revolution of values.'"[42] As will be explained later in this chapter, an earlier fusionist political movement in the nineteenth century also inspired William Barber's assorted coalitions.

Barber frequently cited King in his fiery sermons at Moral Monday protest rallies. Rife with spiritual language and heavy on scriptural references, the rallies were a rebuke to laws proposed by state Republicans and GOP Governor Patrick "Pat" McCrory, newly elected in 2012. Each week, protestors filled the hallways and offices of the N.C. General Assembly, leading to more than 900 arrests by summer's end. The Wake County courts became clogged as the numbers of arrested swelled throughout the summer.[43] Protestors were typically charged with misdemeanors, such as disorderly conduct, second-degree trespass, and violation of building rules.[44]

The first arrests came on Monday, April 29, 2013, when 50 protestors blocked the entrance to the N.C. Senate Chamber.[45] Barber and Duke Divinity Professor Timothy Tyson[46] were among 17 activists who refused to disperse when ordered to do so, and were taken into custody. In the prologue to his book, *The Third Reconstruction: Moral Mondays, Fusion Politics, and the Rise of a New Justice Movement*, Barber writes about that first day: "We did not call it a Moral Monday when we went to the legislature building that day. In fact, it took us nearly three weeks to name what we started with that simple act of protest. But when a small group of us stood together, refusing to accept an extreme makeover of state government that we knew would harm the most vulnerable among us, it was like a spark in a warehouse full of cured, dry tobacco leaves."[47]

Barber had also been arrested two years prior "for interrupting a legislative session to protest the state budget."[48] He called Governor McCrory and Republican legislative leaders "extremists" and this generation's "George Wallaces," a reference to the Democratic Alabama governor notorious for his efforts to prevent school integration in 1963, the year of the March on Washington. "Barber's mode of operation is inclined toward the dramatic gesture," according to Southern politics historian Ferrell Guillory.[49]

On the following Monday, 30 more people were arrested, including Charles van der Horst, MD, an infectious disease specialist affiliated with University of North Carolina Hospitals. Dr. van der Horst recounted his reasons for protesting and consenting to be arrested, despite possibly jeopardizing his career, in an essay for *The New England Journal of Medicine:*

> On May 6, 2013, I was arrested by the North Carolina Capitol Police in front of the doors of the state Senate chamber, protesting our legislature's decision to forgo Medicaid expansion under the Affordable Care Act (ACA) . . .
>
> In February 2013, before a law was passed in North Carolina blocking Medicaid expansion, health care workers and nongovernmental patient organizations held a press conference at the North Carolina General Assembly building. Then we published an editorial arguing that expanding Medicaid would be financially beneficial to North Carolina in the long run. Our legislature plowed on. So on April 29, 2013, the "Moral Monday" protests began, in an attempt to change the minds of Governor Pat McCrory, House Speaker [later U.S. Senator] Thom Tillis, and North Carolina legislators. To academics, such a quest might sound quixotic, but protests (along with common sense) have helped to lead several conservative Republican governors to change their views on Medicaid expansion. . . . We hoped that protests in North Carolina would have a similar effect . . .
>
> Although my personal decision to protest was somewhat spontaneous, the rally was not. The event was carefully planned by a broad coalition of North Carolinians, including environmentalists, voting-rights advocates, leaders in reproductive health, educators, workers, and immigrants, all led by the North Carolina NAACP. The protest was organized in the tradition of civil disobedience, whose history reaches back through Martin Luther King, Jr., and Mahatma Gandhi to Henry David Thoreau. Physicians and other health care workers chose to participate out of frustration at our inability to protect our poorest patients. . . . These problems are not unique to North Carolina.[50]

Raboteau writes that Martin Luther King "had a remarkable fluency" in both biblical literacy and scholarly discourse, having been tutored in both the pulpit and "the philosophical and theological traditions acquired at Morehouse College, Crozer Theological Seminary, and Boston University." His ability to quote scripture, Plato, and Thoreau, as well as cite principles embedded within the nation's founding documents, were a "major factor in the effectiveness of King's rhetoric," according to Raboteau.[51]

"To his admirers, Dr. Barber, a gifted preacher with a big-tent vision, is the strongest contender for King's mantle. And he invites the comparison," *New York Times* religion reporter Laurie Goodstein wrote in a profile. "In April [2017], to mark the 50th anniversary of the landmark sermon at Riverside Church in Manhattan in which King denounced the Vietnam War, saying, 'I cannot be silent,' Dr. Barber preached against [President Donald] Trump from the same pulpit and denounced what he saw as pervasive racism across the political right."[52] Goodstein described Barber's image of himself and his religious social justice activism:

> Loath to be labeled left-leaning or liberal, Dr. Barber cites the Constitution and the common good as freely as the Bible. "We use the words that progressives have thrown away—morality, welfare, poor, faith—because those are soul words," he says.
>
> He calls himself an evangelical "who takes seriously the Old Testament and Jesus." Yet he has fully embraced gay and transgender rights—and in North Carolina, home of the law restricting bathroom use by transgender people. The Bible, he notes, says far more about caring for the needy than it does about homosexuality or abortion.
>
> "How do you take two or three Scriptures and make a theology out of it, and claim it is the moral perspective, and leave 2,000 on the table?" he said. "That is a form of theological malpractice."[53]

Barber again echoes King's sentiments here when he chastises those who use Scripture selectively. King expressed similar disdain for fellow clergy in his much anthologized "Letter from Birmingham Jail":

> In the midst of a mighty struggle to rid our nation of racial and economic injustice, I have heard many ministers say: "Those are social issues, with which the gospel has no real concern." And I have watched many churches commit themselves to a completely other-worldly religion which makes a strange, un-Biblical distinction between body and soul, between the sacred and the secular.[54]

There have been modern political protests leading to massive rallies in state capitals, notably in Wisconsin in 2011.[55] But few if any of those protests matched the size and religious fervor of North Carolina's Moral Mondays.

REPUBLICANS TAKE THE REINS IN RALEIGH

Legislators nationwide frequently pass laws unpopular with various constituencies with little pushback beyond letters to the editor, social media rants, phone calls, or speeches at public meetings. Why was there such an intense, sustained backlash against Republican legislators in this instance? Part of the explanation lies in the fact that the Democratic Party had dominated North Carolina politics for nearly a century, and many longstanding laws and progressive policies implemented over the course of decades were reversed in short order after Republicans were swept into office in 2012.[56] Barber decried these "immoral" reversals as intentional targeting of vulnerable populations. "With a Republican newly elected as governor and a Republican-controlled legislature, North Carolina, long a politically moderate player in the South, will soon have its most conservative government in a century," the *New York Times* reported in December 2012.[57]

The sheer number of bills introduced in a short time span stunned even supporters who had put a Republican majority into office. Some of the proposed legislation Moral Monday activists found objectionable included:

- A repeal of the state Earned Income Tax Credit, which benefited the working poor, and provided a refundable tax credit to nearly 907,000 workers in 2011;
- A proposal to tighten Medicaid eligibility requirements for poor women;
- A plan to reduce unemployment benefits from 26 weeks to 12–20 weeks;
- A voter ID bill, effective in 2016, requiring a government-approved photo identification card to cast a vote, ostensibly to cut down on voter fraud, that also eliminated straight-ticket voting and shortened the period of time for early voting, provisions favored heavily by Democrats and black voters who tended to vote Democrat;[58]
- Repeal of the requirement that campaign ad disclosures must appear in or on an ad identifying who paid for it, reducing transparency;
- Loosening of gun restrictions to allow concealed carry permit holders to carry a firearm into restaurants and bars that serve alcohol as long as the permit holder is not consuming alcohol;
- Repeal of the Racial Justice Act that allowed death row inmates to use statistical evidence of racial discrimination in death penalty appeals.[59]

"We are protesting for things that my mother won," Barber told a reporter for *The New Yorker* magazine in 2016, "Like voting rights."[60]

As journalist Rob Christensen noted, "Through the 1930s, most black voters identified with the party of Abraham Lincoln. But that began to change during the New Deal and particularly gained momentum when Democrats began championing civil rights legislation and Republicans began

Chapter 1

courting disaffected conservative Democrats with their 'Southern Strategy.'"[61] Democrats nationwide ultimately became more identified with progressive causes, and remained in the majority in North Carolina until 2010. The state's centrist reputation, molded by a succession of mostly Democratic politicians in charge for a hundred years, produced education and economic reforms. The Research Triangle Park, the University of North Carolina system, and the N.C. Community College system were all established or refined under primarily Democratic administrations.

That changed in 2012, when for the first time since 1870, Republicans controlled both the General Assembly and the governor's office. As Rob Christensen put it in June 2013, "Numerous programs, laws and initiatives started by Democratic governors and Democratic legislatures are now on political life support as the first unified Republican government in Raleigh in more than a century gives new scrutiny to what has gone before.

"Generations of programs involving education, the environment, health care, election laws and economic development are being eliminated or gutted in the budgets proposed by either Governor Pat McCrory, the Senate or the House."[62]

"North Carolina has never had a problem bragging about its progressive history," Mary C. Curtis wrote in the *Washington Post* later that fall. "In 1960, when George Wallace was formulating the hard-line segregationist stand that would propel him to multiple terms in the Alabama statehouse, North Carolina was electing as its governor Terry Sanford, who was an advocate of education, an opponent of capital punishment and took moderate but definite steps toward integration, at the time a risk in the South."[63]

The state's progressive streak is also evident in its historical protest movements, Curtis said:

> In the early 1970s, Mecklenburg County liked to contrast pictures of the relative calm that greeted its busing of students to achieve school integration with the violence and vandalism up North in Boston's busing battles.
> And 50 years ago, in May 1963, a year before the Civil Rights Act of 1964 ended segregation in public accommodations, Charlotte leaders—black and white—paired up for two-by-two integration of restaurants, called "eat-ins," a name that played off the "sit-ins" of three years before at a Greensboro, N.C., Woolworth's counter.[64]

David Zucchino, writing in *The Los Angeles Times*, stated that, "North Carolina has long portrayed itself as a progressive former Confederate state—a moderate Southern beacon in civil rights and social justice. That image has been challenged since November [2012], when Republicans won the governor's race and took control of both the Legislature and governor's mansion for the first time since Reconstruction."[65]

John Hood, head of the John Locke Foundation, a conservative think tank in Raleigh, disagrees with the storyline of positive Democratic reform vs. negative Republican dismantling. "North Carolina's economic history is not an uninterrupted climb until 2007, when suddenly we fell," he said. The state's economic history "has been filled with peaks and dips, which can be attributed to factors ranging from state highway spending to international manufacturing trends." Hood maintained that, "Texas and Virginia have developed strong economies with more conservative governance."[66]

Republicans became the majority party in part due to outside campaign cash and GOP strategizing, but Democrats in state government also had high profile scandals that led to voter disenchantment. A Democratic leader of the state House of Representatives and an agriculture commissioner both went to jail on corruption charges. Two-term Democratic governor Michael Easley pled guilty in 2010 to filing a false campaign finance report.[67] His successor, former lieutenant governor Beverley Perdue, voluntarily served one term as North Carolina's first female governor, one poll designating her "the most unpopular Governor in the country."[68]

VALUES AND PRIORITIES OF RELIGIOUS CONSERVATIVES AND PROGRESSIVES

In his book, *Touchdown Jesus: The Mixing of Sacred and Secular in American History* (2003), R. Laurence Moore observes that, "For a long time, adherents of very conservative religious groups were less likely to be politically active than members of religious denominations that modernized their doctrines."[69]

> For much of American history it was not just the Jeffersonians who protected the wall of separation. It was religious conservatives who carefully cordoned off church work from the howling wilderness of the world where politicians raked their muck. They wanted no advice from the state about what it meant to be a good Christian. Suspicions about the dangers of a strong state were precisely what drove Americans to separate church and state in the first place. Southern Protestants had particular reasons to resist political moves that might impose someone's moral standards on others. Casting themselves as the victims of abolitionism and other Yankee crusades, they were historically conditioned to treat religion as a private matter. Only in the 1890s did they show much interest in moral legislation. And they did so then because laws against gambling and alcohol and prostitution were seen as ways to control African Americans.[70]

Moore writes that in the early 1960s, many white Christians in both conservative and liberal congregations were racist, and their churches were segregated. "Later, [conservatives] were prepared to acknowledge, along with other Americans, that religious politics had their finest hour in the civil rights campaigns. . . . What is more important, King had shown conservative Christians that the conscience of America could be altered."[71]

As noted earlier, those in conservative and progressive religious camps often reject right/left terminology, even though religion is often explained using these tropes. Below is a broad, generalized dichotomy of contemporary political worldviews of Christian conservatives and liberals. These frames appear often in news coverage of religion:

- CONSERVATIVES: Christianity in the United States is more closely associated with the Republican Party. Some members of the GOP identify as conservative evangelical Protestants who believe in Biblical inerrancy and the creationist theory that the world is about 6,000 years old and was created by God in six days as recorded in Genesis. (This perspective is on display at The Creation Museum in Petersburg, Kentucky.) Most Republican Catholics and Protestants alike speak of abortion as murder, although many Protestants are pro-death penalty, while Catholic doctrine is anti-death penalty. Politically conservative Protestants and Catholics consider homosexuality an aberrant lifestyle. Religiously conservative people abide by the dictum of loving the sinner, hating the sin. Evangelicals are compelled by their faith to spread the good news of Jesus Christ as personal savior to others. Charity is important, and philosophically should come from churches and individuals, not the government. Many believe that God's judgment will come to the wicked, and believers will be raptured into heaven (beliefs vary widely on this), while sinners left behind endure hell on earth, until the anti-Christ is defeated.

- LIBERALS: Liberal Christians tend to be less dogmatic and rule bound. Progressive politicians of faith typically reconcile modern science with religion, believe in evolution and protecting the environment, and support tolerance for those of different faiths, or of those with no faith. Equal rights for all, regardless of ethnicity, gender, or religious belief. Many progressives are "cafeteria Christians," cobbling together practices from various faith traditions to create unique and personalized belief systems, such as combining Methodism and Buddhism. Many liberals, indeed many Americans, see themselves as "spiritual" instead of religious, open to a variety of faith experiences.[72] They are typically pro-choice on abortion and accepting of gay people, and in one study, about 70 percent of gays identified as Christian.[73] There is an emphasis on good works, particularly helping the poor and feeding the hungry. The government is seen as a politically acceptable conduit for sharing wealth through progressive taxation and social programs. Many see the redistribution of wealth as a scriptural mandate that follows Jesus's admonition to care for the poor.

Writing about this bifurcation of Christianity, Australian theologian Michael Frost pointed out that NFL football players Tim Tebow and Colin Kaepernick are both devout Christians, and both are known for taking a knee on the field. Tebow kneels for public prayer. Kaepernick kneels for public protest. "Beginning in 2016, he refused to stand to attention during the playing of the American national anthem," Frost wrote in a column for the *Washington Post.* "Kaepernick decided to either remain seated or kneel during renditions of the *Star Spangled Banner* in support of Black Lives Matter and to protest police violence against black people."[74] As Frost points out, Tebow has received mostly praise while Kaepernick has received mostly condemnation, including death threats and accusations of being a traitor.

> It seems to me that Tim Tebow and Colin Kaepernick represent the two very different forms that American Christianity has come to.
>
> And not just in the United States. In many parts of the world it feels as though the church is separating into two versions, one that values personal piety, gentleness, respect for cultural mores, and an emphasis on moral issues like abortion and homosexuality, and another that values social justice, community development, racial reconciliation, and political activism . . .
>
> One is listening to Eric Metaxas and Franklin Graham. The other is listening to William Barber and John Perkins.
>
> One is rallying at the March for Life. The other is getting arrested at Moral Monday protests.[75]

In his 1997 book, *Stealing Jesus: How Fundamentalism Betrays Christianity*, author Bruce Bawer writes,

> Conservative Christianity understands a Christian to be someone who subscribes to a specific set of theological propositions about God and the afterlife, and who professes to believe that by subscribing to those propositions, accepting Jesus Christ as savior, and (except in the case of the most extreme separatist fundamentalists) evangelizing, he or she evades God's wrath and wins salvation (for Roman Catholics, good works also count); liberal Christianity, meanwhile, tends to identify Christianity with the experience of God's abundant love and with the commandment to love God and one's neighbor. If, for conservative Christians, outreach generally means zealous proselytizing of the "unsaved," for liberal Christians it tends to mean social programs directed at those in need.[76]

The cutting of social programs and the curbing of what Moral Monday protestors viewed as basic rights led to the culture clash between religious and secular progressives vs. political conservatives in North Carolina government.

THE RELIGIOUS ORDER OF MORAL MONDAYS

The Moral Monday rallies of 2013, which grew as the weeks passed, often had the feel of a Christian revival, despite attracting both religious and nonreligious adherents. There was a liturgical aspect to the highly organized and choreographed protests, a Kabuki-like rhythm that followed a prescribed script. "The throngs of demonstrators who flock to the grassy knoll outside the North Carolina Statehouse each Monday know the drill," begins a story by Yonat Shimron of Religion News Service. "They listen to a fiery speech denouncing the Republican majority's legislative actions. They sing freedom songs and chant civil rights slogans. Then they march two by two into the legislative building to be handcuffed by police and arrested for failing to obey orders to disperse."[77]

Marchers assembled each week in various churches near the capitol that opened their doors for the occasion. Barber briefed the crowd and asked for volunteers to be arrested for acts of civil disobedience. Colored armbands were distributed to those who chose not to be arrested. All marched to a large public space near the N.C. General Assembly building where the House and Senate were in session. Then Barber's sermon/address began.

In a piece for the progressive religious *Sojourners* magazine, Barber summed up some of the themes he reiterated at Moral Monday rallies. "We must remind those who make decisions regarding public policy what the prophet Isaiah said 'Woe unto those who legislate evil. . . . Rob the poor of their rights . . . make children and women their prey.'" Isaiah 10: 1–2.

"Martin Luther King Jr. said 46 years ago in one of his last sermons that if you ignore the poor, one day the whole system will collapse and implode. The costs are too high if we don't address systemic racism and poverty. It costs us our soul as a nation."[78] Barber stressed that, "Our agenda, by necessity, is based on hope not fear," and the movement uses "moral language to frame and critique public policy, based on our deepest moral and constitutional values, regardless of who is in power."[79]

Writing in the liberal web magazine *Salon*, freelance writer Kristin Rawls pointed out the progressive religious convictions of the Moral Monday movement. "It might surprise you to know that Jesus is frequently and unabashedly invoked in a protest movement that includes support for LGBT and abortion rights, but such is a simple fact of life in North Carolina. The Moral Monday protests here seek to reclaim the rhetoric of morality and—often explicitly Christian—spirituality in ways that are confounding to the Tea Party."[80] Rawls, who lives in North Carolina, described Moral Mondays as "[a] left-wing protest that seeks to reclaim the banner of prayer and morality."[81]

After each open-air rally, protestors entered the legislative building on Jones Street, which Barber called "the People's House," and sang hymns and chanted slogans. When the order came from state and police authorities to disperse, most of the crowd departed, while those who volunteered to be arrested that day clasped their hands behind them to await the zip ties that bound their wrists. Supporters would line the road beside the buses that transported those being detained to the Wake County jail, shouting words of encouragement and thanks.

By mid-June, there had been more than 350 arrests at Moral Monday events. Clergy from various faiths took the lead at a rally on June 10, 2013 with statements of support for Barber and the movement, signed by seven rabbis and Catholic and Episcopal bishops. One of the signees was Bishop of the Episcopal Diocese of North Carolina, Michael Bruce Curry, who was elected the first African-American presiding bishop of the Episcopal Church two years later in June 2015.[82]

"At a time when the country is becoming less religious and liberal politicians shy away from faith-based rhetoric, this Disciples of Christ minister [Barber], steeped in the activist traditions of the black church, has emerged as a galvanizing force in North Carolina's pushback against the Republican-dominated legislature," Shimron wrote.[83] Author and Christian activist Jonathan Wilson-Hartgrove, Barber's friend and frequent co-author and collaborator, echoed Cornel West when he told Shimron, "He communicates the message of the South with a power I had heard only in recordings of Dr. Martin Luther King."[84]

In an interview with Chapel Hill, North Carolina-based magazine *The Sun*, Wilson-Hartgrove said of Barber, "He's for real." Wilson-Hartgrove, who is white, was raised as a conservative evangelical in the rural foothills of North Carolina. At the age of sixteen, he became interested in politics, and got a summer job as a Senate page for South Carolina Republican Senator Strom Thurmond, known for his opposition to integration and civil rights legislation.[85]

Shortly after his page job in Thurmond's office ended, Wilson-Hartgrove returned home and heard Barber speak for the first time at a gathering in the North Carolina governor's office. "I found his words compelling. This was not the sort of politics I had seen in Washington. It was different," Wilson-Hartgrove said. "I came to see him as my spiritual mentor. As a teenager I began preaching at his church. We've been friends ever since."[86]

BACKLASH AGAINST THE RADICAL CHRISTIANITY OF MORAL MONDAYS

"This is our Selma," Barber said of the Forward Together Moral Movement in press interviews and public speeches.[87] The February 2014 Moral Monday march that brought some 80,000 people to the streets of Raleigh was billed by organizers as the largest civil rights gathering in the South since the 1965 Selma to Montgomery march.[88]

There were actually significant differences between Moral Monday protests and those of the 1950s and 1960s, including the level of risk involved. Those arrested at Moral Monday rallies, despite taunts from critics, had little chance of being beaten or killed by racists and complicit lawmen. In addition, most of those arrested were white. From the first Moral Monday protest on April 29 through the 11th protest on July 15, for example, 83 percent of those arrested were white and 11 percent were black.[89] The movement "is far more deeply interracial and multicultural than the civil-rights movement ever was, in its dreams on its best day," admitted Duke Professor Timothy Tyson, who is white, and was arrested with Barber on the first Moral Monday.[90] One similarity between the two eras was the disdain for each movement's tactics expressed by their respective opponents. Although Moral Monday marchers were not met with physical violence, there was resistance, rebuke, and ridicule, in legacy media outlets and especially online.

One notable critic was former Republican state senator, former Marine, Citadel graduate, and attorney Thom Goolsby. He penned op-eds, widely reprinted in newspapers throughout North Carolina, calling the protests "Moron Mondays" and "Money Mondays." Goolsby, sponsor of the legislation that repealed the Racial Justice Act and supporter of mandatory, transvaginal ultrasounds for women seeking abortions, wrote the following:

> The circus came to the State Capitol this week, complete with clowns, a carnival barker and a sideshow. The "Reverend" Barber was decked out like a prelate of the Church of Rome (no insult is meant to Catholics), complete with stole and cassock. All he was missing was a miter and the ensemble would have been complete.
>
> Several hundred people—mostly white, angry, aged former hippies—appeared and screeched into microphones, talked about solidarity and chanted diatribes. It was "liberal theater" at its best . . .
>
> Never short on audacity, the Loony Left actually named their gathering "Moral Monday." Between the screaming, foot stomping and disjointed speeches, it appeared more like "Moron Monday."[91]

The Civitas Institute, a nonprofit conservative think tank in Raleigh, set up a mock gaming website consisting of mug shots of arrested Moral Monday protestors. Called "Pick the Protestor," the site revealed that "98 percent of those arrested are from North Carolina, that the majority live in the Triangle, are employed, and are Democrats," according to one television news report.[92] Civitas inadvertently supported Barber's contention that most protestors were state residents, rather than outside agitators, as some had claimed. Another news station noted that, "high-profile Republicans, including state party Chairman Claude Pope, have dismissed the protesters as 'outsiders.'

That line has been refined in recent days to say that there are 'outside influences' on the protests."[93]

The Voter Integrity Project of North Carolina (NCVIP), a group affiliated with the conservative Tea Party movement, wrote and posted online a satirical song called "Marxist Mondays" to the tune of "Manic Monday," penned by the musician Prince and originally recorded by The Bangles. "Marxist Mondays" contained the lyrics:

> *It's just another Marxist Monday*
> *It's a staged movement*
> *Astroturf moment.*[94]

"The song accuses protesters of 'throw[ing] a tantrum,' worrying about 'look[ing] real hot,' and wanting to 'just live off food stamps and unemployment,'" according to a blog post by The Institute for Southern Studies. The post also notes that, "NCVIP campaigns against voter fraud, recruiting volunteers to serve as poll monitors. Its tactics have sometimes been criticized as voter intimidation. The group promotes strict voter ID laws, which have been among the targets of the Moral Monday protesters because of their disproportionate impact on people of color, the elderly, students, and people with disabilities."[95]

FUSION POLITICS AND THREE RECONSTRUCTIONS

As noted earlier, fusion politics, cited frequently by Barber, was originally a movement in 1890s America when various parties with some disagreements but with many common interests formed coalitions. When asked by Lynn Stuart Parramore of *The American Prospect* to describe the philosophy behind Moral Mondays, Barber, like King, cited both secular and sacred sources:

When we looked at the preponderance of this legislation that was passed and was being planned, we said, let's look at the deep values of our constitution. We read where it says that in North Carolina, all political power should only be used for the good of the whole. We saw that our constitution of 1868, passed by blacks and whites, guaranteed equal protection and it guaranteed public education, both as a constitutional value and a moral value. Then we looked at the federal constitution and saw that the deep values in that are the common good—promoting the general welfare. The first word, before you even get to freedom and liberty, is the establishment of justice.

Then we went to the Bible. We saw that every major faith says that love and justice should be at the center of public policy. Isaiah 10 says, "Woe unto those who make unjust laws that rob the right of the poor." And we said, wait a minute, when you look at these policies, it's not only bad policy, but it's immoral and extreme. And we said that we had to stand up as a coalition—not liberal vs. conservative (that's too small, too limited, too tired), or Republican vs. Democrat. We had to have a moral challenge because these policies they were passing, in rapid-fire, were constitutionally inconsistent, morally indefensible, and economically insane.[96]

In his writings and speeches, Barber has laid out three specific eras of Reconstruction. The first took place in the period following the end of the Civil War in 1865. The second was in the mid-1950s. Schools were desegregated by the U.S. Supreme Court's *Brown v. Board of Education* decision in 1954, followed the next year by the death of Emmett Till for allegedly insulting a white woman. In a speech to the liberal gathering Netroots Nation 2014, Barber outlined the history this way:

> Two things fueled the civil rights movement. The Brown decision, and the acquittal of the people that killed Emmett Till. . . . Both of these things result in the kind of creation of a second reconstruction. A new fusion, moral fusion politics. . . . We saw affirmative action, we saw the committee on equal employment, we saw civil rights connected morally to economic justice, we saw the Social Security amendments of 1965, we saw the creation on a moral basis of Medicare and Medicaid . . . we saw the Civil Rights Act of '64 and the Voting Rights Act of '65 . . .[97]

These programs were soon under attack by racists who marginalized the programs' beneficiaries and demonized their otherness, he said. He delineated the Southern Strategy being employed in the present by some conservative politicians, making this the right time for a third Reconstruction. Cutting benefits and slashing tax breaks for low- and middle-income families violates Christ's teaching to care for the least among us, he said. That viewpoint clashes with "another school of Christian thought followed by many Southern conservatives: The best way to help the poor is through private charity, providing jobs and promoting self-reliance, rather than government programs," according to an Associated Press story in June 2013 amid the Monday rallies.[98] This storyline echoes previous comparisons of progressive evangelicals vs. conservative evangelicals.

In February 2016, three weeks before the North Carolina Presidential Primary, Barber and Wilson-Hartgrove co-authored an op-ed piece in the Raleigh *News & Observer* titled, "Holding Candidates Morally Accountable." The essay noted the 10th Annual People's Assembly March that had occurred on February 13, "made up of black, white and brown, gay and straight, rich and poor, labor and civil rights Democrats, Republicans and independents, people of faith and people whose moral visions are rooted in reason or politics."[99] Revisiting the theme of fusion politics, they wrote,

We knew it had been done before. After the Civil War, newly freed African-Americans found common cause with white North Carolinians, wrote a new state constitution and founded the South's first public school system. In the 1890s, their political descendants formed an interracial "fusion coalition" of white populists and black Republicans, which won the governorship and every statewide office in 1896. White conservatives overthrew the Fusionist government by force and fraud, installing a one-party state that disenfranchised blacks and ushered in lynch law and Jim Crow segregation. [100]

BLACK SOCIAL GOSPEL

As ethics scholar, theologian, and Episcopal priest Gary Dorrien has pointed out, "Martin Luther King did not come from nowhere, nor did the embattled theology of social justice he espoused." [101] Just as Barber built on King's and others' legacies, King inherited the legacy of the "wrongly and strangely overlooked" black social gospel, as Dorrien called it. Prominent African-American figures associated with the black social gospel movement include Booker T. Washington, Ida B. Wells-Barnett, and W. E. B. DuBois among many others.

Writing in the *Harvard Divinity Bulletin*, Dorrien outlined the evolution of American civil rights and black religious activism:

> The "civil rights movement" actually began in 1884 with a call for what became the National Afro-American League in 1890, which was followed by a brilliant moment of hope in the Niagara Movement of 1905 to 1909. A second phase of activism occurred in 1910 with the founding of what became the National Association for the Advancement of Colored People (NAACP). The historic mass movement that exploded in December 1955 was a third phase. In every phase, the movement had leaders that espoused the social ethical religion and politics of modern social Christianity. [102]

These three phases of the civil rights movement dovetail with Barber's thesis of three eras of Reconstruction, both locating activist roots in the nineteenth-century post-Civil War era. "Though the black social gospel grew out of the abolitionist tradition," Dorrien writes, "it responded to new challenges in a new era of American history: the abandonment of Reconstruction, the evisceration of constitutional rights, an upsurge of racial lynching and Jim Crow abuse, struggles for mere survival in every part of the nation, and the excruciating question of what a new abolition would require." [103]

LIBERATION THEOLOGY AND MORAL MONDAYS

There is more than a hint of Liberation Theology in the rhetoric of Moral Mondays. Liberation Theology grew out of a Catholic movement in

1950–1960s Latin America, the same period in which Martin Luther King Jr. was leading protests against oppression of blacks in the United States. Third World adherents of Liberation Theology who were poor, persecuted, and oppressed found in Christianity a relevant revolutionary and emancipatory power. Establishment political and religious leaders, particularly those in the West, saw the movement as socialist or Marxist.

American James Cone of Union Theological Seminary published, among other works, *A Black Theology of Liberation* in 1970. Cone wrote in part:

> Christian theology is a theology of liberation. It is *a rational study of the being of God in the world in light of the existential situation of an oppressed community, relating the forces of liberation to the essence of the gospel, which is Jesus Christ* [Italics in the original].[104]

The Latin American Pope Francis embraced tenets of Liberation Theology in the twenty-first century with his frequent pleas on behalf of the poor, and in his criticism of capitalism. "While the earnings of a minority are growing exponentially, so too is the gap separating the majority from the prosperity enjoyed by those happy few," Francis wrote in his *Apostolic Exhortation*.[105] Gustavo Gutierrez, the "father" of the controversial Liberation Theology movement, at age 85 was invited by Pope Francis to the Vatican in May 2015 to address the press about ministering to the poor.[106]

"I had sensed in him what I've come to learn is the long tradition of Black liberation preaching," Jonathan Wilson-Hartgrove said of Barber in an interview. "He inherited that from his father, and is, in terms of the Black social gospel, I think, one of its greatest living preachers."[107]

CONSERVATIVE PASTORS AND THEIR MESSAGE

Nationwide, religious conservatives run for local, state, and national offices in order to influence legislation, and some seek to evangelize through politics. In July 2015, some 300 conservative evangelical pastors attended a training session held in Orlando, Florida on how to run for public office. As reported by NPR, this was just "one in a series of workshops being held around the country in an effort to build a movement of pastor politicians who will promote conservative ideas at all levels of government."[108] Mike Huckabee, a 2016 Republican presidential candidate and ordained Baptist minister, was the keynote speaker.

According to the NPR story, workshop organizer and political operative David Lane "calls these Issachar workshops after one of the 12 tribes of Israel, a tribe that, according to the Bible, was led by men who understood the times and knew what Israel should do." At the time of the 2015 Orlando session, the U.S. Supreme Court had ruled in favor of legalizing gay marriage, the national deficit was nearing $500 billion for the year, and the number of abortions was about 730,000 per year.[109] Lane opened with a prayer addressing all of these issues:

> Fifty-five million babies dead, red ink as far as the eye can see, homosexuals praying at the inauguration . . . [110]

Mark Harris, pastor of the First Baptist Church in Charlotte, North Carolina and failed 2014 Republican senatorial candidate, tried to enlist the pastors in the audience in a call and response to the children's hymn, "This Little Light of Mine." When the audience gave a lukewarm response, he said, "Oh, that was pathetic. No wonder the liberals are kicking our tails. Come on." The purpose of these workshops is twofold: to get more conservative evangelical voters to the polls, and to get more evangelical pastors in office. The ministers at the workshops are primarily Protestants, as the Catholic Church forbids its clergy from running for public office.[111]

THE PRESS AND THE PROTESTS

Joshua Clark Davis is co-director of the North Carolina-based *Media and the Movement: Journalism, Civil Rights, and Black Power in the American South*, described on its website as "an oral history project that aims to understand the media and activism ecosystem of the American South during the civil rights movement of the 1960s, 1970s, and 1980s."[112] The day before the 50th anniversary of the March on Washington on August 28, 2013, Davis published an essay with *Huffington Post* titled, "The March on Washington, Moral Mondays and the Media."

Davis, who had been arrested at the June 17 Moral Monday rally for "peaceful civil disobedience," discussed the public relations boost received by both the March on Washington and Moral Mondays via media coverage. He noted that mainstream media covered the main event in 1963, but the black press had been there all along:

> King was already famous for his leadership in the nonviolent, direct action civil rights movement. But the March on Washington was King's, and the movement's, ultimate public relations victory. Never before had national media—particularly television—given the movement so much sustained coverage. As much of this week's commentary will suggest, the March on Washington might have even failed without television cameras there to broadcast it.
>
> But this narrative leaves out a key ingredient of the March's success. More than any other journalists, reporters from black newspapers helped to make the March happen in the first place. Television cameras captured the March, but they missed most of the weeks, months, and years of organizing that prompted hundreds of thousands of people to go to Washington on August 28.[113]

Davis recognized and appreciated the fact that the press boosted the popularity and name recognition of Moral Mondays. "These weekly protests . . . started April 29. Moral Mondays began to enjoy sustained national and international coverage as the protests grew substantially in June. Since then, *New York Times* published no fewer than six articles and editorials that mention Moral Mondays. NPR, MSNBC, Fox News, London's *Guardian* newspaper, and numerous other major news outlets featured stories and opinion pieces on Moral Mondays, too."[114]

Conservatives claimed favoritism in the press toward the movement. "When you start to use inflammatory rhetoric and you try to fan the flame that brings up a history of racism or violence perpetrated by folks who are no longer here, no longer around—to try to bring that kind of inflammatory rhetoric back and justify what they feel today—is totally off base," State Republican Party Chairman Claude Pope said in September of 2013 of the Jim Crow and civil rights era language used by Moral Monday marchers. "And one of the issues is the press seems to be buying into it."[115]

Activist media, Davis says, "made Moral Mondays the top American social protest story of the summer."[116] Durham, North Carolina-based online magazine *Facing South* is an independent social justice and progressive voice put out by the Institute of Southern Studies (ISS). *Facing South*, begun by civil rights activists in 1970, had published nearly twenty stories mentioning the Reverend Barber in the previous six years.

"National television cameras and reporters might show up to cover marches and rallies the day they happen. But if you're looking for the stories behind these movements, you're more likely to get them from independent activist journalists," Davis writes.[117]

The Raleigh *News & Observer*, whose offices were just blocks from the capitol, ran some 30 articles, including straight stories, editorials and first-person op-eds, between the first Monday rally on April 29 and the thirteenth on July 29. Stories focused on the size of the crowd, the number of arrests, and quotes by supporters angry with the legislature over issues such as refusal to expand Medicaid for some 500,000 uninsured citizens; tax cuts that trimmed public school budgets; the elimination of teaching assistant positions; and revocation of a teacher pay hike for those who earned a master's degree.

HOUSE BILL 2

In February 2016, the Charlotte, North Carolina City Council passed an ordinance on a 7–4 vote to expand a non-discrimination ordinance to include protections for lesbian, gay, bisexual, and transgender (LGBT) individuals. Among other items covered under the ordinance was the provision that transgender people could use public restrooms that coincided with the gender with which they identify.[118]

In March, Republicans in the State General Assembly quickly passed HB2, which nearly as quickly became known nationwide as "the bathroom bill."[119] The purpose was to nullify the Charlotte ordinance, but its provisions went further. In an opinion piece for *Charlotte Magazine*, HB2 opponent Greg Lacour wrote,

> Here's what the North Carolina General Assembly did today, in your name, with your money: passed a bill that effectively defines "transgender" out of existence; forces transgender men to use women's rooms and transgender women to use the men's; allows private businesses to discriminate against gay and transgender people; prohibits local governments from preventing such discrimination; prohibits local governments from setting any employment standards, including minimum wage, for businesses they hire as contractors; jeopardizes $4.6 billion in federal Title IX funding for schools; nullifies every nondiscrimination ordinance ever passed by any local government in the state; allowed legislators five minutes to read the bill; allowed the public 30 minutes to comment on it . . . and declared "that the general welfare of the State requires the enactment of this law under the police power of the State"; all predicated on their genuine or feigned horror over a presumed danger that has been shown, definitively, not to exist.[120]

HB2 became a moral issue for both sides, but for diametrically opposed reasons. "Advocates of HB2 have called it a bill that protects women and children in restrooms and locker rooms from men who might pretend to be transgender for illegal motives," reporter Anne Blythe wrote in *The News & Observer*.[121] At an April 2016 rally that drew about 60 people in Asheville in the western mountains, proponents of HB2 focused on keeping families safe from sexual predators in bathrooms. Rally organizer Pastor Andrew Sluder said, "This bill protects all citizens across NC. It keeps school locker rooms safe from the possibility of sexual predators. It is sad that things like this must be brought to the table for discussion, but I thank God for our legislators, Lieutenant Governor, and Governor McCrory for passing this bill." Attendees carried signs that said, "Pray for our state" and "Thank you Governor for keeping families safe."[122]

In May, 11 protestors were arrested during a Moral Monday rally against HB2. Barber consistently called for repeal of HB2. "We know the difference between racism and homophobia . . . we must all stand together," he said.[123] In July, GOP Governor Pat McCrory signed a change to HB2 restoring the right of employees who believe they've been fired because of discrimination to sue in state courts instead of having to seek relief in federal court, but left the exclusionary bathroom provision in place.[124] The bill was repealed and replaced in 2017 after McCrory lost the 2016 gubernatorial election to Democrat Roy Cooper, formerly state attorney general.[125]

CONCLUSION

How effective was William Barber and his Moral Monday movement in sparking social and political change in North Carolina in 2013 and beyond? Four themes were explored in this chapter concerning Moral Monday protests in North Carolina: 1) the role religious rhetoric played in this twenty-first century protest movement; 2) the tone of news media coverage; 3) how social and digital media was used by both protestors and their critics; and 4) the political effectiveness of the protests. Results indicate the following:

1) Religious language was an essential ingredient at Moral Mondays that attracted people of faith and secularists alike, united against changes implemented by Republicans in the state legislature. The primary driver of this rhetoric was the Reverend Dr. William Barber II. In the 2016 presidential contest, Barber continued to employ religious language for commentary, decrying Republican candidates' use of coded language about race. With 2016 GOP presidential contenders Ted Cruz, Marco Rubio, and Donald Trump (who eventually won) using Christian terminology on the campaign trail, Barber wrote in *The Nation*, "Presidential candidates of all political stripes have long courted what the media calls the 'evangelical voters' in the South, using the language of morality."

> Well, I am an evangelical. I have been born again. . . . I learned that persons who claim to be evangelicals are anointed to preach good news to the poor. . . . Evangelism always starts with Jesus's words: "When I was hungry did you feed me? When I was naked, did you clothe me?" In North Carolina, even our state constitution notes, in Article 11, "Beneficent provision for the poor, the unfortunate, and the orphan is one of the first duties of a civilized and a Christian state."[126]

2) Coverage of Moral Monday protests spread across national media, and occupied local newspaper front pages and television news lead status on many days. Davis noted that Moral Mondays had sustained national and international coverage as the protests grew substantially in June. *The New York Times* published six articles and editorials that mention Moral Mondays between June and August 2013. NPR, MSNBC, Fox News, *The Los Angeles Times*, London's *Guardian* newspaper, and many others also ran stories, including the local Raleigh *News & Observer*. Republican legislators accused the news media of bias toward the protestors. Opposing viewpoints to Moral Mondays came from op-eds and news quotes by current and former GOP lawmakers.

3) Both Moral Monday organizers and their opponents employed tech-savvy strategies to forward their respective messages. Barber authored and co-authored op-eds, and he gave frequent interviews. A website was created, and social media employed to inform supporters of upcoming rallies. News outlets often printed stories ahead of marches, informed by emails to reporters. Pushback came from conservatives who created satiric websites that used arrested protestors' mug shots and recorded songs parodying Moral Mondays as "Marxist Mondays." This rhetoric is reminiscent of accusations in the 1950s that the Reverend Martin Luther King Jr. had communist ties.

4) Despite the Moral Monday protests, Republicans remained firmly in charge after the 2014 midterm elections. Had the movement made a difference? In 2015, Barber told the Huffington Post that, "The group was not deterred by GOP wins in the state in 2014."[127] The HKonJ website offered its nationwide following and frequent protests as evidence the movement was a change agent:

> After an avalanche of extreme and immoral policies passed during the 2013 Legislative Session, under the leadership of the NC NAACP, the HKonJ Coalition continued their work under the banner of the Forward Together Moral Movement and organized 13 Moral Mondays and over 25 local Moral Mondays across the state once the session ended. This nationally known movement has spread to other southern states and has inspired people across the nation.[128]

The Moral Monday movement, and Barber, did indeed succeed in attracting national attention, including that of Robert Reich, former Secretary of Labor under President Bill Clinton. In a 2015 Facebook post, Reich wrote:

> A few days ago in Raleigh, North Carolina, I met Reverend William Barber . . . president of the North Carolina NAACP and a leader of the "Moral Mondays" movement that's fighting both for voting rights and for a $15 minimum wage. "This is our Selma," says Barber. "Everything they won in Selma is now being attacked and North Carolina is the clearest example of that." Since taking over state government in 2013, North Carolina Republicans have enacted the toughest voting restrictions in the country, declined Medicaid expansion for 500,000 people, ended unemployment benefits, cut public education funding and slashed taxes on the wealthy. Barber and his Moral Monday activists are fighting those policies in the streets, in the courts and at the ballot box. Over 1,000 people have been arrested during demonstrations at the legislature. . . . A large progressive convergence is occurring.[129]

One significant effect of the Moral Monday movement was victory in a lawsuit that required Republican Legislators to redraw voting districts ruled by the court to have been gerrymandered on the basis of race.[130] "This state's citizens have the right to vote in districts that accord with the Constitution,"

Circuit Judge James A. Wynn, Jr. wrote. "We therefore order that new maps be drawn that comply with the Constitution and the Voting Rights Act."[131] This decision was partly confirmed by the U.S. Supreme Court in 2017.[132]

AFTERMATH

During an appearance on Comedy Central's *The Daily Show* in 2017, Barber told host Trevor Noah, "I don't know any way to be a person of faith and not be concerned about how we're treating the poor, how we're treating the least of these."[133]

"You're doing all of this work in North Carolina, which in many ways has become a microcosm for everything that America is," Noah said to Barber. "You have the imbalances between rich and poor, you have a Democratic state that votes a Democrat for a long time and then all of a sudden switched and voted for Donald Trump and voted Republican. You have a place where there has been gerrymandering, where there is a lot of racial discrimination."

"North Carolina has had an interesting history," Barber responded. "It's not as progressive as people tend to think." He continued,

> You know, we elected [conservative Republican Senator] Jesse Helms for years. The only Democratic candidate that won for presidency other than Jimmy Carter was Barack Obama. But that's significant. When President Obama broke through in the South, in North Carolina in 2008, we had just passed same-day registration and early voting. Two thousand and ten, during redistricting, Trevor, they [Republicans] went redistricting-crazy. They created apartheid districts. Right? And that stacked and packed black voters in a way that in the 2012 election, more progressives voted for progressives.
>
> But because of the redistricting, we ended up with a supermajority extremist legislature. That extremist legislature then passes every law they could. They were anti-Medicaid expansion, anti-immigrants, anti-gay, anti-public education, anti-living wage. Then they decided to pass the worst voter suppression law in the country. . . . 22 states passed racist, voter suppression laws and racially driven redistricting laws. . . . Racism hacked this system before [Donald] Trump was ever elected. . . . And you know what? The people who got hurt the most by the policies that have been elected by these so-called, what I call these "unconstitutionally constituted" legislatures have been poor whites.[134]

After the 2013 Moral Monday rallies, Barber's national, and international, recognition was raised considerably. His profile rose even higher when he was chosen for a plum speaking slot during the 2016 Democratic National Convention. The televised speech was a stirring sermon that echoed his Moral Monday themes and brought roars of approval from the convention floor.

"Good evening, my Brothers and Sisters," he began. "I come before you tonight as a preacher, the son of a preacher, a preacher immersed in the movement at five years old. I don't come tonight representing any organization, but I come to talk about faith and morality."[135]

Barber continued in that vein, throwing attendees at the secular convention a bit off-balance:

I'm a preacher and I'm a theologically conservative liberal evangelical biblicist. I know it may sound strange, but I'm a conservative because I work to conserve a divine tradition that teaches us to do justice, love mercy, and walk humbly with our God.

I've . . . had the privilege of traveling the country with the Reverend Dr. James Forbes, and Reverend Dr. Traci Blackmon and Sister Simone Campbell as we are working together in the revival and calling for a revolution of values. And as we travel the country, we see things. That is why I'm so concerned, about those that say so much—about what God says so little, while saying so little—about what God says so much. And so in my heart, I'm troubled. And I'm worried about the way faith is cynically used by some to serve hate, fear, racism and greed.

We need to heed the voice of the Scriptures. We need to listen to the ancient chorus in which "deep calls unto deep." The prophet Isaiah cries out, "What I'm interested in seeing you doing, says the Lord, as a nation is, 'Pay people what they deserve,' 'Share your food with the hungry.' Do this and then your nation shall be called a repairer of the breach."

Jesus, a brown skinned Palestinian Jew, called us to preach good news to the poor, the broken, and the bruised, and all those who are made to feel unaccepted . . .

I say to you tonight, there are some issues that are not Left versus Right, Liberal versus Conservative, they are "right versus wrong."

We need to embrace our deepest moral values and push for a revival of the heart of our democracy . . .

And so, and so I stop by here tonight to ask,

- Is there a heart in this house?
- Is there a heart in America?
- Is there somebody that has a heart for the poor, and a heart for the vulnerable?

Then Stand up. Vote together. Organize together. Fight for the heart of this nation. And while you're are fighting, sing that old hymn. "Revive us again. Fill each heart with Thy love. May each soul be rekindled with fire from above." Hallelujah! Find the glory.[136]

Reporter Janell Ross, writing in the *Washington Post* stated, "Well, America, what the Reverend William Barber II stopped by the Democratic National Convention Thursday night to tell you was just about the most engaging version of everything that every other speaker touched on over the course of

the four day event. . . . What he delivered—eight years after this brand of
liberation theology took a beating from uninformed corners of the conservative commentariat—was evidence of a long tradition of liberal, religious
patriotism. It was a call to action that, in Barber's view, serves this cause—an
articulation of a liberal and patriotic philosophy with what Barber said was
the moral force to shock and resuscitate the heart of the nation."[137]

On the national NAACP website, Barber's accomplishments were listed
as part of a Divine Plan:

> By the grace of God, Rev. Dr. Barber, along with local, state, and national
> NAACP leaders, has helped to lead the fight for voter rights, just redistricting,
> health care reform, labor and worker rights, protection of immigration rights,
> and reparation for women survivors of Eugenics, release of the Wilmington
> Ten and educational equality. Rev. Dr. Barber has been arrested three times for
> civil disobedience as he stood for educational, economic and equal justice.[138]

In June 2017, Barber stepped away from the leadership of North Carolina's
NAACP chapter to help organize a Poor People's Campaign in Washington,
D.C. and 25 states, akin to Martin Luther King's 1967/1968 Poor People's
Campaign for economic justice, carried out by the Reverend Ralph Aberna-
thy after King's assassination.

In a press release, Barber said, "This moment requires us to push into the
national consciousness a deep moral analysis that is rooted in an agenda to
combat systemic poverty and racism, war mongering, economic injustice,
voter suppression, and other attacks on the most vulnerable. . . . While I am
stepping down as president, I will continue working to advance the moral
movement here at home as well as support the leadership in our conference
to move North Carolina forward together."[139]

On a website with videos, blogs, and historical resources, the new Poor
People's Campaign lays out its vision:

> We are fighting on many fronts of this struggle, including for good affordable
> homes, water, nutritious food, health, and education, for racial, gender and
> LGBTQ justice, for a humane immigration system and an end to mass incar-
> ceration, for living wages and good jobs, for a healthy environment, for peace,
> and for a more genuine democracy. We look to the example of the Forward
> Together/Moral Mondays movement in North Carolina, the struggle against
> water shut-offs in Detroit, the campaigns in Vermont, Maine, Pennsylvania,
> and Maryland to make healthcare a human right, and many others which show
> the power that comes when we're able to see all the problems our communities
> are facing as deeply inter-connected and organize on that basis.[140]

This new fusion movement that brings together a variety of constituencies
and causes is consistent with Barber's message of equality. The New Poor
People's Campaign is associated with another social justice organization

titled Repairers of the Breach. "Repairers of the Breach staff and volunteers conduct trainings, town hall meetings, panels, and participate in other activities with state-based moral movement leaders across the country," according to the group's website, which touts Barber's books.[141]

As nineteenth-century abolitionist and Unitarian minister Theodore Parker said, "The arc of the moral universe is long, but it bends towards justice."[142] The quote was a favorite of King's, and has been used by Barber and many other activist ministers. Barber has stressed time and again that he rejects the narrow frame of left/right politics. Despite his resistance to partisan labels, though, Repairers of the Breach states that part of its mission is to, "Challenge the version of the ultra-conservatives who have misinterpreted Christianity and other faith traditions as a faith that hates the poor. They call 47 percent of us 'Takers,' and they want to shut down any government agency that tries to provide for the general welfare and just economic systems."[143]

"The real conflict isn't Christianity versus Islam or Christianity versus a liberal secular state; it's one version of Christianity versus another," says Jonathan Wilson-Hartgrove.

> As I've said, the abolition movement was one kind of Christianity; the pro-slavery movement, another. If you don't acknowledge this story, then you end up trying to bring people together without a story, which is sort of what the secular state has been attempting. And yet the secular state in the U.S. developed very much within the context of Christian values. The challenge for the Moral Movement is how to have a public discourse that appeals to those values without excluding Jews, Muslims, Buddhists and people who don't adhere to any faith tradition.[144]

Barber "often says left vs. right is too puny for the moral challenge of our day," Wilson-Hartgrove notes. "Sometimes we need language to name right vs. wrong."[145]

That language for Barber is one of morality, and of religion.

NOTES

1. "The Court and its Procedures," U.S. Supreme Court website, accessed January 16, 2016, https://www.supremecourt.gov/about/procedures.aspx; for an analysis of the way some presidents use the National Prayer Breakfast, see Nneka Ifeoma Ofulue, "President Clinton and the White House Prayer Breakfast," *Journal of Communication and Religion* 25, no. 1, March 2002, 49–63.

2. Aleksandra Sandstrom, "Faith on the Hill," Pew Research Center, Religious Landscape Study, January 3, 2017, http://www.pewforum.org/2017/01/03/faith-on-the-hill-115/.

3. 410 US 113 (1973).

4. Mike Wynn and Chris Kenning, "Timeline of a Kentucky Clerk's Gay-Marriage Defiance," The (Louisville, Ky.) *Courier-Journal*, September 3, 2015, accessed March 15, 2016, http://www.usatoday.com/story/news/politics/2015/09/03/ky-clerk-gay-marriage-timeline/

71670068/; David Masci, "5 Questions About the Contraception Mandate," Pew Research Center, August 5, 2015, http://www.pewresearch.org/fact-tank/2015/08/05/contraception-mandate-questions/.

5. Franklin Graham became president of the Billy Graham Evangelistic Association upon his father's retirement from active ministry. Jerry Falwell founded Liberty University in Lynchburg, Va. After his death, his son, Jerry Falwell Jr., became president. Bob Jones was succeeded in the presidency of his eponymous university by his son and grandson, Bob Jones Jr. and Bob Jones III.

6. See, for example, Adelle M. Banks, "Black Churches Split Over Gay Marriage and Obama," Religion News Service, August 7, 2012, http://religionnews.com/2012/08/07/black-churches-split-over-gay-marriage-and-obama/; Laurie Goodstein, "Unions That Divide; Churches Split Over Gay Marriage, *New York Times*, May 13, 2012, http://www.nytimes.com/2012/05/14/us/gay-marriage-issue-divides-churches.html; Harriett Sherwood, "Anglican Church Avoids Split Over Gay Rights—But Liberals Pay Price," *The Guardian*, January 14, 2016, https://www.theguardian.com/world/2016/jan/14/anglican-church-sanctions-against-liberal-us-church-same-sex-marriage.

7. Albert J. Raboteau, *American Prophets: Seven Religious Radicals & Their Struggle for Social and Political Justice* (Princeton, NJ: Princeton University Press, 2016), 150.

8. For a basic history of Occupy Wall Street and the Occupy Movement in general, see Heather Gautney, "What is Occupy Wall Street? The History of Leaderless Movements," the *Washington Post*, October 10, 2011, accessed July 10, 2015, http://www.washingtonpost.com/national/on-leadership/what-is-occupy-wall-street-the-history-of-leaderless-movements/2011/10/10/gIQAwkFjaL_story.html; Tom Burgis, "Origins of the Occupy Movement," *The Financial Times*, January 18, 2012, accessed July 10, 2015, http://www.ft.com/cms/s/0/90108158–41f7–11e1-a1bf-00144feab49a.html#axzz3fVNZFdeM.

9. Quoted in Tommy Tomlinson, "Reverend Resistance," *Esquire*, April 25, 2017, http://www.esquire.com/news-politics/a54573/reverend-william-barber-progressive-christianity/.

10. William J. Barber II with Barbara Zelter, *Forward Together: A Moral Message for the Nation.* (St. Louis, MO: Chalice Press, 2014), 178.

11. Eric C. Miller, "The Origin Story of the Evangelical Mindset: A Conversation with Frances FitzGerald," *Religion Dispatches*, May 31, 2017, http://religiondispatches.org/the-origin-story-of-the-evangelical-mindset-a-conversation-with-frances-fitzgerald/?utm_source=Religion+Dispatches+Newsletter&utm_campaign=dd7c19e658-RD_Weekly_Newsletter&utm_medium=email&utm_term=0_742d86f519-dd7c19e658-84559769. FitzGerald was being interviewed about her book, *The Evangelicals: The Struggle to Shape America* (New York: Simon & Schuster, 2017).

12. Pew Research Center, Religious Landscape Study, May 30, 2014, http://www.pewforum.org/religious-landscape-study/party-affiliation/. The majority of evangelical Christians who lean toward the Democratic Party are nonwhite. According to the U.S. Census, whites are nearly 77 percent of the population, but non-Hispanic or Latino whites comprise only 61 percent. See: https://www.census.gov/quickfacts/fact/table/US/PST045216.

13. Robert P. Jones, *The End of White Christian America* (New York: Simon & Schuster, 2016), 88; Merle Black and Earl Black, *The Rise of Southern Republicans* (Cambridge: Harvard University Press, 2003), 4.

14. Kenneth L. Woodward, *Getting Religion: Faith, Culture, and Politics from the Age of Eisenhower to the Era of Obama* (New York: Convergent Books, 2016), 339.

15. Ibid., 340.

16. Ibid., 341.

17. Jones, *The End of White Christian America*, 89.

18. Woodward, *Getting Religion*, 344–45.

19. Ibid.

20. "1980 Presidential General Election Results," U.S. Election Atlas, https://uselectionatlas.org/RESULTS/national.php?year=1980; "1984 Presidential Election," *270toWin.com*, https://www.270towin.com/1984_Election/.

21. Thomas Jefferson, Letter to the Danbury, Connecticut Baptist Association, January 1, 1802. Full text may be found at Library of Congress website, https://www.loc.gov/loc/lcib/9806/danpre.html.

22. Jones, *The End of White Christian America*, 91.

23. Ibid., 92–93.

24. "2016 Year in Review," Tyndall Report, http://tyndallreport.com.

25. "News Coverage of the 2016 Presidential Primaries: Horse Race Reporting Has Consequences," Shorenstein Center on Media, Politics, and Public Policy, July 11, 2016, https://shorensteincenter.org/news-coverage-2016-presidential-primaries/.

26. Diane Winston, "'There is Sin and Evil in the World': Reagan, Trump, and the News Media," *Los Angeles Review of Books*, September 30, 2016, https://lareviewofbooks.org/article/sin-evil-world-reagan-trump-news-media/#.

27. Michael P. Young, "Confessional Protest: The Religious Birth of U.S. National Social Movements," *American Sociological Review* 67 (October 2002): 660.

28. Ibid., 662. For background on contentious politics, see: Sidney Tarrow, "Modular Collective Action and the Rise of the Social Movement: Why the French Revolution Was Not Enough," *Politics and Society* 21 (1993), 69–90; Charles Tilley, *Popular Contention in Great Britain, 1758–1834* (Cambridge: Harvard University Press, 1995).

29. Ibid., 666.

30. Kraig Beyerlein, Sarah A. Soule, and Nancy Martin, "Prayers, Protest, and Police: How Religion Influences Police Presence at Collective Action Events in the United States, 1960 to 1995," *American Sociological Review* 80, no. 6 (2015): 1250. See also: Daniel M. Cress and David A. Snow, "Mobilization at the Margins: Resources, Benefactors, and the Viability of Homeless Social Movement Organizations," *American Sociological Review* 61, no. 6 (1996): 1089–1109; Rory McVeigh, *The Rise of the Ku Klux Klan* (Minneapolis: University of Minnesota Press, 2009); Aldon Morris, *The Origins of the Civil Rights Movement* (New York: Free Press, 1984); Christian Smith, *Resisting Reagan* (Chicago: University of Chicago Press, 1996); Mayer N. Zald and John D. McCarthy, "Religious Groups as Crucibles of Social Movements," in *Social Movements in an Organizational Society*, eds., M. N. Zald and J. D. McCarthy (New Brunswick, NJ: Transaction, 1987), 67–95.

31. Beyerlein, Soule, and Martin, "Prayers, Protest, and Police," 1252.

32. See, for example: Steve Herbert, *Policing Space* (Minneapolis: University of Minnesota Press, 1996); Peter K. Manning, *Policing Contingencies* Chicago: University of Chicago Press, 2003); Robert Putnam and David E. Campbell, *American Grace* (New York: Simon & Schuster, 2010).

33. Will Huntsberry, "The Rev. William Barber Leads a New Era of Progressive Politics in North Carolina," *Indy Week*, July 24, 2013, accessed July 13, 2015, http://www.indyweek.com/indyweek/the-rev-william-barber-leads-a-new-era-of-progressive-politics-in-north-carolina/Content?oid=3681510.

34. Daniel C. Vock, "With Hundreds of Arrests, North Carolina Preacher Ups the Stakes in Showdown With Republicans," The Pew Charitable Trusts, July 9, 2013, accessed June 30, 2015, http://www.twincities.com/politics-national/?third_party=north-carolina-preacher-raises-the-stakes-in-legislative-showdown.

35. "Rev. Dr. William J. Barber II, President of the NC NAACP," North Carolina NAACP website, accessed June 26, 2015, http://www.naacpnc.org/president; Kirsten West Sivali, "William Barber II, Legendary Civil Rights Leader, Steps Down From NC NAACP Leadership Role," *The Root*, May 11, 2017, http://www.theroot.com/rev-william-barber-ii-legendary-civil-rights-leader-1795137036. Barber stepped aside from the NC NAACP to assist in leading the New Poor People's Campaign.

36. The Rev. William Barber, interview by Lynn Stuart Parramore, "The Man Behind Moral Mondays," *The American Prospect*, June 17, 2013, accessed June 26, 2015, http://prospect.org/article/man-behind-moral-mondays. See also, http://www.hkonj.com.

37. Raboteau, *American Prophets*, 150.

38. "Poor People's Campaign," *King Encyclopedia*, The Martin Luther King, Jr. Research and Education Institute, Stanford University, http://kingencyclopedia.stanford.edu/encyclopedia/encyclopedia/enc_poor_peoples_campaign/.

39. Ibid.

40. Rob Christensen, "MLK's Fateful Decision," *News & Observer*, August 19, 2015, 2A, 11A. Christensen cites research by historian T. Evan Faulkenbury, whose 2012 master's thesis was titled "'Telenegro': Reginald Hawkins, Black Power, and the 1968 North Carolina Gubernatorial Race."

41. Ibid.

42. Drew Dellinger, "Dr. King's Interconnected World," *New York Times*, December 23, 2017, A23. Dellinger was quoting from King's Christmas Eve 1967 sermon at Atlanta's Ebenezer Baptist Church.

43. According to a Friday, September 19, 2014 *News & Observer* story, "The Wake County district attorney announced Friday that he would dismiss all but about 50 cases against protesters arrested at the N.C. Legislative Building in 2013. District Attorney Ned Mangum announced his decision four days after the first case to reach Wake County Superior Court was dismissed. Mangum said he planned to proceed with cases against the demonstrators arrested July 22, 2013, and July 24, 2013, because the evidence is different in about 50 cases." Anne Blythe, "Wake DA agrees to dismiss all but about 50 'Moral Monday' cases from 2013," *News & Observer*, September 19, 2014, accessed June 29, 2015.

44. "North Carolina's Moral Monday Movement," Progresivo blog, accessed July 5, 2015, https://progresivoblog.wordpress.com/north-carolinas-moral-monday-movement/. The Moral Monday Protests and Arrests in 2013:

April 29: 1st Wave—17 arrested

May 1: NC Student Power Union demonstration against the NC General Assembly—5 arrested*

May 6: 2nd Wave—30 arrested

May 13: 3rd Wave—49 arrested

May 20: 4th Wave—57 arrested

June 3: 5th Wave—151 arrested, 1600 in attendance

June 10: 6th Wave—84 arrested,"several thousand"in attendance

June 12: 1st Witness Wednesday,8 arrested

June 17: 7th Wave—84 arrested

June 19: 2nd Witness Wednesday

June 24: 8th Wave—120 arrested, 2500–3000 in attendance

June 26: 3rd Witness Wednesday,3 cited

July 1: 9th Wave—82 arrested

July 3: 4th Witness Wednesday

July 8: 10th Wave—64 arrested

July 15: 11th Wave—101 arrested

July 22: 12th Wave—73 arrested

July 24:6 arrestedwhile occupying Speaker Thom Tillis's office, requesting a meeting with him about the voter suppression bill HB 589

July 29: 13th Wave—none arrested (General Assembly closed)

August 5:Mountain Moral Mondayin Asheville—none arrested; 6,500–10,000 estimated in attendance

August 19: Moral Mondays in Charlotte, Manteo, and Burnsville

August 28: 13 simultaneous rallies around the state on the 50th anniversary of the March On Washington

September 9: Moore County Moral Monday

TOTAL arrested: 936**

TOTAL cited: 3

*This protest was not organized by the NC NAACP, yet the organization publicly supported it.

**Tallies vary slightly among the news coverage. Some estimates are as high as 945.

45. Sue Sturgis, "A Year In, Moral Monday Movement Plans New Protests, More Organizing," *The Institute for Southern Studies*, April 29, 2014, accessed March 10, 2016. http://www.southernstudies.org/2014/04/a-year-in-moral-monday-movement-plans-new-protests.html.

46. Tyson, who is white, is Visiting Professor of American Christianity and Southern Culture at Duke University and has a joint appointment in American Studies at the University of North Carolina at Chapel Hill. He is the author of a memoir, *Blood Done Sign My Name*, about the murder of a black man in Oxford, North Carolina when Tyson was a youth.

47. William Barber with Jonathan Wilson-Hartgrove, *The Third Reconstruction: Moral Mondays, Fusion Politics, and the Rise of a New Justice Movement* (Boston: Beacon Press, 2016), x.

48. John Frank, "NC NAACP president, 16 other protestors arrested outside NC Senate," *News & Observer*, April 29, 2013, accessed June 9, 2015. http://beavercountyblue.org/2013/05/04/naacp-president-arrested-at-nc-protest-of-medicaid-cuts/.

49. Vock, "With Hundreds of Arrests."

50. Charles van der Horst, "Civil Disobedience and Physicians—Protesting the Blockade of Medicaid," *The New England Journal of Medicine* 371, no. 21 (November 20, 2014): 1958–1959.

51. Raboteau, *American Prophets*, 142.

52. Laurie Goodstein, "Religious Liberals Sat Out of Politics for 40 Years. Now They Want in the Game," *New York Times*, June 11, 2017, A22.

53. Ibid.

54. Martin Luther King, Jr., "Letter from Birmingham Jail," *Why We Can't Wait* (New York: Mentor, 1964), 90.

55. James B. Kelleher, "Up to 100,000 protest Wisconsin law curbing unions," Reuters, March 12, 2011, accessed June 9, 2015. Protestors occupied the state capitol in Madison, Wisconsin in massive rallies against a law curbing the union rights of public employees. An unsuccessful recall election was later held for Republican Gov. Scott Walker. http://www.reuters.com/article/2011/03/13/us-wisconsin-protests-idUSTRE72B2AN20110313.

56. The Democratic Party in North Carolina, as in many states, was for years identified with racism prior to the mid-twentieth century. "The ideology of the North Carolina Democratic Party during the first half of the twentieth century was a mix of economic progressivism and conservative retrenchment, particularly on issues of race," according to historian Richard D. Starnes. See Richard D. Starnes, "Democratic Party," NCPedia, 2006, http://www.ncpedia.org/democratic-party; article originally published in *Encyclopedia of North Carolina* ed. William S. Powell (Chapel Hill: UNC Press, 2006). After President Richard Nixon's Watergate scandal in the 1970s and President Ronald Reagan's association with the Rev. Jerry Falwell's Moral Majority in the 1980s, Republicans became identified with evangelical religiosity as well as conservative racial policies, such as the desire on the part of many in the GOP to abolish Affirmative Action. In North Carolina in 1972, ultraconservative Jesse Helms, often labeled a racist and homophobe by his opponents because of his writings, rhetoric, political ads and speeches, was elected to the U.S. Senate. Helms never lost an election, serving until 2003.

57. Kim Severson, "G.O.P.'s Full Control in Long-Moderate North Carolina May Leave Lasting Stamp," *New York Times*, December 11, 2012, accessed January 16, 2017, http://www.nytimes.com/2012/12/12/us/politics/gop-to-take-control-in-long-moderate-north-carolina.html.

58. HB 589, July 26, 2013, http://www.ncga.state.nc.us/Sessions/2013/Bills/House/PDF/H589v8.pdf. The NAACP and other plaintiffs opposed to North Carolina's voter ID law sued. On April 25, 2016, a federal judge upheld the law. U.S. District Judge Thomas Schroeder issued a 485-page ruling dismissing all claims challenging the state's 2013 election law overhaul. On July 29, 2016, the three-judge panel of the U.S. 4th Circuit Court of Appeals reversed that decision and struck down the law, declaring that voter ID was adopted with "discriminatory intent" despite GOP lawmakers' claims that the provision and other voting changes were designed to prevent voter fraud. The 4th Circuit judges said limiting voting options and requiring voters to show photo ID at the polls "target African Americans with almost surgical precision."

59. Rob Christensen, "State GOP rolls back era of Democratic laws," *The Courier-Tribune* (Asheboro, NC), June 18, 2013, accessed June 9, 2015, http://courier-tribune.com/sections/news/north-carolina/state-gop-rolls-back-era-democratic-laws.html. Repeal of the Racial Justice Act was particularly galling to Barber, as Gov. Pat McCrory signed the repeal order on

June 19, 2013—Juneteenth. Juneteenth is the name given to the date of June 19, 1865, the day Union General Gordon Granger landed at Galveston, Texas to inform slaves that the war was over and they were now free. This announcement came two and a half years after President Abraham Lincoln signed the Emancipation Proclamation. In an NAACP press release dated June 21, 2013, Barber said, "Gov. Patrick McCrory picked Juneteenth—of all the days in the year,—to reinstate North Carolina's proven race-based system of death, to sign an unconstitutional and flawed law that repeals North Carolina's nationally-acclaimed Racial Justice Act."

60. Benjamin Wallace-Wells, "The Limits of Protest in Charlotte," *The New Yorker*, September 23, 2016, https://www.newyorker.com/news/benjamin-wallace-wells/the-limits-of-protest-in-charlotte.

61. Rob Christensen, "N.C. GOP Has New Diversity," *News & Observer*, July 1, 2015, 2A.

62. Rob Christensen, "State GOP Rolls Back Era of Democratic Laws," *The Courier-Tribune*, June 18, 2013, accessed June 26, 2015, http://courier-tribune.com/sections/news/north-carolina/state-gop-rolls-back-era-democratic-laws.html.

63. Mary C. Curtis, "Is North Carolina Moving Backward on Civil Rights?" *She the People, Washington Post Blogs*, washingtonpost.com, October 3, 2013, accessed July 13, 2015.

64. Ibid.

65. David Zucchino, "N.C. Legislature Draws Protests; Clergy, Others Welcome Arrest at 'Moral Monday' Demonstrations Against GOP Policies," *The Los Angeles Times*, June 13, 2013, accessed July 13, 2015, A14.

66. Barry Yeoman, "The End of Moderation?" *Duke Magazine*, November 14, 2013, accessed July 13, 2015, http://dukemagazine.duke.edu/article/end-moderation.

67. David Whisenant, "Former NC Gov. Mike Easley enters felony plea agreement," WBTV.com, December 23, 2010, accessed June 26, 2015, http://www.wbtv.com/story/13554761/former-governor-easley-expected-to-pla.

68. "North Carolinians on Perdue, Rivalries," Public Policy Polling, June 15, 2012, accessed June 26, 2015, http://www.publicpolicypolling.com/main/2012/06/north-carolinians-on-perdue-rivalries.html.

69. R. Laurence Moore, *Touchdown Jesus: The Mixing of Sacred and Secular in American History* (Louisville, Westminster John Knox Press, 2003), 184.

70. Ibid., 184.

71. Ibid., 185.

72. See "'Nones' on the Rise," Pew Research Center, Religion and Public Life, October 9, 2012. http://www.pewforum.org/2012/10/09/nones-on-the-rise/.

73. Barna Group, "Spiritual Profile of Homosexual Adults Provides Surprising Insights," June 20, 2009, accessed July 10, 2015, https://www.barna.org/barna-update/article/13-culture/282-spiritual-profile-of-homosexual-adults-provides-surprising-insights#.VZ_7zXhNV6N.

74. Michael Frost, "Colin Kaepernick vs. Tim Tebow: A Tale Of Two Christians On Their Knees," the *Washington Post*, September 24, 2017, https://www.washingtonpost.com/amphtml/news/acts-of-faith/wp/2017/09/24/colin-kaepernick-vs-tim-tebow-a-tale-of-two-christianities-on-its-knees/.

75. Ibid.

76. Bruce Bawer, *Stealing Jesus: How Fundamentalism Betrays Christianity* (New York: Three Rivers Press, 1997), 5. On his website, Bawer describes his philosophy: "As far as I am concerned, the left-right dichotomy has become meaningless anyway. Read *A Place at the Table* and *Stealing Jesus* and *While Europe Slept* and *Surrender* one after the other and you will see that all four books are motivated by a dedication to individual identity and individual freedom and an opposition to groupthink, oppression, tyranny." See Bruce Bawer, "Bio," http://brucebawer.com/bio/.

77. Yonat Shimron, "NAACP's William Barber Emerges as Leader of Moral Monday Protests," June 24, 2013, accessed July 13, 2015, http://www.religionnews.com/2013/06/24/naacps-william-barber-emerges-as-leader-of-moral-monday-protests/.

78. William J. Barber II, "We Are In a Crisis—A Moral Crisis," *Sojourners*, May 13, 2014. See also: William J. Barber II with Barbara Zelter, *Forward Together: A Moral Message for the Nation* (St. Louis, MO: Chalice Press, 2014), 159; Isaiah 10:1–2 NIV.

79. Barber and Zelter, 160–161.

80. Kristin Rawls, "The Liberal Protest that Would Shock the Right: Moral Monday," *Salon*, July 23, 2013, accessed June 30, 2015, http://www.salon.com/2013/07/23/moral_mondays_the_liberal_protest_that_would_shock_the_right/.

81. Ibid.

82. Brady McCombs and Rachel Zoll, "Episcopal Church Elects Michael Curry, Its First Black Presiding Bishop," Associated Press, *Huffington Post Religion*, June 27, 2015, accessed June 29, 2015. http://www.huffingtonpost.com/2015/06/27/episcopal-church-michael-curry-black_n_7679264.html.

83. Ibid.

84. Shimron, Wilson-Hartgrove, an evangelical Christian writer, activist, and leader in the New Monasticism movement, has known Barber since high school.

85. Strom Thurmond served as a South Carolina senator from 1954–2003. He conducted the longest filibuster ever by a lone senator, at 24 hours and 18 minutes, in opposition to the Civil rights Act of 1957. Thurmond also opposed civil rights and voting rights bills passed in 1964 and 1965.

86. Amanda Abrams, "Love Thy Neighbor: Jonathan Wilson-Hartgrove on Race, Faith, and Resistance," *The Sun*, September 2017, 9.

87. Barber has used the "Selma" phrase many times since 2013, including in an open letter posted on the NC NAACP website on March 7, 2015. In a nod to novelist William Faulkner, Barber wrote that, "Selma is not dead. It's not even past. It is alive in North Carolina." March 7, 2015, accessed June 8, 2015. http://www.naacpnc.org/northcarolinaisourselma.

88. Zoe Schlanger, "North Carolina's Moral Mondays are Back with Massive March," *Newsweek*, February 10, 2014, http://www.newsweek.com/n-carolina-progressive-group-kicks-2014-massive-march-228585.

89. Abby Rapoport, "Moral Mondays and the South's New Liberal Gospel," *The American Prospect*, July 29, 2013, accessed June 9, 2015, http://prospect.org/article/moral-mondays-and-south's-new-liberal-gospel.

90. Timothy Tyson, interview by Abby Rapoport, "Moral Mondays and the South's New Liberal Gospel," *The American Prospect*, July 29, 2013, accessed June 9, 2015, http://prospect.org/article/moral-mondays-and-south's-new-liberal-gospel.

91. Thom Goolsby, "Moron Monday Shows Radical Left Just Doesn't Get It," *The Chatham Journal*, June 7, 2013, accessed June 26, 2015, http://www.chathamjournal.com/weekly/opinion/myopinion/moron-monday-shows-radical-left-just-does-not-get-it-130607.shtml.

92. Angelica Alvarez, "Website Mocks Moral Monday Protests," *ABC 11 Eyewitness News*, June 19, 2013, accessed March 9, 2016, http://abc11.com/archive/9145248/. The site has since been removed from https://www.nccivitas.org/moralmonday/.

93. Mark Binker, "Researchers Find 'Moral Monday' Crowd Mostly from North Carolina," *WRAL*, June 18, 2013, accessed March 9, 2016, http://www.wral.com/researchers-find-moral-monday-crowd-mostly-from-north-carolina/12562184/. The report cited research conducted by Fred Stutzman of Eighty Percent Solutions in Chapel Hill, NC, who found that at one Monday protest, 311 of 317 protestors surveyed were from North Carolina.

94. "It's Time to Laugh at the Marxist Monday Crowd!" The Voter Integrity Project of North Carolina, July 8, 2013, accessed March 9, 2016, http://voterintegrityproject.com/its-time-to-laugh/#more-673.

95. Sue Sturgis, "Tea Party Group Responds to NC Protest Movement with 'Marxist Mondays' Song," *The Institute for Southern Studies*, July 8, 2013, accessed March 9, 2016, http://www.southernstudies.org/2013/07/tea-party-group-responds-to-nc-protest-movement-wi.html.

96. The Rev. William Barber, interview by Lynn Stuart Parramore, "The Man Behind Moral Mondays," *The American Prospect*, June 17, 2013, accessed June 26, 2015, http://prospect.org/article/man-behind-moral-mondays.

97. TrueBlueMajority, "I'm Glad I Didn't Miss it: Transcript of The Rev. Dr. William Barber at NN14," *Daily Kos*, July 24, 2014, accessed June 29, 2015. TrueBlueMajority is an alias for a *Daily Kos* writer self-described as "a 'spiritual activist': a faithful Christian, a lifelong liberal, and a proud Democrat." The transcript is a volunteer effort by TrueBlueMajority, rather than being professionally transcribed. A video of the speech is available on the *Daily Kos* website. http://www.dailykos.com/story/2014/07/24/1316230/-I-m-glad-I-didn-t-miss-it.

98. Chris Kardish, "NC Protests Split on Bible's Message to Help Poor," Associated Press, *Yahoo! News*, June 12, 2013, accessed June 30, 2015, http://news.yahoo.com/nc-protests-split-bibles-message-help-poor-161430742.html.

99. William J. Barber II and Jonathan Wilson-Hartgrove, "Holding Candidates Morally Accountable," *News & Observer*, February 21, 2016, 15A.

100. Ibid.

101. Gary Dorrien, "Recovering the Black Social Gospel," *Harvard Divinity Bulletin*, Summer/Autumn 2015, 34. Dorrien is associated with Union Theological Seminary, where Barber was named a 2015–2016 Distinguished Scholar-Activist Fellow.

102. Ibid.

103. Ibid., 35.

104. James H. Cone, *A Black Theology of Liberation* (Philadelphia: J.B. Lippincott, 1970), in *A Documentary History of Religion in America Since 1865*, ed. Edwin S. Gaustad, 2nd ed., (Grand Rapids: Eerdmans, 1993), 555.

105. Pope Francis, *Evangelii Gaudium: Apostolic Exhortation on the Proclamation of the Gospel in Today's World* (November 24, 2013), accessed June 29, 2015. http://w2.vatican.va/content/francesco/en/apost_exhortations/documents/papa-francesco_esortazione-ap_20131124_evangelii-gaudium.html.

106. There were numerous press accounts of the positive and negative reactions to the invitation. See, for example: Barbie Latza Nadeau, "Is Pope Francis a Commie? A Liberation Theology Hero Returns to Rome." *The Daily Beast*, May 12, 2015; Stephanie Kirchgaessner and Jonathan Watts, "Catholic Church Warms to Liberation Theology as Founder heads to Vatican," *The Guardian*, May 11, 2015.

107. Jonathan Wilson-Hartgrove, telephone interview, January 12, 2017.

108. Tom Gjelten, "Evangelical Pastors Gather To Learn Another Calling: Politics," *NPR*, July 10, 2015, accessed July 10, 2015, http://www.npr.org/2015/07/10/421684410/evangelical-pastors-gather-to-learn-another-calling-politics?utm_source=npr_newsletter&utm_medium=email&utm_content=20150710&utm_campaign=npr_email_a_friend&utm_term=storyshare.

109. Obergefell *v.* Hodges, 576 U.S. ____ (2015); Congressional Budget Office figures for the deficit, cbo.gov; Centers for Disease Control abortion figures reflect the year 2011, cdc.gov.

110. Gjelten, "Evangelical Pastors Gather." The homosexual prayer refers to gay Cuban poet Richard Blanco reciting a poem at President Barack Obama's second inaugural in 2013.

111. Ibid.

112. *Media and the Movement: Journalism, Civil Rights, and Black Power in the American South*, accessed June 29, 2015, http://mediaandthemovement.unc.edu.

113. Joshua Clark Davis, "The March on Washington, Moral Mondays, and the Media," *Huffington Post Blog*, August 27, 2013, updated October 27, 2013, accessed June 29, 2015, http://www.huffingtonpost.com/joshua-clark-davis/the-march-on-washington-m_b_3818222.html.

114. Ibid.

115. Mark Binker, "Republicans decry harsh rhetoric at 'Moral Monday' events," *WRAL.com*, September 17, 2013, accessed June 29, 2015, http://www.wral.com/republicans-decry-harsh-rhetoric-at-moral-monday-events/12896893/#p1AwQMjXhA32gwsW.99.

116. Ibid.

117. Ibid.

118. Sarah Delia, "City Council Approves Changes To Non-Discrimination Ordinance," WFAE, February 23, 2016, http://wfae.org/post/city-council-approves-changes-non-discrimination-ordinance.

119. See "A BILL TO BE ENTITLED AN ACT TO PROVIDE FOR SINGLE-SEX MULTIPLE OCCUPANCY BATHROOM AND CHANGING FACILITIES IN SCHOOLS AND PUBLIC AGENCIES AND TO CREATE STATEWIDE CONSISTENCY IN REGULATION OF EMPLOYMENT AND PUBLIC ACCOMMODATIONS," NC House Bill 2, March 23, 2016.

120. Greg Lacour, "Opinion: The N.C. 'Bathroom Bill,' In Sum," *Charlotte Magazine*, March 23, 2016, accessed January 5, 2017, http://www.charlottemagazine.com/Charlotte-Magazine/March-2016/Opinion-the-NC-Bathroom-Bill-In-Sum/.

121. Anne Blythe, "Moral Monday Rally Against HB2 Brings 11 Arrests," *News & Observer*, May 16, 2016, accessed January 5, 2017, http://www.newsobserver.com/news/politics-government/article77988752.html.

122. K. Morgan, "Asheville Supporters Demonstrate in Favor of HB2 Bathroom Bill," *The Tribune Papers*, April 6, 2016, accessed January 5, 2017, http://www.thetribunepapers.com/2016/04/06/asheville-supporters-demonstrate-in-favor-of-hb2-bathroom-bill/.

123. Blythe, "Moral Monday Rally Against HB2 Brings 11 Arrests."

124. For a timeline related to the Charlotte ordinance and HB2, see Greg Lacour, "HB2: How North Carolina Got Here (Updated)," *Charlotte Magazine*, December 21, 2016, accessed January 5, 2017, http://www.charlottemagazine.com/Charlotte-Magazine/April-2016/HB2-How-North-Carolina-Got-Here/. In response to HB2, performers, sports events, and businesses announced cancellations in North Carolina, citing state sponsored discrimination. According to Raleigh television station WRAL, Bruce Springsteen cancelled a concert in the state, the first domino to fall. Charlotte lost a 400-job expansion by PayPal; Raleigh lost $5.6 million in direct costs from 18 canceled conventions; Greensboro lost $6 million from six conferences that moved elsewhere; Cary lost a planned 250-job expansion from Deutsche Bank, totaling $27 million in payroll and construction; Asheville estimated a loss of close to $2 million in cancellations; and the National Basketball Association moved the 2017 All-Star Game from Charlotte to New Orleans, losing Charlotte an estimated $90 million. Losses from these cancellations top $505 million overall. "While half a billion dollars is a significant figure that's harmed businesses directly affected by cancelations, it's a tiny fraction of the state's overall economy. According to the U.S. Department of Commerce, North Carolina's gross state domestic product for 2015 was $510 billion. So, even at $500 million, House Bill 2's impact on the state economy has been about 0.1 percent." See Laura Leslie, "Cancellations over HB2 Make Headlines but Barely Dent NC Economy," *WRAL.com*, September 21, 2016, accessed January 5, 2017, http://www.wral.com/cancellations-over-hb2-make-headlines-but-barely-dent-nc-economy/16035660/.

125. See Craig Jarvis, Colin Campbell, and Lynn Bonner, "HB2 Off The Books As Gov. Roy Cooper Signs Compromise Into Law," *News & Observer*, March 30, 2017, http://www.newsobserver.com/news/politics-government/politics-columns-blogs/under-the-dome/article141716579.html; Text of HB 142: http://media2.newsobserver.com/content/media/2017/3/29/H142v1-HB2changes.pdf.

126. Rev. Dr. William J. Barber II, "It's Not About Trump. Our Political Culture is Corrupt," *The Nation*, March 12, 2016, accessed March 12, 2016, http://www.thenation.com/article/north-carolinas-new-moral-majority-goes-to-the-polls/.

127. Samantha Lachman, "Moral Monday Returns With Public Opinion, If Not The North Carolina Legislature, On Its Side," January 28, 2015, accessed January 16, 2017, http://www.huffingtonpost.com/2015/01/28/moral-monday-north-carolina_n_6564352.html.

128. Historic Thousands on Jones St. People's Assembly Coalition, http://www.hkonj.com/about.

129. Robert Reich, Facebook post, November 1, 2015, https://www.facebook.com/RBReich/?fref=photo

130. "Public Policy in North Carolina," Ballotpedia, accessed March 15, 2016, https://ballotpedia.org/Redistricting_in_North_Carolina.

131. Covington v. North Carolina. 161 (M.D.N.C. Aug. 11, 2016).

132. 581 US____(2017). The court struck down two North Carolina congressional districts, ruling that lawmakers had violated the Constitution by relying too heavily on race in drawing them.

133. *The Daily Show*, Comedy Central Network, airdate June 5, 2017.

134. Ibid. Transcript from author's notes.

135. Transcript adapted from liberal Dailykos.com website. Underlines and boldface omitted. Ellipses indicate omitted lines. For video and full transcript, see: Leslie Salzillo, "Watch Rev. Barber 'Shock' the DNC, Shame Religious Hypocrisy & Lead with Love," Dailykos.com, July

28, 2016, accessed January 5, 2017, http://www.dailykos.com/story/2016/7/28/1553896/-Moral-Monday-s-Rev-William-Barber-IGNITES-the-DNC-Lead-With-Love.

136. Ibid.

137. Janell Ross, "The Rev. William Barber Dropped the Mic," *Washington Post*, July 28, 2016, accessed January 5, 2017, https://www.washingtonpost.com/news/the-fix/wp/2016/07/28/the-rev-william-barber-dropped-the-mic/?utm_term=.187a19ad21e7.

138. "Dr. William Barber," NAACP website, accessed January 12, 2017, http://www.naacp.org/naacp-board-of-directors/board-member-dr-william-barber/.

139. Press release, "The REV. DR. WILLIAM J. BARBER II, TO TRANSITION FROM PRESIDENT OF THE NORTH CAROLINA NAACP STATE CONFERENCE TO JOIN LEADERSHIP OF THE POOR PEOPLE'S CAMPAIGN CALL FOR A NATIONAL MORAL REVIVAL," NCNAACP, May 11, 2017.

140. A New Poor People's Campaign for Today, website accessed June 14, 2017, https://poorpeoplescampaign.org/new-poor-peoples-campaign/.

141. "Our Mission," Repairers of the Breach, website accessed June 14, 2017, http://www.breachrepairers.org.

142. "Theodore Parker And The 'Moral Universe,'" NPR, September 2, 2010, accessed January 16, 2017, http://www.npr.org/templates/story/story.php?storyId=129609461.

143. "Our Mission," Repairers of the Breach.

144. Abrams, "Love Thy Neighbor," 11.

145. Jonathan Wilson-Hartgrove, telephone interview, January 12, 2017.

Chapter Two

So Blessed by God

Adding the Almighty to the Pledge of Allegiance to the Flag

I Pledge Allegiance to the Flag of the United States of America and to the Republic for which it stands, one Nation under God, indivisible, with liberty and justice for all. [1]

—Final version of the Pledge of Allegiance to the Flag, adopted 1954

INTRODUCTION

One winter evening in 1969, comedian Red Skelton (1913–1997) performed a nostalgic monologue about the Pledge of Allegiance on his long running CBS variety television show. Long before the advent of YouTube, the audio clip was later released on a 45-rpm vinyl record.[2] Growing up in Vincennes, Indiana, Skelton said, he and his classmates routinely recited the pledge at school. One day, his principal, Mr. Lasswell, gave a speech about the pledge, saying, "Uh, boys and girls, I have been listening to you recite the Pledge of Allegiance all semester, and it seems that it has become monotonous to you. Or, could it be, you do not understand the meaning of each word? If I may, I would like to recite the pledge, and give you a definition for each word."[3]

Skelton, in the guise of his elderly principal, then explained each segment of the pledge:

I—Me; an individual; a committee of one.
Pledge—Dedicate all of my worldly good to give without self-pity.
Allegiance—My love and my devotion.

To the Flag—Our standard. "Old Glory"; a symbol of courage. And wherever she waves, there is respect, because your loyalty has given her a dignity that shouts "Freedom is everybody's job."
of the United—That means we have all come together.
States—Individual communities that have united into 48 great states; 48 individual communities with pride and dignity and purpose; all divided by imaginary boundaries, yet united to a common cause, and that's love of country.
Of America.
And to the Republic—A Republic: a sovereign state in which power is invested into the representatives chosen by the people to govern; and the government is the people; and it's from the people to the leaders, not from the leaders to the people.
For which it stands
One Nation—Meaning "so blessed by God."
Indivisible—Incapable of being divided.
With Liberty—Which is freedom; the right of power for one to live his own life without fears, threats, or any sort of retaliation.
And Justice—The principle and qualities of dealing fairly with others.
For All—That means, boys and girls, it's as much your country as it is mine.

Skelton concluded the skit by breaking character and speaking directly to the studio audience:

Since I was a small boy, two states have been added to our country, and two words have been added to the Pledge of Allegiance: *Under God*. Wouldn't it be a pity if someone said, "That is a prayer"—and that be eliminated from our schools, too?[4]

"UNDER GOD"

Americans often show their patriotism—and piety—through public recitations of the Pledge of Allegiance to the flag. The current pledge is the fourth incarnation of a flag oath composed by a clergyman, who was also a magazine staff writer, for school children in the nineteenth century. Some 50 years later, the secular patriotic pledge took on a religious dimension with the addition of the phrase "under God." This final alteration was an official act of Congress passed during the tense years of the Cold War, a time of increased public religiosity.[5]

The idea of adding God originated in the early 1950s within the Catholic fraternity the Knights of Columbus, and nationwide adoption of the phrase was championed by the Hearst newspaper chain and other media outlets, both religious and secular. The addition of a deity to the pledge was accepted in most quarters, but rejected in others.

Another half-century later, controversy concerning "under God" in the pledge continued. In the summer of 2002, the federally-inserted phrase was challenged by self-described atheist Michael Newdow on behalf of his school-aged daughter. On June 26 of that year, the Ninth U.S. Circuit Court of Appeals banned the use of "under God" in public school recitations of the pledge on the grounds that the First Amendment forbids "an establishment of religion" by government. Many groups—including members of Congress—defied the Court and kept the pledge intact, prompting the Court to stay the decision pending appeals, including one by the U.S. Justice Department.[6]

On Flag Day, June 14, 2004—the 50th anniversary of the inclusion of "under God" in the Pledge of Allegiance—the U.S. Supreme Court, sidestepping church-state issues, reversed the lower court 8–0, and dismissed the challenge to the use of the phrase on other grounds.[7]

This chapter explores and explains how "under God" found its way into a secular flag pledge, and how the decision to add these two words to the pledge influenced and often divided American society over the next century.

THE EVOLUTION OF THE PLEDGE OF ALLEGIANCE

Written by a Christian socialist clergyman, the original pledge was conceived as a secular document. When the Reverend Francis Bellamy composed what he called the "Pledge to the Flag" for *The Youth's Companion* magazine in August 1892, it read:

> I pledge allegiance to my flag and the Republic for which it stands: one nation indivisible, with liberty and justice for all.[8]

"In a marketing gimmick, the *Companion* offered U.S. flags to readers who sold subscriptions, and now, with the looming 400th anniversary of Christopher Columbus' arrival in the New World, the magazine planned to raise the Stars and Stripes 'over every Public School from the Atlantic to the Pacific' and salute it with an oath," writes journalist Amy Crawford.[9]

Bellamy's cousin was author Edward Bellamy, a leading American socialist and writer of the utopian novels *Looking Backward* (1888) and *Equality* (1897). Francis Bellamy was a Baptist minister who, like Edward, believed in economic equality. Instrumental in forming the Christian Society of Socialists, Francis served as the group's vice president. What is considered to be a patriotic oath is actually "a statement of an American Socialist, and more specifically, a Christian Socialist," according to pledge historian John W. Baer.[10]

Bellamy actually resigned from the Society of Christian Socialists nearly two years prior to writing the pledge. Later in life, he was a successful advertising man in New York City, and edited the book *Effective Magazine Advertising*.[11] In light of anti-communism campaigns of the 1950s, it is striking that Bellamy's early political leanings were never called into question.

Bellamy's original pledge was first modified at the inaugural National Flag Conference, under the leadership of the American Legion and the Daughters of the American Revolution, in 1923 to read:

> I pledge allegiance to the Flag of the United States and to the Republic for which it stands: one nation, indivisible, with liberty and justice for all.

The following year at the Second National Flag Conference the identifying words "of America" were inserted after "United States." Congress formalized the use of the pledge for all flag raising ceremonies in 1942. [12]

In April 1951, the Knights of Columbus in New York adopted a resolution to amend the pledge for use at their own assemblies by adding the words "under God" after the word "nation" and before the word "indivisible." [13] Subsequent resolutions by the Catholic organization led to a campaign to urge Congress and President Dwight Eisenhower, who was raised a Jehovah's Witness but later converted to Presbyterianism, to change the pledge officially. The Knights also sent letters to every member of Congress in 1952 urging the change. [14]

In April 1953, a Republican senator from Michigan, Homer Ferguson, and Democratic Congressman Louis C. Rabaut, also of Michigan, sponsored joint legislation to insert the phrase "under God" into the Pledge of Allegiance. Representative Rabaut's House bill was the one signed into law by President Eisenhower on Flag Day, June 14, 1954. [15] This final change created the pledge as it reads today:

> I Pledge Allegiance to the Flag of the United States of America and to the Republic for which it stands, one Nation under God, indivisible, with liberty and justice for all. [16]

As John Baer put it, "The pledge was now both a patriotic oath and a public prayer." [17]

In his seminal study on interfaith relations, *Protestant, Catholic, Jew* (1955), Will Herberg wrote, "The identification of religion with the national purpose is almost inevitable in a situation in which religion is so frequently felt to be a way of American 'belonging.'" He continued,

> In its crudest form, this identification of religion with national purpose generates a kind of national messianism which sees it as the vocation of America to bring the American Way of Life, compounded almost equally of democracy and free enterprise, to every corner of the globe; in more mitigated versions, it sees God as the champion of America, endorsing American purposes, and sustaining American might. [18]

Although many faithful still argue that God has been removed from American public life, and some Christians maintain that their religion in particular is under attack from atheists, secularists, media, and government, religious influence is ever present in our pledge, on our currency, and in our politics.

THE COLD WAR SETTING FOR ADDING GOD

Headlines in newspapers and on the cover of newsweeklies in the spring and summer of 1954 were filled with stories about the Army-McCarthy Hearings, looking into alleged infiltration of the federal government by communists. World War II had been over for less than a decade, and it had ended with the deadly explosion of two atomic bombs in Japan. Now in peacetime, the country was becoming increasingly paranoid once again.

Senator Joseph McCarthy, a Wisconsin Republican, had in 1952 launched an anti-communism crusade. Hundreds were accused—justly or unjustly—of being communists or communist sympathizers. He became a nationwide celebrity, partly because "McCarthy's effort succeeded in exploiting a climate of fear that surrounded the cold war and everything that had to do with domestic subversion," according to Donald Crosby. "In such an atmosphere it was inevitable that McCarthy's sensational charges would find a ready (even fanatical) audience."[19] The Catholic press largely supported McCarthy, particularly the conservative periodical *Brooklyn Tablet.* Bucking this trend was the liberal Catholic magazine *Commonweal*, which stated in a June 18, 1954 editorial, "Some honestly believe that he is a great national asset; others, like the editors of this magazine, are convinced that he is a dangerous demagogue."[20]

Alongside these events were scattered stories on an issue that literally linked God and Country. Through a letter writing campaign begun in 1951 by the Catholic fraternal order the Knights of Columbus and championed by others, a bill sped through both houses of Congress amending the Pledge of Allegiance to the Flag, adding the words "under God." Prior to the bill being signed into law by Eisenhower, the president's pastor, the American Legion, and the Hearst newspaper chain would all claim partial credit for adding God to the pledge.

When Congressman Rabaut introduced the original House resolution in April 1953 he said, "You and I know that the Union of Soviet Socialist Republics would not, and could not, while supporting the philosophy of communism, place in its patriotic ritual an acknowledgement that their nation existed 'under God.'"[21]

During the Cold War, the United States had a collective case of nerves because of national and international unrest, and citizens were seeking spiritual, not just patriotic, guidance from their government. The annual National Day of Prayer was instituted by Congress in 1952; in 1956, "In God We Trust" officially became the national motto, replacing the unofficial "E Pluribus Unum"; and in 1957, paper currency began bearing the slogan, "In God We Trust," matching the existing phrase on coins, which had been mandated in 1864 during the Civil War.[22]

One could argue the nation moved from seeing itself united by a common humanity to a fearful one seeking the protection of God. This mid-twentieth century national paranoia has parallels in the post-September 11, 2001 United States, with rising public fears of terrorist attacks and widespread resistance to immigration, particularly of Muslims.[23]

"The late 1940s and '50s were also the years in which Billy Graham was filling stadiums and making his first visits to the White House," Jon Meacham writes, "when President Eisenhower opened Cabinet meetings with prayer (on one occasion, however, deep into a session, he said, 'Jesus Christ! We forgot the prayer!'), when Congress voted to make 'In God We Trust' the national motto, and the phrase 'under God' was added to the Pledge of Allegiance—all signs of a vital public religion."[24]

As Richard J. Ellis has written, "Inserting the words 'under God' into the Pledge of Allegiance must be understood as only one of many actions taken in the early years of the Eisenhower presidency that were designed to inject religious faith into public life."[25] Ellis also places the Pledge in the context of anticommunist sentiment:

> The history of the Pledge of Allegiance, from its inception, has mirrored the history of American anxieties . . . the creation of the Pledge of Allegiance stemmed in large part from the anxiety about the threat that new immigrants posed to the American way of life. . . . The addition of "under God" to the Pledge in 1954 emerged out of an anxiety about the threat of Soviet Communism.[26]

In his book, *One Nation Under God: How Corporate America Invented Christian America*, Princeton history professor Kevin M. Kruse disagrees with this assessment. Scholars, he writes, have "the mistaken idea that the pledge change was largely, or even solely, a result of Cold War anticommunism. But in reality it was the result of nearly two decades of partisan fighting over domestic issues. The Cold War contrasts were largely a last-minute development, one that helped paper over partisan differences."[27]

Kruse also notes that, "In short order, the phrase 'one nation under God' quickly claimed a central position in American political culture. It became an informal motto for the country, demonstrating the widespread belief that the United States had been founded on religious belief and was sustained by religious practice."[28]

LEGAL CHALLENGES TO THE PLEDGE

Of all the religious symbolism officially added to public life in the 1950s, the addition of "under God" to the Pledge has caused the most turmoil—and litigation. Jerry Bergman has studied religious groups that object to saluting the flag of the United States and the harm to children caused by societal attitudes of intolerance toward differences of opinion. He writes that the first recorded instances of refusals to salute the flag occurred in 1918. "The flag salute issue is only one of many which has surfaced in the endless conflict between church and state. . . . The flag as a symbol typically elicits strong emotional feelings on the part of both those who feel all should salute as well as those who feel saluting is wrong."[29]

Children are often caught between the demands of parents and the demands of school authorities, Bergman notes. The lawsuit brought by Michael Newdow in 2002 to remove "under God" from the Pledge of Allegiance, for example, was an attempt to shield his daughter from pledge recitations in school.

Notable conflicts between parental teachings and the required recitation of the Pledge of Allegiance arose from two 1940s-era U.S. Supreme Court cases involving Jehovah's Witness families. In *Minersville School District v. Gobitis* (1940), the court dealt with the issue of the refusal to recite the pledge by two elementary school children.[30] The Gobitas children's parents had taught them Witness doctrine that God is the supreme authority, and saluting the flag is not Scriptural. The basis for this belief is a literal interpretation of Exodus: "Thou shalt not make unto thee any graven image, or any likeness of anything that is in heaven above, or that is in the earth beneath, or that is in the water under the earth; thou shalt not bow down thyself to them nor serve them."[31] In the view of Witnesses, the United States flag represents an "image." The court ruled against the Gobitas family, and in favor of compulsory recitation if required by a school district. The court noted, "National unity is the basis of national security."

Three years later, the court reversed itself in *West Virginia State Board of Education et al. v. Barnette et al.* (1943). Following the *Gobitis* decision, the West Virginia Board of Education had made the flag salute mandatory in public schools. Ironically, the original "salute" was an outstretched hand resembling the Nazi salute to Adolph Hitler.

Protests from Jehovah's Witness families and others were viewed as insubordination by the school board. This time, the court acknowledged civil liberties, writing that, "the refusal of these persons to participate in the ceremony does not interfere with or deny rights of others to do so. . . . The sole conflict is between authority and rights of the individual." Instead of promoting national unity, the court recognized that, "Government of limited power need not be anemic government." The most often-quoted passage from this case foreshadows the Ninth Circuit decision some 60 years later:

> If there is any fixed star in our constitutional constellation, it is that no official, high or petty, can prescribe what shall be orthodox in politics, nationalism, religion, or other matters of opinion or force citizens to confess by word or act their faith therein. If there are any circumstances which [sic] permit an exception, they do not now occur to us. [32]

Writing just after that 2002 Ninth Circuit decision eliminating "under God" from the pledge, Peter H. Schuck asserted that the decision *should* be reversed, but for the right reasons. He said the original legislation to insert the phrase in 1954 "was a clear governmental endorsement of religion," but the best reason to reverse the decision is that the phrase is not compulsory. "[T]he Pledge and the words 'under God' are voluntary and thus do not impose an orthodoxy on those who are asked to recite them." [33]

Contradicting that argument as well as earlier rulings, the U.S. Court of Appeals for the Fourth Circuit in August 2005 upheld a Virginia law requiring public schools to lead a daily recitation of the Pledge, rejecting a claim that its reference to God was an unconstitutional promotion of religion. A suit filed by Edward Myers, a Mennonite father of three, objected to the phrase "one nation under God" on grounds that it supports civic religion and violates the establishment clause of the First Amendment.

But the court ruled that the Pledge is a patriotic exercise, not an affirmation of religion. "Undoubtedly, the pledge contains a religious phrase, and it is demeaning to persons of any faith to assert that the words 'under God' contain no religious significance," the court ruled. "The inclusion of those two words, however, does not alter the nature of the pledge as a patriotic activity." [34]

THE PRESS AND THE PLEDGE

How did the legal and political maneuvering over the pledge play out in the press? It is instructive to explore framing of the "under God" issue in both religious and secular periodicals of the period leading up to the passage of the "under God" legislation.

Religious publications active during this period include:

* The nondenominational religion magazine *The Christian Century* (founded 1884) projects a progressive social gospel viewpoint, reflecting many of Bellamy's early views. The small circulation magazine contains informed commentary, and is read by seminarians and theologians as well as by a general audience.

- The *Christian Science Monitor* (founded 1908) is a newspaper published by Mary Baker Eddy's Christian Science Church. Along with the Mormon-owned *Deseret News* and the Unification Church's *Washington Times, The Christian Science Monitor* "generally adhered to professional norms for objective reporting, but evidence of religious influence could be seen in their advertising policies and, to a lesser extent, in story selection and framing," according to scholar Judith M. Buddenbaum.[35]

- The leading weekly Unitarian publication *The Christian Register* (1821–1957), published by the American Unitarian Association, opposed the pledge bill adding God. Despite its title, the magazine touted church/ state separation.

- Catholic sources of the period include the respected National Catholic Welfare Conference (NCWC) News Service; *The Catholic Standard*, the weekly newspaper of the Archdiocese of Washington, D.C., founded in 1951 when the "under God" movement began; the *Beehive*, a publication of the Catholic Maccabees organization; the conservative *Catholic World;* and the liberal *Commonweal*. The Knights of Columbus (founded 1882) took a leadership role in urging acknowledgement of God in the Pledge, and their publications *Columbia, The Fraternal Age*, and *The Fraternal Monitor* all touted the K of C party line. *The Catholic Transcript* is the official newspaper of the Archdiocese of Hartford, Connecticut, which includes New Haven, where the Knights are headquartered.

Secular news sources that reported on the pledge include:

- The Hearst newspaper chain, particularly the flagship *New York Journal-American* and *The Detroit Times*, crusaded for the change in the pledge with editorials and front-page stories. Hearst papers had long ago mastered the art of mounting Crusades with the zeal of a Christian martyr, especially publicly popular ones that boosted circulation.

- *Time* and *Newsweek* were well established as journalistic entities by the mid-1950s when print was King, providing analysis as well as weekly news summaries. Both magazines reached a large, national audience of millions.

RELIGIOUS MEDIA RESPOND TO THE PLEDGE CHANGE

A May 1954 item by the NCWC News Service discussed a bill passed unanimously by the Senate that was awaiting passage in the House. The House version of the bill, introduced by liberal Representative Louis C. Rabaut, D-Michigan, a devout Catholic, would insert the words "under God" into the Pledge of Allegiance. The story explains how the bill came about:

> According to Luke E. Hart, Supreme Knight of the Knights of Columbus, the Pledge of Allegiance to the Flag was originated by Francis Bellamy of Rochester, N.Y., who was associated with *The Youth's Companion*, a popular magazine for young people. The pledge was recited for the first time at a Columbus Day rally in 1893.
>
> The idea of having the pledge changed so as to give recognition to God originated with the Knights of Columbus, according to Mr. Hart, and then was taken up by other fraternal, patriotic, religious and similar organizations. [36]

Knights of Columbus publications were predictably enthusiastic about the legislation adding "under God," and also touted the fraternity's involvement and initial efforts to change the pledge. An article in *The Fraternal Age* notes that the U.S. House bill was introduced only after the change was approved two years prior by the Catholic National Fraternal Congress. [37] *The Fraternal Monitor* was equally effusive, running a story about Senate passage of the amendment that covered most of a page with a photo of Supreme Knight Luke Hart. [38]

A survey of all issues of the conservative magazine *Catholic World* for 1954 and 1955 finds many references to, and defenses of, Joseph McCarthy, but none to the pledge issue. The liberal Catholic periodical *Commonweal* also carried no news of the pledge during this period.

Non-Catholic religious sources were muted or played a contrarian role. *The Christian Science Monitor* (1954) ran a five-line brief on page one after Congress approved the bill. The sentence read in its entirety, "Now in the White House awaiting President Eisenhower's signature is a resolution passed by Congress which adds the words 'under God' to the pledge of allegiance to the flag, so those taking the promise would henceforth pledge devotion to 'one nation under God.'" [39] This was the extent of the paper's reporting on the measure.

An editorial in the progressive *Christian Century* stated that the pledge bill "is the sort of proposal against which no member of Congress would think of voting," and that,

> It will be hailed in some church quarters as another triumph for religion—and perhaps it is. But we would be more excited if schools and civic associations

were to direct their attention into putting real meaning into the last six words.[40]

Those last six words are, of course, ". . . with liberty and justice for all." The Unitarian publication *The Christian Register* (1954) ran an account of the annual meeting in Boston of the American Unitarian Association. The pledge change, the religious slogan "in God We Trust" on money, and other religious displays in American public life were criticized by speakers at the convention. The coverage of a keynote speech quoted Agnes E. Meyer, a Washington-based writer: "Religion can and should be democracy's strongest ally. . . . Yet freedom of religion would not long survive unless our country is sufficiently united to withstand the ever growing power of communism." On that point, Meyer and the backers of the Pledge amendment were likely in agreement.

However, Meyer also told the assembly that religious orthodoxy is becoming the "latest fad" in America, and that, "if you don't bring God into every cabinet meeting, political convention or other assembly, it is bad public relations."[41]

THE HEARST CRUSADE

Acknowledgement of the Knights of Columbus as the impetus of the Pledge change movement eventually came from various news sources and even the president himself.[42] Before the final bill was signed by President Eisenhower, and for weeks afterward, however, various news organizations would get the originator of the "under God" idea wrong, and one initially took all the credit. William Randolph Hearst Jr. carried on his father's long tradition of latching onto a pet issue and promoting it, and his newspaper chain claimed the movement to insert the phrase as its own. As Ronald Bishop notes, "Hearst reporters were carrying out a directive from management to convince Americans that the Pledge of Allegiance must reflect our devotion to God, and God's ongoing role in our national affairs."[43]

The Hearst pledge crusade may have been part of an effort to stem falling circulation and profits. "Nineteen fifty-four was a dismal year for Hearst, a year pervaded by the awful sensation that the world of the old man's [W.R. Hearst Sr.] dream had at last begun to disintegrate," according to Hearst biographers Lindsay Chaney and Michael Cieply.[44] While the newspaper industry as a whole was healthy, the 11-newspaper Hearst chain posted a $340,000 loss for 1954.[45]

In April, a month prior to the NCWC release, Hearst's *New York Journal-American* ran an editorial announcing its intent: "It seems to us that in times like these when godless Communism is the great peril this nation faces, it becomes more necessary than ever to avow our faith in God and to affirm the recognition that the core of our strength comes from him."[46]

The next day, a story ran in the paper with the headline, "Legion Head Supports Change in Allegiance Pledge." The kicker headline adds, "Hearst Campaign to Stress Faith in God." The second paragraph reads: "The campaign, launched yesterday by the Hearst Newspapers, seeks early action by the Senate and House Judiciary Committee on a joint resolution introduced by Senator [Homer] Ferguson (R.-Mich.)." The article ends with an exhortation to local citizenry to get involved: "Readers desiring to lend their personal support to the Ferguson resolution are urged to write their Senators who, from this State, are Herbert H. Lehman and Irving M. Ives."[47]

The appeal worked. As Ellis notes, "[T]hrough the determined efforts of various civic, veterans, and fraternal organizations, as well as the Hearst newspapers, House and Senate members found themselves deluged by letters urging support for adding the words 'under God' to the Pledge."[48] Two weeks later, the *Journal-American* ran a front page, bylined article with a Washington dateline announcing that the Senate had voted unanimously to add "under God" to the pledge. "The measure now goes to the House and if approved there will be sent to the White House for the signature of President Eisenhower, which will make it the law of the land. . . . The Hearst newspapers *sponsored the legislation* [emphasis added] in a nationwide campaign which resulted in unprecedentedly heavy mail to all Congress members."[49]

In an editorial the next day, the *Journal-American* continued to applaud its own efforts. "It is, of course, a matter of deep gratification to the Hearst Newspapers that our national campaign, undertaken less than a month ago, for inclusion of the two supremely important words in the Pledge has moved so swiftly toward success." The editorial cast the paper as "a very strongly interested intermediary" between readers and the U.S. Congress that functions "for the nation's good."[50] Protestant, Catholic, and Jewish groups generally were recognized in the piece for their part in the campaign, as were various veterans groups such as the American Legion. In the same edition of the paper, a report revealed that the million-member women's American Legion Auxiliary was ready to distribute copies of the amended pledge to the country's schools.[51]

No mention of the Knights of Columbus.

Not until five days later on May 18 did the *Journal-American* acknowledge the Knights. A brief ran as an addendum to stories previously published. Quoting Supreme Knight Luke E. Hart, the organization was labeled a "pioneer" in the effort to add "under God" to the pledge. K of C involvement dating from 1951 was reported, as was the brotherhood's mass mailings to members of Congress and the president. The story mentioned in the fourth paragraph that, "The Hearst newspapers have been conducting a drive to have Congress amend the oath *in conformity with the nation's traditional faith in God"* [Emphasis added].[52]

Three days before President Eisenhower signed the bill into law, another Hearst paper, *The Detroit Times*, ran an editorial with six small American flags streaming across the top of the page. Above the flags in bold print were the words, "MONDAY IS FLAG DAY! Get Ready to Fly Yours." The editorial was entitled "Under God" and made no mention of the Knights:

> THE NATIONAL CAMPAIGN of the Hearst newspapers and their readers to include the words "Under God" in the Pledge of Allegiance to the Flag has been all but won. . . . We began this campaign on direction of William Randolph Hearst Jr., April 28. Less than a month and a half later it arrived at realization . . .
>
> Leaders of the three great faiths, powerful veterans' organizations, civic groups, educators and literally thousands of patriotic men and women joined in the demand on Congress to adopt the resolution. To all these our deep thanks.[53]

According to Bishop, "Reporters for Hearst's newspapers put aside the journalistic convention of objectivity to openly promote patriotism in the face of the largely imagined threat posed by Communism."[54]

NEUTRAL VOICES: NON-HEARST SECULAR NEWS MEDIA AND THE PLEDGE

In May, about three weeks before the bill became law, the *New York Times* ran stories about the proposed change in the Pledge that were free of the religious and patriotic advocacy omnipresent in the Hearst papers. A story deep inside a Sunday edition noted the volume of mail being received from all over the country urging Congress to add "under God" to the pledge. "Congress is being flooded with mail, but on a subject far removed from the McCarthy-Army hearings that hold the headlines," ran the lead. The number of letters was recorded as "by the thousands daily," and the writers were "demanding" that the Pledge be changed. The *Times* said the Senate quickly adopted the resolution and sent the measure on to the House because of "the great influx of letters."[55]

According to the *Times*, Michigan Senator Homer Ferguson, chairman of the Senate Republican Policy Committee, introduced the bill on February 10, "just three days after the change was urged in a Lincoln Day sermon by the Reverend George M. Docherty, pastor of the New York Avenue Presbyterian Church here [Washington], where President Eisenhower worships." Eisenhower heard Docherty say "There [is] something missing in the pledge" that characterizes the American way of life:

> Indeed, apart from the mention of the phrase "the United States of America," it could be the pledge of any republic. In fact, I could hear little Muscovites repeat a similar pledge to their hammer-and-sickle flag in Moscow. Russia is also a republic that claims to have overthrow [sic] the tyranny of kingship. Russia also claims to be indivisible.[56]

The *Times* story went on to report that, "The churches backed it. So did veterans groups, civic clubs, patriotic organizations, fraternal organizations, labor unions, trade associations. Newspapers, individually and by chains, backed it editorially."[57]

Two stories in the *Times* related the criticism of the Pledge change resolution by speakers at the Boston American Unitarian Association meeting. The Unitarian Ministers Association, "went on record as being opposed to the insertion of 'under God,' in the Pledge of Allegiance to the Flag. . . . The ministers held that this was an invasion of religious liberty."[58]

On the same Sunday as the story about the flood of supportive mail to Congress, the *Times* ran a story about the address at the Unitarian Association meeting by Agnes Meyer. "The frenzy which has seized America to legislate Christianity into peoples [sic] consciousness by spurious methods, both at home and abroad . . . will harm the Christian religion more than the persecution it is now suffering under the tyranny of Communists," Meyer said. The story reported that Meyer called religion among some people "the latest fad," and said "She cited as being contrary to the principle of separation of church and state Senator Homer Ferguson's resolution to insert 'under God' in the pledge of allegiance."[59]

The day after the bill became law on June 14, 1954, the *Times* ran a ten-paragraph front-page story highlighting the ceremony that accompanied the signing. The lead was objective: "The Pledge of Allegiance to the flag hereafter will give recognition to God as well as country" The text of the pledge was printed, and there was an account of Rabaut and Ferguson, who were in dispute over the bill's authorship, putting aside their differences to recite the new pledge on the Capitol steps. A four-paragraph presidential statement was printed in full, in which Eisenhower said, "From this day forward, the millions of our school children will daily proclaim . . . the dedication of our nation and our people to the Almighty."[60]

TIME magazine ran two stories in May. The first was two paragraphs in the Religion section and began with the existing pledge plus a brief history. The pledge bill was in subcommittee at the time, and the magazine quoted Congressman Rabaut as saying "democratic . . . institutions presuppose a Supreme Being."[61]

Two weeks later a three-paragraph story in the newsweekly's National Affairs section, closer to the front of the book, declared that the drive for the change in the Pledge "has swept Capitol Hill, with all signs pointing to early approval by Congress" ("Nation 'Under God,'" 1954). The story recounted the tale of the Reverend Docherty planting the seed with Eisenhower. "Sen. Homer Ferguson, Michigan Republican, took it from there," the story said.[62] *Newsweek* ran the same three-paragraph story in the Religion section of its May 31 issue.[63]

Four things support the idea that this particular story could have come from Ferguson's office. First, Ferguson, a Senate Republican, and Louis Rabaut, a House Democrat, were debating whose version of the bill would be sent to the president, a dispute eventually won by Rabaut. Second, the wording of the story—"Sen. Homer Ferguson, Michigan Republican, took it from there"—gives rise to the suspicion that his office sent out a press release that was then reprinted by the competing weekly news magazines. Third, besides the wording of the texts being the same, so were the headlines, "Nation 'Under God.'" Finally, in an effort to correct the record, a press release dated May 25, 1954 from Rabaut's office calls his bill, introduced April 20, 1953, "the granddaddy of them all," yet there was no mention of Rabaut in *Time* or *Newsweek.*

A letter appeared in *Newsweek* at the end of June from Luke Hart, spelling out the chronology of the pledge change, beginning with the Knights' meetings in 1951 through the order's 1953 mass mailings to Congress. "Therefore, the idea did not originate with Reverend Docherty nor with Senator Ferguson," Hart wrote. "It had its origin with the Knights of Columbus . . ."[64]

CONCLUSION

As journalist Amy Crawford noted, the pledge to the flag began as a way to market *Youth's Companion* magazine. It has been used as a marketing tool ever since, for political causes, pop and country songs, governmental protests, and for numerous commercial products. In 2016, an election year, Budweiser temporarily changed the name of its beer to "America," adorning its cans with phrases from the Pledge of Allegiance and lyrics from *The Star-Spangled Banner* and *America the Beautiful*. "We are embarking on what should be the most patriotic summer that this generation has ever seen, with Copa America Centenario being held on U.S. soil for the first time, Team USA competing at the Rio 2016 Olympic and Paralympic Games," said Ricardo Marques, vice president of Budweiser. "Budweiser has always strived to embody America in a bottle, and we're honored to salute this great nation where our beer has been passionately brewed for the past 140 years."[65]

Flag symbolism has long been a part of American culture, and holding the flag sacred is a form of Civil Religion, a term that came into widespread academic use after sociologist Robert Bellah published his 1967 essay, "Civil Religion in America." Bellah wrote that civil religion was "an institutionalized collection of sacred beliefs about the American nation."[66]

Of the phrase's assorted definitions, one is the invocation of a deity in political speeches, and it certainly applies to public oaths. Since the September 11, 2001 attacks, Americans of all stripes have come together in public spaces to confess their "faith" in America. Of the demonstrations of public faith post-September 11, religion journalist Mark Silk has written, "[T]he readiness of Americans, from inside the Beltway to the hinterlands, to incorporate a diversity of faiths into their public ceremonies has been impressive."[67]

Historian John E. Semonche, writing about flag burning protestors and the First Amendment, put his finger on the symbolic importance of the flag in American culture:

> While the First Amendment is an important part of the theological core of the civil religion, its preeminent symbol is the flag. Reflect for a moment on its primacy in the culture. *What* object do Americans annually celebrate? *To what* do Americans, alone among all nationals of the world, pledge allegiance, *with what* do Americans drape the coffins of those who have died in service of their country, and *upon what* object is both the American national anthem and the national march focused? Only by understanding the position of the national emblem in this religious structure can we begin to make sense of the heated debate over flag-burning. Few on either side of the controversy denied the symbolic importance of the American flag, least of all the burners themselves.[68]

"Some of life's most important decisions are sealed not with logical comprehension but with emotional response to symbolic speech," former Southern Baptist Convention President Jimmy R. Allen wrote in 2000 concerning proposed anti-flag burning amendments to the Constitution. Allen argued that the flag is not a religious symbol, and "others have the right to voice unpopular opinions," including through protest by flag burning. "Our nation needs to get on to more significant matters," he concluded.[69] Flag burning as a form of protest comes and goes in American culture, and since September 11, 2001 is more often seen in other countries with which the United States is at war.

As mentioned earlier, of all of the religious conventions created for American public life in the 1950s, the addition of "under God" to the Pledge is the one that keeps recurring as a major divisive issue. As R. Laurence Moore (2003) has written,

> If the health of religion in the United States depends on two words inserted into the Pledge of Allegiance, then American religion is surely running on empty. On the other hand, secularists who think that the same two words endanger the American republic are ignoring the many ways that religion is already embedded in American culture.[70]

The Knights and other conservative religious organizations saw no conflict of church and state interest in the recognition of God in a public pledge in the 1950s. Many Americans still hold such a view. Conversely, Unitarians, atheist organizations, and assorted people of faith firmly believe there is a basic conflict between the current version of the pledge and the establishment clause of the First Amendment. It's important to remember that the pledge, though ubiquitous, is not compulsory.

Religion permeates American culture, as Moore asserts, but rarely is God such a prominent part of public life as in the case of the Pledge of Allegiance.[71]

NOTES

1. Public Law 396, 83rd Cong., 2nd sess., Cong. Rec. 249. *Joint resolution to codify and emphasize existing rules and customs pertaining to the display and use of the flag of the United States of America*, amendment of sec. 7, H.J.R. 243 (1954) (enacted).

2. Red Skelton, "The Pledge of Allegiance As Reviewed By Red Skelton On The Red Skelton Hour, Jan. 14, 1969," *CBS Television Network*. 7-inch vinyl record, Columbia 4–44798, February 25, 1969.

3. Red Skelton, "Commentary on the Pledge of Allegiance," transcript, American Rhetoric Online Speech Bank, http://www.americanrhetoric.com/speeches/redskeltonpledgeofallegiance.htm.

4. Ibid. In *Engel v. Vitale*, 370 U.S. 421 (1962), the U.S. Supreme Court had ruled that it was unconstitutional for governmental bodies to write a school prayer and compel its recitation in public schools.

5. John W. Baer, email interview by author, October 20, 1996. See also John W. Baer, *The Pledge of Allegiance: A Centennial History, 1892–1992* (Annapolis: J.W. Baer, 1992); Jerry Bergman, "The Modern Religious Objection to Mandatory Flag Salute in America: A History and Evaluation," *Journal of Church and State* 39 (1997): 215–236; Richard J. Ellis, *To the Flag: The Unlikely History of the Pledge of Allegiance* (Lawrence: University Press of Kansas, 2005).

6. *Newdow v. U.S. Congress*. 292 F.3d 597 (9th Cir. 2002); *Newdow v. U.S. Congress*. 328 F.3d 466 (9th Cir. 2002).

7. *Elk Grove Unified School Dist. v. Newdow*, 542 US 1 (2004). The U.S. Supreme Court reversed the federal court's decision that a reference to God in the pledge turned its daily recitation in public schools into a religious exercise that violated the separation of church and state, but not specifically on those grounds. Eight justices took part in the case, with only three of the justices offering an opinion on the merits of adding "under God" to the pledge, agreeing that the addition of the phrase in 1954 was constitutional. Five justices, however, held that the U.S. Court of Appeals for the Ninth Circuit should not have heard the case at all because the

plaintiff, Michael A. Newdow, lacked the legal standing to bring it. Newdow sued on behalf of his daughter, whose primary custody rested with the child's mother.

8. Jeffrey Owen Jones, "The Man Who Wrote the Pledge of Allegiance," *Smithsonian Magazine*, November 2003, Smithsonian.com. The word "to" was added after the first "and" in October 1892.

9. Amy Crawford, "Anatomy of an Oath: How a PR Gimmick Became a Patriotic Vow," *Smithsonian Magazine*, September 2015, 9.

10. Baer, email interview by author.

11. Francis Bellamy, *Effective Magazine Advertising: 508 Essays About 111 Advertisements* (New York: Mitchell Kennerley, 1909).

12. Although codified for civilian use on June 22, 1942 by a joint resolution of Congress, the Pledge was not compulsory. Many school systems required it, however—some students who refused were suspended or expelled—until the requirement was declared unconstitutional in 1943 in *West Virginia State Board of Education v. Barnette*.

13. "Let's Get This Clear," *Columbia*, August 1955, 3.

14. C. Knowles, "Big issue in D.C.: The Oath of Allegiance: Proposal to Change it Draws Heavy Mail on Capitol Hill," *New York Times*, May 23, 1954, E7.

15. "Congress Wins Point of Order from Senate," the *Washington Post*, June 9, 1954, A2.

16. Public Law 396, 83rd Cong., 2nd sess., Cong. Rec. 249. *Joint resolution to codify and emphasize existing rules and customs pertaining to the display and use of the flag of the United States of America*, amendment of sec. 7, H.J.R. 243 (1954) (enacted).

17. Baer, interview.

18. Will Herberg, *Protestant, Catholic, Jew* (Garden City, NY: Anchor Books, 1955, rpt. 1960), 264.

19. Donald Crosby, *God, Church, and Flag: Senator Joseph R. McCarthy and the Catholic Church 1950–1957* (Chapel Hill: UNC Press, 1978), 44.

20. Editorial, "McCarthyism against McCarthy," *Commonweal*, June 18, 1954, 260–261. This was one of several anti-McCarthy stories and editorials published in *Commonweal*. See, for example, Shannon, "McCarthy and His Friends," April 16, 1954, 42–44; "The McCarthy Committee," August 20, 1954, 477–478.

21. John W. Baer, *The Pledge of Allegiance: A Centennial History, 1892–1992* (Annapolis: J.W. Baer, 1992), 62.

22. Latin for "Out of many, one." The phrase "E pluribus unum" is on the Great Seal of the United States and has been since the eighteenth century, but was never formally adopted by Congress as a national motto. This ad hoc national motto has been ingrained in popular culture, notably in the film *The Wizard of Oz*, in which the Wizard gives Scarecrow a diploma from the university committee of *E Pluribus Unum*. As historian Kevin M. Kruse has written, "[T]he new pledge moved well beyond that original base of conservative Protestants to unite Americans from across the religious and political spectrum. Soon this unofficial motto was joined by an official one." See also "History of 'In God We Trust,'" at https://www.treasury.gov/about/education/Pages/in-god-we-trust.aspx.

23. On September 11, 2001, 19 militants associated with the Islamic terrorist group al-Qaeda attacked the United States, killing nearly 3,000 people. In November 2015, after deadly attacks in Paris and San Bernardino, California by followers of the so-called Islamic State terror group ISIS/ISIL, and amidst a heated presidential election season, 83 percent of registered voters in a Washington Post/ABC News Poll said they believed "a terrorist attack in the United States resulting in large casualties is likely in the near future." http://apps.washingtonpost.com/g/page/politics/washington-post-abc-news-poll-nov-15–19–2015/1880/; a Public Religion Research Institute poll in December 2015 found that "Three-quarters (75 percent) of Americans say that terrorism is a critical issue in the country," while 41 percent identified illegal immigration as a critical issue, http://publicreligion.org/research/2015/12/survey-nearly-half-of-americans-worried-that-they-or-their-family-will-be-a-victim-of-terrorism/#.VnGQkjYzx6N.

24. Jon Meacham, *American Gospel: God, the Founding Fathers, and the Making of a Nation* (New York: Random House, 2006), 175.

25. Richard J. Ellis, *To the Flag: The Unlikely History of the Pledge of Allegiance* (Lawrence: University Press of Kansas, 2005), 126–127.

26. Ibid., 213.

27. Kevin M. Kruse, *One Nation Under God: How Corporate America Invented Christian America* (New York: Basic Books, 2015), 109.

28. Ibid., 111.

29. Jerry Bergman, "The Modern Religious Objection to Mandatory Flag Salute in America: A History and Evaluation," *Journal of Church and State* 39, no. 2 (Spring 1997), 235.

30. *Minersville School District v. Gobitis*, 310 U.S. 586 (1940). The surname Gobitas was misspelled as "Gobitis" throughout the family's various court battles. See Shawn Francis Peters, *Judging Jehovah's Witnesses: Religious Persecution and the Dawn of the Rights Revolution* (Lawrence: University Press of Kansas, 2000), 19.

31. Exodus 20:4–5 (KJV).

32. *West Virginia State Board of Education et al. v. Barnette et al*, 319 U.S. 624 (1943).

33. Peter H. Schuck, "The Pledge on the Edge," *American Lawyer* 24, September 2002, 65.

34. *Myers v. Loudoun County Public Schools*, No. 03–1364 (August 10, 2005).

35. Judith M. Buddenbaum, "Religious Journalism," *History of the Mass Media in the United States*, ed. Margaret A. Blanchard (Chicago: Fitzroy Dearborn Publishers), 581.

36. "Measure Asks Words 'Pray for Peace' Be Used To Cancel Postage: Bill Adding 'Under God' To Flag Pledge Near Approval, NCWC News Service, May 17, 1954.

37. *The Fraternal Age*, June 1954, 2.

38. "K. of C. Sponsored Amendment to Pledge of Allegiance Adopted Unanimously by U.S. Senate," *The Fraternal Monitor*, June 1954, 16.

39. "Washington: Pledge Resolution in White House," *The Christian Science Monitor*, June 9, 1954, 1.

40. "Insert 'Under God' in Flag Pledge," *The Christian Century*, May 26, 1954, 629.

41. J. Hopkins, "Unitarians Call for Courage, Confidence, Common Sense to Face World Crisis, Build Future of Brotherhood," *The Christian Register*, July 1954, 24–27.

42. In a letter to Luke Hart dated August 6, 1954, President Eisenhower wrote, "[T]his year we are particularly thankful to you for your part in the movement to have the words 'under God' added to our Pledge of Allegiance." From archives of Knights of Columbus Supreme Office, New Haven, CT.

43. Ronald Bishop, "That is Good to Think of These Days: The Campaign by Hearst Newspapers to Promote Addition of 'Under God' to the Pledge of Allegiance," *American Journalism* 24, no. 2 (2007): 81.

44. Lindsay Chaney and Michael Cieply, *The Hearsts: Family and Empire: The Later Years* (New York: Simon and Schuster, 1981), 142.

45. Ibid.

46. "Under God," *New York Journal-American*, April 28, 1954.

47. "Hearst Campaign to Stress Faith in God: Legion Head Supports Change in Allegiance Pledge," *New York Journal-American*, April 29, 1954, 10.

48. Ellis, *To the Flag* 134–135.

49. W.P. Flythe, "Senate Votes to Add 'Under God' to Pledge," *New York Journal-American*, May 12, 1954, 1.

50. "Under God," Editorial, *New York Journal-American*, May 13, 1954, 10.

51. "Legion Auxiliary Joins Pledge Drive: Will Distribute Copies of 'Under God' Flag Oath," *New York Journal-American*, May 13, 1954, 10.

52. "K. of C. Urged Revised Oath," *New York Journal-American*, May 18, 1954, 10.

53. "Under God," Editorial, *Detroit Times*, June 11, 1954, 10.

54. Bishop, "That is Good to Think of These Days," 64.

55. C. Knowles, "Big Issue in D.C.: The Oath of Allegiance: Proposal to Change it Draws Heavy Mail on Capitol Hill," *New York Times*, May 23, 1954, E7.

56. Ibid.

57. Ibid.

58. "Congress Proposals Hit By Unitarians," *New York Times*, May 22, 1954, 29.

59. "Surpass Orthodoxy, Christianity Urged," *New York Times*, May 23, 1954), 30.

60. "President Hails Revised Pledge," *New York Times*, June 15, 1954, 1.

61. "Under God," *Time*, May 17, 1954, 101.

62. Ibid.

63. Ibid.

64. Luke E. Hart, "Pledge of Allegiance" [Letter to the Editor], *Newsweek*, June 21, 1954, 10.

65. "Budweiser Emblazons America on Cans and Bottles to kick off its Most Patriotic Summer Ever," Anheuser-Busch press release, PR Newswire, May 10, 2016, accessed May 23, 2016.

66. Robert Bellah, "Civil Religion in America," *Daedalus* 96, no. 1 (Winter 1967): 1–21. Reprinted with commentary and rejoinder in Donald R. Cutler, ed., *The Religious Situation 1968* (Boston: Beacon, 1968), 388–393.

67. Mark Silk, "The Civil Religion Goes to War," *Religion in the News* 4, no. 5 (Fall 2001): 1.

68. John E. Semonche, "The Flag as Religious Symbol Versus the First Amendment as Holy Writ: A Battle Among the Faithful," *North Carolina Humanities* 1, no. 1 (Fall 1992): 59.

69. Allen, 47, 50.

70. R. Laurence Moore, *Touchdown Jesus: The Mixing of Sacred and Secular in American History.* (Louisville: Westminster John Knox Press, 2003), 27.

71. Author's note: An early version of this chapter was published in *Journal of Media and Religion*, 7, no. 3 (July–September 2008), 170–189.

II

Religion and Entertainment

Chapter Three

God Wants His Stars Everywhere

The Media Mission of Actors, Models, and Talent for Christ

Let your light so shine before men, that they may see your good works, and glorify your Father which is in heaven.

—Matthew 5:16, KJV

INTRODUCTION

"Go because Jesus said to go. How better to reach all nations than through media? Go because the entertainment industry raises our kids and controls our culture. Go because the average teen spends 75 hours a week in media. Go because Jesus went. Become a hip, talented, non-judgmental ambassador for Christ in a world that desperately needs Good News!"[1]

This exhortation is one of many such enthusiastic declarations on the website of Actors, Models, & Talent for Christ (AMTC).[2] Billing itself as a "talent development ministry," AMTC isn't exactly a Christian talent agency, and it isn't exactly a Christian talent school, although it resembles the latter more than the former. AMTC is a mix of *American Idol, Dancing with the Stars,* and *The Voice,* if each of those competitions opened with prayer. There is some crossover to those secular, yet family-friendly shows. AMTC alum and country singer Brandon Chase appeared on *The Voice,* and was chosen to work with artist and celebrity judge Blake Shelton. Singer Tim Urban, who attended and performed at an AMTC conference, was on the 2010 season of *American Idol.*

How to adequately explain this nonprofit, nondenominational, Tyrone, Georgia-based talent ministry? Here's how AMTC describes itself:

> *AMTC is much more than an agency*. In fact, we don't recommend you try for an agent before you're ready. Why? #1. You might get the wrong one. #2. You might make the wrong first impression and hinder your future success . . . because you weren't ready.
>
> *AMTC is a talent development ministry* that finds, prepares and launches God's performers into the mission field of media.[3]

According to religion and media scholar Daniel A. Stout, "Religious groups are often at odds with popular culture, but they also help create and sustain it. . . . It is insufficient to examine religious groups only as critics; they must also be studied as creators of and participants in popular culture. In some ways, *religion is popular culture* and can never be completely detached from it"[4] [Italics in original]. As noted in the Introduction to this book, communication scholar Quentin Schultze maintains that, "Religious groups have always expressed a love-hate relationship with American popular culture."[5] Rather than keeping popular culture at arm's length, AMTC embraces media, especially entertainment media, which is the opposite of what many mainline and conservative congregations preach. "Sadly, many churches have avoided the worldly business of entertainment," according to AMTC's website. "But Jesus said to Go (sic) unto all nations. How? In media, with Spirit, talent, love, truth and excellence."[6]

This chapter explores mission and ministry in the context of entertainment media, specifically the training of performers by AMTC to enter into successful show business careers while maintaining religious conviction and ethical boundaries.

AMTC AS A CHRISTIAN MINISTRY

Carey Lewis Arban cofounded AMTC, along with her late mother Millie Lewis, a former fashion model. Arban goes by the title of "Chief Serving Officer." Her son-in-law, Adam She, is the executive director, and both of Arban's daughters have a hand in the business. AMTC employs about 30 full-time people and about 100 part-timers to work with performers who enroll in various classes.[7] A detailed history of AMTC is outlined later in this chapter.

AMTC's mission statement is clear in its intent to prepare believers for the "mission field of media":

> Actors, Models and Talent for Christ (AMTC) is a non-profit ministry dedicated to making good bolder in film, fashion, music and theater. We seek, find

and prepare performers to go into the world's most influential mission field: entertainment. Our faith-based education programs, international conference and focus on fellowship set the stage for God's stars to rise and shine as reflections of His Truth.[8]

"All faiths are welcome," Arban maintains, despite the decidedly Christian focus.[9] AMTC consultant, talent scout, actress, and evangelical Christian Jenn Gotzon says the ministry is a good first step for people of faith who want to be entertainers. Gotzon had a nonspeaking role as Tricia Nixon in the 2008 Ron Howard film *Frost/Nixon*, and is featured in the small budget faith-based film *Unbridled*, starring actor Eric Roberts.[10] "It's a wonderful place for people who love God and want to use their gifts that God has given them in acting, modeling, singing, dancing, standup comedy, hosting, and might not know, 'How do I go about learning these skills? How do I get into an industry to work in a safe environment? What do I need to even begin this journey?'"[11]

"AMTC creates a bridge," Gotzon said, "taking the mother, father of a child who knows zero about the entertainment industry except what media tells them and educates them through industry professionals that are working, who also love God, that are then there as consultants to teach the performer from young to very mature, all the way up into the 80s, 90s. . . . AMTC will take anyone who has a similar heart, and their heart is that they want to use their gifts to be able to impact and make a positive difference in media."[12]

The ages of applicants range from 4 to 80, Executive Director Adam She confirms, and there has been a rise in the number of older performers since AMTC became a ministry in 1982. "So, even with a large number of teens and kids our average age range is in the early 20's," he said.[13]

Planting Bible-believing Christians in entertainment media is at the core of the organization's mission. AMTC repeats the phrase "making good bolder" throughout its promotional literature, advertising its fee-based services through digital and print media, as well as on billboards along major interstates. Focusing mostly on younger clients, AMTC offers training and education that "set the stage for God's stars to rise and shine as reflections of His Truth."[14]

"There is no better way to go out to all the world than through media and the entertainment industry. . . . It's where all the role models are at," Adam She told *The Atlanta Journal-Constitution* in 2015. "(Hollywood) is a mere reflection of the world it portrays. The darkness is not just (in) Hollywood. It's the whole world," he said.[15]

"No life goes untouched by media. Film, fashion, music and theater influence us like never before," AMTC declares. "Their stars have become the standard bearers for our children. . . . At AMTC, we believe God has allowed such a time as this. Earth's stage is set. The King is coming. Actors, models and talent for Christ are called to prepare the way of the Lord. . . . 'Arise, shine; for your light has come, and the glory of the Lord has risen upon you' (Isaiah 60:1)."[16]

There is a three-step process in working with AMTC, as outlined in the organization's annual report:

* *Auditions, aka "searches."* In 2014, there were 124 searches held in 63 cities across the United States involving 34,495 applicants.

* *Bridge Training Program.* From the nearly 35,000 hopefuls, 2,928 people enrolled in the Bridge Training Program in New York, Los Angeles, Atlanta, Chicago, Dallas, Denver, Seattle, and Orlando. "Performers received professional talent consultation, online curriculum, a national photo session and marketing materials," according to AMTC's 2014 Annual Report. "More importantly, they received spiritual preparation and an ongoing fellowship of performers to help them stay true to God's purpose. After successful completion of The Bridge, performers further their education and receive introductions to entertainment industry professionals at AMTC's bi-annual SHINE Conference. At SHINE the journey into the mission field of entertainment begins safely and effectively."

* *SHINE Conference.* Performers who completed the Bridge Program (a requirement) attended the Orlando, Florida-based SHINE Conference in either January or July. They auditioned post-training for agents, managers, casting directors, and music industry professionals from both mainstream and faith-based media organizations. Between the two 2014 SHINE events, 1,226 performers attended. More than $250,000 in scholarships was awarded to attend schools as diverse as the New York Academy of Performing Arts, and Liberty University, the conservative Christian college in Lynchburg, Virginia operated by Jerry Falwell, Jr.[17]

AUDITIONS

Depending upon area of talent, an applicant's audition will consist of one of the following:

Actors: Prepare a 30 second monologue, or read a script provided by AMTC.
Models: Walk for our Scout. Special shoes are unnecessary. Stay natural.
Singers: Prepare a 30 second song without accompaniment. (Exceptions: songwriters may bring guitars or keyboards.)
Dancers: prepare a 30 second choreographed routine. (Bring music and your own speakers.)
Comedians: prepare a 30 second standup routine.

NOTE: Models, singers, dancers and comedians must also prepare or read a 20–30 second script. [18]

Auditions are a hybrid of a theatrical cattle call and a revival meeting. There are typically two scheduled audition times per day, and each session takes 3–4 hours to get through. After a general information session, applicants are separated according to talent, and then perform for a scout.

An open talent audition held in Durham, North Carolina in February 2016 illustrates the inner workings of this process. [19] A little more than 100 people gathered in a ballroom at the DoubleTree by Hilton Hotel on a cold Saturday morning to perform for AMTC scouts. Minors were accompanied by at least one parent, and most everyone had a friend or relative along for moral support. Gotzon was there, as were other AMTC representatives. Husband and wife Prayer Team members Willie and Sandra were present to greet attendees. Prayer Team members, or Prayer Warriors as they are known, receive weekly email newsletters from AMTC and assist with events and personnel. [20]

Talent hopefuls were asked to fill out a form at the registration table, which required completion of this phrase: "My #1 Goal from AMTC is . . ." Applicants could select from one of the following listed responses: "Self-Improvement," "Education," "A Career," or "To see how far I can go." A slide show highlighted the opportunities available to performers to be Christian witnesses as part of the entertainment industry, as much by their choices as by their words. Before being split up to perform monologues, sing, walk, or do standup comedy, Gotzon gave instructions to applicants for an efficient and successful audition. When their turn came, they were to give their name and age, and say something interesting about themselves prior to performing for a scout.

Gotzon discussed fundraising and other ways to help pay for classes, should they get a callback. Applicants were told to consider whether "God is putting it on your heart to enroll" in AMTC training, and to "pray to determine if you're right for us." She said that enrollees "have to be the right caliber" of talent to go further. AMTC stresses morality, but is serious about having talent. Amateurs must demonstrate aptitude and potential for success.

Following a pep talk and a group tension-releasing stretch, Gotzon prayed aloud:

> Father God . . . fill everyone right now with your peace. . . . Let them experience the gift you've given them, and let them get excited to share those gifts today. Father God, give us as scouts your wisdom and discernment to know how to best help each performer where they're at. . . . Guide them and give them clarity today. Father, if this is a program that will really be helpful to them, let them know in their heart, Father God, and let us know so we can do

what's best for them. . . . Father, thank you so much for this time. . . . In the
name of Jesus. Amen.[21]

"Prayer is often stereotyped in our culture as a form of pietism, a lamentable
privatization of religion," writes Kathleen Norris in *Amazing Grace: A Vocabulary of Faith.* "Even many Christians seem to regard prayer as a grocery
list we hand to God, and when we don't get what we want, we assume the
prayers didn't 'work.' . . . Prayer does not 'want.' It is ordinary experience
lived with gratitude and wonder, a wonder that makes us know the smallness
of oneself in an enormous and various universe."[22] Gotzon's simple prayer
was instructional as well as communal. Meant in part to reassure hopefuls
that AMTC is a Christian talent ministry, the prayer also reinforced the fact
that not all who audition are accepted.

After a chorus of "Amens," hopefuls scattered to audition in assorted
event rooms. AMTC staffer John Montes hosted singing auditions in the
main hotel ballroom while Gotzon ushered actors into an adjacent room. As
with *American Idol* and other such televised contests, applicants sang a Cap-
pella in front of Montes, who watched, listened, and took notes. Other hopefuls and their supporters watched from folding chairs in the cavernous room.
After the first young woman completed her song, silence fell. "You guys can
clap now," Montes told the audience, and they did. Whether hopefuls pass or
fail the audition, the atmosphere is one of support and respect.

BRIDGE TRAINING PROGRAM AND SHINE CONFERENCE

Those who receive callbacks after the initial audition return the next day for
registration and orientation. AMTC offers classes through the *Bridge Training Program* that develops and showcases talented people of faith, and pairs
them with professional agencies with the goal of launching their professional
entertainment careers. The premiere event preparing media missionaries for
the world of show business is the *SHINE Conference*, available to those who
attend the Bridge Program and are deemed sufficiently talented and adequately prepared. This six-day conference has been going on for nearly 40
years, and takes place twice a year at the Gaylord Palms Resort in Orlando,
Florida. This showcase is where "Christians get screen, stage, seminar and
one-on-one time with entertainment industry executives. If you're a performer wondering how to take your talent to the world and maintain your focus on
God, SHINE makes it possible."[23] Agents and managers from both religious
and mainstream media organizations attend SHINE each year to scout for
new faces.

If a performer's goal is to make a positive impact on media, Gotzon says,
AMTC's goal is to develop the performer's talent and moral judgment:

AMTC, after they go through an audition process, and are evaluated on their skill, will determine if they get to be invited to be a part of this talent development program, which includes an online curriculum full of a gazillion videos from the consultants teaching the performers via webinars to tutorials teaching on the subject of modeling: "What do I do if I go onto a closed set and someone asks me, I need to take my clothing off. . . . We govern and help guide them on biblical principle. . . . How do you bring your agent, your manager in to ensure something like that never happens. How do you protect yourself? Before arriving on sets, you'd never enter into a situation like that, and if you do, how do you exit professionally if that is something you're not interested in doing?

AMTC helps create very clear boundaries with the performer and their relationship with God, knowing what they should do and what they shouldn't do.[24]

Such ethical advice has even more resonance in the wake of the #MeToo movement, launched in 2017 after allegations of sexual harassment, assault, and impropriety surfaced against a slew of powerful men in various media and entertainment professions, beginning with movie mogul Harvey Weinstein.[25]

"Some performers feel called only to faith-based music and film," Gotzon added. "Some performers are called to mainstream, and AMTC also teaches that no one is to be judging or condemning anyone for the choices that they make because it's part of the journey of the individual as God is leading them."[26] Rather than giving in to every demand made on a performer, AMTC trainees are taught to act as an example for others by maintaining their moral principles, even if they lose an opportunity. Whether this actually occurs is up to the individual. Successful entertainers who have spent time at AMTC include actors Megan Fox (*Transformers*), T.C. Stallings (*War Room*), and Matt Czuchry (TV's *The Good Wife*); Broadway dancer, choreographer, and actress Chryssie Whitehead; model and athlete Omarr Dixon; and comedian Antoine Scott.

One AMTC alumnus who chose the faith-based entertainment route is T.C. Stallings. Stallings, who acted in school and church plays as a youth, is featured in AMTC promotional material, including its 2014 Annual Report. A scholarship athlete at the University of Louisville, Stallings went on to play in the Canadian Football and European Arena Leagues. "T.C.'s life changed forever the day he heard God calling him back to acting, via a commercial for AMTC," according to his biography in the 2014 Annual Report. "One SHINE conference later, doors of opportunity opened."[27] Stallings had major roles in the faith-based movies *Courageous* and *War Room*, both produced by the successful Christian film company Kendrick Brothers Productions. Fellow AMTC graduate Ben Davies also appeared in 2015's

War Room, a TriStar Pictures release that cost $3 million and grossed $67 million.[28]

"The bottom line is that all these gifts and talents that God has blessed me with—my goal now is just to use them to glorify Him," Stallings says. "My platform now is to glorify God."[29]

There is another bottom line at AMTC, and that is the cost of classes. AMTC is a 501c3 non-profit ministry supported by fees from programs and services, as well as through donors. Salaries and other operating expenses are paid from these funds. Those invited to become part of AMTC are told how much they must pay for the amount of training they wish to receive. If invitees do not have the financial means right away, they do personal fund-raising and enter at a later date. Prices vary, as students must pay for training, plus travel and lodging expenses:

> Actors, Models and Talent for Christ offers various events, courses, programs, ranging from no cost to $5245 for our flagship event: The SHINE Conference, which includes the Bridge Prep Program, Signature Photo Shoot and Brand Consult. Performers must audition for acceptance. If accepted, payment plans, discounts (up to $1500) and fund-raising options are available. In addition, AMTC offers a unique Faith/Works Program as funding assistance for those in need. Details are fully explained from an Admissions Director if you receive a callback.[30]

"Performers are [enrolled] and prepare on the Bridge [program] for SHINE as little as 2 months for qualified performers to more than a year for those that need more time," according to Adam She. "Those that enroll for the upcoming conference received a $500 discount."[31]

AMTC'S HISTORY, FROM MODELING TO MINISTRY

Bits of AMTC's history appear in the organization's literature, in books and magazines, and on various websites. What follows is an account of AMTC's founding and evolution to a Christian nonprofit assembled from these various sources, as well as from author interviews with ministry personnel.

"My mother was a New York fashion model in the late 1940s," according to AMTC co-founder Carey Lewis Arban. Arban's mother, Millie Lewis, started a chain of successful modeling agencies in the Southeast in the 1960s, and Carey later joined the family business. "In the years that followed, she (and I) launched streams of models into the industry. In some ways, my life has been wrapped around the business of appearance: how it affects every area of our lives, including the business of show business."[32]

Millie and Carey eventually expanded their modeling business and began hosting conferences that paired talented clients with agents. Over time, this secular, successful, commercial venture evolved into the nonprofit ministry Actors, Models, & Talent for Christ. AMTC is now separate from the independent modeling agencies that continue to operate under the Millie Lewis name.

The website of Millie Lewis Modeling and Development Center of Savannah, Georgia, notes that Millie, "a former international model and cover girl, started her school and agency business over 30 years ago in her four original schools, all now independently owned. Her legacy continues through instruction of etiquette, fashion and modeling." Millie Lewis, who died in 2001, appeared in print ads in the 1940s as one of the DuBarry cosmetics "Who is She?" girls. Her image graced the pages of such magazines as *Vogue, Harper's Bazaar*, and *Life*.[33]

Millie, whose maiden name was Mildred Lucille Runnion, was a New York fashion model. She later met and married an Air Force pilot named John Earle "Jack" Lewis. "My fighter-pilot dad became a stunt pilot for the newly formed U.S. Air Force (his ending rank was major), and my mom was the model hired to stand on his float in a NYC air show," Arban said.[34] The couple moved to Jack's hometown of Columbia, South Carolina and had three children, John, Bob, and Carey, the youngest, who was born in 1955. "As God would have it, it's a unique story. I was only 5 when my mother started teaching modeling and personal development at a highly-touted dancing school in Columbia, called Calvert-Brodie."[35] Beginning in 1960, Millie Lewis opened five eponymous modeling and finishing schools in South Carolina and Georgia. When Carey was older, she joined her mother's modeling business.

The first Millie Lewis Convention was held at the Sheraton Hotel in Charleston in 1982 with 150 Contestants and 15 New York Agents. "It was a safe and cost-effective way for local talent to meet national agents in one time and one place—to see how far they could go without the travel and risk of trying to do it alone," Arban says on AMTC's website.[36] "Eventually, the Convention expanded in 1987 to become the Mid-South Models Convention (MSMC), and in 1992 the convention went national, evolving into AMTC: the American Modeling & Talent Convention.

"While the convention's early years focused mainly on models, increasing numbers of actors, singers, dancers, and comics were attending . . . and becoming stars. Young unknowns like Megan Fox, Mena Suvari, and Matthew Underwood were early graduates who set the stage for the rising stars of today," according to Christian online database 'Ndiepedia.[37]

With a goal of expanding its impact on the entertainment industry, the company renamed itself again. AMTC became Actors, Models, & Talent Competition, signaling another new era for the Millie Lewis brand. The growing convention eventually drew thousands of performers and families each year, as well as top agents and managers seeking fresh talent. When both the business and Carey Lewis Arban reached middle age, AMTC morphed a third time. As recounted on the 'Ndiepedia site:

> The company's growing success in the industry ultimately became hollow for its founder, Carey Lewis. She had accomplished what she'd set out to do. She could look back to that day she told her mother they could "do it better," and know with confidence it was true. But it wasn't enough.
>
> In this desert, the true shaping of AMTC began. Carey Lewis, who at the age of 51 saw herself as a burned out CEO, turned her life and her company over to God. She became a committed Christian and the mission of the company changed course, again. In a few short years, one more name change would forever define the company's core focus. Throughout the years, the "C" part of AMTC had never quite gelled. Other "C's," like "convention," "conference," or even "coalition" were offered in addition to "competition." It turns out the right "C" was finally found in "Christ." A divine path had been ordered all along, even if no one had recognized it.
>
> "Even more, the deep roots that AMTC grew into fashion and entertainment through its first 24 years would now be used for God's purposes—to promote His stars into key positions in the most pivotal mission field in the world: media. I was transformed, and so was AMTC—both for such a time as this," says Carey. [38]

That final name change came in 2010, and Actors, Models, & Talent for Christ became a nonprofit corporation in 2012.

Christian writer Os Hillman in his 2011 book, *Change Agent: Engaging Your Passion To Be the One Who Makes a Difference*, profiled Arban's transformation, both personal and professional. According to Hillman, Arban had her Christian conversion experience around 2005–2006. (AMTC's website says Arban "became a late-in-life committed Christian in 2006.") Hillman writes that, "Her daughter and son-in-law, who both work with her in the business, also came to faith in Christ not long after."[39] Arban and her daughters, Glynis and Lexy, and son-in-law, Adam She (who is married to Lexy), now run AMTC.

In AMTC's 2014 Annual Report, Carey—whose marriage fell apart prior to her religious conversion and is variously billed as Carey Lewis and Carey Lewis Arban—lays out her personal testimony:

> I looked like I was at the top, but I was really at the bottom. In brokenness I met Jesus, and I was transformed—from a burned-out 51-year-old CEO to now a 58-year-old girl on a mission. God had a plan. . . . I was thrilled, but my daughters and son-in-law were part of AMTC, and they weren't Christians yet. What would they think? Well, God took care of that. Within two years, they were committed to Christ and were baptized. [40]

Adam She, who joined AMTC in 2004, is now the executive director. Along with Arban, he was instrumental in guiding AMTC's transformation from a company into a ministry. Not raised as a believer, She says on AMTC's website that he met God in a dream in 2008. "Today, Adam's skills in business rest upon his dependence on Jesus and commitment to prayer. He is an extraordinarily humble, fair-minded and gifted man of God. Adam is generation #3 in this 34-year-old family dynasty turned talent ministry."[41]

Dreams loom large at AMTC. "I believe AMTC (the ministry) was born by a dream God put in my mom's heart as a girl," Arban said. "Apparently, she was quite devout at that time. She told me when I was a teen she wanted to be a missionary. Instead, we were nominally Christian, in a cultural way. So to a truth-seeking teenage[r], her dream seemed crazy to me. Even so, God can give us visions that are fulfilled beyond our lifetimes. So, it did come true in a most unusual way. AMTC is now raising an army of missionaries in arts and entertainment."[42]

The AMTC narrative features God appearing not only in dreams, but also during what Arban calls her "Treadmill Experience." "A few months after surrendering to Jesus, God spoke to me on a treadmill," she says of her transformation. "He told me the name of AMTC would change. We were AMTC before we were for Christ, but the 'C' stood for 'Competition.' God said we would no longer be 'Actors, Models & Talent Competition.' We would become 'Actors, Models & Talent for Christ' because that's what the 'C' was always meant to be."[43]

Arban continues:

> I was thrilled. . . . I finally knew my purpose. Friends and co-workers were initially negative—afraid that our mainstream talent executives would not support a boldly Christian company.
>
> But my friends were wrong. The agents who had been with us for so long stayed loyal, and what they discovered at the "new" AMTC surprised them. They saw a face for Jesus they never knew: they saw beauty, talent, love, integrity and purpose. They didn't feel judged, but inspired!
>
> Pretty soon, Christian casting directors wanted to support this movement, too. So today's AMTC now hosts both mainstream and Christian media executives, because God wants His stars everywhere.[44]

CRITIQUES OF AMTC

Slaughter of the Sheep is a blog operated by Chrystal Whitt, a writer who calls out those she deems false prophets who misuse Christianity. Both the *Slaughter* blog and its Facebook page feature the tagline, "Endeavoring to warn the lambs away from the slaughter . . ."[45] Whitt has written critical pieces about televangelists Paul and Jan Crouch of the Trinity Broadcast Network (TBN) and megachurch pastor Creflo Dollar, and tackled assorted controversial religion-oriented subjects. The first and last of her six rules for posting on her personal blog are:

1. Be nice.

6. If you send me a scathing e-mail with the sole intention of telling me how horrible I am for attacking your favorite false prophet, be warned . . . it may show up in one of my posts. If you would like to discuss things intelligently, we will discuss them. (See rule number 1.)[46]

Her review of AMTC is itself scathing. She questions whether Christ has anything to do with the ministry, quoting James 4:4: *"You adulteresses, do you not know that friendship with the world is hostility toward God? Therefore whoever wishes to be a friend of the world makes himself an enemy of God"* [Italics in original].

"I was over at *Benediction Blogs On* reading some great posts when I came across [Actors, Models, and Talent for Christ]," Whitt writes. "It is a website/talent agency for men, women, and children who are supposedly actors, actresses, and models for Christ. That's Christ Jesus in case anyone is wondering."[47]

Whitt calls AMTC a "talent agency" and seizes upon the resume of AMTC alum Mena Suvari, one of the actresses the ministry highlights as a success story. "For those who don't know, Suvari has appeared in such 'sex romps' as *American Pie* and *American Beauty.* These films aren't fit for anyone to watch, much less act in . . ."[48] Whitt quotes a long description of Suvari from the AMTC site that includes her appearance in another sex-related film and her marriage to a much older man.

"What sickens me is this . . . where is Christ in all of this?" She goes on to ask, "How can a company say it is 'for Christ' when one of their top success stories is an actress of sinful morals, and they even brag about that sinful behavior in her profile description as if it's something to be proud of?

"Would you say this is a success or that they are sold out to the world?

"They need to take Christ out of their name."[49]

Debbie Sikkema is the mother of actress Brooke Sikkema, and the proprietor of a website called YourYoungActor.com. The Sikkemas moved from South Carolina to Los Angeles to develop Brooke's career after a good experience with AMTC. Debbie Sikkema's open letter to visitors on the site reads in part:

> We've learned so much during this journey into acting, and there are so many things I wish I'd known sooner. We had to try to figure out most things on our own as we encountered them. We did not know where to go to get assistance, and we did not always make the best decisions. I want to share our experiences with others so that they can learn from our mistakes and our successes.[50]

Brooke took part in AMTC auditions and classes through the Millie Lewis Model & Talent Agency in 2002 and attended a SHINE convention in January 2003. An inquiry on YourYoungActor.com as to whether AMTC is a "scam" prompted a long response from Debbie Sikkema. "It is a very well-run, family-friendly and safe event," Sikkema writes of the classes and convention. She says the price is high, and suggests that there are other avenues to getting into show business if people can't afford AMTC rates. As to the question of whether AMTC is a scam, Sikkema addresses the issue this way:

> *AMTC is* not a scam *in terms of making false promises.*
> *What does AMTC promise?*
> What AMTC promises is that you will compete in front of numerous industry judges from around the world—talent agents, talent managers, casting directors, and other entertainment industry professionals. And on that part they do deliver.
> If you compete and do well, the results from the convention can be life-changing. These things are all absolutely true.
> *AMTC Does Not Promise*:
>
> 1. *To make you a star* if you attend.
> 2. *That you will get a talent agent* if you attend.
> 3. *That you will get a talent manager* if you attend.
> 4. *That you will get a job* if you attend.
> 5. *That you will be "discovered"* if you attend.
>
> And it is important for you to seriously consider the fact that none of the above things are promised to you if you attend.[51]

Christian entertainment website *Rockin' God's House* founder Abbie Stancato wrote an essay on his blog about AMTC in 2013 titled, "The Truth, the Myths, and the Facts About Actors, Models & Talent for Christ (AMTC)." Stancato had seen ads for the ministry and wanted to find out what it was all about. "I went to my old friend Google," he wrote, "and began to scan the web to discover a wide range of opinions, from loved them to utter hatred! The polarization was too far apart, to believe the legitimacy of many comments."[52] So Stancato contacted Adam She directly, and came away impressed:

> Here is my summary of the interview. I asked difficult questions, and I believe Adam was honest and straight forward. Their skills guidance is not cheap . . . several thousand. Many websites will instruct you to never pay to find opportunities. They claim any legitimate company should only take a percentage for the work they find, not an entrance fee. I agree in most cases. . . . I disagree here. AMTC is a training ground providing a service. They introduce people to large stage, high pressure auditions, and will introduce you to industry professions. They do not provide work, nor do they contractually bind you to artists' contracts beyond their training. Any contract or work offered from the attending industry professionals are between you and them. AMTC does offer ministry, military and family discounts. Additionally, scholarships are given to

those who qualify based on merit, financial need, and/or life circumstances. They have a very large organization, designed to offer an extensive look into a very complex and sophisticated industry.[53]

Stancato says that not everyone has the talent to make it in professional entertainment, and the cost of AMTC's services can be off-putting. "Here is your line of caution," he writes. "American Idol has no shortage of contestants who are delusional when it comes to a personal self-evaluation of talent. Just because you have a burning desire for success as an entertainer, doesn't guarantee you have the talent to make the big time."[54]

Actors, Models, & Talent for Christ is an enterprise that focuses on talent, image, appearance, showmanship, and branding, merged with Christian outreach. "We want to give performers marketability so they may have the largest potential sphere of influence," Adam She told Stancato. "[B]y gaining fame, or influence we get the opportunity to reach people in the mainstream . . . not everyone who enters the program is seeking fame. Some come with the humble desire to hone their skills for positions in the church, ministry or anywhere God leads them."[55]

CONCLUSION

In his book, *Eyes Wide Open: Looking for God in Popular Culture*, William D. Romanowski notes that when Martin Scorsese's controversial 1988 film *The Last Temptation of Christ* opened, some Christians saw it as blasphemous while others considered the portrayal of Christ as both human and divine, consistent with Christian theology. "Christian cultural engagement is as varied and conflicted as are attitudes toward popular art," Romanowski writes.

"According to Scripture, culture has much to do with faith; it is part of being 'fearfully and wonderfully made' in the image of God." He continues:

> That we are God's cocreators is an overarching theme in the Bible and a fundamental assumption of a Christian approach to culture, so culture refers to the way that we define and live in God's world. An understanding of what the Bible says about culture provides a justification for Christian engagement with popular art and also a basis for both production and criticism.[56]

Entertainment as evangelistic outreach is at the heart of Actors, Models, & Talent for Christ. "Publicly professing Christians are now seen at the top of film, fashion, music, theater and sports. But many more performers are needed, because this mission field is vast," She says. "'The harvest is plentiful, but the workers are few' (Luke 10:2). Through the movement of actors, models and talent for Christ, millions upon millions of lost and prodigal children will enter the Kingdom of God."[57]

As Stancato correctly pointed out, "AMTC is a training ground providing a service." In the 2014 Annual Report for Actors, Models, & Talent for Christ, Adam She described AMTC as both a ministry and a mission. "AMTC is now a training ground for missionaries: media missionaries to be exact. To get them prepared spiritually and physically. To learn how to succeed in this world, but not be of it. Because the most influential mission field on earth is media, and it's not wise to enter it unprepared. It's not godly to leave it alone."[58]

To learn how to succeed in this world, but not be of it. How does one do that in a profession that often breeds immodesty and egocentrism? "Obviously, Christians who believe they are called to work in popular culture need to be certain they are not suffering from its debilitating effects," warns evangelical writer and editor Kenneth A. Myers, author of *All God's Children and Blue Suede Shoes: Christians & Popular Culture*. "They also ought to find ways of communicating to their public that there is more to life than seeking entertainment."[59]

As detailed by Myers, Shultze, Romanowski, and others, the devout, regardless of religious affiliation, have a complex relationship with media and popular culture, especially entertainment. In the mid-twentieth century, the Catholic Church's Legion of Decency dictated which movies were off limits to the faithful, and there remain religious institutions and denominations with objections to entertainment perceived as immoral. Conversely, many churches feature liturgical dance, Christian rock and hip hop, light shows, and other theatrical elements in their services.

AMTC not only straddles the line between sacred and secular media, but sees entering secular culture as vital to its mission. Talented Christian faithful are coached and trained so they can compete at the highest professional levels of entertainment, yet are urged to maintain their integrity while sharing their faith with others. Just as religiously affiliated law and journalism training programs attempt to influence those professions, AMTC is contributing to the cadre of faith-based actors, musicians, and models.

More and more entertainment media are being produced by Christian-based companies. Even as the Christian entertainment industry grows, it remains apart from the secular mainstream. If AMTC succeeds in its stated goals, faith-based entertainment and entertainers will *become* the mainstream.

NOTES

1. "Why Should You Go?" AMTC website, accessed May 25, 2016. AMTC cites the Kaiser Family Foundation for its figure of 75 hours per week. A 2010 Kaiser report states 7.5

hours of engagement with media per day for 8–18 year olds. See https://kaiserfamilyfounda-tion.files.wordpress.com/2013/04/8010.pdf. In 2015, Common Sense Media published a study saying teens (ages 13–18) spend 9 hours per day with various forms of entertainment media. See https://www.commonsensemedia.org/about-us/news/press-releases/landmark-report-us-teens-use-an-average-of-nine-hours-of-media-per-day#.

2. In 2018, Actors, Models, and Talent for Christ closed after 35 years in business.

3. "Is AMTC a Talent Booking Agency?" AMTC website, accessed May 23, 2016.

4. Daniel A. Stout, "Beyond Culture Wars: An Introduction to the Study of Religion and Popular Culture," *Religion and Popular Culture: Studies on the Interaction of Worldviews* (Ames, IA: Iowa State University Press, 2001), 8.

5. Quentin J. Schultze, "Touched by Angels and Demons: Religion's Love-Hate Relation-ship with Popular Culture," in *Religion and Popular Culture*, eds. Daniel A. Stout and Judith M. Buddenbaum (Ames, IA: Iowa State University Press, 2001), 46.

6. "Talent Missionaries Wanted," AMTC website, accessed May 25, 2016. AMTC's 2014 Annual Report lays out the ministry's evangelical beliefs in a section titled "What We Be-lieve": "AMTC believes the entire Bible is the infallible Word of God. We recognize and follow the precepts of God's holy scripture; from the wisdom and prophecies of the Old Testament, in the life, death, and resurrection of Jesus Christ. As an organization we seek to obey the words of Jesus Christ and His teachings."

7. Daniel Miller, "Selling Stardom: A Christian Pathway to Hollywood," *Los Angeles Times*, December 30, 2015, accessed June 8, 2016, http://www.latimes.com/entertainment/la-et-ct-selling-stardom-christian-talent-seminar-20151230-story.html.

8. "Mission Statement," Actors Models & Talent for Christ, 2014 Annual Report.

9. Quoted in Os Hillman, *Change Agent: Engaging Your Passion To Be the One Who Makes a Difference* (Lake Mary, FL: Charisma House, 2011), 152.

10. *Unbridled* (2017) is based on a real ranch in Cary, North Carolina that pairs troubled teen girls with horses that need attention, as a form of emotional therapy. The plot focuses on a girl who is the victim of sex abuse and trafficking. The film came in second at the 2017 International Christian Film Festival. Eric Roberts explained to reporter Jessica Banov of the Raleigh *News & Observer* why he appeared in the small, independent film. "In between the bigger productions Roberts is known for, such as 2008's Batman film, 'The Dark Knight,' or one of his recurring TV roles, he said he likes to find projects from new or first-time directors. His wife, who is his manager, calls such projects his 'giving back films.' . . . 'The industry has been too good to me and my family,' said Roberts, whose sister is actress Julia Roberts and whose daughter is actress Emma Roberts." Jessica Banov, "Movie Filming in Triangle Inspired by Cary's Corral Riding Academy," *News & Observer*, February 25, 2016, http://www.newsobserver.com/news/local/news-columns-blogs/article62274017.html.

11. Jenn Gotzon, telephone interview by author, February 11, 2016.

12. Ibid.

13. Adam She, email interview by author, February 18, 2016.

14. "Our Mission & Vision," AMTC website.

15. "Taking a Christian Path to Hollywood," *AJC.com*, January 8, 2016, accessed May 25, 2016, http://www.ajc.com/news/lifestyles/religion/taking-a-christian-path-to-hollywood/npymx/.

16. "Entertainment Matters," AMTC website, accessed May 25, 2016.

17. "AMTC at Work," Actors Models & Talent for Christ, 2014 Annual Report.

18. "How Will I Perform?" AMTC website, accessed May 25, 2016.

19. The author attended and observed the February 27, 2016 North Carolina audition with the permission of AMTC officials. Information comes from author's notes and recorded inter-views with participants. The audition schedule for 2016 included more than two dozen stops nationwide in cities as varied as Phoenix, Arizona; Dallas, Tyler, and San Marcos, Texas; Portland, Oregon; Wichita, Kansas; Chicago, Illinois; and Anaheim, California. All have major airports and nearby hotels with space for auditions.

20. Willie and Sandra did not give their last names.

21. Author's notes, February 27, 2016.

22. Kathleen Norris, "Prayer as a Mystery," *Amazing Grace: A Vocabulary of Faith* (New York: Riverhead Books, 1998), 351.

23. "Connecting Christians with the World," AMTC website, accessed May 25, 2016.

24. Gotzon, telephone interview.

25. For information and background on #MeToo: See the MeToo website at https://metoomvmt.org; Sophie Gilbert, "The Movement of #MeToo," *The Atlantic*, October 16, 2017, https://www.theatlantic.com/entertainment/archive/2017/10/the-movement-of-metoo/542979/. The *TIME* magazine "Person of the Year" for 2017 was a collective group of "silence breakers," women who had gone public, or gone through spokespeople, to level charges of harassment and assault, http://time.com/time-person-of-the-year-2017-silence-breakers/.

26. Ibid.

27. "T.C. Stallings: An AMTC Story," Actors Models & Talent for Christ, 2014 Annual Report, 7.

28. *War Room*, Box Office Mojo, accessed June 8, 2016, http://www.boxofficemojo.com/movies/?id=warroom2015.htm.

29. "T.C. Stallings: An AMTC Story."

30. "What is the cost for the Bridge Prep Program and SHINE Conference?" AMTC website, accessed May 25, 2016. Four salaries are listed in the 2014 Annual Report: Carey Lewis, Chief Serving Officer, $74, 484; Adam She, Executive Director, $60,000; Julia Keeley, Logistics Director, 42,084; Nerissa Heil, Accounting Director, $41,414.

31. Adam She, email interview by author, February 18, 2016.

32. Carey Lewis Arban, "The Business of Branding," *Backstage.com*, February 23, 2016, accessed May 23, 2016, http://www.backstage.com/advice-for-actors/backstage-experts/business-

33. Millie Lewis Modeling and Development Center website, accessed May 26, 2016.

34. Carey Lewis Arban, email interview by author, May 31, 2016.

35. Ibid.

36. "AMTC's Tranformation," AMTC website, accessed May 25, 2016.

37. "(AMTC) Actors, Models, and Talent for Christ," 'Ndepedia, Taylor Bear Publication, November 30, 2013, accessed May 26, 2016, https://ndiepediablog.wordpress.com/2013/11/30/amtc-actors-models-and-talent-for-christ/. 'Ndepedia describes itself on its website as "an independent Christian / Gospel artist and Christian business entrepreneur online database and only exists to help in giving added exposure to those artists and organizations that strive to spread the Word of God."

38. Ibid.

39. Hillman, *Change Agent* 151–152.

40. "Family is Key," Actors Models & Talent for Christ, 2014 Annual Report, 6.

41. "About: Our Leadership," Actors Models & Talent for Christ website, http://amtcworld.org/ministry/about/.

42. Arban, email interview by author.

43. "AMTC's Transformation: The Treadmill Experience," Actors Models & Talent for Christ website, http://amtcworld.org/mission/amtcs-transformation/.

44. Ibid.

45. The blog's homepage is https://slaughteringthesheep.wordpress.com, accessed June 9, 2016. The concept of believers exposing those considered to be false Christians is explored further in the chapter titled, "Jesus Laughed: The Uses and Abuses of Religious Satire."

46. "Rules for Posting," *Slaughtering the Sheep*, https://slaughteringthesheep.wordpress.com/rules-for-posting/.

47. Chrystal Whitt, "Actors, Models, and Talent for Christ?" December 22, 2010, accessed June 9, 2010, https://slaughteringthesheep.wordpress.com/2010/12/22/actors-models-and-talent-for-christ/.

48. Ibid.

49. Ibid. Suvari was married to cinematographer Robert Brinkmann, 17 years her senior, for five years.

50. Debbie Sikkema, "About," *YourYoungActor.com*, accessed June 9, 2016, http://www.youryoungactor.com/about/.

51. "Is AMTC a Scam?" *YourYoungActor.com*, September 10, 2009, accessed June 9, 2016, http://www.youryoungactor.com/2009/09/10/is-amtc-a-scam/.

52. Abbie Stancato, "The Truth, the Myths, and the Facts About Actors, Models & Talent for Christ (AMTC)," *Rockin' God's House*, March 31, 2013, accessed June 8, 2016, http://rockingodshouse.com/the-truth-the-myths-and-the-facts-about-actors-models-talent-for-christ-amtc/.

53. Ibid.

54. Ibid.

55. Ibid.

56. William D. Romanowski, *Eyes Wide Open: Looking for God in Popular Culture* (Grand Rapids: Brazos Press, 2001), 35–36. The quoted Bible verse comes from Psalm 139, verse 14: "I will praise thee; for I am fearfully and wonderfully made: marvelous are thy works; and that my soul knoweth right well" (KJV).

57. Stancato, "The Truth, the Myths, and the Facts."

58. "Family is Key," Actors Models & Talent for Christ, 2014 Annual Report, 6.

59. Kenneth A. Myers, *All God's Children and Blue Suede Shoes: Christians & Popular Culture* (Westchester, IL: Crossway Books, 1989), 185.

Chapter Four

Sacramental Pilgrimage

Catholicism, Humanism, Spirituality, and Community *Along* The Way

Jesus saith unto him, I am the way, the truth, and the life: no man cometh unto the Father, but by me.

—John 14:6, KJV

Keep yourself a stranger and pilgrim upon earth, to whom the affairs of this world are of no concern.

—Thomas a Kempis
(Book One, Chapter 23, "A Meditation on Death")

INTRODUCTION

In 2010, American actor, writer, producer, and director Emilio Estevez made a small budget independent film called *The Way* along Europe's Camino de Santiago, an ancient religious pilgrimage route referred to for centuries as "The Way of St. James."[1] The movie stars Estevez's father Ramon Estevez, who goes by his stage name of Martin Sheen, and is best known for television's *The West Wing* and the films *Badlands* and *Apocalypse Now.*

This chapter offers a case study of the intimate, character-driven film *The Way*, arguing that its subtle spiritual and religious messages more genuinely reflect the lived human experience than those of overtly Christian movies, or tangentially Biblically-based Hollywood blockbusters. The myriad ways in which faith has been depicted onscreen, along with the motivations of the various creators of Christian-themed entertainment, will also be discussed.

CHRISTIANITY IN MAINSTREAM FILM

Thousands of films with religious and spiritual themes have been produced from the Silent Era to the present, and more than a hundred of those have contained portrayals of the life and death of Jesus Christ.[2] Many of these projects have been welcomed by Christian believers, while others stirred controversy.

In the mid-1970s, famed Italian film director Franco Zeffirelli (*The Taming of the Shrew; Romeo and Juliet*) made a six-hour television miniseries based on a script by novelist Anthony Burgess (*A Clockwork Orange*), screenwriter Suso Cecchi D'Amico, and Zeffirelli himself, called *Jesus of Nazareth*. As is often the case with religiously-themed films, Zeffirelli's *Jesus* was criticized before anyone saw it.

According to media historian Harold (Hal) Erickson, when Zeffirelli "noted publicly that he intended to depict Jesus Christ as a human being rather than a religious icon, his expensive made-for-TV miniseries *Jesus of Nazareth* fell victim to protestors long before its April 3, 1977, debut. Despite the pullout of several sponsors, *Jesus of Nazareth* was aired as scheduled, sweeping the ratings in the process."[3]

The late theologian William Barclay, Professor of Divinity and Biblical Criticism at Glasgow University and the author of Bible commentaries, wrote a narrative version of the script, essentially a movie tie-in book. In his introduction, Barclay wrote,

> It may well be that there are some who think it is an irreverence to make the life of Jesus into a film. However, there are fewer and fewer people who read and more and more who learn by looking at pictures. I therefore regard the writing of this book as an opportunity to be seized . . .
>
> In the film and in this book the story of Jesus is told simply and straightforwardly. There is no attempt at sensationalism.[4]

The pious, particularly conservative evangelicals, initially fretted over portraying Jesus as human, even though such an interpretation is Biblically-based. Erickson points out that concerned audience members need not have worried. "In avoiding the usual overproduced Hollywood approach to the Gospels, Zeffirelli offers one of the most sensitive and reverent portrayals of Jesus ever seen on film."[5] Despite taking some dramatic license concerning invented characters and situations, viewers eventually came to embrace Zeffirelli's low-key vision of Christ's life.[6]

Hollywood regularly churns out sand and sandals spectaculars with special effects and major stars, such as Joseph Fiennes as a Roman Military Tribune in the resurrection film *Risen*, and Ewan McGregor as Jesus in *Last Days in the Desert*, as well as the big budget epics *Noah* and *Exodus: Gods and Kings*, starring Russell Crowe and Christian Bale, respectively.[7] In another era, popular Bible-inspired mainstream movies such as Cecile B. De-Mille's remake of *The Ten Commandments* were welcomed by the faithful as celebrations of Holy Scripture, and by studio heads as box office gold. When *The Ten Commandments* was released in 1956, it was the most expensive film of any genre ever made up until that time. State of the art effects and a massive star-studded cast attracted the religious and secular alike to theatres, and the film was an evergreen on television for decades, usually shown during Christian Holy Week.[8] At the film's premiere, DeMille said, "What I hope for our production of *The Ten Commandments* is that those who see it shall . . . not only be entertained and filled with the sight of a big spectacle, but filled with the spirit of truth."[9] Sixty years on, journalist David Walters wrote in *Bloomberg Businessweek* that "Cecil B. DeMille's *The Ten Commandments* was nominated for the Academy Award for Best Picture in 1956, and it's still the sixth-highest-grossing movie of all time domestically when adjusted for inflation."[10]

"Filmmakers aspiring to capture Christian history onscreen have adopted both subtle and spectacular styles," writes scholar and filmmaker Craig De-tweiler, author of *A Matrix of Meanings: Finding God in Pop Culture* (2003). "Hollywood directors like Protestants Cecil B. DeMille and D.W. Griffith turned Bible stories into the most opulent productions possible. They employed special effects and a cast of thousands to bring audiences to their feet (and the box office). The abundant means of biblical blockbusters often emphasize spectacle over spirituality."[11]

Other directors choose a sparse style to convey meaning "in an effort to pull audiences beyond their own egotism. This strand is found in the films of French Catholic Robert Bresson, Dutch Lutheran Carl Theodor Dreyer, and Russian Orthodox Andrei Tarkovsky," according to Detweiler.[12]

The spare filmmaking style is described in detail by screenwriter and film theorist Paul Schrader in his book *Transcendental Style in Film* (1972). "Perhaps the most enduring form of Christianity onscreen adheres to what Paul Schrader defined as "the transcendental style," Detweiler notes. "These austere films refrain from telegraphing emotions via established notions of acting, music, or plot. . . . Audiences are invite into the drama, given room to discover themselves within the (in)action."[13] As Schrader himself put it, "Most movies lean towards you. They lean towards you aggressively with their hands around your throat, trying to grab every section of your attention." Transcendental films are quieter, and linger on a scene longer. "These types of films lean away from you, and they use time, and as other people would call it, boredom, as a technique."[14]

While not in the same category with Ozu, Bresson, or Dreyer, Emilio Estevez directed *The Way* at a deliberate pace, utilizing extended shots of people walking the Camino, at a distance and in close-up, marking the ordinary task of making one's way through the European countryside. Contemplation is seen on the primary characters' faces. "Estevez's narrative is dominated by master shots of the landscape capturing Tom and his pals wandering through the wilderness and small villages, exploring ancient cathedrals and local traditions," Eric Kohn wrote in his review of The Way on filmmaking website IndieWire. "That decision lends a documentary quality to the journey, but the plot gives it a precise context not solely based around touristic indulgences. Instead, Esetevez has made a travelogue that celebrates the act of traveling, both literally and otherwise, regardless of the destination."[15]

By contrast, reality show producer Mark Burnett and his actress wife Roma Downey, both professed Christians, favor highly produced, biblically-based narrative films for TV and theatrical release. Downey previously starred in the syrupy CBS series Touched by an Angel that ran from 1994–2003.[16] The Bible, their 10-hour scripted miniseries, aired on The History Channel in 2013 and drew some 95 million cumulative viewers.[17]

The next year, Burnett released for theatrical exhibition Son of God, a pieced together movie culled from the New Testament installments of his Bible miniseries. The year 2014 was dubbed by some as "the year of the Christian film" or "the year of the Bible."[18] In addition to Son of God, Noah, and Exodus: Gods and Kings, films released in 2014 with religious themes included Heaven is for Real, Left Behind and God's Not Dead.

THE CHRISTIAN FILM INDUSTRY

What is a "Christian film?" How does a Christian movie differ from other movies in purpose and message? And how is The Way, as asserted in this chapter, a more authentic picture of Christ-like humanity, redemption, forgiveness, and community than a straightforward Christian film?

In their in-depth history of Christian film, Celluloid Sermons: The Emergence of the Christian Film Industry, 1930–1986 (2011), Terry Lindvall and Andrew Quicke highlight journalist Milton Anderson's 1935 book The Modern Goliath, which blasted the lax morals of Hollywood "talking pictures" and urged churches to make their own movies. Anderson echoed Dr. Franz Kordac, the archbishop of Prague, when he said that "if St. Paul were alive at this hour he would use talking pictures to spread the gospel of Jesus Christ."[19]

Many believers responded by filming pastoral sermons for distribution. As Lindvall and Quicke noted,

Christians of all denominational stripes and theological persuasions would respond to [Anderson's] call to make celluloid sermons for various audiences. The concept of celluloid sermons is grounded in the historical Protestant roots of an evangelistic rhetoric of conversion. It refers to the corpus of film work generated by religious groups that seek to evangelize, preach, teach, provoke, or convert, rarely to just entertain. The historian Harry Stout has revealed the potent effect of early American sermons as a "public act of cultural formation, not just religious expression." The people and organizations that made these religious films sought to convert their spectators, to draw them into their spheres of influence in both ecumenical and sectarian ways.[20]

As will become evident later in this chapter, Anderson's admonition for individual churches to make inspirational films continues in the digital era.

As early as 1929, prominent evangelist Aimee Semple McPherson of the Foursquare Angelus Temple in Los Angeles formed her own film company. *Celluloid Sermons* traces the roots of the post-Depression Christian film industry to pioneers of the 1940s, such as the Reverend James Friedrich, Carlos Baptista, and Irwin Moon. Their work was followed by a Christian studio system, consisting of a variety of organizations and denominations. One of the more unusual moguls in this venture was Sam Hersh. Hersh, who was Jewish, founded Family Films in 1946. He later converted to Christianity, made films for the National Council of Churches, and was instrumental in the Lutheran television show, *This is the Life;* the Southern Baptist show *This Is The Answer;* and the Methodist series *The Way.*[21]

One of Hersh's early successful movies was *Bible on the Table* (1951), about a grocery delivery boy who asks a mother at one of his stops why a Bible is always on her breakfast table. The mother then explains that the Bible is an essential part of the home, just like furniture and appliances.[22] Such obvious heavy-handedness characterizes many Christian films, and is appreciated by many Christian audiences.

Ken Anderson's Gospel Films opened its first studio in the 1950s, growing over the course of a decade to "the largest Christian film production and distribution center in the world."[23] Gospel Films became a professionally run organization, striking rigid business deals with libraries for rentals to churches, garnering solid profits. The popularity of television spelled the beginning of the end of this arrangement. "[W]ith the demise of Sunday evening services in the late 1950s, and with family shows like *Bonanza* and *The Wonderful World of Disney* dominating television, rentals fell off considerably."[24] Anderson left Gospel Films by 1960, establishing a film company under his own name, and continued to produce movies with the axiom, "The message is always first," above profits.[25]

Gospel Films acquired Thomas Nelson Communications in 1989, grew into Gospel Communications International in 1998, and continued to embrace emerging technologies like the internet. By 2008, Zondervan had purchased Gospel's internet holdings, and all other assets were put up for sale.

Instructional films had begun to dominate the Christian film market by the 1970s. Educational psychologist James Dobson, founder of Focus on the Family, was a major purveyor of such films. Dobson's film series featured "his pop-psychology Christian teachings on family issues, which positioned him as the new Dr. Benjamin Spock. For a production cost of about $30,000, Dobson's seven-part series established a norm of biblical instruction regarding raising children and communicating with one's spouse."[26] Titles included *The Strong-Willed Child; Christian Fathering;* and *What Wives Wish Their Husbands Knew about Women.*

As the end of the millennium approached, a plethora of Rapture-focused Christian films appeared in theaters, on VHS tapes, and eventually on DVD. "Russ Doughten and Don Thompson are credited for developing a whole new genre, the apocalyptic or Christian horror picture," according to Lindvall and Quicke. Akin to the *Left Behind* books (16 novels published from 1995–2007) and films popularized by Tim LaHaye and Jerry B. Jenkins, Doughten and Thompson's successful *A Thief in the Night* (1972) was the first of a series of apocalyptic end-times movies.[27] The Trinity Broadcasting Network had a hit with *The Omega Code* (1999), which involves a plot by the Antichrist to take over the world. While not a Christian film per se, the Hollywood blockbuster *End of Days* (1999) starring Arnold Schwarzenegger attracted Christian and action viewers alike.

Of this dispensational fundamentalist, and quite bleak, perspective of the end of the world, Lindvall and Quicke observed, "With the dramatic tendency among end-times filmmakers, echoing and exploiting Darby's nineteenth-century notion of the Rapture, this apocalyptic genre attracted an anxious and gullible audience. In contrast to the early Christian belief of the blessed hope of the Second Coming, these cinematic interpretations triggered fear and restlessness."[28]

Baptist Evangelist Billy Graham understood the power of film for conversion early in his long career. The Billy Graham Evangelistic Association (BGEA) began producing films with a moral message in 1953. BGEA's film arm, World Wide Pictures (WWP), distributed the 1975 film *The Hiding Place* about Corrie Ten Boom, a Dutch woman whose family hid Jews during the Nazi Holocaust. Many WWP-produced films showed a lost soul, such as a rebellious teenager who ran away from home. After a series of letdowns, the protagonist would wind up at a Billy Graham Crusade, incorporating actual Crusade footage. By the end, the lost soul would reconcile with his family. These releases were often followed by an altar call in the theater, where a minister or counselor would pray with filmgoers. Through its cinematic ministry, BGEA claims to have brought more than 2 million souls to Christ.[29]

Affordable and portable digital technology has made it easier for independent films to be made by small Christian companies and even individual churches. "Frustrated with the movies Hollywood has been releasing, more and more congregations are making their own feature films," religion reporter Kim Lawton wrote in *Christianity Today*.[30] Lawton, a longtime host and correspondent for the PBS show *Religion & Ethics Newsweekly*, detailed the genesis of church-as-film-studio trend in 2011 for *The Christian Century* magazine:

> The church filmmaking trend began at Sherwood Baptist in Albany, Ga., where associate pastors and brothers Alex and Stephen Kendrick have released three feature films since 2003. They are finishing the fourth one, "Courageous," about policemen struggling to be good fathers.
>
> In Sherwood films, volunteer church members make up nearly all the cast and crew and do everything from catering to building sets. Sherwood teamed with Provident Films, a division of Sony, and found a very receptive audience. Their third film, "Fireproof," starring Kirk Cameron, was made on a $500,000 budget, and it took in more than $33 million at the box office, making it the highest-grossing independent film of 2008.
>
> Sherwood films have a specific message, and making their own movies allows them to express it. The films have an overtly Christian tone, and the upcoming "Courageous" continues that.[31]
>
> There is a Churches Making Movies Film Festival that nurtures this niche industry. "Churches Making Movies is a cultural movement of churches harnessing the power of films to impact culture," according to the festival's website. "We screen films from across the country produced by churches, media ministries and Christian Non-Profits. In addition to movie screenings, we offer several learning experiences for church-based filmmakers and writers." The festival began in 2013 in New Jersey, and in 2017 held a West Coast festival in Los Angeles. "The success of the film festival is a result of the entire team's personal relationship with Jesus Christ and our passion for movie evangelism. Our desire is for more churches to use films specifically to inspire people around the world to find and maintain true relationships with God."[32]

The festival's mission statement notes that just as Jesus was a storyteller, filmmakers can spread the gospel through their films:

> One of the most effective and important activities Jesus did for people was to tell them stories. He was the master storyteller. Through His stories, Jesus transformed hearts, renewed minds, and saved souls. In the 21st Century, filmmakers are some of our most influential storytellers. Through their stories, filmmakers heavily influence our beliefs, establish some of our traditions, and define many of our values. The ability of these stories to change the world is a testament to why churches should make movies.[33]

The 2015 film *War Room* by the Kendrick brothers is about using prayer to repair a broken family. *War Room* was produced for $3 million, and earned $67.7 million domestically.[34] The Internet Movie Database (IMDB) described the plot succinctly: "A seemingly perfect family looks to fix their problems with the help of Miss Clara, an older, wiser woman."[35] There's a little more than that going on in this unabashedly Christian film. This is how co-writer and producer Stephen Kendrick described *War Room*, the brothers' fifth film project:

> On Aug. 28, 2015, we had the privilege of releasing a feature film entitled WAR ROOM into U.S. theaters and over a dozen international markets. The movie introduces viewers to the concept that prayer can be a powerful weapon that will positively impact every area of our lives. In WAR ROOM, an elderly widow named Miss Clara shows a young woman her "wall of remembrance" in the foyer of her house. It's a collage of pictures that serve as mementos of specifically answered prayers in her life. [36]

Kendrick went on to describe how he and his brother Alex were inspired to go into the film business:

> During the 1990s, we watched our father, who didn't have the money, books, or classrooms launch an independent, private Christian school through prayer. They just celebrated their 25th anniversary. Once, when he needed funds to rent a modular classroom, Dad prayed for the $7,000 needed to set it up. A few days later, a married couple, unaware of the need, dropped by his office said, "We believe God is leading us to give this to you." The man placed a check written out for $7,000 on dad's desk. Not a penny more or less than what dad had requested. Not a year too early or a month too late. We were in awe.
>
> In 2002, following in our father's footsteps, we were privileged to launch a faith-based movie ministry through our church with no money, no professional experience, and no film school training. But we had learned that God could provide at every level, and so we laid every need before Him at each phase of the production.
>
> Now, after 13 years, five films, and international distribution in 76 countries, we continue to be in awe of God's precise provision in response to specific prayer. [37]

Other successful films in the Christian category include *God's Not Dead* (2014) and its sequel, *God's Not Dead 2* (2016), which were produced by Pure Flix for $1.1 million and $5 million, respectively. The first film earned more than $63 million worldwide, and the sequel brought in $23.5 million. These earnings don't match Marvel and Disney movie numbers, but by any accounting, they were financial, if not critical, successes. [38] *God's Not Dead* "is the fifth-most-profitable movie by percentage in cinema history, with a return on investment of 2,627 percent," according to *Bloomberg Businessweek*. [39]

Many secular reviewers were not kind to either film. "Even by the rather lax standards of the Christian film industry, God's Not Dead is a disaster," Todd VanDerWerff wrote on the *A.V. Club* website. "Resembling a megachurch more than a movie, it's been designed not to convey any particular message, but to reinforce the stereotypes its chosen audience already holds." [40]

Each *God's Not Dead* film has a plot revolving around someone who stands up for belief in God. In the first film, a college freshman and devout Christian finds his faith challenged by an atheistic philosophy professor named Radisson, who tells the class they must disavow the existence of God or face a failing grade. "Lacking only glowing red eyes to complete the effect (rather like the Jews in the wartime Nazi propaganda films), Radisson sinisterly strokes his goatee while lecturing his impressionable students on the triumph of science and reason over the ancient 'superstition' of Christianity," wrote *Variety* critic Scott Foundas.[41] When the young student refuses to write "God is Dead," he is tasked with proving God's existence through research and argument in a debate with the professor in front of the class.

The sequel turns the tables and features a Christian teacher named Grace who faces a court case for sincerely answering a question about Jesus in her public-school classroom. The plot of each of the *God's Not Dead* movies involves seemingly Godless educational institutions that require Christian students and teachers to disavow their faith. This viewpoint is reinforced by the homeschool curriculum resources offered by Pure Flix, which includes videos for reinforcing lessons of faith.[42]

Pure Flix, headquartered in Scottsdale, Arizona, describes itself as "a Christian movie studio that produces, distributes, and acquires Christ centered movies." As noted on the studio's website, "Our VISION is to influence the global culture for Christ through media. Our MISSION is to be the world leader in producing and distributing faith and family media. Since day one, we continue to strive to make a difference for His name."[43]

Pure Flix also posted a message on its website that it labeled "The Pure Flix Challenge":

Hollywood has played a major role in shaping our current culture by controlling most of the media we experience today.

We challenge you to stand up for Christ and share these heart-felt movies with your families, friends, communities and church to impact our world for Christ.

We hope you enjoy our morning devotionals as well as our behind the scenes videos and blogs, live from the set of our new movies.

We want to thank you personally, if not for your support, prayers, and purchases of our DVD's, Pure Flix would be unable to continue making Christ centered films with positive messages that share the Gospel of Jesus Christ.

On behalf of the Pure Flix Family, God bless.

Our best regards,

—Pure Flix[44]

In an essay for *Vox* titled "Why Are Christian Movies So Painfully Bad?" religion and culture writer Brandon Ambrosino details the plot of *Old Fash-*

ioned, a film meant to be the "Christian response" to the sexually explicit—
and highly profitable—*Fifty Shades of Grey*.[45]

> In the film, Clay, a former frat boy who runs an antique store, meets Amber, a
> restless spirit who wanders around the country. When Amber rents an apart-
> ment from Clay, she quickly realizes everything she's heard about him is
> right—he has really outdated, and unrealistic theories of love, mostly centered
> on "old-fashioned" courtship.
>   Amber learns of Clay's theories firsthand when she asks him to come over
> to fix something in her house. Before he can enter her home, he makes Amber
> leave. He has made a promise to himself that he will never be alone in a house
> with a woman. He's saving himself for marriage, you see.
>   Clay's ideas are intriguing to Amber, who finds herself drawn to the
> throwback gentleman. But both of them have skeletons in their closet, and
> need to deal with those first if there's any chance of making their old-
> fashioned courtship work.[46]

"Fans of *Fifty Shades* might see echoes of that book in this basic plot summary," Ambrosino writes. "In both stories, a man with unconventional notions of romance and sex woos a woman, getting her to at least consider his
viewpoint. Except in *Fifty Shades*, this involves lots of sex, and in *Old
Fashioned*, this involves, well, no sex at all."[47]

Ambrosino acknowledges that there is nothing inherently wrong with a
movie plot about chastity, and "if Hollywood is serious about cultivating
diversity of perspective, then it needs to tell more stories that portray lesser-
known walks of life on screen—including religious ones," he says.

"But *Old Fashioned*'s problem isn't that it's telling a religious story. The
biggest problem here is it's desperately trying to invalidate a secular one."
Freestyle Releasing, the film's distributor, admitted that its marketing plan
involved "counter-programming" to *Fifty Shades*. "It's as if the Christian
movie industry pays attention to mainstream cinema just long enough to see
what it's up to," Ambrosino notes, "before raising funds to do slightly different versions of the same thing, only with less famous actors, more Jesus, and
rocking chairs. (There are always rocking chairs.)"[48]

Ambrosino cites Christian film critic Alissa Wilkinson, who wrote in an
essay about Christian artists, "Over the past few decades, Christians, and
evangelicals in particular, have been really, really prolific in making pop
culture products that parallel what's going on in mainstream cultural production."[49] This is the pattern—for nearly every secular entity, there is likely a
religious parallel, especially an evangelical Christian parallel.

"The goal, in other words, isn't to make a movie," Ambrosino writes.
"The movie is only the vehicle for achieving the goal. The real goal is
engaging and converting secular culture." He goes on to indict *Old Fashioned* as a prime example of how amateurish Christian film can be:

> A good deal of what [Christian] actors and directors know about their trade comes from on-the-job training, from working on set and in production studios under filmmakers with decades of experience. By isolating themselves from Hollywood, Christian filmmakers are passing up not only on "secular messages," but on the mentoring that other budding talent are receiving.
>
> As a result, *Old Fashioned*, rife with cliché, feels forced and unnatural at every turn.[50]

Christian films, Ambrosino argues, try too hard, focusing too much on the literal word of God as opposed to making good art. "As a result, the lessons at the heart of the story—i.e., the *whole reason the film exists* in the eyes of its core audience—are easily dismissed by the secular masses the film is ostensibly meant to reach. This is the irony of the Christian film industry: movies that appeal mostly to Christians are marketed as if capable of bringing sinners to repentance."[51]

Christian films, whether made by established production companies or tech savvy congregations, are often so didactic they frequently turn off the very people Christians hope to reach through entertainment evangelism. Reporter Kim Lawton explored this conundrum in an interview with writer Cathleen Falsani, author of *The Dude Abides: The Gospel According to the Coen Brothers*. "I think artistically when you go into any kind of creative act with an agenda, you run the risk of whatever it is that you produce being inauthentic," Falsani told Lawton. "And I think audiences—particularly filmgoers, particularly young filmgoers—can smell inauthenticity from ten miles away."

Falsani suggested to Lawton that conservative Christians look more closely for spiritual themes in secular Hollywood movies. "One of the ways that I find my faith most enlivened is when I engage with art, particularly with film, and my favorite films in terms of what I think are faith messages, Christian messages, messages about God's grace and love—not a single one of them is a Christian film."[52]

Two of the more commercially successful films targeting both mainstream and Christian audiences are *Miracles from Heaven* (2016) and *The Shack* (2017), both of which deal with elements of the supernatural. *Miracles from Heaven: A Little Girl, Her Journey to Heaven, and Her Amazing Story of Healing* is a nonfiction book published in 2015 by Christy Beam about her young daughter Annabel. Annabel survived both a serious illness and a fall from a tree, after an out-of-body encounter with God. The Sony/Columbia Pictures release had major players attached to it. The film starred Jennifer Garner and Queen Latifah, and was co-produced by Bishop T.D. Jakes of Texas megachurch The Potter's House (with 30,000 members), who is also a bestselling author and television host. *Miracles* cost $13 million, and earned $73.9 million worldwide.[53]

The Shack is based on a 2007 self-published novel by Canadian author William P. Young that became a bestseller.[54] The plot concerns a father named Mack, whose young daughter Missy is abducted during a camping trip and murdered by a serial killer. Her bloodied clothing is found in an abandoned shack in the woods, but not her body. His life shattered, Mack receives a letter from "Papa," which is his wife's nickname for God. Mack answers the summons to return to the cabin where his daughter was apparently murdered. There, he meets God in the form of an African-American woman, as well as Jesus and the Holy Spirit—the Trinity. Beginning with this encounter, Mack finds healing and the capacity for forgiveness. *The Shack* starred Oscar-winning actress Octavia Spencer and Australian actor Sam Worthington, and was distributed by Summit Entertainment. Domestic box office was $57.3 million, followed by $39.5 million in foreign earnings, for a worldwide total of nearly $97 million.[55]

By contrast, *The Way* earned $4.4 million.[56]

THEORETICAL APPROACHES TO RELIGION AND FILM

Catholic priest, sociologist, and novelist Andrew M. Greeley saw the potential in popular culture, especially popular film, to become a "sacrament," a tangible and visible sign of inward grace. Greeley developed what he called a theology of the religious imagination. As he wrote in his 1988 book, *God in Popular Culture*, "Film is especially well disposed for the making of sacraments, for the creating of epiphanies, because of its inherent power to affect the imagination. . . . [T]he pure, raw, power of the film to capture the person who watches it, both by its vividness and by the tremendous power of the camera to concentrate and change perspectives, is a sacramental potential that is hard for other art forms to match."[57]

Robert K. Johnston, professor of theology and culture and co-director of the Reel Spirituality Institute at Fuller Theological Seminary, notes that, "the focus on film's sacramental possibilities to mediate the presence of God has particularly been the purview of Catholic critics. In the writings of Andrew Greeley, John May, Richard Blake, and Thomas Martin, the focus has been not simply on a film's morality or on its religious content and themes. These writers have instead turned to consider the observer-critic's experience of the Divine."[58]

Johnston developed a five-way typology that characterizes how religious people respond to film: *Avoidance; Caution; Dialogue; Appropriation; Divine Encounter.*[59] The Fundamentalist leans toward *avoidance*. Evangelicals are *cautious*. Progressives encourage *dialogue*. Catholics *appropriate*. Liberal Protestants often have a *divine encounter*. "The diversity of genres for the term 'theology' finds its analogue in the diversity of interests among theology and film scholars," he writes. He continues:

> Some would concentrate on theology as a discipline—on the use of film as an aid for theological reflection. Others would focus their attention on practical know-how pertinent to ministry—on film's ecclesial and missional potential. And still others would have us concentrate on a first-order knowledge of God—on film as revelatory. The concerns of "theology and film" can, thus, be understood as threefold in nature—reflection, faithful practice, and contemplation.[60]

Both Johnston and Peter Malone, president of SIGNIS (the World Catholic Association for Communication) and an author who has examined film through a Catholic lens, have cited John May's descriptions of the emerging field of religion and film analysis. May, a Roman Catholic literature professor, laid out five categories of writing about religion and film:

1. *Religious Discrimination*—Moralizing as opposed to deep moral evaluation. An example is conservative critic Michael Medved's *Hollywood Vs. America: Popular Culture and the War on Traditional Values*.

2. *Religious Visibility*—Refers to praise for films with religious themes such as *The Ten Commandments* and *King of Kings* that are not necessarily religious films. The two examples given here were mainstream studio productions meant to appeal to all audiences, especially the devout. These were also meant to be family-friendly, despite their scenes of biblical violence.

3. *Religious Dialogue*—Malone describes this approach as, "the viewer brings a moral and religious perspective to a film. . . . This opens up the possibility of dialogue between religious and secular critics and filmmakers in their pursuit of a common humanity and morality."

4. *Religious Humanism*—This approach "encourages audiences to deepen their 'spiritual' more than their 'religious' response."

5. *Religious Aesthetics*—This approach looks at cinematic language of film as an art form as opposed to an overt Christian perspective.[61]

"Those theologians focusing on the aesthetic begin with the film text itself, and discover theology within it. This sacramental approach is more typically Roman Catholic," Johnston writes.[62] The Religious Humanism, Visibility, and Dialogue categories apply to the sensibilities of *The Way*, as spirituality, redemption, community, and forgiveness are recurring themes in the film.

Greg Garrett finds moments of grace in violent mainstream films such as *The Matrix, Pulp Fiction,* and *The Godfather,* as well as in films with more obviously redemptive plots, including *Dead Man Walking, It's a Wonderful Life,* and *Tender Mercies.* As Garrett wrote in *The Gospel According to Hollywood,*

> *Pulp Fiction* is, in fact, filled throughout with examples of grace, unexpected moments when unexpected things happen. Vincent [played by John Travolta] not only saves the life of Mia (Uma Thurman), the wife of his boss Marcellus Wallace (Ving Rhames), but he administers the adrenaline shot to her heart himself. Butch (Bruce Willis) goes back into the basement of a creepy pawn shop to save Marcellus, the very same gangster who has put out a death sentence on him for not throwing a fight. [63]

Christopher Deacy, who has published widely on theology and film, writes that "Films can thus engender serious reflection on what it means to be rescued or redeemed from sin, suffering, and alienation in a manner that corresponds to the basic tenet of redemption in Christianity that the 'redis-covery of life and life's purpose—to love and to live in peace with God and all people—is not something that it is possible to do unaided.'"[64]

Dietrich Bonhoeffer wrote in *The Cost of Discipleship* (1937) that "As Christ bears our burdens, so ought we to bear the burdens of our fellow-men."[65] As the pilgrims in *The Way* progress in their journey (see the plot outline below), they hear each other's stories and bear each other's burdens.

THE PLOT OF *THE WAY*

The Way depicts Christian community, with all its flaws, as it is lived on the ground by believers, nonbelievers, spiritual seekers, and casual observers. Just as it defies categorization as a Christian film, *The Way* is also not a biblically based story. It is a familial story, starring real life father and son Martin Sheen and Emilio Estevez. Estevez directed the film from his original screenplay. An outline from *The Way's* website:

> Martin Sheen plays Tom, an irascible American doctor who comes to France to deal with the tragic loss of his son (played by Emilio Estevez). Rather than return home, Tom decides to embark on the historical pilgrimage "The Way of St. James" to honor his son's desire to finish the journey. What Tom doesn't plan on is the profound impact this trip will have on him . . .
>
> Inexperienced as a trekker, Tom soon discovers that he will not be alone on this journey. On "The Way," Tom meets other pilgrims from around the world, each with their own issues and looking for greater meaning in their

lives: a Dutchman (Yorick van Wageningen), a Canadian (Deborah Kara Unger) and an Irish writer (James Nesbitt), who is suffering from a bout of writer's block. . . . Through Tom's unresolved relationship with his son, he discovers the difference between "the life we live and the life we choose."[66]

As this synopsis states, Sheen plays Tom Avery, an American ophthalmologist and single father to Estevez's character, Daniel. The two clash on most everything, including their values and how to live life. Daniel gives up his graduate studies in order to travel, choosing to walk the Camino de Santiago. Tom wants his son to settle down, like him.

As Daniel embarks on his pilgrimage on the Camino, he gets caught in a storm on his first day and is killed. Instead of retrieving his son's body and returning it home for burial as he originally planned, Tom changes his mind and has Daniel cremated and the ashes placed in a box. Literally putting himself into Daniel's shoes, Tom packs up his son's gear, stuffs the box of ashes into the pack, and sets out to complete the journey Daniel began. Tom, a lapsed Catholic, scatters Daniel's ashes as a sacrament and a tribute at strategic points along the way.

CHRISTIAN PILGRIMAGE AND THE CAMINO DE SANTIAGO

Although *The Way* is not a Christian, or more specifically, Catholic, film in the conventional sense, "messages about God's grace and love," as Falsani puts it, can be found in this modest movie shot on location across France and Spain in a biblical 40 days, "and 40 nights," as Sheen quipped in several interviews. Christians have been making the 800-kilometer (approximately 500 miles) pilgrimage on the Camino de Santiago since the Middle Ages. The ultimate destination is Santiago de Compostela, allegedly the burial place of Jesus's apostle James the Greater. Santiago is the capital of Galicia, Spain, where star Martin Sheen's father was born. The idea for the film came about after Sheen visited his father's homeland with his grandson Taylor Estevez (Emilio's son) and the pair drove along sections of the Camino.[67] When Sheen returned home, he pitched script ideas to Emilio about a modern-day pilgrimage along the Camino, and eventually they returned to make *The Way*.

The theology expressed in *The Way* is primarily Catholic, though the main character of Tom, played by Sheen, has strayed from the church. The film foreshadowed the era of the humble prelate Pope Francis, elected in 2013, whose messages of non-judgment, reconciliation, and care for others over self, elevated the pontiff's popularity among Catholics and non-Catholics alike.[68] Although the film is a product of Estevez's imagination, he used various nonfiction source materials for his screenplay, including writer

Jack Hitt's 1994 nonfiction book about his hike along the Camino called, in a nod to Jack Kerouac, *Off the Road.*[69]

The Way is a film about four dissimilar pilgrims with various motives for walking the Way of St. James, as the Camino de Santiago is also known. The physical experience of pilgrimage is, as Greeley said of the art of film, a powerful influence on the imagination. Religious pilgrimage, however, involves the body as well as the mind. A pillar of Islam, for example, is the hajj, or pilgrimage to Mecca. Millions of Christians travel to Lourdes in the French Pyrenees yearly to visit the Catholic holy site where in 1858, the Virgin Mary is said to have appeared to a 14-year-old peasant girl named Bernadette. Geoffrey Chaucer's *Canterbury Tales* is perhaps the best-known literary example of a pilgrimage account. Chaucer's diverse band of storytellers was traveling to visit the relics of Saint Thomas Becket in Canterbury Cathedral. We learn that one of the travelers, the Wife of Bath, had previously made the pilgrimage along the Camino.

From the twelfth century, Santiago de Compostela has been one of Christendom's primary pilgrimage destinations. Yet, just as non-Christians travel to Lourdes for tourism, so do many non-Christians make the trek along the Camino. They do it for reasons ranging from seeking purpose, to shedding pounds, to contemplation, to achieving the sense of accomplishment akin to completing the Appalachian Trail. Pilgrims begin at various points along the route, and in earlier centuries simply began the journey from their homes.

Pilgrimage predates Christianity, but as a word, "its initial origins are with Christianity, and associated with early Christian travel to places associated with significant figures (from Jesus to the multitude of saints) and key events and stories in the tradition," according to religious studies scholar Ian Reader.[70] "Pilgrimage is a global phenomenon found almost universally across cultures," Reader notes. "Thousands of walkers and cyclists follow the Camino, the pilgrim's way across Europe to the cathedral at Santiago de Compostela in north-west Spain, which is said to hold the relics of St. James, while many more go there each year by bus, plane and train."[71]

"The origins of Santiago de Compostela and of the ensuing pilgrimage are to be found, as so often in Christian hagiography, in a supernatural occurrence," Spanish travel writer Sergi Ramis writes in his guidebook to the Camino de Santiago (Camino is Spanish for "path" or "journey").[72] As Ramis relates the story, in the ninth century shepherds noticed a "mysterious glow" in Padron, a town located in the Galicia area of northwest Spain. They informed the religious authorities, who found a sarcophagus at the site with the remains of three people. The bishop of nearby Iria Flavia traveled to the spot and declared that the marble coffin contained the bones of St. James the apostle and his two disciples, Atanasio and Teodoro. King Alfonso II the Chaste shortly thereafter ordered that a sepulcher and church be constructed at the site.[73]

How could the bones of James, who is the patron saint of Spain and Portugal, wind up on the Iberian Peninsula? The Gospels tell us that James, son of Zebedee the fisherman, was one of the first to follow Jesus and one of only three apostles to witness Jesus's transfiguration. He may have also been one of the first of the 12 disciples martyred for his beliefs and preaching. After Jesus's crucifixion, James departed for the Roman province of Hispania. After a short visit there, he returned to Jerusalem where, "About that time Herod [Agrippa] the king laid violent hands on some who belonged to the church. He killed James the brother of John with the sword," according to Acts 12.[74]

"At that time it was a common practice for an apostle to be buried where he had preached and it was in connection with this that a miracle occurred," Ramis writes. Several legends surround the "miracle" relocation of James's remains for burial from Jerusalem to Iberia. These legends all have some variation on the idea that James's sarcophagus floated in a boat down the Mediterranean where, after quite the journey across the Strait of Gibraltar and the Atlantic Ocean, it ran aground at Galicia. The burial spot of James's remains was not discovered until about 800 years later.

After the relics were recovered, "Pilgrims came from all over Europe following the *Camino de Santiago* to reach the city born around the Holy Tomb, exercising a great influence on the surrounding area," notes a history of the Camino by the United Nations Educational, Scientific, and Cultural Organization (UNESCO). "This is evidenced in the small towns, churches, hospitals, and monasteries that were built near the *Camino* to attend to the thousands of pilgrims who came to visit the tomb."[75]

The site was destroyed by Muslim troops at the end of the tenth century, and rebuilt in the next century. "Until the 18th century, Santiago de Compostela was the most important pilgrimage destination in the entire Christian world," according to the Organization of World Heritage Cities.[76] Subsequent wars and the plague ensued, and the relics of the apostle were actually missing from 1588–1879. When the cathedral was being remodeled in the nineteenth century, some bones were discovered and Pope Leo XIII declared these the bones of James.[77] This declaration, and the eventual designation of The Way as a World Heritage site in 1993, revitalized the Camino and secured its importance as a religious pilgrimage.

In 2014, more than 235,000 people completed the pilgrimage.[78] Despite being so well traveled, the Camino requires precautions beyond physical preparation and securing the right gear. Theft and physical danger from humans as well as weather—both are plot devices in *The Way*—can be obstacles. Ramis refers to conmen who have taken advantage of pilgrims "for a thousand years."[79]

"The Camino has been promoted by Galician tourist authorities and in travel magazines as an ideal setting for walking holidays," writes Ian Reader.

This consumerist attitude toward pilgrimage sets the stage for twenty-first century pilgrimage depicted in *The Way.*

MAKING *THE WAY*

The Way was shot on location along the Camino de Santiago in just under six weeks (it really did take 40 days), on a shoestring budget with little equipment and a skeletal crew of about 50. By contrast, the average number of credits in the top 1,000 films shot between 1994 and 2013 was 588.[80] The $150 million *Noah*, a 2014 film starring Russell Crowe, lists hundreds of cast and crew.

Sheen, in his third film with son Emilio as director, worked essentially for free. People making the pilgrimage to Santiago de Compostela were enlisted as extras. Even with few principal actors and a focus on character rather than plot, *The Way* conveys reverence and unabashed respect for religion, more so than many over-the-top extravaganzas or comparable small religious films with obvious storylines.

In various interviews, Estevez compared *The Way*'s characters to those in *The Wizard of Oz*:

> [Sheen's character Tom is a] stranger in a strange land. . . . He finds himself in Spain alone; and he wants to be alone. Unlike Dorothy who invites the other three to come along, Tom doesn't want to have anything to do with them. They invite themselves; and isn't it true that sometimes people come into our lives who we don't want to have anything to do with, ultimately teach us the greatest lessons. So the idea was through these three individuals, Tom would become a father to them in many ways that he was never able to be a father to Daniel [the character played by Estevez] . . .
>
> [Sarah] was broken, fragmented, and self-flagellating, if you will. So, when we meet her, she's got a hole in her heart, and she is our Tin Man. . . . We meet the Cowardly Lion in Joost in that he's big, and lovable. And when [Tom] says, "What are you, all five?" He says, "No, I'm just scared." Then, Jack, of course, is our Scarecrow, suffering from writers block, not having a brain . . .
>
> The theme is that it's OK to be exactly who you are, that God loves you no matter how broken, no matter how imperfect you are.[81]

Concerned about *The Way* being pigeonholed as a "religious movie," Estevez rejected that notion in an interview with the secular website *The Daily Beast.* He said *The Way* is "about being human. It's less about religion and faith and more about spirituality and living life. I've been reading things online accusing us of being too religious and it's kind of offensive."[82] The thought of the film being "too religious" was anathema to Estevez, even "offensive." As a Hollywood filmmaker, Estevez was well aware of the labels that can cripple the box office. Categories such as "religious," "family," or "adult," attached to a movie can limit audience appeal. In other interviews, he stressed the film's spirituality and the minor miracles that occurred during filming. Such is the turmoil inherent in religious commodification.

The Way premiered to mixed reactions at the 2010 Toronto International Film Festival and opened theatrically in October 2011 in New York and Los Angeles. The film was released through Producers Distribution Agency, founded in 2010 by producer John Sloss "to offer an alternative theatrical distribution model for unique films in a constantly changing marketplace."[83] Despite a marketing strategy that took Sheen and Estevez by bus to various cities and colleges for personal appearances accompanied by a screening, the film barely grossed $4.4 million, tiny compared to even some independent church-produced movies.[84] In its widest release, *The Way* opened in 283 theaters, was in circulation for 23 weeks, and closed in March 2012.[85] By comparison, *Noah* (2014) made $43.7 million in its *opening weekend*, played in 3,571 theaters, and closed after 12 weeks.[86]

The Way obviously lacked for an audience, Christian or otherwise. Despite weak attendance, this chapter argues that this tiny, personal nontheistic film is more realistic than comparable melodramatic Christian films, while still delivering a Christian message more closely aligned with everyday lived experience.

DISCUSSION OF *THE WAY*

Jesus is not a character in *The Way*, but Christianity is, specifically Catholicism. The Cathedral of Santiago de Compostela, the ultimate destination of Camino pilgrims, is a Catholic cathedral; Sheen's character Tom is a lapsed Catholic; Jack, the Irish writer with writer's block, is a bitter ex-Catholic; Tom encounters an ailing Catholic priest along the journey; and so on.

The opening scenes of *The Way* show Tom finishing up with a patient in his ophthalmology office in sunny Ventura, California. His son Daniel has called from France, his assistant tells him, but again failed to leave a number. "Everyone on the planet has a mobile phone except my son," Tom mutters. "We're all on Daniel's terms."

In the next scene, Tom is playing a round of golf with three fellow doctors who banter with one another. Tom is teased for being an eye doctor rather than a "real" doctor, and he responds by saying the eyes are the windows to the soul. When a golf shot leaves his ball nearby, he rides the cart to retrieve it, causing more gentle derision from his foursome. "I'm old and tired," Tom responds.

Within minutes of the film's opening, several things are established:

- Tom and his adult son Daniel have a strained relationship.
- We know what Tom does for a living, we know he lives alone, and we see that he has a comfortable and sedentary lifestyle, which makes his later decision to walk the Camino seem rash, yet ultimately unselfish and meaningful.

Tom's cell phone rings as he's putting, and a French police official on the other end of the call tells him his son has died on the Camino de Santiago. Uncomprehendingly, Tom jumps into one of the carts and drives away, leaving his three puzzled companions behind.

We next see Tom telling his assistant to cancel appointments for the week while he flies to France to retrieve Daniel's body for burial in the United States. "He wanted to see the world," he says, sardonically.

"And he did," she replies.

Cut to Tom sitting in a church pew with a priest who appears to know him well. "Would you like to pray with me, Tom?" the priest asks.

"What for?" Tom replies.

In a series of flashbacks, we see Daniel and Tom in conversations that offer a stark contrast in the two men: In a scene played out in semi-darkness in Tom's kitchen (budgetary constraints required the use of natural light, which turned out to be a positive artistic choice for setting the mood), Daniel tells Tom he is giving up his doctoral studies to travel and experience life. As Tom drives Daniel to the airport for his pilgrimage on the Camino, Tom asks him what his plan is. Receiving a vague answer, Tom says, "So, you don't have a plan." To which Daniel replies, "Don't judge me."

Daniel says he consented to let his father drive him to the airport only if "you wouldn't lecture me about how I'm ruining my life."

"I lied," Tom retorts. Daniel urges Tom to drop everything and come with him, making this a father/son journey. "My life here might not seem like much to you," Tom says, "but it's the life I choose."

Daniel glances across the front seat of the car and delivers the tagline of the film: "You don't choose a life, Dad. You live one."

Their relationship thus established, we return to the present to see Tom in France speaking with Police Captain Henri Sebastian (Tchéky Kario), the official who called to notify him of Daniel's death. "What was he doing out there?" Tom asks, clueless about the Camino's history. Captain Sebastian gently explains the ancient legacy of the path. "The Way is a very personal journey," especially for Christian believers, he says. Sebastian says he has "walked three times to the Atlantic Ocean and back," and "will do it once more on my 70th birthday. God willing, of course."

Later that night, Tom is alone in his hotel going through Daniel's backpack, and we see him break down at the loss, and the remembrance of their strained relationship. He decides in the middle of the night to have Daniel cremated and spread his ashes along the Camino—completing the pilgrimage together.

When an unprepared and out-of-shape Tom leaves the next morning, the skeptical yet supportive Sebastian sees him off. Revealing that he too has lost a child, Sebastian hands Tom a scallop shell for the journey.

Variations of the story of the martyrdom of St. James in 44 C.E. have led to the symbolism of the shell. Two commonly cited ones are:

> *Version 1:* After James's death, his disciples shipped his body to the Iberian Peninsula to be buried in what is now Santiago. Off the coast of Spain, a heavy storm hit the ship, and the body was lost to the ocean. After some time, however, the body washed ashore undamaged, covered in scallops.

> *Version 2:* After James's death his body was mysteriously transported by a ship with no crew back to the Iberian Peninsula to be buried in what is now Santiago. As James's ship approached land, a wedding was taking place on the shore. The young groom was on horseback, and on seeing the ship approaching, his horse got spooked, and the horse and rider plunged into the sea. Through miraculous intervention, the horse and rider emerged from the water alive, covered in seashells. [87]

As Tom begins his trek along the Camino, his plan is to be alone with Daniel's ashes and his own regrets. Instead, using *The Wizard of Oz* analogy, he gradually collects three companions on the journey. Unlike Dorothy in Oz, Tom scorns the companionship at first, but gradually and grudgingly welcomes their company.

Joost the Dutchman (Yorick van Wageningen) tells Tom he is walking the Camino to lose weight. He needs to fit into a suit for an upcoming relative's wedding, and admits his own wife no longer wants to have sex with him because of his flab. A happy-go-lucky man, Joost has a variety of drugs with him, from pills to pot, and indulges in bread and pastries and other culinary delights at every stop. Joost shows little inclination toward religion, but no hostility, either. Mostly, he eats.

Sarah the Canadian (Deborah Kara Unger) is a bitter, guarded woman. She is seeking redemption and solace on the Camino for aborting her child in order to spare her offspring the physical abuse she endured from her ex-husband, facts we learn late in the film. Playing against the easygoing Canadian stereotype, Sarah is a chain-smoking, brittle, hurting woman when we first meet her. She declares to others that she is on the trail to quit smoking, but admits in the end the pilgrimage was never about giving up cigarettes. Sarah sarcastically nicknames Tom "Boomer," as in Baby Boomer, at their first meeting in a hostel. As she spouts her disdain for Americans of his generation, Tom quietly gets up and walks away, leaving Sarah surprised at his lack of an aggressive retort. Tom's action mirrors Sheen's personal belief in peaceful passive resistance. Ignoring Sarah's taunts startles her by upending her expectations of verbal assault.

Jack the Irishman (James Nesbitt) is by turns a jolly and melancholy would-be novelist who likes to drink and pontificate—like Joost, a more stereotypical character, but also like Joost, a character imbued with humanity. As a young man, Jack wanted to be the next James Joyce, but wound up a magazine travel writer for the past 20 years. He is on the Camino to cure his writer's block by finding a new story to tell. When that story becomes Tom's journey along the Camino with Daniel's ashes, Tom is angry and resistant, protective of both Daniel and his own emotions. Fancying himself a literary historian of sorts, Jack is constantly reading from an early guidebook about the Camino and urging his compatriots to have a "true pilgrim experience" by camping and roughing it. A true pilgrim, he says theatrically, "is poor and must suffer." There is no initial trace of religiosity in Jack, and he later expresses antipathy toward the Catholic Church.

Early on, Tom walks with Joost and Sarah periodically, but travels various stretches in solitude prior to acquiring Jack. Camino pilgrims often walk at different paces. Eventually, the four walk together out of choice.

Encountering an unstable innkeeper one evening who has conversations with an imaginary female companion, the four freaked-out pilgrims beat a hasty retreat and decide camping out overnight is a better idea. As Tom gathers his pack the next morning, the box containing Daniel's ashes falls to the ground. Sarah reaches for it at the same time Tom does and he pushes her hand away. Sarah reflexively strikes Tom hard across the face.

Saying nothing, he packs his gear and walks away, resisting for a second time the temptation to lash out at Sarah. Later along the trail, Sarah attempts a clumsy apology, citing the physical abuse she endured during her marriage. Tom, who has forged ahead, doesn't want to hear it, until she stops him in his tracks with the confession of guilt she feels over aborting her unborn daughter.

"I didn't want the SOB to have two of us to beat on," she tells Tom. "Sometimes I hear her voice, my baby."

"Sorry about your baby," Tom says.

"Sorry about yours," Sarah replies.

"My son was almost 40."

"Yeah, but he'll always be your baby."

Tom nods his head to indicate that Sarah should walk with him, and they continue down the path in silence.

After days and miles of getting along reasonably well with his three hangers-on, Tom lashes out in a memorable episode. The Camino landscape is by turns rural fields, mountains, highways, small towns and larger cities. Coming into a town for the night, the wine flows as Jack reads loudly from his historical guidebook and bloviates about the Camino. Tom gets progressively drunker on wine and reflects on both Daniel's fate and his own. How did he, a prosperous eye doctor with a comfortable suburban life, wind up sleeping in hostels and camping out with strangers on a 500-mile journey through the Pyrenees?

"Christ, you're a bore," he suddenly exclaims to Jack. "An arrogant bore."

Sarah and Joost are amused at first, until Tom becomes progressively nastier. Tom continues to berate Jack's yearning to be a "true pilgrim" on the Camino.

"Like you would know. What did you use to pay for this wine? How many credit cards do you have in your wallet, Jack from Ireland? How many true pilgrims used their true credit cards to get out of a true jam along the Camino back in the Middle Ages, you Jackass from Ireland? You are a true fraud," Tom says, becoming increasingly agitated.

"Friends," Tom continues, "the question is, what does it take for someone to become a true pilgrim on the Camino? Is that right, Jack? How about death? How about dying on the Camino? Would that make someone a true pilgrim? Would that qualify for your damn book?"

As Jack looks stricken, Tom shouts to some policemen standing nearby to arrest this "fraud." Instead, it is Tom who is arrested for public drunkenness. As Tom sits in the lobby of the police station handcuffed to a bench, he has a vision of Daniel sitting across the room, shaking his head and looking disapprovingly at his father's predicament.

Jack pays Tom's bail. Wearing his sunglasses to hide his shame, Tom approaches Jack outside of the police station after his release. "Thank you for bailing me out," Tom says.

"You can thank my credit card," Jack replies, walking away.

Later on the Camino, Tom assures Jack he will reimburse the bail, and they strike a deal—Jack gets to write the story of Tom and Daniel and the debt is settled. Tom reluctantly agrees. As they walk, Jack pulls out his pen and notebook and asks Tom what Daniel meant to him.

"He was my son. What do you think he meant to me?" After a pause, Tom says in a quieter voice, "Daniel was a lot like you. Smart, confident, stubborn. Pissed me off a lot."

Jack then confesses to Tom that he's not only suffering writer's block, but is a failed novelist.

You know, when I was an undergraduate at Trinity College, Dublin, I wanted to be W. B. Yeats. Or James Joyce. But good writers usually die broke, so after I left college, I wrote for travel mags. Thought I'd do that for a while, put some money away and then get down to the novel. Twenty years later, here I am still writing for travel magazines. I'm not feeling sorry for myself. It's the life I chose.

Hearing his own voice echoed in, "It's the life I chose," Tom tells Jack to write the truth of this journey he's taking with—and for—Daniel.

"Jack, you write whatever you want about all this," Tom says. "What you saw, how you felt. You write it like it happened. You write the truth."

"I'll do my best," Jack says solemnly.

As they walk, Tom encounters an older hiker wearing a yarmulke and greets him as a rabbi. The man tells Tom he is actually a Catholic priest with brain cancer, and he wears the yarmulke to cover a surgery scar.

"I don't practice anymore," Tom says.

"Lots of lapsed Catholics out here on the Camino, kid," the priest replies.

The priest then offers Tom a rosary, but he is resistant. The priest smiles and reaches into his coat, revealing a pocketful of them. When the two meet up later, it is Tom who smiles as he pulls the rosary out of his coat pocket to show the priest he still has it.

"They came in handy," Tom tells him.

"They usually do," the priest replies.

Tom nearly loses Daniel's ashes twice along *The Way*. Early in the journey, Tom was unaccustomed to carrying Daniel's heavy pack and accidentally drops it off a bridge into a stream below. Tom wades in to retrieve it, camping along the banks as his clothes dry out overnight.

Much later, when the four protagonists stop in the town of Burgos, Spain, a boy steals the pack from atop a pile of other pilgrim's bags. Tom and his three companions chase the young boy through the streets into an alley, where he disappears. The boy is a member of the Roma, the gypsies, who are often regarded in European society as thieves and beggars. Tom stands in the alley, looking up at the empty windows, and pleads with the boy to just return the box. Joost puts his arm around Tom and they walk away.

In a pub that evening, a Roma father and son walk in carrying Tom's pack. The father, Ishmael (Antonio Gil), has made his son return the pack to Tom and apologize. "Everything is there," Ishmael says, making eye contact with Tom. "Everything."

As Tom pulls out the box with Daniel's remains, Ishmael bows his head and crosses himself.

"My son has dishonored himself and his family," he says, looking at the boy. "A very bad day for me." As a means of atonement, Ishmael invites Tom and his friends to join his family for dinner and dancing by firelight, and they accept.

At the feast that evening, Ishmael encourages Tom to go beyond the Santiago de Compostela Cathedral to Muxia and spread his son's ashes in the sea for a proper final burial.

"I'm not a religious man," Tom says, again.

"Religion has nothing to do with this. Nothing at all." Do it for him and for you, Ishmael urges.

Forgiveness and reconciliation are recurring themes in *The Way:* between Tom and his three companions (who supplant his golfing buddies as a foursome); Tom and the Roma; fathers and sons.

There are many extended walking sequences in *The Way*, some without dialogue, showing stages of the journey. After leaving Burgos, Spain, Tom glances to his right at a tree, and we glimpse Daniel leaning against it and smiling as Tom passes. Tom stops and turns to see that Daniel is not really there.

At another point, self-flagellating monks dragging a cross walk through a square as the foursome watch. We see the bloody backs of the monks, practicing the rarely performed medieval practice of symbolic penance.

Having walked for hundreds of miles, camped out and slept in hostels and small inns, the four dirty pilgrims pause in front of a large luxury hotel. Staring up at the elegant building's exterior, Jack says aloud that true pilgrims wouldn't feel right to stay there.

"My treat," Tom says.

Cut to Jack ordering booze in his private room, Sarah luxuriating in a bath in hers, and Joost ordering an enormous, sumptuous meal from room service. After Joost finishes his feast, he sits and stares ashamedly at the empty plates on the cart.

We see Tom watching television when there is a knock at his room door. It is Sarah, who invites herself in and stretches out on a couch in front of the TV. A second knock at the door reveals Joost who, upon seeing Sarah in Tom's room, misunderstands and thinks he has interrupted a romantic encounter. Tom tells him to come in, and as the intruders settle in, there is a third knock—Jack bearing bottles of wine. Tom tells him to join the party. As Jack takes his place beside and Sarah and Joost, Tom watches the three of them with a bemused look on his face, like a benevolent father whose adult children have decided to move back home.

The next morning, freshly rested and closer than ever, the four pilgrims continue the next leg of the journey. They encounter La Cruz de Ferro, a large iron cross dating from the eleventh century atop a wooden pole that once served as a marker during winter passages, and is at one of the highest points on the Camino. Pilgrims typically leave a stone here, symbolically unburdening their cares as they make a prayer or wish and prepare for rebirth.

Sarah recites the traditional prayer, inscribed at the cross site:

> Dear Lord, may this stone, a symbol of my efforts on the pilgrimage, that I lay at the feet of the cross of the Savior, weigh the balance in favor of my good deeds that day when the deeds of all my life are judged. Let it be so.

All four leave their stones at the base of the cross, joining thousands of others left by previous travelers.

In the next scene we see Tom, Joost, and Sarah coming out of a small church they have encountered along the way. Jack remains outside resting on a low wall. "It's a beautiful church, Jack," Tom says. "Have a look."

"Where I come from, the church has a lot to answer for," Jack says. "Temples of tears, Tom. I don't go in them anymore."[88]

Nearing Santiago de Compostela, Tom tells the group that Ishmael told him to take Daniel's ashes all the way to the sea in Muxia. "Oh, it's all Gypsy hocus-pocus, man," Joost insists. "Well, you're on your own, Tom. Santiago is as far as this Dutchman is going." The others agree—Santiago de Compostela is the end of the line.

When they reach the cathedral, Jack pauses at the entrance. He then cocks his head and utters, "Oh, well, I'm here now," and enters with the others. The four pilgrims approach the statue of St. James, and Joost reads from his guidebook that early pilgrims approached the statue on their knees. Tom and Sarah walk up and touch the statue, and she lays her leather cigarette pack holder at St. James's feet.

As the camera pans around the interior and angles upward, we see Tom, Sarah, and Jack admiring the elaborate and ornate building. Hanging back, Joost approaches James's statue alone, on his knees.

In an interview, Sheen discussed watching that scene over and over in the completed film:

> When the Dutchman falls to his knees, what was your reaction? Me too. I've seen it a half a dozen times, I know it's coming. As soon as he starts doing this, "Is anybody looking?" Boom, I'm gone. It's in the dark, and I'm allowed to do it again. That moment, you fall to your knees in thanksgiving and praise. You fall to your knees for help, for mercy. You fall to your knees when you finally surrender and say, "I don't have it. Lord, take my hand. Lead me on." It's our own personal hymn. And this film just rings with it. It's just so deeply personal.[89]

Meanwhile, Tom holds tightly to Daniel's ashes as he gazes toward the saint's ancient relics. Sarah prays. A close-up of Jack shows him sitting in a pew looking up, his tears flowing freely. They don't discuss their feelings—we just see their outward responses to this sacred space. No exposition necessary.

A giant incense holder is hoisted high above the parishioners by a group of monks holding a rope. As the incense container swings like a giant pendulum spreading its scent overhead, Tom looks at the group of monks pulling on the rope.

He momentarily sees Daniel's smiling visage among them, as he did in the police station and along the trail, and he crosses himself. Daniel has completed the journey with his father's help.

Outside the church the four stand around silently fidgeting, as if they cannot bear to separate. They smile, stare at each other knowingly, and begin to laugh. And then they continue on together to Muxia. The film ends with the four standing seaside, staring as the waves crash on gigantic rocks.

Jack, staring in the distance: "Writers. They always want the last word. But this?" Overwhelmed, he walks out of the frame.

Sarah, lighting a cigarette: "This was never about quitting these things. But you knew that." She walks away as well.

Joost, reflecting on all of the calories he consumed along the Way: "I needed a new suit anyway."

After Joost departs, Tom makes his way down the slippery rocks to the water's edge. He pulls the plastic bag containing what's left of Daniel's ashes from the box, kisses it, and scatters the remains into the sea. He forms his hands into a gesture of prayer and walks away.

The final scene of the film shows Tom walking solo in what appears to be a country in the Middle East, or perhaps India. It doesn't matter.

Taking Daniel's advice, he's living life.

MARTIN SHEEN AND CATHOLIC ACTIVISM

Martin Sheen was 69 when he took on the role of a reluctant pilgrim in *The Way.* After working on the film together, Sheen and Emilio Estevez coauthored an autobiography called *Along the Way: The Journey of a Father and Son.*[90] Sheen relates his life story in the book, as well as what it was like to work on the film with his son. Sheen is a devout Catholic, and what follows is a brief biographical sketch highlighting his activist brand of Catholicism.

Born in Dayton, Ohio in 1940, one of ten children of immigrant parents, Sheen's legal name is Ramon Gerard Estevez. His Irish mother, Mary Ann Phelan, died from a cerebral hemorrhage when he was 11, and his Spanish father, Francisco, raised the family while working for the National Cash Register Company. Mary Ann's family had ties to the Irish Republican Army, and her family sent her to live with cousins in Dayton at the age of 18 to avoid the troubles.[91]

As mentioned earlier, Francisco was originally from Galicia in Northern Spain, where the Santiago de Compostela resides. He left Spain for Cuba in 1916, and landed in the United States three years later. Francisco met Mary Ann after making his way to Ohio, and Sheen writes that his parents "didn't share a common language but they were both devoutly Catholic and both had been shaped by the solid community ties of rural village life."[92]

Despite his father's encouragement to attend college, the rebellious Sheen left home early to pursue a career in New York theatre and television. Father Alfred Drapp, a priest in Dayton who had become a friend and mentor, lent him $300 to get a foothold in New York. He had trouble getting both apartments and acting jobs with the name Ramon Estevez, so he chose "Martin Sheen" as a stage name to honor two men he admired. One was a supportive CBS casting director named Robert Dale Martin, and the other was Catholic televangelism pioneer Bishop Fulton J. Sheen.[93]

Sheen soon became involved in The Living Theatre, whose productions carried political and socially relevant messages. In a 2003 interview with *The Progressive*, Sheen said of this theatre experience,

> It had a very profound effect on me. I started with them when I was nineteen and spent two-and-a-half years with them. Through them, I was introduced to Women's Strike for Peace, the ban the bomb movement. It was an avant-garde theater, filled with very liberal, progressive, intelligent, passionate, heroic people. Julian Beck was one of my mentors and heroes. He introduced me to the Catholic Workers' movement.[94]

That progressive impulse has, if anything, intensified. Sheen has been arrested more than 60 times over the years for his activism on behalf of a variety of causes. In numerous interviews, he has said, "Your faith has to cost you something, otherwise you have to question its value." Sheen counts social activist priests Daniel and Phillip Berrigan, as well as their fellow Jesuit Priest and activist John Dear, among his inspirations. All three became Sheen's close friends. Sheen's activism has extended to protests against various wars, nuclear proliferation, social injustice, homelessness, apartheid, and other causes.

Sheen's religious devotion is borne of a long and difficult path. All of Sheen's siblings wrestled with alcohol, and he was no exception. He eventually attended a 12-step program and reverted to the Catholic Church in 1981. As he told the *National Catholic Register* during the bus tour to promote *The Way*:

> It began after my illness in the Philippines while filming *Apocalypse Now*. I began going to Church because I was afraid of dying. Then I stopped going for a long time. My eyes were first reopened when I was in India filming *Gandhi*. Then, in 1981, while in Paris, I read the book *The Brothers Karamazov*. I had been given the book by director Terrence Malick. The book kept me up. After reading it, I went to see a priest and told him I wanted to come home. He looked at me with eyes that said, "This is what I do." He told me to return the next day at 4 p.m. as he had a wedding at 4:30 p.m. He told me not to be late. I went to confession with him and wept. I came back to a Church that was very different. I left a Church of fear and returned to a Church of love.[95]

As Sheen biographer and friend Sister Rose Pacatte, Director of the Pauline Center for Media Studies in Los Angeles, notes in her short biography of Sheen, he often quotes the French Jesuit priest and philosopher Pierre Teilhard de Chardin (1881–1955): "Someday, after mastering the winds, the waves, the tides and gravity, we shall harness for God the energies of love, and then, for a second time in the history of the world, man will have discovered fire."[96]

Sheen described for Sister Pacatte his personal understanding of God. He related an experience he had while attending a mass at St. Monica's Church in Santa Monica years earlier. "There was this guy behind me, who knew all the prayers of the Mass and was so loud and overbearing, well, I just sat in silence. When we got to the part of the Creed where it used to say, 'He was born of the Virgin Mary and became a man,' this annoying man said with great passion instead, 'and he was born of the Virgin Mary *and became human!*' [italics in original]. I was so struck by that."

It made me reflect on what it truly meant for God to become like one of us! Now every time I pray the Creed I say *human* because when you think of the difference between "man" and "human," well, it's remarkable. Jesus became one of us!

When I think of Jesus as human, I think of the mystery of God becoming human. Did you ever think of how long God may have been trying to send the Messiah, but because God would not force himself on anyone, because we have free will, it didn't work. And maybe the person God asked said, "No" or "Are you kidding? You want me to do what?" And then an angel goes to this little girl, Mary, and asks her, and she says, "yes."[97]

In another interview with Sister Pacatte, Sheen discussed his 1981 return to the church, highlighting what he views as its activist aspects. "I came back to the church of compassion, love and service, not a church that had me waiting to be condemned for my sins. I found the church of Mother Teresa and Daniel Berrigan. Mother Teresa drove me back to Catholicism and Dan Berrigan keeps me here. I became very active at that time."[98]

"Martin is certainly a family man but he comes to Mass mostly by himself, though Emilio accompanies him sometimes," Priest William Kerze told Sister Pacatte. Father Kerze coached Sheen when he played a priest in the films *Stella Days* (2011) and *Trash* (2014). "When there are family funerals, then the whole family comes. I know it sounds like a cliché, but Martin walks the talk; he is a man of integrity and what you see is what you get."[99]

Sheen has been married to his wife, Janet, since 1961 and is father to four children, Charlie, Emilio, Renee, and Ramón.

"People don't have any idea how important his faith is to him, that it comes before everything," says Father Michael Kennedy, head of the Jesuit

Restorative Justice Initiative in California, a longtime friend. "He reads so much on spirituality. He's not fake; he's totally committed."[100]

"When we're on the set people say that sometimes it's easy to forget who's the father and who's the son," Estevez wrote in *Along the Way: The Journey of a Father and Son*. "That doesn't mean we always get along. We don't. We disagree, a lot. He's a devout and practicing Catholic, whereas I have my own ideas about spirituality and a strong connection to the earth."[101]

In one of many interviews to promote the film, Estevez said, "I'm on a spiritual journey and am very much in touch with that. There was a point in the production process where I stopped calling what happened along the way coincidences and began calling them miracles. Things like that happened daily, things that were just supposed to be."[102]

Estevez said his son meeting the love of his life on the road trip with his Grandfather Martin in Spain was a good omen for the film. "While there, the innkeeper's daughter walked into the room, and when she and my son met, it was love at first sight. They ended up getting married. That's the first miracle of the Camino. Afterwards, Martin kept giving me the nudge that we should make a movie about the Camino."[103]

Estevez referred to the assorted happy incidents during the film shoot as "milagros," Spanish for miracles. "We had two crew members who met and fell in love on the way. We were warned it would rain every day. It only rained two days, and on those days, we filmed our interior shots. There were many *milagros*. We were charmed and blessed and paid attention to them," he said.[104] The notion of minor miracles, blessings, and spiritual journeys is reflective of what many people mean when they refer to being spiritual rather than religious. Estevez is on the spiritual path, while Sheen has chosen religious commitment within the realm of his liberal Catholicism.

A movie company had never before been allowed inside the cathedral at Santiago. Sheen said the Catholic Church was concerned the filmmakers might take a cynical approach to religion. Estevez explained what happened next:

> We had the whole crew praying, even the atheists. Twenty-four hours before we filmed, we got approval, and they allowed us to go into the Cathedral in Santiago de Compostela. The world premiere took place in Spain on Oct. 11, 2010. When the movie ended, the archbishop stood up, gave Martin a hug and said, "This film is a gift." They were relieved that we hadn't denigrated the Camino.[105]

The Independent Catholic News, the first daily online Catholic news service in the United Kingdom, covered a screening of *The Way* in London, followed by a Q&A with Sheen and Estevez. Franciscan Sr. Janet Fearns from overseas charity mission Missio, asked, "Those of us who can identify with *The Way* through a journey of faith can see one of the beauties of this film and of the film *Of Gods & Men*—is its quiet understatement—but also its profound meaning. How much of a challenge is it to get that out on to audience?" "That is the challenge," Estevez responded. "Do you have any ideas? This film has no car chases or special effects, bad language or scenes of sexuality. The only reason we have an adult rating is that the Dutchman smokes a little grass. That's one of his characteristics. He's an agnostic, yet one of the most moving moments in the film is when he drops to his knees at the doorway of the Cathedral. We didn't want to hit people over the head with spirituality but to offer a quiet sense of something they can relate to." [106]

At the same event, in response to a congratulatory remark for "resisting the temptation to throw in extra drama," Estevez remarked, "Nobody is going to give you 200 million for a film on the Camino. It's a tough sell. But we also don't want to just appeal to one demographic. Our film is pro people, pro life—not anti-anything. It invites you to grab a backpack and jump on the screen with us." [107]

RELIGIOUS AND SECULAR MEDIA REVIEWS OF *THE WAY*

Critic Scott Feinberg covered a special premiere of *The Way* at a 2011 fundraiser for the Walkabout Foundation in New York the day before it opened nationwide in the United States. Walkabout, a nonprofit that provides wheelchairs to those who cannot afford them, was founded by siblings Luis and Carolina Gonzalez-Bunster. Luis, who is paralyzed and uses a wheelchair, became the first person to cross Spain using only the strength of his arms when he and Carolina completed the Camino de Santiago de Compostela to launch their foundation. [108]

Writing in *The Hollywood Reporter*, Feinberg said, "The film is surprisingly moving (thanks to a tour de force performance by 71-year-old Sheen, who inherently engenders more goodwill than just about any actor I can think of) and funny (thanks, above all, to a great supporting performance by Dutchman Yorick van Wageningen), and you will be hardpressed to find a better story about a father and son, friendship, and faith this year." [109] The Walkabout premiere was attended by former president Bill Clinton, who spoke at the event: "I thank the people who made this beautiful movie. . . . I want you to know you did a good thing tonight. . . . Thank you again Martin. Thank you Emilio for making this movie." [110]

The filmmakers did interviews with a wide variety of outlets. Televangelist Pat Robertson's conservative Christian Broadcast Network (CBN) praised *The Way* as a film "you can take your elderly parents and high school kids to see." [111] Estevez told CBN.com, "Kids are posting on Facebook saying, 'I've never heard of this before. Thank you for making the film. I'm going to Santiago. I'm taking my parents to the movie. I finally found a movie that I can take my parents to that is not vulgar, that's not so CGI-driven or about outer space, that they can relate to.'"[112]

Sheen was asked by a reporter for *The Daily Beast* if he and Estevez were "spiritual people." Sheen replied, "I've never met anyone that wasn't! I think we believe in mystery. But religion, unfortunately, because of dogma, tends to divide us, and spirituality and humanity is what unites us."[113]

In a review of *The Way* in the *National Catholic Register*, Steven D. Greydanus wrote:

> The catchphrase "spiritual but not religious" is among the most glib and insipid pieties of our times. *The Way*, with its centuries of tradition, its ritual gestures and formalities, its institutions and symbols, its physically demanding regimen, and its cultural, Christian and Catholic particularity, is a gratifying reminder of how religion grounds and enriches us in ways that "spirituality" can't. "Spirituality" has no traditions or rituals, makes no demands, gives us nothing to *do* in times of crisis. Spirituality itself points beyond spirituality to religion—a point *The Way* makes with unforced persuasiveness.[114]

As this review targets a Catholic audience, Greydanus adds a precaution concerning the spreading of Daniel's ashes: "Well-instructed Catholics may be taken aback by the manner in which Tom seeks to honor his son's final intention of traveling the Camino. Tom, a lapsed Catholic, presumably isn't aware of his obligations under Church law, and while it might or might not make a difference if he did know, his actions don't necessarily reflect a rejection of the relevant Catholic beliefs, and we need not judge him—or the film—harshly in this connection, though, of course, this example shouldn't be followed by Catholics."[115]

After 1963 and Vatican II, the Catholic Church no longer forbad cremation of bodies after death. The scattering of human ashes is seen as desecration, however. According to the guidelines set forth in *The Order of Christian Funerals*,

> Since the human body has an eternal destiny in any form, the Church requires that cremated remains of a body be buried or entombed immediately after the Funeral in the same timely manner as a body. Cremated remains of a loved one are not to be scattered, kept at home or divided into other vessels among family members, just as it is clear that these practices would desecrate a body in a casket. The Church allows for burial at sea, providing that the cremated remains of the body are buried in a heavy container and not scattered.[116]

Violating this Catholic dictate, Tom spreads Daniel's ashes as a dramatic device as they make the journey along the Camino de Santiago "together." Sister Pacatte dismisses the ashes argument with a sort of "It's only a movie" defense:

Some folks are concerned that Tom leaves little handfuls of Daniel's ashes along with way, at different roadside shrines, and then at the end, tosses them into the crashing waves near a Catholic church along the northern coast of Spain. Yes, the Catechism of the Catholic Church teaches that the cremated ashes are to be kept and buried together so that the integrity of the body is maintained. But that's the whole point, isn't it? Tom is way out of touch with his faith, and this pilgrimage was his way of finding his way home again.

To quote the film critic Roger Ebert: We don't go to the movies for Sunday school. However, films often provide a means to talk about things that truly matter.

I think "The Way" expresses well what the Catholic author Flannery O'Connor once wrote, that most people come to the Church (or return to the Church) by means that the Church does not approve.

When it comes to God's grace, there are no limits for God is all-powerful and colors outside the lines to get our attention. The movie offers us so much to talk about. "The Way" is a movie full of grace. [117]

Despite his objections to depictions of spirituality and cremation, Greydanus is optimistic about the film's message. "If there is a glimpse of transcendence in *The Way*, it is at the climax, in the Cathedral of Santiago de Compostela," he writes. "While the film stops well short of a profession of faith, it does offer an affirmation of sorts of the human value, especially in times of crisis, of some kind of faith or religious heritage, and in particular of Catholic cultural accoutrements, of traditions like pilgrimages and the sign of the cross, and of beautiful cathedrals and such. This is a salutary thought, as far as it goes, and a welcome one in our cultural moment." [118]

Greydanus sees religion as something that makes demands on us, but ultimately enriches us, while spirituality is unable to feed our souls. *The Way* is about humanity, community, self-discovery, healing, forgiveness, and being set free of burdens. Are those religious or spiritual things? Both? Greydanus confesses he would have liked to see more digging into the souls of the characters, but the film suffices as a valentine to the Camino. It will inspire others to take the journey, he writes. "Count me among them." [119]

Jack is perhaps the best example of transcendence and affirmation in *The Way*. Bitter about the sins of the Catholic Church in Ireland, he nonetheless weeps and finds a measure of peace inside the Cathedral. His connection is with his fellow pilgrims and with God, not a religion.

Francis Phillips is a freelance book reviewer and blogger who writes for the British magazine *Catholic Herald*. She wrote about *The Way* in 2012, focusing on Sheen himself and what she sees as his flawed faith. Her opinion can be summed up by her essay title: "Martin Sheen is a better actor than theologian: The actor, like so many liberal Catholics, seems to have lost his Way." [120]

Phillips gives a brief plot summary before attacking Sheen's liberality. "It seems that Sheen goes along with the attempts to redefine marriage," Phillips wrote. As evidence, she quotes from an interview Sheen gave to *Life Site News* about gay marriage:

> My religion's highest standard is conscience. Nothing can get between your conscience and God, not even the Church. . . . The Church is a conduit, and it is a spiritual journey, but it is not the end of the journey. The Church is an institution, primarily of men . . . and so they are flawed, obviously. And so they are not authorized from preventing any member from following their conscience no matter what that is. You can't get between a person's conscience and their God. Nobody can do that.[121]

Phillips will have none of it. "'Conscience' as we know, has to be 'informed'; i.e. we can't make up our own rules and then describe this as 'following our conscience'. Whenever I have met people whose 'conscience' has led them away from Church teaching, it has been apparent, to me at least, that it has been used as an excuse to evade hard issues."[122]

Phillips picked up on the film's *Oz* analogy, saying, "Like the characters in *The Wizard of Oz* they all stumble along the pilgrim way, fighting, arguing—and finally bonding, as they reach the great cathedral in Compostella (sic) and recognise that a kind of healing process has taken place in all of them." She is charitable toward Sheen's character Tom, if not toward the actor himself. Like Greydanus, Phillips notes that spreading a loved one's ashes along the Camino de Santiago is "unlawful from an ecclesiastical point of view, but I have to say I had a sneaking sympathy with the aging doctor—played in the rugged, macho American fashion by Sheen—who is desperate to make amends to his dead son for the failures in their relationship when he was alive."[123]

Christianity Today, the magazine founded in 1956 by Protestant evangelist Billy Graham, gave *The Way* a four-star rating. Reviewer Kenneth R. Morefield called it "One of the best films of the year."[124] Morefield, an associate professor of English at Campbell University, is the editor of *Faith and Spirituality in Masters of World Cinema, Volumes I, II and III* (2008, 2011, 2015, Cambridge Scholars Publishing). In his review, he explores the bonds among the characters, particularly between Sarah and Tom.

> As we learn more about Sarah and her reasons for walking the Camino, we not only understand her character better but also why these two people are well suited to understand and help each other. Grief and sorrow often alienate those who feel it from others; words of sympathy grate when we feel those expressing them cannot truly understand what we are going through. When Sarah finally shares a difficult part of her past with Tom, it is one of the more powerful moments in the film because the emphasis within the story is less on what she did than on the devastating emotional consequences of her actions.[125]

Morefield notes that the film is about intimacy, not of a sexual nature, but "particularly about how grief removes some of the social boundaries we keep up." He also explores the idea of *The Way* as a Christian film. Moving beyond the more legalistic religious points expounded by Greydanus and Phillips, Morefield says the film explores spirituality in a specifically Christian manner:

> Is this a "Christian" film? Probably not, at least not in the niche-marketing sense of the word. It is not constructed to lead audiences to affirm a particular answer so much as to depict people asking the most fundamental of spiritual questions. I would argue that it is Christian but not evangelistic. That is, it is situated in a place in which spiritual questions are framed in a Christian context, but it does not attempt to compare religions or emphasize the notion that Christian answers to universal questions may have singular distinctives.
>
> I am tempted to argue that the film isn't really ecumenical so much as it is specific, concrete. If we hear more about (or are prompted to think more about) God in general than about Jesus specifically, that has more to do with where these characters are on their path than it does about what path they are on. [126]

Finally, Morefield expounds on the central thesis of this chapter, the notion that "*The Way*, though, is not (just) a good film because of its subject matter or in comparison to some other, more overtly self-conscious (and self-proclaiming) Christian films." He goes a step further by proclaiming, "It is a great film, period." [127]

The Pulitzer Prize-winning film critic Roger Ebert was less effusive. "Audiences seeking uplift will find it" in *The Way*, he wrote. "It's a sweet and sincere family pilgrimage, even if a little too long and obvious." [128] Ebert saw vagueness in the film's message:

> Your response to it may depend on how receptive you are to the idea of the journey. Since both Sheen and Estevez are public about their Catholicism, I'm not sure what the point was of making Tom so firmly secular; perhaps so that even he, following so many centuries of footsteps, can sense some of their spirituality. "The Way" is a nice film. Not great, not urgent, but quietly positive. [129]

Ebert hints at a "conversion" experience, not so much as a coming to Christ moment, but as a spiritual awakening. Sheen himself reverted to the Catholicism of his youth when he was approaching middle age, and as has been noted, *The Way* parallels that experience.

"The Way occupies that nebulous territory between labour of love and vanity project. A sincere, well-intentioned story about grief and faith, it feels almost daringly old-fashioned," said David Gritten in the British newspaper, *The Telegraph*. Various critics have noted how little happens in the movie,

similar to Paul Schrader's theory of the transcendental style, and Gritten
addresses that filmic contradiction head on:

> *The Way* is rather an odd film, which frequently feels closer to the long
> stretches of boredom and sporadic magic of real life than to cinematic conven-
> tion: this is, I think, the secret of its success . . .
>   The main factor that makes this film work is Sheen himself: his character
> is a tetchy, uptight old guy, but—unlike his curiously orange, Donald Trump-
> ish hair—he exudes the stubborn whiff of authenticity. Sheen is directed by his
> own son in real life, Emilio Estevez, who also appears in flashback playing
> Daniel, and the film dwells unshowily on the necessary exorcism of regret
> when death arrives in the midst of a family dispute. [130]

Gritten observes that *The Way* unfolds its story in an "unshowily" fashion to
relate life as it is, not as we wish it might be. As an example, Gritten writes
that Tom "finds his new companions irritating as hell, but as time wears on
he learns to bear them, and finally to spare them a little kindness from his
sparse store." The shots of Tom learning to care for these new friends "are
hard-won and strangely moving," he says. [131]

Not for everyone, though. "For a self-proclaimed spiritual film, Emilio
Estevez's *The Way* proves to be, well, not so spiritual," David Roark wrote in
Paste, a magazine devoted to covering music, movies, and other popular
entertainment. "The slow, hackneyed drama, instead, turns out to be one
giant cliché, void of any insights into human experience but full of political
correctness." [132] After bashing the "sappy" Adult Contemporary soundtrack,
which includes James Taylor's "Country Road," Roark offers an alternative
film choice: "For a more personal, more effective, far superior film about
death, family and spirituality that actually makes use of its international
setting, see Wes Anderson's *The Darjeeling Limited*." [133]

Finally, online aggregator Rotten Tomatoes recorded scores of 82 percent
and 83 percent for collective positive reviews given by film critics and the
website's users, respectively. The capsule "Critics Consensus" of all reviews
on the site reads: "It may be a little too deliberately paced for more impatient
viewers, but *The Way* is a worthy effort from writer/director Emilio Estevez,
balancing heartfelt emotion with clear-eyed drama that resists cheap sentiment." [134]

Three of the film's characters—Sarah, Captain Sebastian, and Tom—
have all lost a child, and their sadness is expressed in an emotional, yet
underplayed manner. The film gives us loss, and it fills the loss not with
romance or sentimentality, but with bonds of friendship, respect, and new-
found community. Spiritual community. Christian community.

CONCLUSION

Catholic writer Tim Drake called *The Way* "a refreshingly beautiful and respectful treatment of the Church, telling the story of a father who decides to take the Camino de Santiago walking pilgrimage in honor of his deceased son."[135] The key word here is "refreshingly," hinting that the United States' movie industry is not always kind to Catholicism in particular, or Christianity in general. In turn, audiences are often unhappy with Hollywood, particularly religious audiences.

Actor/director Mel Gibson ran into various roadblocks with his controversial film *The Passion of the Christ* (2004). Gibson, who can arguably be described as an ultraconservative Catholic, founded the independent Catholic Church of the Holy Family in California, which is not affiliated with an archdiocese or the Holy See, and rejects Vatican II reforms.[136]

Despite his status as a bankable star, no Hollywood studio would back Gibson in his personal chronicle of the last 12 hours of Jesus's life, so he spent $45 million of his own money to produce, direct, and market a film with lesser-known actors, shot in Aramaic and Latin with subtitles. He shunned a traditional big budget promotional campaign by appealing directly to Protestant and Catholic churches and their respective religious leaders.

It worked. Churches bought blocks of tickets for their members, and some rented entire theatres for their congregations. As Jerry Cobb of CNBC noted when the film debuted, "Many Christian groups are using the film to promote themselves. One religious Web site calls it 'perhaps the best outreach opportunity in 2,000 years.'"[137]

Passion opened on Ash Wednesday in February 2004. More than a decade after its premiere, it was still ranked as one of the top-grossing R-rated films (for graphic violence) of all time alongside decidedly secular movies such as *Fifty Shades of Grey* (2015) and *American Sniper* (2014). In its opening weekend, *Passion* earned more than $83 million. Worldwide, it brought in more than $600 million.[138]

In 2004, *the National Catholic Register* and *Faith & Family* magazine polled more than 1,000 people online "for films that best celebrate Catholic life," and generated a list of 100 movies. As the *Register* explained, "These are movies with specific Catholic references, not simply with Catholic themes." *The Passion of the Christ* was ranked number one, albeit with an asterisk denoting that it may not be "family-friendly."[139] Gibson's version of a suffering Christ was a quite human depiction, but the film was not to everyone's taste, primarily because of the graphic violence during the scourging and crucifixion scenes.

Two years later, *Entertainment Weekly* labeled *The Passion of the Christ* the most controversial film of all time, primarily for its grisly close-ups of Jesus Christ's bloody body and Gibson's perceived anti-Semitism.[140] His film broadly portrays the Jewish authorities as viciously condemning Jesus.[141] Many conservative Christian viewers of Gibson's highly produced and brutal film saw it as an accurate depiction of Christ's suffering. Gibson was widely praised by many Protestant evangelicals, Catholics, and other religious communities for his gritty portrayal of Christ's death.

Gibson was also singled out for personal criticism from other quarters. Arrested for drunk driving in 2006, he launched into an anti-Semitic rant against the Jewish policeman who pulled him over, though he later apologized. The tirade was fodder for those who saw him—and his movie—as prejudiced against Jews. Complicating matters, Gibson left his wife after having an affair, and was accused of domestic abuse and sexist phone calls to his mistress, Oksana Grigorieva, the mother of his out of wedlock child. Tabloid newspapers and Hollywood gossip mills had a field day.

Bishop Robert Barron, founder of Word on Fire Catholic Ministries, and next to Pope Francis, the most-followed Catholic leader on social media, surmised that some of the animus directed toward Gibson has to do with anti-Catholic bias in Hollywood.[142] "I've suspected that the obsessive interest in Mel Gibson's dysfunction might be a function of (anti-Catholic) prejudice. Let's face it. Hollywood is filled with dozens, hundreds, of dysfunctional people," Barron said in an online video.

This is not a new argument. In 1992, film and cultural critic Michael Medved published *Hollywood vs. America*, declaring in its opening lines that, "America's long-running romance with Hollywood is over."

> As a nation, we no longer believe that popular culture enriches our lives. Few of us view the show business capital as a magical source of uplifting entertainment, romantic inspiration, or even harmless fun. Instead, tens of millions of Americans now see the entertainment industry as an all-powerful enemy, an alien force that assaults our most cherished values and corrupts our children.[143]

There is a section in Medved's book called "Kicking the Catholics" wherein he details the "anticlerical impulse in Hollywood" that resulted in a number of Catholic-bashing movies. Among the examples cited are: *The Runner Stumbles* and *Monsignor*, both dramas that center on priests who fall in love with nuns and are complicit in their deaths; *We're No Angels* and *Nuns on the Run*, comedies with criminals posing as holy men in a monastery and a convent, respectively; and *Heaven Help Us*, a raunchy teen comedy set in a 1960s parochial school.[144]

Medved, who is Jewish, was a strong defender of *Passion of the Christ* despite cries of anti-Semitism from Jewish groups. After Gibson's rant against the Jewish policeman who arrested Gibson for driving drunk, Medved said Gibson should seek reconciliation with the Jewish community. "Those of us who have defended and praised Gibson for his outspoken Catholic commitment, and for his efforts to use the movie medium to convey religious messages, feel inevitably betrayed and, yes, a bit humiliated," Medved wrote in a *USA Today* opinion piece.

"My own acquaintance with Gibson suggests that at this tortured moment in his life, he sincerely craves an opportunity to deepen his obviously pathetic understanding of Jewish identity and history," Medved continued. "In any event, the process of reconciliation he proposes—no matter how difficult or incomplete—can only be good for Gibson, and good for the Jews."[145]

Making a Christian-themed or Christian-related movie, indeed a movie highlighting any religion, is not for the faint of heart. Hollywood is an industry town, and its primary focus is on making money. If art results along the way, that's icing on the cake. Hollywood film and television executives typically shy from controversy, as any financially fickle, high stakes, commercial industry would.

Emilio Estevez expressed his frustration in numerous promotional interviews for *The Way* about trying to sell the movie to studio executives. He told Drake in 2011:

> When we pitched it to studio representatives you could see their eyes glaze over. They'd say, "It's about spirituality." So we decided to shoot it digitally and independently. I believe this movie plays between Glenwood and Newark. Beverly Hills and New York can take a walk. Hollywood makes a lot of garbage. We know because we've been in some of it. There are less and less movies to go to—films without overt sexuality and language that won't make me blush. We're all tired of what's coming out of Hollywood. Word of mouth will help this film make it.[146]

The Way is one of those films that comes and goes at the multiplex and the art house without making much of a stir among the general public. It was reviewed widely in both religious and mainstream secular publications, but made little financial or cultural impact, unlike *Passion of the Christ*. In a way, this is what makes the film *worthier* of examination. Hollywood has tremendous cultural influence, and the American film industry drops in on religion occasionally, often in an overblown or distorted manner.

"This is not an 'inspirational film' in the usual, syrupy sense; none of these people are overtly finding God on this trek," Neil Genzlinger wrote in a *New York Times* review of *The Way*. "The beauty of the movie, in fact, is that Mr. Estevez does not make explicit what any of them find, beyond friendship. He lets these four fine actors convey that true personal transformations are not announced with fanfare, but happen internally."[147]

"[P]ilgrimage, although it's a physical endeavor, for the most part, it's an interior pilgrimage," Martin Sheen told author and *On Being* host Krista Tippett in a 2015 interview. "It's an interior journey, and all the pilgrims who've ever done it have come to that realization. You're walking physically, that's something you're doing outside. But there's something else going on inside. And it's the journey to your true self, I think, we begin to realize. Because we're quiet and focused in a way that we normally are not. So you get six, eight, ten weeks on pilgrimage to learn about yourself and to celebrate your life."[148]

The Way producer David Alexanian, echoing critic David Gritten, stressed the film's "authenticity":

> You spend so much time trying to convince others of something in Hollywood, trying to sell somebody something. This film is not trying to sell anybody anything. Martin's performance is not a sales pitch. This film isn't religious or preachy. It's an authentic film, which is what's unique about it. It's a film that's dedicated to a grandfather, inspired by a great-grandson. You've got four generations. And the authenticity of that, I think, people are responding to. One of the reasons that documentaries do well—and this film is far from a documentary—is, we're tired of the stuff that seems hokey and contrived. And I don't blame Hollywood for doing that, but they've just stopped creating, and they've started re-creating, or copying . . .
>
> And nobody said no to us when we were pitching this film, but they surely didn't say yes. So we had to go out and make it happen. And to your point of how difficult it was, we just stopped trying to convince people who didn't get it, and we just said yes to the believers. We allowed the believers to get involved. Not believers in the religious sense, but believers in this project.[149]

The Way does not fit into the narrow Christian film category, and targets a broader audience than *War Room, God's Not Dead*, and similar productions. Major Hollywood films with religious bases, such as *Last Days in the Desert* (2016) with Ewan McGregor as Jesus avoiding temptation while wandering the desert for 40 days, explore themes of humanity, but are less relatable than *The Way.*

Though *The Way's* anemic box office may not have inspired movie executives, its depiction of walking the Camino inspired new pilgrims. American journalist Carol Frey wrote of the journey along the Camino she and her husband Ed took a year after seeing the film. "Invariably, today's pilgrims explain their decision starting with 'The Movie,'" Frey wrote, describing the film's influence. "If you haven't seen 'The Way'—and most people haven't—the story begins with the death of the doctor's son only a few days after he started his spiritual journey on the Camino."[150] Frey covered the basic plot points, detailing the transformation of the film's characters, and that of friends and acquaintances who have completed the journey. "None is overtly religious, though," she says of these transformations. "What they are doing is portrayed as a pilgrimage, so that people of faith recognize its significance, but *others are not excluded.* [emphasis added] . . . Though we are churchgoers, Ed and I didn't feel the need to walk the Camino for religious reasons, but we craved time away from duties and distractions to reflect on our purpose in life. And it delivered, just as in the movie."[151]

While *The Way* is arguably more spiritual than religious, it offers scenes of faith, hope, forgiveness, love, and redemption, without using a bludgeon on the audience. At times painful, at other times joyous, deliberately paced, and somewhat flawed, it more closely resembles genuine life than either Hollywood epics or church-centered films that preach to the choir.

NOTES

1. Kathleen Ashley and Marilyn Deegan, *Being a Pilgrim: Art and Ritual on the Medieval Routes to Santiago* (London: Lund Humphries, 2009); Emilio Estevez, dir., *The Way*, ARC Entertainment, 2010.
2. Lloyd Baugh, "The African Face of Jesus in Film: Two Texts, a New Tradition," in Richard Walsh, Jeffrey L. Staley, and Adele Reinhartz, *Son of Man: An African Jesus Film* (Sheffield: Sheffield Phoenix Press, 2013), 120.
3. Harold Erickson, *Jesus of Nazareth:* Review Summary, *New York Times*, accessed August 5, 2015, http://www.nytimes.com/movies/movie/26102/Jesus-of-Nazareth/overview.
4. William Barclay, *Jesus of Nazareth* (New York: Ballantine Books, 1977).
5. Erickson, *Jesus of Nazareth.*
6. See John 1:14 (NIV): "The Word became flesh and made his dwelling among us. We have seen his glory, the glory of the one and only Son, who came from the Father, full of grace and truth." Other New Testament verses also refer to Jesus's humanity, particularly his suffering on the cross.
7. A partial list of Hollywood movies with overt Christian and Jewish themes from the early twentieth century to the early twenty-first includes:

* *The Life and Passion of Jesus Christ* (1902–1905; silent)
* *The King of Kings* (1927; silent)
* *The Jazz Singer* (1927; early talkie; partially silent)
* *Quo Vadis* (1951)
* *The Robe* (1953)
* *The Ten Commandments* (1956)
* *Ben Hur* (1959)
* *King of Kings* (1961)
* *The Greatest Story Ever Told* (1965)
* *Fiddler on the Roof* (1971)
* *Jesus Christ Superstar* (1973)
* *Godspell* (1973)
* *The Messiah* (1976)
* *The Chosen* (1981)
* *Chariots of Fire* (1981)
* *Yentl* (1983)
* *The Last Temptation of Christ* (1988)
* *The Prince of Egypt* (1998; animated)
* *The Passion of the Christ* (2004)
* *Soul Surfer* (2011)
* *Noah* (2014)
* *Exodus* (2014)
* *Son of God* (2014)
* *Left Behind* (2014)
* *Heaven is for Real* (2014)

- *God's Not Dead* (2014)
- *War Room* (2015)
- *90 Minutes in Heaven* (2015)
- *Faith of Our Fathers* (2015)
- *God's Not Dead 2* (2016)
- *Miracles from Heaven* (2016)

8. "DeMille on Film," Cecile B. DeMille website, cecilebdemille.com, accessed August 9, 2015. DeMille previously shot a silent version of *The Ten Commandments* in 1923.

9. Ibid.

10. David Walters, "Why Audiences Flock to Faith-Based Films," *Bloomberg Businessweek*, March 30, 2016, https://www.bloomberg.com/news/articles/2016–03–30/why-audiences-flock-to-faith-based-films.

11. Craig Detweiler, "Christianity: The Subtle and the Spectacular," *The Routledge Companion to Religion and Film* (Abingdon: Routledge, 2011), 109.

12. Ibid.

13. Ibid., 123.

14. Paul Schrader, interview, *Transcendental Style in Film*, TIFF Originals, YouTube, April 26, 2017, https://www.youtube.com/watch?v=mFcCs8c2n6I.

15. Eric Kohn, "Emilio Estevez's 'The Way' Is A Lot Better Than It Looks," *IndieWire.com*, October 7, 2011, http://www.indiewire.com/2011/10/review-emilio-estevezs-the-way-is-a-lot-better-than-it-looks-51769/.

16. Succinct plot description of *Touched by an Angel* from imdb.com: "Monica, Tess, and Andrew are a trio of angels sent to Earth to tell depressed and troubled people that God loves them and hasn't forgotten them."

17. "The Bible," *Hollywood Jesus*, April 8, 2013, accessed July 21, 2015, http://www.hollywoodjesus.com/the-bible-11/.

18. See Hollie McKay, "Is 2014 the year of the Christian film?" FoxNews.com, April 11, 2014; Jonathan Merritt, "5 films that will make 2014 'the year of the Bible,'" Religion News Service, January 3, 2014; Andrew Romano, "Hollywood Declares 2014 the Year of the Bible," *The Daily Beast*, January 9, 2014.

19. Terry Lindvall and Andrew Quicke, *Celluloid Sermons: The Emergence of the Christian Film Industry, 1930–1986* (New York: New York University Press, 2011), x; see also, Milton Anderson, *The Modern Goliath: A Study of Talking Pictures with a Treatment of Non-Theatrical Talking Pictures Especially Talking Pictures for Schools and Churches and Some Chapters on Character Education and Values* (Los Angeles: David Press, 1935). Lindvall and Quicke's book offers an in-depth look at the development of the Christian film genre, and is recommended for those who wish to delve more deeply.

20. Lindvall and Quicke, x–xii; Harry Stout, *The New England Soul: Preaching and Religious Culture in Colonial New England* (Oxford: Oxford University Press, 1986).

21. Lindvall and Quicke, *Celluloid Sermons* 116–119.

22. Ibid., 118. *Bible on the Table*, Broadman Films, 1951; YouTube, A/V Geeks, avgeeks.com, July 8, 2017, https://www.youtube.com/watch?v=yjWqokxP1nk.

23. Lindvall and Quicke, 126.

24. Ibid., 127–128.

25. Ibid., 138–139.

26. Ibid., 131–132.

27. A summary on the Internet Movie Database (IMDB) summarizes the plot of *A Thief in the Night* this way: "The story of Patty, a young woman caught up in living for the present with little concern for the future. She meets and marries a young man and her life seems great, until one moment she awakens to find her husband gone and the radio reporting millions of people have mysteriously disappeared. As dramatic, earth shaking events begin to unfold around her, Patty realizes she is living in the end times spoken of in biblical prophecy. Adventure and suspense build to a though-provoking climax in this powerfully gripping film." Films based on LaHaye and Jenkins's *Left Behind* novels are *Left Behind: The Movie* (2000), *Left Behind II: Tribulation Force* (2002), *Left Behind: World at War* (2005), and a remake of sorts, also titled

Left Behind (2014). A video game called *Left Behind: Eternal Forces* went on the market in 2006.

28. Ibid., 186–187.

29. World Wide Pictures, Billy Graham Evangelistic Association website, accessed August 5, 2015, http://billygraham.org/tv-and-radio/worldwide-pictures/.

30. Kim Lawton, "Church Movies Keep Coming," *Christianity Today*, April 20, 2011, http://www.christianitytoday.com/ct/2011/aprilweb-only/churchmoviescoming.html.

31. Kim Lawton, "Fed Up with Hollywood, Churches Make their Own Films," *The Christian Century*, March 11, 2011, accessed January 6, 2017, https://www.christiancentury.org/article/2011-03/fed-hollywood-churches-make-their-own-films.

32. "About the Festival," Churches Making Movies website, accessed January 6, 2017, http://www.churchesmakingmovies.com/about-us.

33. Ibid.

34. *War Room*, Box Office Mojo, http://www.boxofficemojo.com/movies/?id=warroom2015.htm.

35. "War Room," Internet Movie Database, http://www.imdb.com/title/tt3832914/.

36. Kendrick Brothers website, http://kendrickbrothers.com/news/provision-through-prayer, accessed February 4, 2016. Originally published in Published in *The Washington Times*, November 30, 2015. The brothers also produced *Courageous* (2011), *Flywheel* (2003), *Fireproof* (2008), and *Facing the Giants* (2006).

37. Ibid.

38. Financial information from *The Numbers: Where Data and the Movie Business Meet*, http://www.the-numbers.com/movie/Gods-Not-Dead#tab=summary.

39. Walters, "Why Audiences Flock to Faith-Based Films."

40. "*God's Not Dead* is a Mess Even by Christian Film Standards," Todd VanDerWerff, *The A.V. Club*, March 24, 2014, https://film.avclub.com/god-s-not-dead-is-a-mess-even-by-christian-film-standar-1798179908.

41. Scott Foundas, "Film Review: 'God's Not Dead," *Variety*, March 22, 2014, http://variety.com/2014/film/reviews/film-review-gods-not-dead-1201142881/.

42. See Pure Flix website, https://offers.pureflix.com/christian-homeschool-curriculum-movies.

43. "About Us," Pure Flix website, http://pureflixstudio.com/about-us/. Arizona-based Pure Flix defines its movie ministry on its web page, Pureflixstudio.com: "Our passion is to create films that impact our culture for Christ. From the founding of Pure Flix it has always been our vision and calling to serve alongside the church by providing affordable and effective Movie Ministry solutions to use for Outreach, Church Growth, Fellowship Opportunities, Small Group Ministry and Sermon Messages."

44. Ibid.

45. According to Box Office Mojo, *Fifty Shades of Grey* was the number one film when it opened on Valentine's Day weekend in 2015, bringing in $85 million. The final domestic gross was $166.2 million. *Old Fashioned* had a domestic gross of $1.9 million.

46. Brandon Ambrosino, "Why Are Christian Movies So Painfully Bad?" *Vox*, April 1, 2016, https://www.vox.com/2015/2/15/8038283/christian-movies-bad-old-fashioned-fifty-shades.

47. Ibid.

48. Ibid.

49. Alissa Wilkinson, "Why Christian Artists Don't Want to be 'Christian Artists,' *IndieWire.com*, November 11, 2013, http://www.indiewire.com/2013/11/why-christian-artists-dont-want-to-be-christian-artists-127322/.

50. Ambrosino, "Why Are Christian Movies So Painfully Bad?"

51. Ibid.

52. Kim Lawton, "Church Movies Keep Coming," *Christianity Today*, April 20, 2011, accessed August 11, 2015, http://www.christianitytoday.com/ct/2011/aprilweb-only/churchmoviescoming.html.

53. *Miracles from Heaven*, Box Office Mojo, http://www.boxofficemojo.com/movies/?id=miraclesfromheaven.htm.

54. *The Shack* joined the Evangelical Christian Publishers Association list of Diamond Award Winners for selling more than 10 million copies, http://christianbookexpo.com/salesa-wards/.

55. *The Shack*, Box Office Mojo, http://www.boxofficemojo.com/movies/?id=theshack.htm.

56. *The Way*, Box Office Mojo, http://www.boxofficemojo.com/movies/?id=way2011.htm.

57. Andrew M. Greeley, *God in Popular Culture* (Chicago: The Thomas More Press, 1988), 251.

58. Robert K. Johnston, "Theological Approaches," *The Routledge Companion to Religion and Film*, Ed., John Lyden (London: Routledge, 2011, pbk), 321.

59. Ibid, 314.

60. Ibid, 314–315.

61. See: John May, *New Images of Religious Film* (Kansas City: Sheed & Ward), 1997; Peter Malone, "The Roman Catholic Church and Cinema (1967 to the Present), *The Routledge Companion to Religion and Film*, Ed., John Lyden (London: Routledge, 2011, pbk), 57–59; Robert K. Johnston, "Theological Approaches," 313.

62. Ibid.

63. Greg Garrett, *The Gospel According to Hollywood* (Louisville: Westminster John Knox Press, 2007), 87.

64. Christopher Deacy, "Redemption," *The Routledge Companion to Religion and Film*, Ed., John Lyden (London: Routledge, 2011, pbk), 356; quoting Clive Marsh, *Theology Goes to the Movies: An Introduction to Critical Christian Thinking* (London: Routledge, 2007), 104.

65. Dietrich Bonhoeffer, *The Cost of Discipleship* (London: SCM Press, 1959), 80.

66. "About the Film," *The Way* website, http://www.theway-themovie.com/film.php.

67. Taylor wound up meeting the woman who would become his wife on the trip with Sheen, and relocated to Spain. He wound up working as an associate producer on the film, making *The Way* a true family affair.

68. The Argentinian-born Francis, the first Latin American pope, began his papacy in March 2013. "Francis's approach marks a sharp departure from that of the last two popes [Benedict and John Paul II], who saw the church as a bulwark against secular culture and cast themselves as God's messengers of moral code," writes Alan Zarembo of *The Los Angeles Times*. "He wore frayed cassocks and asked people to pray for him—and for nonbelievers to at least think good thoughts. He ministered to prisoners and turned down lunch with Washington dignitaries Thursday to dine with the homeless. . . . The message, from the church, is that its appeal is simple and authentic. Francis, in essence, is a rebranding of Catholicism." Alan Zarembo, "With Pope Francis, Catholicism has a New Brand— an Everyman's Pope," *The Los Angeles Times*, September 28, 2015, accessed September 29, 2015, http://www.latimes.com/nation/la-na-pope-visit-assess-20150928-story.html.

69. Jack Hitt, *Off the Road: A Modern-Day Walk Down the Pilgrim's Route into Spain* (New York: Simon & Schuster Paperbacks, 2005; originally published 1994).

70. Ian Reader, *Pilgrimage: A Very Short Introduction* (Oxford: Oxford University Press, 2015), 20.

71. Ibid., 1.

72. Sergi Ramis, *Camino de Santiago*, trans. Peter Barraclough (London: Aurum Press, 2014), 20. According to the United Nations Educational, Scientific, and Cultural Organization (UNESCO), the site was discovered when "a hermit called Pelagius saw a mysterious light shining over a Roman tomb forgotten in the middle of a forest." The *Lonely Planet* guidebook refers to the hermit as "Pelayo."

73. Ibid.

74. Acts 12:1–2, ESV. The Acts of the Apostles is the fifth book of the New Testament and records the establishment of the Christian Church and its message preached throughout the Roman Empire.

75. Santiago de Compostela (Old Town), UNESCO, http://whc.unesco.org/en/list/347. Santiago de Compostela became a World Heritage Site in 1985. The Way, or the Camino, was added as a WHS in 1993.

76. Santiago de Compostela, Spain, Organization of World Heritage Cities, http://www.ovpm.org/en/spain/santiago_de_compostela.

77. Ramis, *Camino de Santiago*, 25.

78. Ashifa Kassam, "Mounted Police to Patrol Spain's Camino de Santiago Amid Security Fears," *The Guardian*, August 11, 2015, accessed August 12, 2015, http://www.theguardian.com/world/2015/aug/11/mounted-police-patrol-spain-camino-de-santiago-security-fears.

79. Ramis, *Camino de Santiago*, 5.

80. Stephen Follows, "How Many People Work on a Hollywood Film?" Blog post on stephenfollows.com, February 24, 2014, accessed September 22, 2015, https://stephenfollows.com/how-many-people-work-on-a-hollywood-film/.

81. Hannah Goodwyn, "Emilio Estevez and Martin Sheen on Faith and Filming *The Way*," *CBN.com*, n.d., accessed August 11, 2015, http://www.cbn.com/entertainment/screen/emilio-estevez-martin-sheen-faith-the-way-goodwyn.aspx.

82. Marlow Stern, "Sheen Family's Epic Journey," *The Daily Beast*, October 6, 2011, accessed September 9, 2015, http://www.thedailybeast.com/articles/2011/10/06/the-way-martin-sheen-emilio-estevez-on-charlie-sheen-occupy-wall-street.html.

83. PDA website, http://www.cineticmedia.com/pda/4572794171.

84. Figure as of March 2012. Source: Box Office Mojo, http://www.boxofficemojo.com/movies/?id=way2011.htm.

85. Source: Box Office Mojo.

86. Source: Box Office Mojo, http://www.boxofficemojo.com/movies/?id=noah.htm.

87. "Symbols of the Camino." Caminoteca, accessed September 15, 2015, http://caminoteca.com/en/about-the-camino/symbols-of-the-camino.

88. Jack's reference could mean any of a variety of issues concerning the Catholic Church in Ireland—sexual abuse and cover up; oppression and subjugation of women; authoritarian tendencies; violence. For a sympathetic yet critical analysis, see John P. McCarthy, "The State of the Catholic Church in Contemporary Ireland," *The Catholic World Report*, March 16, 2017, http://www.catholicworldreport.com/Item/5500/the_state_of_the_catholic_church_in_contemporary_ireland.aspx.

89. Tasha Robinson, "Martin Sheen & Emilio Estevez Interview," *A.V. Club*, October 6, 2011, accessed September 29, 2015, http://www.avclub.com/article/martin-sheen-emilio-estevez-62918.

90. Martin Sheen and Emilio Estevez with Hope Edelman, *Along the Way: The Journey of a Father and Son* (New York: Free Press, 2012). Sheen has also appeared in various acting projects with his other son, Charlie Sheen.

91. Ibid., 13–15.

92. Ibid., 16.

93. Rose Pacatte, *Martin Sheen: Pilgrim on The Way* (Collegeville, Minnesota: Liturgical Press, 2015), 21.

94. Martin Sheen, interviewed by David Kupfer, *The Progressive*, July 2003. Julian Beck (1925–1985) was co-founder and director of The Living Theatre.

95. Tim Drake, "Emilio Estevez and Martin Sheen Talk of Faith," Blog post, *The National Catholic Register*, September 14, 2011, accessed August 12, 2015, http://www.ncregister.com/blog/tim-drake/emilio-estevez-and-martin-sheen-talk-of-faith. Sheen had a heart attack at age 37 on the set of *Apocalypse Now* and nearly died.

96. Quoted in Pacatte, *Martin Sheen*, 109.

97. Pacatte, *Martin Sheen*, 99–100.

98. Rose Pacatte, "On 'The Way' with Martin Sheen, *National Catholic Reporter*, October 7, 2011, accessed September 8, 2015, http://ncronline.org/news/spirituality/way-martin-sheen. Daniel Berrigan died April 30, 2016.

99. Pacatte, *Martin Sheen: Pilgrim on The Way*, 100.

100. Ibid., 109.

101. Sheen and Estevez, *Along the Way*, 4.

102. Drake, "Emilio Estevez and Martin Sheen Talk of Faith."

103. Tim Drake, "Emilio Estevez and Martin Sheen Talk About 'The Way,'" *The National Catholic Register*, September 14, 2011, accessed September 29, 2015, http://www.ncregister.

com/daily-news/martin-sheen-and-emilio-estevez-talk-about-the-way. Estevez often calls his father "Martin" in interviews.

104. Ibid.

105. Ibid.

106. Jo Siedlecka, "A Father and Son Project: Martin Sheen, Emilio Estevez Discuss *The Way*," *Independent Catholic News*, February 24, 2011, https://www.indcatholicnews.com/news.php?viewStory=17731.

107. Ibid.

108. "About Us," Walkabout Foundation, https://walkaboutfoundation.org/about-us.

109. Scott Feinberg, "Bill Clinton Attends Premiere of 'The Way,' Cheers Film and Related Foundation," *The Hollywood Reporter*, October 7, 2011, https://www.hollywoodreporter.com/race/bill-clinton-attends-premiere-way-245255.

110. Ibid.

111. Hannah Goodwyn, "Emilio Estevez and Martin Sheen on Faith and Filming *The Way*," *CBN.com*, n.d., accessed August 11, 2015, http://www.cbn.com/entertainment/screen/emilio-estevez-martin-sheen-faith-the-way-goodwyn.aspx.

112. Ibid.

113. Stern, "Sheen Family's Epic Journey."

114. Steven D. Greydanus, "Martin Sheen and Emilio Estevez Travel the Ancient Pilgrimage Route Together and Finish their Journey of Faith with a Flourish," *National Catholic Register*, October 7, 2011, accessed August 9, 2015, http://www.ncregister.com/daily-news/sdg-reviews-the-way.

115. Ibid.

116. "The Catholic Way of Death & Burial," Catholic Cemeteries, Archdiocese of Washington website, accessed August 3, 2015, http://www.ccaw.org/wayofdeath_cremation.html.

117. Rose Pacatte, "The Way," *AmericanCatholic.org*, n.d., http://www.americancatholic.org/Entertainment/entertainment.aspx?id=13045.

118. Greydanus, "Martin Sheen and Emilio Estevez."

119. Ibid.

120. Francis Phillips, "Martin Sheen is a Better Actor than Theologian: The Actor, Like So Many Liberal Catholics, Seems to have Lost His Way," *Catholic Herald*, April 9, 2012, accessed August 9, 2015, http://www.catholicherald.co.uk/commentandblogs/2012/04/09/martin-sheen-is-a-better-actor-than-theologian/#.VcGD7XnMDoE.mailto.

121. Kathleen Gilbert, "Catholic Actor Martin Sheen: 'The Church is not God' on Gay 'Marriage' Issue," *Life Site News*, April 3, 2012, accessed August 9, 2015, https://www.lifesitenews.com/news/catholic-actor-martin-sheen-the-church-is-not-god-on-gay-marriage-issue, quoted in Phillips.

122. Phillips, "Martin Sheen is a Better Actor."

123. Ibid.

124. Kenneth R. Morefield, "The Way: A Poignant Drama about the Journey Toward Healing, Wholeness, and the Help We Find Along The Way," *Christianity Today*, October 7, 2011, accessed October 20, 2015, http://www.christianitytoday.com/ct/2011/octoberweb-only/way.html.

125. Ibid.

126. Ibid.

127. Ibid.

128. Roger Ebert, "The Way," *Rogerebert.com*, October 5, 2011, accessed October 20, 2015.

129. Ibid.

130. David Gritten, "The Way, Review," *The Telegraph*, May 12, 2011, accessed October 20, 2015, http://www.telegraph.co.uk/culture/film/filmreviews/8510077/The-Way-review.html. Note that Gritten used Donald Trump as a comparative figure five years before he was elected president.

131. Ibid.

132. David Roark, "The Way," *Paste*, October 10, 2011, http://www.pastemagazine.com/articles/2011/10/the-way.html.

133. Ibid.

134. *The Way*, Rotten Tomatoes, www.rottentomatoes.com.

135. Drake.

136. Kate O'Hare, "'The Passion of the Christ,' Mel Gibson and Hugging the Cactus," *CatholicVote.org*, March 11, 2014, accessed August 3, 2015, https://www.catholicvote.org/the-passion-of-the-christ-mel-gibson-and-hugging-the-cactus/.

137. Jerry Cobb, "Marketing 'The Passion of the Christ,'" *CNBC*, February 25, 2004, accessed July 30, 2015, http://www.nbcnews.com/id/4374411/ns/business-cnbc_tv/t/marketing-passion-christ/#.VbpsfXhNV6M.

138. Figures from boxofficemojo.com.

139. "Top 100 Pro-Catholic Movies," *National Catholic Register*, accessed July 30, 2015, http://www.ncregister.com/info/top_100_pro_catholic_movies/.

140. "'Passion of the Christ' is most controversial; *Entertainment Weekly* ranked films; 'Clockwork Orange' came in second," Today.com, June 9, 2006, accessed July 30, 2015, http://www.today.com/id/13231682#.VbpzmnhNV6N.

141. John 18:33–36 (NIV), reads: 33 Pilate then went back inside the palace, summoned Jesus and asked him, "Are you the king of the Jews?"

34 "Is that your own idea," Jesus asked, "or did others talk to you about me?"

35 "Am I a Jew?" Pilate replied. "Your own people and chief priests handed you over to me. What is it you have done?"

36 Jesus said, "My kingdom is not of this world. If it were, my servants would fight to prevent my arrest by the Jewish leaders. But now my kingdom is from another place."

142. Word on Fire website. See http://www.wordonfire.org/about/fr-robert-barron/.

143. Michael Medved, *Hollywood vs. America*. (New York: HarperPerennial, 1993), 3. According to the Internet Movie Database, the top ten highest grossing films of 1992 were a mixed bag of comedy, fantasy, violence, sequels, and sexuality. The top 10, in order from most popular, are: *Aladdin; Home Alone 2; Batman Returns; Lethal Weapon 3* (with Mel Gibson); *A Few Good Men; Sister Act; The Bodyguard; Wayne's World; Basic Instinct; A League of Their Own.* Boxofficemojo.com reports that movie ticket sales in 1992, the year Medved's book was published, were up by 2.9 percent.

144. Ibid., 52–53.

145. Michael Medved, "Reconciliation Should Follow Mel's Malibu Meltdown," *USA Today*, August 2, 2006, accessed August 5, 2015, http://usatoday30.usatoday.com/news/opinion/editorials/2006–08–02-gibson-edit_x.htm.

146. Ibid.

147. Neil Genzlinger, "A Trek From Loss and Grief to a Life Given Greater Meaning," *New York Times*, October 6, 2011, http://www.nytimes.com/2011/10/07/movies/the-way-directed-by-emilio-estevez-review.html.

148. Krista Tippett, "Spirituality of Imagination," *On Being*, December 17, 2015, https://onbeing.org/programs/martin-sheen-spirituality-of-imagination/8257/.

149. Robinson, "Martin Sheen & Emilio Estevez Interview."

150. Carol Frey, "The Quietly Positive Way," *News & Observer*, November 30, 2014, 19A.

151. Ibid.

III

Sacred and Profane Media

Copyrighting God

Translating, Publishing, Marketing, and Selling the Bible

And further, by these, my son, be admonished: of making many books there is no end; and much study is a weariness of the flesh.

—Ecclesiastes 12:12, KJV

INTRODUCTION

Americans own a boatload of Bibles. Most families who own Bibles often have more than one, usually in multiple versions. There is no one English Bible translation that suits all denominations, nor one that appeals to all adherents of a specific denomination. How important is the Bible in American life? A survey by the American Bible Society (ABS) and the Barna Research Group shows that, "80 percent of Americans view the Bible as sacred literature and 64 percent believe the Bible has more influence on humanity than any other text. Among adults who say their household owns a Bible, the median number they own is three."[1] ABS and Barna parsed that Bible ownership number: "Eighteen percent of Bible owners have one Bible; 33 percent own two to three; 24 percent have four or five; and another 24 percent own more than five."[2]

"The Bible business is booming," declared Daniel Silliman of the Heidelberg Center for American Studies. "There are annual sales of 40 million Bibles—from study Bibles to family Bibles to pocket Bibles. That's not even counting foreign markets."[3] As journalist Daniel Radosh has noted, "The familiar observation that the Bible is the best-selling book of all time obscures a more startling fact: The Bible is the best-selling book of the year, every year."[4]

Owning a Bible, or three, doesn't necessarily correlate with actually reading it. "Slightly more than one in four adults say they never read the Bible (28 percent). One in 10 read the Bible less than once a year and another one in 10 report reading the Bible once or twice a year. These three segments combine to represent 'non-Bible readers' (48 percent), a segment that has grown by two percentage points since 2014."[5] In 2015, a slight majority, 52 percent, reported reading the Bible one or more times a week, with older adults more likely to read it than Millennials. Segments of the population most likely to read the Bible include practicing Protestants and Catholics, Elders, African-Americans, residents of the South, and those making under $50,000 annually.[6]

"When it comes to the reasons people read the Bible, a relatively consistent majority of people does so because it draws them closer to God, though significant minorities in 2016 also point to a need for comfort (16 percent) or direction (16 percent)," according to Barna. "And although just one-third of Americans profess to reading the Bible at least once per week, the majority of Americans (62 percent) express a desire to read the Bible more often."[7]

That desire to read and understand the Bible extends beyond America's borders. More than 5 billion Bibles have been sold globally, and new editions are being sold in the United States every year.[8] "It is common knowledge that the Bible has been translated into more languages than any other piece of literature," the late Bible scholar Bruce M. Metzger wrote in his slim yet thorough volume, *The Bible in Translation: Ancient and English Versions.* "What is not generally appreciated, however, is the great increase in the number of different translations that have been produced relatively recently, that is, during the nineteenth and twentieth centuries," Metzger noted. "Before this period, the church, it must be confessed, had been rather slow in providing renderings of the Scriptures in other languages."[9]

With updates, corrections, and new translations, an accurate number of English-language versions of the Holy Bible is nearly impossible to determine, but the figure is in the hundreds. Not every language on earth has its own translation, but the Old and New Testaments (or Hebrew Bible and New Testament) have been translated whole or in part into more than 2,000 languages worldwide. And many of these translations carry a copyright.

This chapter explores the packaging and marketing of Bibles as commodities for the English-speaking spiritual marketplace, as well as the history of proprietary Biblical translations. Included are profiles of some of the companies, both for-profit and nonprofit, that produce and sell unique Bibles. Which English versions of the Holy Bible sell best in the United States, and what media corporations publish them? How do they differ? Why do people buy one Bible over another? Can you copyright the Word of God?

BUYING AND SELLING THE BIBLE

Selling the Holy Bible for a profit is not equivalent with mammon. There is nothing inherently immoral or greedy about charging customers for a book that costs money to translate, print, bind, distribute, upload, download, record, promote, and revise. Even Bibles given away by churches and organizations such as the Gideons must be paid for by *someone*, typically donors. The Bible is like most consumer media products, in that it is promoted in a variety of forms to appeal to many demographics. Bibles come in paperback, hardcover, leather, imitation leather, zipper pouches, in assorted colors and sizes, in audio versions, and on electronic readers, such as Amazon's Kindle or Barnes & Noble's Nook. There are several Bible apps. A cursory search on Amazon's "Bible Store" turns up nearly 45,000 products.[10] Christianbook.com (1–800-CHRISTIAN®; "EVERYTHING CHRISTIAN FOR LESS!") lists 12,500 Bibles.[11] Many Bibles contain extra material such as commentaries, concordances, meditations, even advice and instruction, all aimed at highly segmented audiences. "Special products" Bibles primarily target Christian audiences, a market segment that will be discussed in detail.

In her 2007 essay "Making Money, Saving Souls: Christian Bookstores and the Commodification of Christianity," Anne L. Borden interviewed four managers and proprietors of Christian bookstores in order to define the negotiation between business and ministry. Books and other products with Christian themes constitute a $4.6 billion industry, and reflecting this expanded line of religious merchandise, the Christian Booksellers Association, founded in 1950, now goes by the moniker of CBA.[12]

Borden notes that, "Christian lifestyle branding emerged as hip retail products came on the market."[13]

> Coffee Mugs, pencils, patches, and bumper stickers promoted sayings such as "God is Alive" and "Jesus Loves You." Some manufacturers borrowed directly from contemporary culture, producing products such as bumper stickers with the slogan "Jesus Christ, He's the real thing" in a style imitative of advertisements for Coca-Cola.[14]

Borden acknowledges the tensions in running a for-profit business with a sacred mission in a secular society. She outlines three Christian merchandising responses to secularization: *resistance, accommodation, and sacralization*. The bookstore manager or owner who practices *resistance* objects to certain materials, such as books that conflict with the proprietor's vision of Christianity. These materials may include certain types of music, such as Christian Hip Hop. *Accommodation* for Christian retail means stocking a variety of merchandise, some of it contradictory, and perhaps opening the shop on a Sunday. To illustrate *sacralization*, in which the bookstore may also operate as a ministry, Borden quotes an owner who sells what he calls "Jesus junk" alongside traditional spiritual books. Poseable Jesus figures, trendy tee shirts, and breath mints in the shape of crosses might fall into this category. "I'm a book and Bible man," the owner tells Borden. "I sell all this other stuff because people want it."[15]

Jerry B. Jenkins, best known for coauthoring the enormously successful *Left Behind* series of books (which in turn spawned movies, calendars, comics, and the like) with the late Reverend Tim LaHaye, in 1974 wrote a twenty-fifth anniversary history of the Christian Booksellers Association. "It's an exciting day to be in the business ministry of Christian bookselling," Jenkins wrote in the introductory chapter. "In the wake of the Jesus Movement of the late sixties and early seventies, distributors of Christian literature, music, jewelry and other products are continually meeting new challenges to reach people who are thirsty for knowledge of the Good News."[16]

"A sizable portion of the Protestant evangelical community has made its peace with commercial culture by deciding to become 'a bigger road side attraction,'" according to R. Laurence Moore and Carol Flake.[17] Moore identifies evangelist Dwight L. Moody's (1837–1899) brother-in-law Fleming H. Revell (1849–1931) as one of the first entrepreneurs to become wealthy by selling religious literature, including tracts of Moody's writings. "What Revell accomplished is apparent in Christian bookstores across the United States."[18] Moore cites early 1990s sales figures in the $200 million range, a benchmark by which to measure phenomenal growth in the now multibillion industry. Because of the wide array of merchandise—"greeting cards, coffee mugs, table mats, and frisbees (sic) with inspirational messages"—Moore observes that, "It is, in fact, difficult to wander through these bookstores and imagine any aspect of popular culture that has been left uncloned."[19] Bibles are often seen as personalized items, similar to other consumer goods we buy that fit and perhaps improve our lifestyle.

POPULAR AND BESTSELLING ENGLISH BIBLE TRANSLATIONS

Various English language Bible translations from original Greek, Hebrew, and Aramaic manuscripts are copyrighted, ostensibly so unauthorized changes cannot be made by rival publishers and sold as an "authorized" version, such as the Revised Standard Version (published 1952), the New King James Version (published 1982), the English Standard Version (published 2001), and so on. Royalties must be paid and permissions obtained when using or quoting these copyrighted religious texts, just as if a publisher other than Scholastic wanted to repackage a book from the *Harry Potter* series.

Muslim scholars and leaders maintain that the only way to understand the actual revelations and meaning of the Qur'an is to read the book in the original Arabic. English language editions of the Qur'an typically come with a caveat that warns the reader he or she is reading only an approximate translation of Muhammad's verses. Of English translations of the Hebrew Torah, Jewish writer Aviyah Kushner, author of *The Grammar of God: A Journey into the Words and Worlds of the Bible*, has written:

> Many English translations only translate the *pshat*, the simplest understanding of the Torah text itself, and do not translate commentary. . . . Instead, the English reader often encounters one single authoritative Biblical text, presented alone. . . . Reading translations should be seen as a window into what millions of readers throughout the world think and feel; at the very least, whether we are Jewish or Christian, religious or secular, we should all be talking about how the particular Bible we read affects what we believe, and how language and translation have shaped us all.[20]

Unlike adherents of the Qur'an or the Torah, Christian missionaries have historically held few such qualms about the Bible, eagerly translating it into the native tongue of whatever population they are attempting to evangelize— or colonize.

This is not to say that Christians are completely indifferent to which translation they use. New English versions and translations of the Bible appear in the United States for many reasons. Ongoing Bible scholarship contributes to scholars' understanding and interpretation of canon manuscripts, and archaeological digs reveal artifacts that place ancient writings in proper historical context. There is also the dynamic nature of language, as meanings shift over time, words become archaic, and early syntax becomes awkward for the modern ear.[21] These factors account for several contemporary English translations, some more successful than others. "The proliferation of Bibles underscores the anxieties people have about whether or not they are reading the right Bible," writes Silliman. "Concerns over accuracy and interpretation are especially true among religious traditions that distrust secular scholarship on the Bible."[22]

"It is estimated that there have been more than five hundred English translations of the Bible, and there has never been a time in American history when so many translations have been in widespread use at once," according to Radosh. "A large Christian bookstore may carry as many as fifteen, although the top six account for ninety-five per cent of sales . . . if a company wants to publish a study Bible or a devotional Bible using a modern translation, it will have to pay royalties to the owner of that translation. Commissioning a proprietary translation is often more cost effective in the long run, especially since it can be licensed out to other publishers."[23]

As Moore astutely observed, "Printing a new edition is an increasingly useful strategy to keep an old book selling."[24]

Each year, the International Christian Retail Show (ICRS) attracts between two and three thousand attendees, and awards are handed out by *Christian Retailing* magazine for top selling merchandise. At the 2016 ICRS in Cincinnati, for example, *Christian Retailing's* Best winners in the Bible categories were the *Jesus-Centered Bible*, a devotional from Group Publishing; *The Notetaking Bible*, by B&H Publishing Group; and *The Action Bible*, voted best in the Teen category and published by the nonprofit David C. Cook organization.[25]

Below in chronological order are the most *widely distributed* translations of the Bible into modern English (including the King James Bible) by version name, abbreviation, publication date, major revision dates, and publisher:

- Authorized King James Version (KJV) 1611 Various publishers
- American Standard Version (ASV) 1901 Thomas Nelson & Sons
- The Amplified Bible (AMP; Based on ASV with explanatory notes and references) 1965 Zondervan and the Lockman Foundation
- Revised Standard Version (RSV) 1947, 1952, 1959, 1971 Thomas Nelson & Sons
- New Jerusalem Bible (NJB) 1985 Doubleday
- New English Bible (NEB) 1970, 1989 Oxford University Press and Cambridge University Press
- New American Standard Bible (NASB) 1971, 1995 the Lockman Foundation
- Living Bible (LB) 1971 Tyndale House Publishers
- Good News Bible (GNB) 1976, 1992 American Bible Society
- New International Version (NIV) 1978, 1984 Zondervan
- New King James Version (NKJV) 1982 Thomas Nelson
- New Century Version (NCV) 1987 Worthy Publishing
- Contemporary English Version (CEV) 1995 American Bible Society
- New Revised Standard Version (NRSV) 1990 Oxford University Press
- New Living Translation (NLT) 1996, 2004 Tyndale House
- New English Translation Bible (NET) 2001, 2005 Biblical Studies Press
- English Standard Version (ESV) 2001 Crossway Bibles
- The Message (MSG) 2002 NavPress
- Holman Christian Standard Bible (HCSB) 2004 Broadman & Holman
- Today's New International Version (TNIV) 2005 Zondervan
- Common English Bible (CEB) 2011 Church Resources Development Corp (Joint Project of Disciples of Christ, Chalice Press; Presbyterian Church U.S.A., Westminster John Knox Press; Episcopal Church, Church Publishing Inc; United Church of Christ, Pilgrim Press; and United Meth-

odist Church, Abingdon Press. Abingdon Press is the sales distribution partner for the CEB.)[26]

Below is a list compiled by the Christian Booksellers Association (CBA) of the *top selling* Bible translations for 2014 based on dollar amounts:

1. New International Version (NIV)
2. King James Version (KJV)
3. New King James Version (NKJV)
4. New Living Translation (NLT)
5. English Standard Version ESV)
6. Holman Christian Standard Bible (CSB)
7. The Voice (a modern "contextual equivalent" translation)
8. New American Standard (NAS)
9. Reina Valera 1960 (Spanish language edition)
10. New International Reader's Version (NIRV; for ages 8 and up)[27]

In mid-2016, the *top ten bestselling individual Bibles* on the CBA list based on Christian retail store sales—followed by the name of the publisher—were:

1. *Church Bible*—NIV, Zondervan
2. *The Story* (Abridged, chronological NIV Bible that reads like a novel), Zondervan
3. *Inspire Bible*—NLT—(Elastic band closure; cloth cover), Tyndale
4. *New Testament and Psalms*—KJV, B&H
5. *Inspire Bible*—NLT—(Imitation leather), Tyndale
6. *Free on the Inside Bible*—NIRV, Zondervan
7. *Thinline Bible*—NIV, Zondervan
8. *Tiny Testament Bible*—NIV—(For christenings), Zondervan
9. *Thinline Bible*—NIV, Zondervan
10. *Tiny Testament Bible*—NIV, Zondervan[28]

The New International Version (NIV) has been the bestselling version of the Bible in the United States for decades, with more than 450 million copies in print.[29] The International Bible Society (IBS), which through various mergers has become part of Biblica, began work on the NIV in the late 1960s and published the first edition of an NIV New Testament in 1973. More about IBS and Biblica later in this chapter.

According to the American Bible Society's 2015 report:

> The New International Version is the preferred version of 13 percent of Bible readers, followed closely by the New King James Version (10 percent) and the English Standard Version (8 percent). All other translations are preferred by 3

percent or less of Bible readers . . . practicing Protestants are more likely than average to mention the New International Version (20 percent). Millennials are less likely to mention the King James Version (28 percent) and more likely to mention the English Standard Version (15 percent). Non-practicing Christians are more likely than average to own a copy of the King James Version.[30]

Note that seven of the bestselling Bibles are published by Zondervan, two by Tyndale, and one by B&H. Along with Thomas Nelson, these four companies are among the dominant names in Christian publishing. Repetitions on this bestseller list result from new printings and editions. The newer books may have similar or nearly identical content, but different ISBN numbers. Corporate ownership of Bible publishers will be discussed in more detail later in this chapter.

COPYRIGHT AND THE KING JAMES BIBLE

Copyrighting a unique translation of the Bible usually leads to making a profit, a financial motive that has led to criticism.[31] Australian patent and trademark attorney Roger Syn asks:

> If religious works can be owned as property, the question remains: is the Bible an exception? While the *laws* allowed the land and chattels to be held privately, it is inconceivable that Moses or the priests would have asserted ownership in the written *laws* themselves, including the Ten Commandments. Does the passage of years—admittedly thousands—change that principle? Bibles sold in bookshops today, after all, contain the laws Moses received on the fiery mountain. God's Word so personifies God Himself that the Bible says: "In the beginning was the Word, and the Word was with God, and *the Word was God.*" Who can *copyright God?*[32]

"Bible copyright, then, divides into two camps," Syn writes. "On one hand, Bible copyright may be justified because ownership is not claimed in the Bible, but merely a translation. On the other hand, many regard even a translation as still the Word of God."[33] Syn acknowledges that those who labor over translations and spend the money to publish a Bible have a right to remuneration. "Practically, it may come down to *how*, rather than *whether* copyright is administered." Even though Biblical copyright exists and others may violate it, Syn cites scripture to caution against lawsuits between believers.[34]

Of the King James Version (KJV), he says, "Over time, the premise of the Bible being free of copyright changed. For nearly three hundred years, the *Authorised Version* of 1611 remained the predominant translation used in churches. In 1881, English scholars produced a revision entitled the *English Revised Version.* This time, copyright was applied."[35]

Today, the 1611 King James Version is in the public domain. "In the United States, after the War of Independence of 1776, English patents were disregarded," according to Syn. "This caused the *Authorised Version*—still protected by royal patents—to enter the public domain outside the United Kingdom. Similarly, without English copyright protection, the *English Revised Version* was tampered with several times, so subsequent translations in the United States were copyrighted. In 1901, American scholars copyrighted the *American Standard Version*, and the *Revised Standard Version* of 1946."[36] The *New Revised Standard Version* "is an authorized revision of the Revised Standard Version, published in 1952, which was a revision of the American Standard Version, published in 1901, which, in turn, embodied earlier revisions of the King James Version, published in 1611."[37]

The text of the KJV is a manuscript translated between 1604–1611 by a committee appointed by England's King James I.[38] "Six panels of translators produced the work, forty-seven men meeting at Oxford and Cambridge with two from each panel as final reviewers," according to a detailed commentary on Biblical translation by Gerard S. Sloyan.

It was meant chiefly to replace the "Geneva Bible" of 1560, the work of William Whittingham, later Dean of Durham, and two other associates in Marian exile, Miles Coverdale, a former Augustinian, and the diocesan priest John Knox. This translation, which remained popular for a century, was dedicated to Queen Elizabeth I and contained extensive marginal notes redolent of the thought of Jean Cauvin and Théodore de Bèze. The English divines could not have suspected that it would sit ill with the queen who had not long been on the throne. It was the first translation in English to divide the Bible into numbered verses and included 1 and 2 Esdras and the six deuterocanonical books, all termed "Apocrypha." The virtue of the Geneva Bible was that it corrected many mistranslations of Hebrew words in previous English Bibles. It was followed shortly by the "Bishops' Bible" of 1571 (Coverdale's revision of the "Great Bible" of 1539), produced in an effort to diminish sales of the Geneva Bible.[39]

"The King James Version of the New Testament was based upon a Greek text that was marred by mistakes, containing the accumulated errors of fourteen centuries of manuscript copying."[40] That indictment of the KJV comes from the preface to the 1952 Revised Standard Version Bible by Thomas Nelson & Sons. New copyrighted translations build on previous ones. Translation work is still done by committees comprised of scholars, just as the KJV was translated by a scholarly meeting of minds.

KJV Bibles are now printed by a variety of publishers in both cheap and expensive editions, and some include additional copyrighted material, such as maps, charts, genealogies, photographs, and other supplements. Those elements are factored into the retail price. The KJV is currently the only translation used by the Church of Jesus Christ of Latter-day Saints (LDS). Since 1979, the church has published an LDS edition with cross-references to the *Book of Mormon*. There are also many independent Protestant churches and religious service organizations that prefer the seventeenth century KJV Bible.

GUTENBERG AND EARLY BIBLE PRINTING AND TRANSLATION

An exhaustive history of early scribal culture and the effect of Johannes Gutenberg's fifteenth century printing press on worldwide religious literacy are beyond the scope of this chapter, so this section offers a brief overview of historical media-related precedents leading up to today's lucrative U.S. Bible publishing industry.

Bible versions over the centuries have been translated from the Greek, Hebrew, Aramaic, or a combination of the three. Some are *formal equivalence* translations, meaning they mimic the linguistic rhythms of the original Hebrew and Greek manuscripts. Others are *functional equivalence* translations, conveying scripture through modern language or paraphrase for clearer understanding. *Optimal equivalence* offers word-for-word translation whenever original meanings are understandable to the modern ear.

"In sum, there is no such thing as a 'literal' translation from one language to another over the length of a biblical book," Sloyan says. "In the nature of the case, it is all a 'dynamic equivalence,' the philologists' term for saying a thing as one might say it in the receptor language. This leads to two conclusions. The first is that all renderings from one tongue to another are approximations. What the generality of people consider a 'good' translation is one that does not strike them amiss in their parent or first language. The practical norm applied to Bible translations by hearers or readers other than scholars of the ancient tongues and their cultures is: 'Does it make good English (French, Finnish) music in my ears?' The scholar asks that question in second place but another one in first: 'Does this Finnish/French sentence say what the sacred writer in Greek or Hebrew wished to say—neither more nor less nor other?'"[41]

"In Europe, Latin was the language of law, science and the Church," book historian Martyn Lyons has written. The Vulgate ("common version"), the fourth century Latin translation from the Greek and Hebrew by St. Jerome (347–420 C.E.), became the Catholic Church's official Bible in the 1500s. "Latin books accounted for 77 percent of all books printed before 1501 (known as the *incunabula*, from the Latin for 'cradle'). Initially, the invention of printing vastly increased production of books in Latin, especially religious books for the established Church. In 1546, the Council of Trent affirmed that the Latin Vulgate Bible was the only authentic version of scripture."[42]

Martin Luther (1483–1546), who translated the Latin Bible into a unifying German vernacular and popularized the notion of *sola scriptura* ("scripture alone"), was hardly the first reformer to defy Church authority over the Bible. Scholar Karen Armstrong writes:

> Marsilio of Padua (1275–1342) was incensed by the growing power of the established Church and challenged papal claims to be the supreme guardian of the Bible. Henceforth all reformers would link their dislike of popes, cardinals and bishops with a rejection of their claim to be the arbiters of exegesis. John Wycliffe (1329–84), an Oxford academic, became enraged by the corruption of the Church and argued that the Bible should be translated into the vernacular, so that the common people did not have to rely on the priesthood but could read the Word of God for themselves. . . . And William Tyndale (c. 1494–1536), who translated the Bible into English, raised the same issues: should the authority of the Church be greater than that of the gospel or should the gospel be elevated above the Church?[43]

An authorized English language version of the Bible for use in Catholic services came in the mid-twentieth century. "The Catholic Biblical Association, upon the publication of the encyclical letter of Pope Pius XII, *Divino Afflante Spiritu* (1943), turned to translating the entire Bible from the original languages. It was a first in English for that church. Successive portions were published under the Confraternity imprint in 1950, 1952, 1955 and 1961. The whole was completed in a fourth volume of 1968, the translation of *Samuel Through Maccabees*. Together with the newly translated New Testament, the *New American Bible* appeared in 1970."[44]

Fourteenth century Oxford cleric and scholar John Wycliffe (c. 1330–1384) is often credited with producing the first handwritten English translation of the Bible from Latin, "though recent scholarship suggests that he was not the actual translator but rather the inspiration and figurehead for that dangerous and secretive undertaking" by Wycliffe's assorted followers, according to Donna Butler and David F. Lloyd.[45] Wycliffe translations were outlawed by the church at the beginning of the fifteenth century, but copies still exist.

As Armstrong noted, William Tyndale (born c. 1492–94) became the first to translate the Bible into English from the original Hebrew. Author Steven M. Wise has praised Tyndale's writing as "extraordinary. His original Bible translations transformed English. Much of the verb-centered, monosyllabic cadence and plain Saxon that forged the beauty of the King James Version of the Bible—'take up they bed and walk,' 'let there be light,' 'salt of the earth,' 'my brother's keeper,' 'blessed are the peacemakers'—beg to be read aloud and were cribbed from Tyndale. Shakespeare knew Tyndale's work well."[46]

Because the Church condemned as heresy any English translations, Tyndale was strangled to death and his body burned in 1536.[47] Tyndale's friend Myles (or Miles) Coverdale is responsible for printing the first complete English edition of the Bible in 1535, borrowing heavily from both Latin sources and Martin Luther's accessible German translation of the previous year. Another Tyndale associate, John Rogers, published the 1537 *Matthew Bible* (aka *Matthew's Version* or *Matthew's Bible*) under the pseudonym Thomas Matthew.[48]

In between Wycliffe and Tyndale, introduction of the printing press into the Western world changed the very nature of books. For thousands of years, scribes wrote on scrolls, and later in bound volumes, and finer handwritten copies of manuscripts contained colorfully vivid illuminations. Books were relatively few and extremely precious prior to the invention of moveable type by Gutenberg in the 1450s.[49] The Gutenberg Museum in Mainz, Germany, located across a square from the city's 1,000-year-old St. Martin's Cathedral, contains the legacy of this native son. The museum contains many artifacts, including two rare copies of the first book Gutenberg printed for commercial sale in the 1450s: a 42-line, double-columned Bible, a Latin edition of the Vulgate. Fewer than 50 intact and partial copies of Gutenberg's Bible exist today.

In addition to fashioning letters and characters from metal rather than carved wooden blocks, Gutenberg used high quality paper for book pages, and he created the Textura typeface that mimicked the skilled handwriting of the painstaking copyists who came before him. "The scale of Gutenberg's achievements is inestimable," writes Simon Garfield in his book on typography, *Just My Type*. "He advanced not only the printing press but also new oil-based inks (thinner water-based inks failed to adhere to metal) in addition to what may be considered to be the first example of book marketing. He employed twenty assistants, some of them in a sales capacity; in an early version of the Frankfurt Book Fair in 1454, all 180 copies of his Bible were sold ahead of publication."[50]

Gutenberg borrowed heavily to finance his work, and eventually lost his print shop to creditor and partner Johann Fust. Although provided for by the local Archbishop in his later years, Gutenberg was unable to profit from his printing venture, despite the impact his inventions made upon the world. Many modern publishers have no such barriers to earning profits from various incarnations of the Bible.

MADE IN CHINA

Gutenberg printed Bibles in his native Germany, and other Bibles that followed were produced all over Europe. But where are most Bibles printed today? "Chances are good that your favorite Bible was printed in China," according to Sarah Eekhoff Zylstra writing in *Christianity Today*. Zylstra quotes Mark Bertrand of the Bible Design Blog as saying, "The overwhelming majority of Bibles sold at Christian bookstores or Barnes & Noble were printed there."[51] She continues:

> "A lot of people have misgivings about that," [Bertrand] said. "Some of it is, 'Oh, our Bibles are printed in Communist China.' Others are concerned about the economic situation, about what conditions these Bibles were produced under."
>
> The Chinese government's restriction of Bible distribution is also troubling, said ChinaAid's Bob Fu. "When brothers and sisters are being persecuted and arrested for their beliefs based on the same Bible, what does it mean to purchase an exported copy that says Made in China?"
>
> Since China's only legal printer of Bibles, Amity Printing Company, published its first Bible . . . 117 million Bibles have followed. More than half of those were printed in the last six years, including 12.4 million in 2013, making China the world's biggest Bible publisher. Three out of four of last year's Bibles were produced for export.[52]

"Amity Printing Company is a joint venture between the Amity Foundation and the United Bible Societies," according to Amity's website. "The company was established in 1988 with an ongoing mission and priority to serve the Christian church in China. Besides our domestic production, Amity is a major exporter of quality Bibles and presently exports internationally to satisfied customers in over 70 countries." Amity surpassed a milestone of 147 million Protestant and Catholic Bibles in April 2016, "in more than 90 different languages such as English, German, Spanish, and French, together with many African languages."[53]

Amity specializes in the thin, gilt-edged paper favored by many Bible publishers. The primary reason Bible printing is outsourced, though, is the same reason so many other manufactured products Americans use are imported from China: It's cheaper. As Zylstra writes:

> Choosing a printer comes down to "quality and competitive price," said Tim Bensen, a buyer at Tyndale House Publishers. "We print all over the world," he said. "Amity does good work."
>
> "Printing Bibles is more difficult than printing other types of books, and requires a certain amount of expertise," he said.[54]

Randy Bishop, director of Bible production at HarperCollins Christian Publishing, agrees. "Bibles have more steps in the production process," he said. "However, the main feature that makes a Bible unique is thin paper. It takes a special expertise to print, fold, gather, and bind Bible paper."[55]

An article in *China Daily* quoted longtime Amity employee Cai Yong-ping as saying the company carefully researched the type of paper it used. "A lot of people use their Bibles for many years, so the paper needs to remain intact even if the book is read frequently. The paper needs to be light, but it must not be too thin or the words on the other side of the page will be visible.

"When we receive orders from clients in mountainous countries and regions, we subject the paper to cold-temperature testing to ensure that it will not become brittle at high altitudes."[56]

CORPORATE MEDIA OWNERSHIP

In the 1980s, more than thirty companies controlled American media assets, including publishing houses, television networks, newspapers, magazines, radio stations, and movie studios. By the early 2000s, that number had dwindled to six conglomerates, each with an international reach. As of 2016, the Big Six were *National Amusements, Disney, TimeWarner, Comcast, News Corp, and Sony.*[57] With mergers and acquisitions being approved every few years, this lineup could shift, and the number of owners could shrink even further. In 2017, for example, AT&T was in negotiations to acquire Time-Warner.

Why is this relevant to Bible translations? Media consolidation means fewer voices and viewpoints control what the public sees, hears, and reads. Additionally, Bibles are a multi-billion-dollar business, and the companies who control Bible publishing also control the retail price of new Bibles. News Corp, the conglomerate run by Rupert Murdoch and his family, owns not only Fox News, Fox Sports, and most all other media named Fox, it also controls a large chunk of the Bible industry. This gives New Corp tremendous marketing power.

As discussed in the next section, News Corp not only publishes Bibles under its HarperCollins imprint, but purchased two additional longtime rivals in the Bible business, Zondervan and Thomas Nelson. Zondervan publishes the popular New International Version in the United States, which is consistently one of the top selling Bible versions in its various packaged incarnations.

MODERN BIBLE PUBLISHERS AND TRANSLATIONS

Britain's *Oxford University Press* dates to 1478—about a quarter century after Gutenberg's first Bible—and claims to be the world's largest university press.[58] Oxford's best-known Bibles are scholarly offerings such as *The Catholic Study Bible* (New American Bible, Revised Edition, or NABRE), which includes study guides, archaeology essays, glossary, and full color maps; *The New Oxford Annotated Bible* (NRSV), with maps, concordance, and index; and *The New Oxford Annotated Bible with the Apocrypha.*[59]

Major American media companies publishing English language Bibles include *HarperCollins* (owner of the *Zondervan* and *Thomas Nelson* imprints); *Tyndale; Crossway; B&H Publishing Group (Holman); Navpress* (operated by interdenominational ministry, The Navigators); and *Hendrickson Bibles.* There are others, but these are the Bible brands found most often in both Christian and secular bookstores. Brief descriptions below of each of these companies include examples of their Biblical products.

The easiest way to get into Bible publishing is to buy an existing Bible publisher. *HarperCollins Christian Publishing,* formed in 2012 and based in Nashville, Tennessee, is the corporate parent of legacy publishing groups *Thomas Nelson* and *Zondervan.* HarperCollins Christian Publishing's corporate parent is *HarperCollins Publishers,* whose corporate parent is Murdoch's *News Corp.*[60] Such are the vagaries of media mergers and acquisitions.

A brief history of the company's foray into religious publishing is outlined on the HarperCollins website:

> In 1798, Thomas Nelson founded his first publishing house in Edinburgh, Scotland, determined to make books, particularly Christian classics, affordable to the common man. In 1931, Pat and Bernie Zondervan began their publishing journey in Grand Rapids, Michigan, where they began buying and selling books and Bibles. HarperCollins Publishers [which dates to 1817] acquired Zondervan Publishers in the 1980s and Thomas Nelson in 2012, integrating the two similar, yet uniquely different, publishing groups under one leadership. Today, the strength of these great names—Thomas Nelson and Zondervan—continue to represent the highest quality in Christian publishing, creating the Company's foundation.[61]

The news of HarperCollins's acquisition of Thomas Nelson in 2012 "stunned many in the industry," according to *Publishers Weekly (PW).* Nelson and Zondervan were the two largest Christian publishers in the world at the time, and the purchase brought the longtime competitors under one corporate roof. The sales implications were staggering, though hard to pin down, as *PW* writer Lynn Garrett reported:

> Harper has another religion-focused unit—its HarperOne division publishes religion books aimed at the general trade and academic markets as well as a small complement of Bibles, including the New American Bible Revised Edition for Catholics and other specialty Bibles in the New Revised Standard Version.
>
> The Nelson acquisition would give HarperCollins a significant chunk of the religion trade and Bible markets, though how big that chunk would be is hard to quantify. The size of those markets is notoriously difficult to estimate;

books with religion content span many genres, and publishers define what is a religion book in different ways. Sometimes they choose not to categorize their books as religion at all, in part because of shelving issues. BookScan does not collect data from religion-specialty stores; generally the acquisition is estimated to capture about 70 percent of known sales in the category.

AAP and BISG, who coproduced the new BookStats report, now agree on an estimate of $1.4 billion for the size of the religion book market in 2010. Reliable Bible sales numbers are even more difficult to come by (BookStats doesn't break those out), but a conservative estimate by the Somersault Group, a consulting and publishing services agency formed by several Zondervan veterans, places unit sales at about 25 million annually.[62]

As Garrett indicated and research bears out, accurate figures for religious books, especially Bibles, can be elusive. Many of these books outsell trade books appearing on the *New York Times* bestseller lists. What is clear is that this market segment is a reliable revenue stream worth tens of millions of dollars to News Corp's bottom line. News Corp boasts annual revenues of more than $8 billion.[63] Revenues for HarperCollins hover around $1.6 billion.[64] The conglomerate's various subsidiaries are well positioned to create and promote new products for the Christian market for years to come.

The Thomas Nelson division (http://www.thomasnelson.com) has a dozen subcategories of Bibles befitting a commercially successful publisher: Audio, Bilingual, Children's, Daily, Devotional, Gift, Bible Handbooks, Large Print, Study, Women's, Teen & Student, and Art Journaling Bibles for note taking or doing "Bible art" as you read. This is typical of contemporary Bible publishing. Thomas Nelson Bibles also come in a variety of translations, although the New King James Version (NKJV) is the company's bestseller.[65]

Zondervan (http://www.zondervan.com) is the North American licensee of the immensely popular New International Version (NIV) of the Bible, and offers at least 18 categories of the 1978 NIV translation, including Travel Bibles (compact size), Bibles for Life Events (mourning, recovery, coping, marriage), and Bibles for New Believers (fast facts, scripture study). As the NIV story goes, "Howard Long, an engineer from Seattle, was known for his passion for sharing the gospel and his love for the King James Bible. One day, he tried sharing Scripture with a non-Christian—only to find that the KJV's 17th-century English didn't connect. In 1955, Long embarked on a ten-year quest for a new Bible translation that would faithfully capture the Word of God in contemporary English. Eventually his denomination, the Christian Reformed Church (CRC), and the National Association of Evangelicals (NAE) embraced his vision for the NIV."[66]

A cadre of scholars met in 1965 to create the NIV. "Instead of just updating an existing translation like the KJV, they chose to start from scratch, using the very best manuscripts available in the original Greek,

Hebrew, and Aramaic of the Bible," according to the Biblica website. Biblica, formerly called the New York Bible Society and then the International Bible Society before settling on its current name in 2009, declares that "Perhaps no other Bible translation has gone through a more thorough process to ensure accuracy and readability."[67]

Who initially paid for the New International Version to be created? According to Biblica:

> In 1968, Biblica (then the New York Bible Society) came on board as the NIV's financial sponsor, mortgaging its office space in Manhattan and New Jersey so that Howard Long's dream of a trustworthy, accessible Bible translation would become reality.
>
> Ten years later, the full NIV Bible was published. The initial print run of over a million copies sold out before they were even done printing. Such was the demand for an accurate, readable Bible. Dozens of evangelical denominations, churches, and seminaries embraced the NIV as their official Bible translation for preaching, study, public reading, and personal use.[68]

Biblica remains the worldwide publisher and copyright holder of the NIV. According to Zondervan, the Committee on Bible Translation meets annually to reevaluate the NIV text.[69]

In addition to the Zondervan and Thomas Nelson imprints, HarperCollins Christian Publishing is also home to Olive Tree Bible Software and Bible Gateway, "the world's largest Christian website."[70] Bible Gateway (https://www.biblegateway.com) "offers free access to the Bible in more than 80 languages and 170 different translations."[71] Finally, HarperCollins has carved out yet another market niche with Harper Bibles, and produces a New Revised Standard Version aimed at Catholic congregations called the *NRSV Catholic Edition*. Special features include scriptures in Catholic canonical order, lightweight Bible paper, and a time line of Church and world history.

LifeWay Christian Resources is the nonprofit retail arm of the Southern Baptist Convention (SBC). In its 2011 annual meeting, the SBC requested that LifeWay bookstores consider not selling the NIV Bible. The Baptists' complaint was that the NIV is partly inaccurate and too gender-inclusive. As Steve Young explained in the American Library Association trade journal *Choice* concerning similar complaints from evangelicals about the NRSV, "Thus, for example, 'brothers' is often translated 'brothers and sisters' when the translators judge the author to be addressing both men and women, with a footnote indicating the Greek word is 'brother.'"[72] Despite the nonbinding resolution, LifeWay trustees voted the next year to continue selling the NIV.[73] That turned out to be a good financial decision, as the NIV is a top selling translation.

B&H Publishing Group, an imprint of LifeWay, is a publisher for trade, church, and academic markets. B&H, also a non-profit, publishes the *Hol-*

man Christian Standard Study Bible and the *NIV Rainbow Study Bible*, which "has a unique color-coding system that allows readers to quickly and easily identify twelve major themes of Scripture throughout the text: God, discipleship, love, faith, sin, evil, salvation, family, outreach, commandments, history, and prophecy. . . . The No. 1 fully color-coded Bible with more than *2 million* combined units sold! [Boldface and exclamation point in original.]"[74]

Illinois-based *Crossway* (https://www.crossway.org) is another nonprofit Christian publisher that holds the copyright on the English Standard Version (ESV). In 1938, Christian printer Clyde Dennis and his wife Muriel began Good News Publishers in Minneapolis, Minnesota to distribute religious tracts to missionaries and others. "Within the first five years, Good News was distributing more than 50 million tracts each year."[75] Clyde died in 1962, and Muriel became president of Good News, serving until her death in 1993. Crossway Books was begun in 1979 and is run by the founders' son, Lane T. Dennis, who is also Chairman of the ESV Bible Translation Oversight Committee and Executive Editor of the ESV Study Bible.

"The vision for the ESV Bible began in the early 1990s as many evangelical Christian leaders saw a need for a new 'word-for-word' Bible translation—one that would be characterized by precision and literary excellence, in the classic stream of the Tyndale New Testament and the King James Version Bible," according to the Crossway website. "The ESV was created by a sixty-member team of the finest evangelical Bible scholars from around the world, with additional review and input provided by the sixty-member ESV Advisory Council," plus a "twelve-member Translation Oversight Committee."[76]

As with the NIV and other copyrighted versions, the translators who created the ESV claim authenticity, scriptural faithfulness, and accuracy.

Tyndale House Publishers, based in Carol Stream, Illinois, began when Kenneth Taylor paraphrased the Bible into modern English as a way to convey scripture to his 10 children, feeling the King James Version was too difficult for them to grasp. He self-published the first edition of *Living Letters* in 1962. When Taylor exhibited the book at the Christian Booksellers Association the following spring, evangelist Billy Graham spotted it and printed a special edition to give away via his televised crusades. Graham distributed 500,000 copies to television and stadium audiences, starting a phenomenon that grew into *The Living Bible*, which has now sold more than 40 million copies.[77] "The spirit of the era is best captured by an edition of the *Living Bible* put out under the title 'The Way' [1971], which features psychedelic lettering and photographs of shaggy-haired young people and describes Jesus as 'the greatest spiritual Activist who ever lived,'" Daniel Radosh wrote in *The New Yorker* magazine.[78]

NavPress is the publishing ministry of international Christian organization The Navigators. "The Navigators is an international, interdenominational Christian ministry established in 1933 as an outreach for followers of Jesus Christ to help others come to know and grow in Him as they navigate through life—a goal embodied by The Navigators trademarked motto, 'To Know Christ and to Make Him Known®.'"[79] NavPress entered into an alliance with Tyndale House in 2014 to improve distribution of their publications.[80]

The Message is NavPress's primary Bible product. "*The Message* is not a study Bible, but rather a reading Bible. It is a version of Scripture translated by Eugene H. Peterson and published by NavPress Publishing Group. The verse numbers, which are not in the original documents, have been left out of the print version to facilitate easy and enjoyable reading. The original books of the Bible were not written in formal language. The Message tries to recapture the Word in the language we use today."[81]

Born in Washington state in 1932, Peterson became a clergyman and author, and in 1962 was a founding pastor of Christ Our King Presbyterian Church in Bel Air, Maryland. After his retirement in 1991, Peterson began work on an ambitious novel-like rendering of the Bible in plain English that was called *The Message*. In his introduction to *The Message: The New Testament in Contemporary Language*, Peterson writes that in the Greek-speaking world of Jesus's time, the stories, letters, and poetry that make up the New Testament were written in "the common, informal idiom of everyday speech, street language."[82] Peterson's version of the New Testament was published in 1993, and the complete *Message* Bible was published in 2002. Peterson goes on in his introduction to explain that:

> This version of the New Testament in a contemporary idiom keeps the language of the Message current and fresh and understandable in the same language in which we do our shopping, talk with our friends, worry about world affairs, and teach our children their table manners. The goal is not to render a word-for-word conversion of Greek into English, but rather to convert the tone, the rhythm, the events, the ideas, into the way we actually think and speak.[83]

Below is an excerpt of Peterson's retelling of the birth of Jesus Christ from the Gospel of Matthew:

> The birth of Jesus took place like this. His mother, Mary, was engaged to be married to Joseph. Before they came to the marriage bed, Joseph discovered she was pregnant. (It was by the Holy Spirit, but he didn't know that.) Joseph, chagrined but noble, determined to take care of things quietly so Mary would not be disgraced.[84]

In a 1995 interview with *The Mars Hill Review*, Peterson describes the gene-sis of *The Message*, which began with a phone call from Jon Stine, who became Peterson's editor at NavPress:

> [Stine] said, "Remember *Traveling Light*, the book you wrote on Galatians? Well, I cut out all the paraphrased parts, Xeroxed them together and I have been carrying them around for ten years showing it to all my friends. I'm just getting really tired of Galatians. Would you paraphrase the whole New Testament?"
>
> Well, it took me a year to do Galatians, so I thought how could I ever do the whole New Testament. He called me three or four months later when in the meantime, for unrelated reasons, I had decided to resign from my parish. . . . I agreed to do ten chapters of Matthew at which time John would show it to his colleagues to see what they thought. . . . Because I love language, I love words, I have always read my Bible in Hebrew and Greek as an adult. So I was always trying to get those languages into American, especially in my preaching and teaching. So as I was doing the Message I often had the feeling of harvest. . . . In some ways it was easy, like walking through an orchard and picking apples off of a tree. [85]

Criticism of Peterson's radical rhetorical approach to scripture has come from various quarters. "Peterson's 'para-translation' of the Bible, *The Mes-sage: The Bible in Contemporary Language*, was published over a span of nine years, from 1993 to 2002," Cathleen Falsani wrote in *Sojourners* maga-zine in 2012. "And even a decade after its completion, critics still are debat-ing the merits and missteps of his translation of Holy Writ into idiomatic, sometimes colloquial, modern English."[86]

"This book should be recognized for what it is," declares Michael Mar-lowe, editor of the *Bible Research* website. "It began as a stimulating para-phrase of the Epistle to the Galatians included in a popular devotional book, and it remains a piece of stimulating devotional literature. But it is not the Word of God."[87]

"*The Message* is not only a poor paraphrase, but it is, in fact, heretical," writes conservative Christian blogger Justin Peters. Peters lives in South Africa and calls his blog, *For the Love of His Truth: A Christian Blog about Fundamental Biblical Facts*. "The question must be asked, 'Would Jesus Christ approve of this rendering of His word?' Certainly any honest intellec-tual assessment would have to lead one to the answer of 'no.'"[88]

An early review of *The Message* by John R. Kohlenberger III in *Christian Research Journal* declares that "not everything in *The Message* should be treated as gospel. . . . So how are we to view *The Message*? It is an expansive paraphrase that is not so labeled, as is *The Living Bible*. Beset with inconsis-tencies, its idiom is not always 'street language'; its terminology is often idiosyncratic to its author. . . . Because of its interpretive and idiosyncratic nature, *The Message* should not be used for study."[89]

"Most of the criticism comes from people who don't understand language," Peterson told Falsani in 2012. "I have to explain to them what a metaphor is. . . . But I try to be courteous and gentle and try to explain what I did."[90]

The goal of creating an approachable Bible that people will actually read is an old impulse. A number of condensations and formats akin to Peterson's have been tried, including one that appeared in 1933 called *The Short Bible: An American Translation in Brief*, edited by Edgar J. Goodspeed and J.M. Powis Smith. A review from the November 11, 1933 *The Literary Digest* magazine notes that "The 2,000 pages of the Standard Bible are reduced to 546 in the short, or a little more than one-fourth."[91] Goodspeed and Smith began the *Short Bible* with the Book of Amos, placing Genesis, traditionally the first book of any Bible, seventeen chapters in. The argument was that the arrangement places the included books in the chronological order in which they were *written*.

"To the man in the street the Short Bible may serve as an introduction to the source of all Christian authority and to the inspiration of English literature," according to *Literary Digest*. "If it does that, it will have served well."[92]

BIBLE SOCIETIES

Bible societies are in the business of translating the Gospel into other languages and placing Bibles in the hands of as many people as possible for evangelistic purposes. Below are snapshots of four such organizations, *The American Bible Society, The United Bible Societies, The International Bible Society*, and *The British and Foreign Bible Society.*

The American Bible Society (ABS) is a 200-year-old nonprofit based in Philadelphia with the mission of making "the Bible available to every person in a language and format each can understand and afford, so all people may experience its life-changing message."[93] ABS has been around since 1816, and first gave Bibles to the U.S. military the following year. In 1842, they provided the first Bibles in braille for the blind, and produced the first audio Bibles on records in 1934. ABS describes its activities this way:

WE SEE A SOLUTION
We work with a global network of partners
to reach the unreached, helping all people engage

> by TRANSLATING the Bible where no translation exists
> by DISTRIBUTING the Bible to people who long for their first copy
> by RESTORING broken lives through God's Word
> by EQUIPPING local leaders to share the transforming power of God's
> Word

by ADVOCATING for the Bible to play a role in culture[94]

The Society rose to prominence 150 years after its founding with the 1966 publication of *Good News for Modern Man: The New Testament and Psalms in Today's English Version*, "a Bible for the young and disaffected," according to Radosh. "It resembled a mass market illustrated paperback novel. A year later, five million copies were in print."[95] That number reached 30 million by 1971, and is now well over 100 million.[96] ABS also has a 45,000-volume collection of Bibles, the largest outside the Vatican.[97] The society hit a low point when it came under criticism for questionable fundraising and spending, and in 2015 moved from its pricy 12-story Manhattan headquarters to Philadelphia, leaving New York for the first time in its history.[98]

According to John Fea, author of *The Bible Cause: A History of the American Bible Society*:

> *Good News for Modern Man* was the brainchild of Eugene Nida, an ABS linguist who pioneered the "dynamic equivalence" approach to Bible translation. At the heart of this theory is the idea that the best translation of a Bible text is one that allows readers to forget they are reading a translation at all. Nida was one of the first Bible translation theorists to take the linguistic position of the reader this seriously. A good translation, he argued, would arouse in the reader the same reaction that the writer of the text hoped to produce in his "first and immediate" readers.[99]

Bible translator and former Southern Baptist Missionary Dr. Robert G. Bratcher created Today's English Version (TEV) for the ABS *Good News Bible* (GNB). "This Translation of the New Testament has been prepared by the American Bible Society for people who speak English either as their mother tongue or as an acquired language," according to the ABS. "As a distinctly new translation, it does not conform to traditional vocabulary or style, but seeks to express the meaning of the Greek text in words and forms accepted as standard by people everywhere who employ English as a means of communication."[100] Since 2001, the TEV has been known in the United States as the Good News Translation (GNT).

An example of The Lord's Prayer from the TEV/GNT: "Father: May your holy name be honored; may your Kingdom come. Give us day by day the food we need. Forgive us our sins, because we forgive everyone who does us wrong. And do not bring us to hard testing."[101]

The GNT has had its share of criticism for being too loose with scripture. "Some scholars thought Bratcher's translation was simplistic, pitched at too low a level of reading ability," according to Fea. "Evangelical scholars worried that a thought-for-thought translation rather than word-for-word translation amounted to a paraphrase of scripture and undermined the conviction that every single word of the Bible is inspired by God."[102] Despite some opposition, Fea writes, *"Good News for Modern Man* set the stage for other dynamic equivalence Bibles and paraphrases such as *The Message*, *The Voice*, *The New International Version*, and *The New Living Translation*. It spurred a rise in Bible sales in the early 1970s, and made the American Bible Society a household name among Christians."[103]

The ABS also publishes the Contemporary English Version (CEV), which is in even simpler English than the TEV/GNT. Citing statistics by the National Center for Education on rates of adult literacy, the ABS determined that "a contemporary translation must be a text that an inexperienced reader can *read aloud* without stumbling, that someone unfamiliar with traditional biblical terminology can *hear without misunderstanding*, and that everyone can *listen to with enjoyment* because the style is lucid and lyrical (italics in original)."[104]

The United Bible Societies "is a global network of Bible Societies working in over 200 countries and territories across the world," according to the UBS website. Translation is an ongoing activity for UBS. "We believe the Bible is for everyone so we are working towards the day when everyone can access the Bible in the language and medium of their choice."[105] Founded in 1946 by Bible societies from more than a dozen countries, the England-based UBS is involved with hundreds of translation projects around the globe. The UBS Mission Statement is simple: "The reason our fellowship of Bible Societies exists is to equip churches worldwide to share God's Word."[106]

Since 1950, UBS has published a refereed journal called *The Bible Translator*, the only such journal "dedicated to the theory and practice of Bible translation."[107] In the UBS tradition of keeping pace with the times, the Digital Bible Library® (DBL) is an online digital licensing management platform developed and maintained by the United Bible Societies. "It is the largest Scripture database with 1,276 total Bible translation items available. . . . Thanks to DBL access, technology developers can create apps that can switch between 422 full Bibles, 800 New Testaments and 54 portions for reading, search and comparison of texts."[108]

As discussed earlier, *The International Bible Society* began life as the New York Bible Society (NYBS) in 1809, predating ABS by seven years. The organization changed to the global name in 1983 to reflect its expanded mission. In 2007, IBS and the British Christian organization Send the Light (STL) merged, and on the 200th anniversary of the society, changed its name to *Biblica*.[109] According to the Biblica website, "Today, Biblica works in 55 countries in six regions of the world. Our global ministry continues to impact various groups such as children, at-risk teens, the unreached, disaster survivors, prisoners, and refugees. Biblica has translated, published, and provided more than 650 million Bibles and biblical resources to bring the good news of God's love and mercy to people worldwide."[110] Biblica, as noted previously, created the New International Version.[111]

The British and Foreign Bible Society, now simply called Bible Society, formed in London in 1804. A founder was British abolitionist William Wilberforce (1759–1833), who became a Christian in his 20s. Focusing on worldwide Bible translation and distribution, the Bible Society, like ABS, is celebrating 200 years of existence. Bible Society has established local Bible Societies in 146 countries.[112]

CREATING AND MARKETING SPECIAL PRODUCTS BIBLES

The concept of creating and copyrighting new Bibles for niche markets is not itself new. "Bibles were commodities in nineteenth-century America," wrote Colleen McDannell in her 1995 book Material Christianity: Religion and Popular Culture in America. "Publishers revamped the Bible, moving it out of the 'unchanging' realm of religion and into the 'ever new' realm of fashion. In doing so they designed Bibles significantly different from those mass distributed by the American Bible Society. Publishers made their Bibles convey messages about status and taste, in addition to spiritual uplift."[113] Bibles for the home were created with pages for family records and photographs, and often had pictorial elements such as illustrations of scenes from scripture.

Such innovations continue more than a century later. "The popularization of the Bible entered a new phase in 2003, when Thomas Nelson created the BibleZine," according to Daniel Radosh.[114] Radosh quotes a story told by Wayne Hastings, then-senior vice president and publisher for the Bible Division of Thomas Nelson Publishers in Nashville:

> Wayne Hastings described a meeting in which a young editor, who had conducted numerous focus groups and online surveys, presented the idea. "She brought in a variety of teen-girl magazines and threw them out on the table," he recalled. "And then she threw a black bonded-leather Bible on the table and said, 'Which would you rather read if you were sixteen years old?'" The result was "Revolve," a New Testament that looked indistinguishable from a glossy girls' magazine. The 2007 edition features cover lines like "Guys Speak Their Minds" and "Do U Rush to Crush?" Inside, the Gospels are surrounded by quizzes, photos of beaming teen-agers, and sidebars offering Bible-themed beauty secrets:
>
> "Have you ever had a white stain appear underneath the arms of your favorite dark blouse? Don't freak out. You can quickly give deodorant spots the boot. Just grab a spare toothbrush, dampen with a little water and liquid soap, and gently scrub until the stain fades away. As you wash away the stain, praise God for cleansing us from all the wrong things we have done. (1 John 1:9)"[115]

Revolve was a success, and Thomas Nelson followed up with *Refuel* for boys, *Blossom* for tweens, *Real* for urban youth that came with a CD of Christian rap, and *Divine Health* with notes by Don Colbert, MD author of *What Would Jesus Eat?*[116] By 2007, only four years after *Revolve* was conceived, Thomas Nelson had sold well over two million BibleZines.[117]

To illustrate what R. Laurence Moore meant when he wrote that it's difficult to "imagine any aspect of popular culture that has been left uncloned"[118] by religion, consider these other creative specialty products Bibles:

- *Extreme Faith Bible: God's Word Knows No Bounds* (CEV, American Bible Society) has a skydiver, a skater, and a rock climber on the cover, all holding a Bible in one hand as they practice their sports. This paperback ABS Bible is in the Contemporary English Version. An excerpt from the story of the adulterous affair between King David and Bathsheba provides a sample of the simplistic, modernized language, resembling a transcript from *The Maury Povich Show*: "She came to him, and he slept with her. Then she returned home. But later, when she found out that she was going to have a baby, she sent someone to David with this message: 'I'm pregnant!'" 2 Samuel 11:4–5, CEV.[119]

- *Teen Study Bible* (NIV, Zondervan) is a hardcover book that has a busy and abstractly colorful dust jacket that resembles a megachurch preacher's tee shirt. This Zondervan product is an exercise in self-promotion, with taglines such as, "#1 SELLING BIBLE FOR TEENS," and "New International Version: Most read. Most trusted." The interior front flap tells a potential buyer that the Bible "has been updated for a NEW GENERATION!" This is the Bible that "will accelerate your faith, getting you up to speed with God and moving your spiritual growth into the fast lane!" All that before you explore inside. Many Bibles have a space for dedications or writing an owner's name. The *Teen Study Bible* has a page for personalization that encourages teens to list "My best feature," "Things I'm good at," "The Bible character most like me," and so on. This allows the Bible to serve as a youthful diary of sorts. Features inserted throughout the text by husband and wife Christian authors Larry and Sue Richards continue this relational tone. Slick pages highlight Bible verses that teens may be able to identify with, such as music: "It is good to praise the Lord and make music to your name (Psalm 92:1)." Another inserted page asks, "What was it like to actually live in Biblical times?" A list includes walking to wells for water, shopping in open markets instead of malls, bathing only once a week, no college, and "Hubs of culture (church, family, etc.) Hmmm, sound familiar?"[120] The Bible also has textbook-like features such as introductions to each book; eight pages of color maps; Bible quizzes; and an explanation of the Apostle's Creed. [121]

- The *Operation Worship Holy Bible* (NLT, Tyndale House) is a mass market paperback Bible targeted at military personnel. Individual churches often buy the Bibles in bulk, paste a bookplate in the front, and ship them to wherever random soldiers are serving. The coated paper cover is in camouflage colors and resists dampness, and inside the typeface is miniscule to keep the overall book size small. This compact Bible is produced by Tyndale in partnership with the nonprofit Open Window Foundation, parent company of the Operation Worship ministry. The ministry has historically shipped 50,000–70,000 Bibles a year, and declared on its website that demand tripled in 2015–2016 due to printing technology that now permits the cover of the Bible to be customized to include the insignia of a specific unit within a branch of the military. [122]

- *The One Year Bible* (NIV, Tyndale House) also comes in mass market paperback size and is arranged by calendar date for 365 daily readings. Each date has a selection from the Old Testament, the New Testament, Psalms, and Proverbs. The Bible can be read straight through, used as a reference, or utilized as a daily devotional. [123]

- *Fellowship of Christian Athletes Coach's Devotional Bible: Daily Game Plans for Coaches* (CSB, Holman Christian Standard Bible) is exactly what it sounds like—a devotional Bible to be used by high school and college coaches associated with FCA. The Holman Christian Standard Bible is a copyrighted translation. In addition to the 66 books of the Old and New Testaments, there is a year's worth of daily inspirational essays written by secondary and college coaches from various sports around the country. The Bible comes in a colorful cardboard gift box. [124]

- *The Green Bible: Understand the Bible's Powerful Message for the Earth* (NRSV, HarperOne, and imprint of HarperCollins) is a variation on the "red-letter" editions of the Bible that printed in bright red the words spoken directly by Jesus Christ. This "green-letter" Bible uses a light green color for references to nature, the environment, and the earth, from Genesis to Revelation. Example of a "Green" passage: "It is he who made the earth by his power, who established the world by his wisdom, and by his understanding stretched out the heavens." [125] Printed in the United States on paper that is 10 percent post-consumer content, its "all-natural 100 percent cotton/linen cover material is produced in a green friendly environment (all air is purified before exhausting into the atmosphere and all water is purified and recycled)." [126] The Foreword is by South African

Bishop Desmond Tutu, and the Bible opens with nature verses from St. Francis of Assisi and American environmentalist/farmer/author Wendell Berry.

• *The Poverty and Justice Bible: Catholic Edition* (NRSV, The British and Foreign Bible Society), though from a different publisher, is a variation on *The Green Bible.* Passages allegedly depicting aspects of poverty and social justice issues are highlighted in orange. When you browse the pages of *The Poverty and Justice Bible,* you can be forgiven for thinking you are looking at a used copy. The orange highlighting is ragged left and right, simulating handwritten marker swipes. An example of a highlighted passage is Luke 4:18: "The Spirit of the Lord is upon me, because he has anointed me to bring good news to the poor. He has sent me to proclaim release to the captives and recovery of sight to the blind, to let the oppressed go free."[127] The center of the Bible features 32 pages printed on heavy stock titled "The Core," featuring inspirational commentary and quotes from U2 musician Bono and *Purpose Driven Life* author and televangelist Rick Warren, among others. The Core is essentially a call to action. Declaring that "God cares passionately about issues of poverty and justice," the Bible challenges readers to focus on these issues "in 3-D": Discover, Dream and Do. "Find out about the issue. Dig into the Scriptures . . . Reflect on the issues . . . Get your hands dirty and get involved! And, of course, pray."[128] The Catholic edition of this Bible includes the Apocrypha as well as a preface explaining that the order of the books is based on the fourth and fifth century Latin Vulgate translation by St. Jerome.

Zondervan also released an audio Bible with an all-black cast called *Inspired By The Bible Experience: The Complete Bible.*[129] Performers included Samuel Jackson as God, with Blair Underwood (Jesus), Forest Whitaker (Moses), Angela Bassett (Esther), Cuba Gooding, Jr. (Jonah), Denzel and Pauletta Washington (Song of Songs), LL Cool J (Samson), Eartha Kitt (Serpent), Bishop T. D. Jakes (Abraham), and Bishop Eddie L. Long (Joel). "The cast is all black," wrote religion writer Ann Rodgers in the *Pittsburgh Post-Gazette,* "but Zondervan has not marketed it as a Bible for African-Americans— figuring, instead, that people of all colors will want to hear Denzel Washington and his wife, Pauletta, for example, read the erotic Song of Songs . . ."[130]

KICKSTARTING SCRIPTURE: THE BIBLIOTHECA BIBLE PROJECT

On June 27, 2014, Santa Cruz, California book designer and graphic artist Adam Lewis Greene launched a campaign on the crowd-funding site Kick-

starter.com to create and sell a new Bible. Greene called the project Bibliotheca, a Latin word meaning "a collection of books."[131] His idea was simple.
He wanted to design a high quality, long-lasting, reader-friendly edition of
the Bible: "The Biblical Literature elegantly designed & crafted for enjoyable reading, separated into volumes, and free of all numbers, notes, &c."[132]
In other words, abandon the reference format and make the Bible into a
narrative, like any trade fiction or nonfiction book.

"People love stories," Greene said in a video posted on the Kickstarter
site. "Could it be that the encyclopedic nature of our contemporary Bibles is
what's driving this idea that the Biblical literature is dry and boring? There
should be an alternative. We should be able to experience these texts in their
original forms as literary works of art, and we should be able to sit down and
lose ourselves in them like we would any good book, or any classic literature."[133]

Compacting the entire Biblical library into one thick volume is an idea
from the Middle Ages, he said, and the time has come to separate them.[134] As
the late Harvard University Preacher and Professor Peter J. Gomes explained
in *The Good Book*, "The Hebrew Bible is organized somewhat differently
from what Christians call the Old Testament. The first five books are called
The Law. The Prophets are divided into The Former Prophets, which include
Joshua, Judges, Samuel, and Kings, The Latter Prophets, composed of Isaiah,
Jeremiah, and Ezekiel, and those prophets called The Twelve, comprising
Hosea, Joel, Amos, Obadiah, Jonah, Micah, Nahum, Habakkuk, Zephaniah,
Haggai, Zechariah, and Malachi." The third section of the Hebrew Bible is
called The Writings, consisting of 12 books, including Psalms and Proverbs.[135] Rabbinical councils assembled the Biblical canon of works that
evolved over time between 70 and 135 C.E. "When Jesus refers to the Scripture, and New Testament Jewish Christians speak of the Law and the Prophets, it is this Bible of which they speak," Gomes wrote.[136]

In his book, *Walking the Bible: A Journey by Land Through the Five
Books of Moses*, author Bruce Feiler summarizes the assemblage of the Hebrew Bible this way: "There are thirty-nine books in the Hebrew Bible. The
books are divided into three categories: the Law (*torah*), the Prophets
(*nevi'im*), and the Writings (*ketuvim*). The Hebrew term for the Bible, *tanakh*, is an acronym for these groups."[137]

The Five Books of Moses that comprise the first five books of the Bible—
Genesis, Exodus, Leviticus, Numbers, Deuteronomy—along with the other
34 books, make up the Hebrew Bible canon. "Early followers of Jesus added
five narratives, twenty-one letters, and a book of visions [Revelation]. Originally, these were viewed as addenda to the Hebrew Scriptures, but as they
gained in importance, Christians began calling the earlier books the 'Old
Testament" and the supplement the 'New Testament,'" notes Feiler.[138]

"The Hebrew Bible is what scholars of all persuasions used to call the 'Old Testament,'" writes poet, biographer, essayist, and translator David Rosenberg, "but that Christian designation is falling away, since *Tanakh* has always been far more than a testament. It is a honed library of thirty-nine books written in the language of ancient Israel, Hebrew (with the tiny exception of a few late passages in Aramaic)."[139]

Greene's custom designed four-volume Bibliotheca set is divided thusly:

Volume One: The Five Books of Moses & The Former Prophets
Volume Two: The Latter Prophets
Volume Three: The Writings
Volume Four: The New Testament

Before and after the advent of printing, Greene said in his video pitch, the notion that a Bible is "holy and set apart" was reflected in the careful selection of paper, ink, and even handwriting. Bibliotheca Bibles would be printed in Germany—just as Gutenberg's were—on fine opaque paper, and the bindings sewn rather than glued. Each volume will lie flat, he said, and the text will be in a specially designed font. As noted above, all footnotes, chapter, and verse numbers will be removed, akin to Peterson's paraphrased *Message* Bible, but with more precision in the complete translation.[140] Greene selected the American Standard Version, a translation decision that will be discussed later. The result, he said, will be a reading experience that is "pure," "elegant," and "simple."

"I want to give people the opportunity to read the Biblical library with a fresh set of eyes," Greene says. "To sort of experience it anew."[141] His solicitation was straightforward:

> If this is something that you're excited about and want to see it made, and you want to hold it in your hand, or you want to give it to your friend or your family member, then this is something that I'm asking you to contribute to.[142]

Greene needed $37,000 to create 500 sets of print Bibles, four volumes in each set, a modest total of 2,000 books. He reached that goal the next day, and still had 28 days of fundraising left to go. Sounding surprised and delighted, he posted a written update on his Kickstarter site:

> We have now far exceeded the goal and are currently the 9th most popular Kickstarter project in the wide world. Again, I want to thank all of you for the support, kind words, encouragement, great questions, and lengths you've gone in spreading this around the world.
>
> I am excited to watch this project expand its reach over the next 28 days.[143]

The orders continued to pour in. After numerous inquiries, Greene decided to offer the New Testament as a stand-alone volume rather than require all backers to purchase a set of four books, the first three containing sections of the Old Testament. He posted a separate update for international backers, asking for patience and saying shipping fees may be prohibitive in some areas.

Potential backers both foreign and domestic who didn't understand that Kickstarter campaigns require pledges paid up front—even after a goal is met—received an explanatory update on June 30 from Greene, who by this point was slightly overwhelmed and continually grateful.

> Everyone,
>
> It seems that there are many who don't know that in order to get the set you have to contribute to the Kickstarter now. Since it is fully funded it is definitely going to happen, and now it is, in effect, a limited-time pre-order.
>
> In other words, there is no guarantee that this set will be available again after the campaign.
>
> I would appreciate any of you who would help me make that more clear as we continue to share!
>
> Again and again, thank you,
>
> —Adam[144]

After five days, Bibliotheca garnered $100,000. By July 12, the project was funded at 540 percent of the original goal, with $200,000 pledged by nearly 2,000 people. By July 25, more than 10,000 people had pledged a total of a million dollars. Greene added a "stretch goal" for this milestone, offering the Deuterocanonical Books, or Apocrypha, as a fifth volume for all who had previously ordered full sets. The final tally on July 27, the closing day of the campaign, was $1,440,346 from 14,884 backers.[145]

Why did a Bible—in a world filled with Bibles—sell that well? The tale of Bibliotheca's success illustrates four things: *1)* there is still a market for well-made print books; *2)* the internet is a powerful sales tool that enables anyone to reach a global audience; *3)* crowdfunding on platforms such as Kickstarter can be an effective online fundraising tool for appealing ideas and products; *4)* no one can predict with certainty which ideas and products will catch fire.

The Bibliotheca project attracted both religious and mainstream press attention. "Introducing the Bible! Now with Less!" screamed a teasing headline in *Christianity Today*, the evangelical magazine founded in 1956 by the Reverend Billy Graham. Reporter Sarah Eekhoff Zylstra zeroed in on two points covered by most other news media writing about Greene: the rapidity of his fundraising and the nature of the text design. "Greene's project, named *Bibliotheca*, is a (mostly) American Standard Version Bible (with the '*thees*' and '*thous*' replaced). But what's catching attention is the layout. Unlike most Bibles printed since Gutenberg, Greene's version has one column, wide margins, a large typeface, and no notes or chapter marks."[146]

"The Bible is sometimes called the greatest story ever told. Its typography, on the other hand, leaves much to be desired," John Brownlee wrote in *Fast Company*, a business magazine. "The idea behind Bibliotheca is simple: What if we printed the Bible as if it were just another long book?"[147]

"'Bibliotheca' Bible Project Blows Up On Kickstarter With Chapterless Bible," was the title of a story on Huffington Post Religion by Associate Editor Yasmine Hafiz. Hafiz quotes three Biblical scholars about the project, including Greg Carey, a professor of New Testament at Lancaster Theological Seminary. "Many of the biblical books were composed as literature rather than for reference purposes: this edition honors that reality," Carey said.[148]

Delivery dates for Greene's Bibles came and went, and in mid-2016, the two-year mark passed. The delays were the result of a combination of factors, including the massive response and the care with which Greene and his small staff took in selecting the vendors and materials. Several Bibliotheca backers expressed their dismay in the comments section of Greene's occasional posts. In response, Dr. David deSilva, Trustees' Distinguished Professor of New Testament and Greek at Ashland Theological Seminary and one of a panel of readers Greene recruited for the project, wrote a post of his own on the Bibliotheca site in May 2016.

> Dear Backers:
> I see that there's some ill feeling about the delay in the publication of this edition of the Bible. I can understand your frustration, but please permit me to share a few things that might help.
> Adam contacted me, together with several other professors of the Old and New Testament who have been involved in Bible translation projects, to do a final read of the text Adam is publishing and do a final "quality control" check. He's taking his work very seriously and wants this not just to be beautifully printed but to be *worth* printing beautifully. I myself read about two-thirds of the Apocrypha/Deuterocanonicals and a few select books of the New Testament, and am so glad that Adam included this time-consuming but project-improving step.[149]

deSilva previously worked on the Common English Bible (CEB) translation. "It took a team of several hundred people involved (under a board of eight) five years to create the Common English Bible" deSilva noted. "Granted, that was a fresh translation, but even the mechanical work of formatting an existing translation to which global changes are going to be made (like dropping the archaic second-person singular pronouns and verb forms) takes an immense amount of time, especially for a handful of people."[150]

Backer Jeremy Lagerman posted the following comment beneath deSilva's post in support of Bibliotheca:

At first, I supported this project to see how badly it would go. Adam had absolutely no idea the amount of work re-writing the book that is the basis for three religions. Then I saw the time frame and laughed. How bad is this going to be. Then the first deadline was missed. Ok, so its (sic) a little late. Then things started to change. Adam figured out how much work it really is and told us. I had mixed feelings at that time. Disappointed that I didn't have a product, glad to see the level of respect he has given this book. I originally purchased this to see how bad it would be, now I'm excited to read what I trust to be the most accurate translation to a language I can read. As far as I'm concerned, take all the time you need to make good on your dream . . . [151]

Lagerman's somewhat sardonic observations reflect the range of both negative and positive feedback from the thousands of backers over the years. A few wondered publicly about getting their money back, while others were frustrated with the lack of communication from Greene.

The initial enthusiasm for yet another new Bible in an already flooded marketplace prompts questions. Greene is a designer, not a theologian. How does his Bibliotheca Bible vary from any other ASV Bible on the market, other than omission of chapter and verse numbers? What distinguishes it from a much less expensive ASV available from nearly any bookseller? Three specific differences concerning the *design, production*, and *translation* are discussed below.

First, Greene designed a new typeface to honor the text. "I started by learning how to hand-write the letterforms that have evolved into our traditional book typefaces, and from there dove into the meticulous world of type design," Greene wrote to backers in the Bibliotheca site. "After over three years in the making and dozens of iterations, this project is the debut of this 'set apart' typeface" akin to Hebrew scribal traditions for holy texts. "Its rhythmic and spacious quality is designed for fluid readability. I have designed accompanying italic and small capital alphabets as well."[152]

Second, much thought went into high quality printing and binding. There are ribbon bookmarks and foil spine stamps, with a rounded spine with flat-opening sewn binding. "It's a more expensive and time-consuming way of building a book, but it immediately creates a more enjoyable experience," Aaron Souppouris wrote of Bibliotheca on *The Verge* website. "The pages are opaque, acid-free book paper, rather than the transparent sheets almost derogatorily referred to as 'Bible paper,' and will be printed using traditional offset printing."[153]

Third, a note on Greene's choice and tweaking of the ASV translation. The American Standard Version is based in part on a British Revised Version of the King James Bible done in the nineteenth century. In 1871, Swiss-born, German educated theologian Philip Schaff (1819–1893), who eventually settled in the United States, oversaw a panel of 30 British and American scholars who set out to create the ASV. When published in 1901, it was copyrighted to protect the text from unauthorized changes, but the copyright has since expired, leaving the ASV in the public domain, and therefore free of royalty fees. The 1901 first edition's full title was *The Holy Bible containing the Old and New Testaments translated out of the original tongues, being the version set forth A.D. 1611 compared with the most ancient authorities and revised A.D. 1881–1885. Newly Edited by the American Revision Committee A.D. 1901.*[154]

The ASV was the basis of two revisions, the *Revised Standard Version* (RSV, 1952) and the Lockman Foundation's *New American Standard Bible* (NASB, 1971). Kenneth Taylor used the ASV as the basis for his para- phrased *Living Bible* (LB, 1971), and the ASV is the root source for the *World English Bible* (WEB, 2000), also in the public domain. Jehovah's Witnesses, for one denominational example, use the ASV translation in addi- tion to *The New World Translation of the Holy Scriptures* (NWT, 1950, 1961).[155]

After receiving concerned emails from some Kickstarter backers about the ASV and Greene's proposed editing methods, Greene posted a long explanation of his rationale. Some excerpts:

> Most of our major contemporary translations come in a direct line from the ASV . . . translators of the ASV were committed to as much formal accuracy as possible, and therefore it is superior to most in preserving the idiom, repeti- tion, and syntax of the original languages.
>
> I will be replacing all of the redundant archaisms with their modern equiv- alents (*you* for *thou*, *does* for *doth*, *sits* for *sitteth*, etc.).
>
> I will occasionally incorporate the syntax (word-order) of Young's Literal Translation (YLT) of 1862 (though I am using the revised edition of 1898), which was even more committed to formal literalism than the ASV.
>
> One very important note: I would like to be clear that the use of the YLT will be *extremely minimal*. I am estimating less than 1 percent. Also, the changes will be mainly to syntax, not vocabulary.
>
> Somewhat controversially, the translators of the ASV chose to represent the name of God as "Jehovah," a word coined in English by Tyndale. Jehovah is the German transliteration of the Hebrew letters (J-H-V-H) with the vowel sounds of Adonai placed between the consonants. This was controversial be- cause adding vowel sounds suggests pronunciation, which is prohibited by Orthodox Judaism; for that matter, the actual pronunciation is lost to us.
>
> I have gone one step further—or one step backward, depending on how you look at it—and will be using the English transliteration of the name of God; that is, YHWH, set in all small capital letters. This way, pronunciation is not suggested, but the name of God is still represented, rather than replaced.[156]

J. Mark Bertrand is a Bible collector who has published the Bible Design Blog (bibledesignblog.com) since 2007. The blog "is dedicated to the physi- cal form of the Good Book," as he puts it. In an online essay published in

July 2014 shortly after Bibliotheca's Kickstarter launch, he wrote of the ASV translation:

> Comparisons to Crossway's recently-released hardcover ESV Reader's Bible are apt, though Bibliotheca represents a more extreme (perhaps the right word is pure) interpretation of the idea. . . . The appeal of the edition is this: you find a secluded nook and find yourself drawn into the biblical narrative, page after page, in a way you've never experienced before.
>
> Frankly, choosing the *American Standard Version* reinforces this goal. . . . Using it doesn't guarantee a loyal fan base like, say, the ESV would. Adam makes a compelling case for his choice. . . . He sees the translation contributing to Bibliotheca's literary experience. For those of us who haven't read the ASV before, this will contribute to the feeling of discovery when you curl up on the couch with a Bibliotheca volume.
>
> If you'd told me a month ago that today I would be anxiously awaiting a new edition of the American Standard Version, I would have been doubtful. But here I am, doing precisely that, and unlike some people I'm not backing Bibliotheca in the hope that its success will lead to a future edition in the translation of my choice. I'm actually looking forward to the entire project as Adam envisioned it.[157]

Bertrand, who later published a two-part online interview with Greene, even compared the Bibliotheca promotional video to that of Crossway's ESV Bible. "The Crossway video is good, but the Bibliotheca video is great," he wrote. "It's a much more detailed and compelling presentation of the reader-friendly design ethic. You come away from the Bibliotheca video a convert to the idea of a readable, novel-like Bible, and new converts love to share. Imagine how differently we'd be talking about Bibliotheca if a publisher had bankrolled the publication, then added the SKU to a dozen others in the catalog, promoted by a paragraph or two of bland copy and a snapshot of the packaging."[158]

Bertrand's Bibliotheca cheerleading appears to be an endorsement of the democratic nature of nonprofit Bible projects, as well as a harsh critique of Crossway's media promotion. Less enamored with Greene's Bibliotheca video was *Fast Company's* John Brownlee, who wrote, "And while Greene's Kickstarter video on the project uses all of the clichéd Christian imagery of an *Arrested Development* gag, the spirit and spirituality behind the project seem earnest."[159]

In his two-part interview with Greene, Bertrand focuses heavily on design, as might be expected from a Bible Design blog. Bertrand also asked about what he thinks "the outpouring of enthusiasm for Bibliotheca signifies to the world of Bible publishing." Greene's reply encompasses format, form, and technology:

I think the response to this project signifies that the biblical anthology is much too large (and I don't mean in a physical sense) to be contained in any one format or type of reading experience. This is a diverse literature, which transcends time, culture and style in a way that very few have done, and none to the same extent. It has always taken on different forms within various contexts—artistic and technical, story-driven and study-driven. These forms will continue to change and, at times, surprise us.

I also believe that the increased ability to dynamically study the biblical literature through web-based technology creates space for a project like this—by which we experience the text exclusively as story—to exist and thrive.[160]

What Adam Greene has wrought is a new Bible design in an old translation, using old media for production and new media for promotion. More than two years after the project launch, Greene sent an email to his backers on September 30, 2016, letting them know the end was near. In both the email and a blog post on the Kickstarter site, he announced the good news:

Hello, everyone. I'm sorry for the long wait between updates. The end is in sight. Here's where we stand. All five volumes are completely printed. Binding is almost finished—three of the five volumes are completely bound, while the remaining two are in the finishing stages and will be bound by October 7.[161]

Greene explained that the Bibles would be shipped from the Kösel book printing plant in Germany to the United States, arriving "in port by late November to early December, which means that U.S. orders and most international orders should arrive in time for Chanukkah and Christmas."[162] He offered his regrets for the long delay, but said the wait would be worth it:

I sincerely wish we had been able to deliver the finished product sooner. We did our best—and I'm confident that because we took the time we did, we *have* made the best books we could have shipped to you. The editorial team, the researchers, the proofreaders, the scholars, and Kösel have all brought their expertise to the table to create something that I trust you'll find enjoyable, enriching, and enduring.[163]

Bibliotheca Project Update #55 arrived in backers' email inboxes on December 17, 2016. "Bibliotheca Is Home," was the title of the message. Instagram photos of Bibliotheca Bibles were pouring in from happy recipients around the country. "I have very much enjoyed seeing Bibliotheca make its way across the US and into many of your homes," Greene wrote. "Although I held the final product several weeks ago, it has never felt more finished than in the past few days as I've seen photos of you—the ones who supported this vision over two years ago—holding it in your hands and placing it on your shelves. And if your books haven't come yet, hold tight—they'll arrive soon."[164]

CONCLUSION

A controversial 2014 *Newsweek* cover story alleging rampant misreading and mistranslating of the Bible, especially by evangelical and fundamentalist Christians, was posted online two days before Christmas and appeared in the print edition the following month. "No television preacher has ever read the Bible," reporter Kurt Eichenwald stated flatly. "Neither has any evangelical politician. Neither has the pope. Neither have I. And neither have you. At best, we've all read a bad translation—a translation of translations of translations of hand-copied copies of copies of copies of copies, and on and on, hundreds of times."[165]

R. Albert Mohler Jr., the conservative president of the Southern Baptist Theological Seminary, wrote a sharp response to Eichenwald on his website just after the *Newsweek* article was posted. "No knowledgeable evangelical claims that the Bibles we read in English are anything other than translations," Mohler said. "But it is just wrong and reckless to claim that today's best translations are merely 'a translation of translations of translations.' That just isn't so—not even close. Eichenwald writes as if textual criticism is a recent development and as if Christian scholars have not been practicing it for centuries. He also grossly exaggerates the time between the writing of the New Testament documents and the establishment of a functional canon. He tells of the process of copying manuscripts by hand over centuries as if that seals some argument about textual reliability, wrongly suggesting that many, if not most, of the ancient Christian scribes were illiterate."[166]

Asbury Theological Seminary Bible Scholar Ben Witherington criticized both Eichenwald's accuracy and his journalistic integrity:

> There is, in short, no evidence whatsoever in this article that 'scores' of theologians and scholars' [*sic*] have been consulted. There is also no evidence that there was any attempt to be fair and balanced in the scholars one would cite or draw on to base conclusions in this lengthy article . . .
>
> One of the typical missteps in arguing about the Bible, that Eichenwald falls prey to is the argument that all we have are bad translations of the Bible. Here's what he claims. . . . "About 400 years passed between the writing of the first Christian manuscripts and their compilation into the New Testament. (That's the same amount of time between the arrival of the Pilgrims on the Mayflower and today.)"
>
> This is not merely misleading, it's historically incorrect! It is not true that the original manuscripts are hopelessly remote from us and cannot hope to be recovered. Nor is it the case that the vast majority of modern preachers are oblivious to the actual state of the Biblical text that stands behind various

modern translations. This is not only a caricature of the majority of America's clergy, it is an even worse caricature of the state of play in regard to the text criticism of the Bible. [167]

Newsweek editors claimed that a goal in publishing the piece was to stimulate discussion, and they invited the responses. One detailed reply published on *Newsweek's* website was by Michael L. Brown, evangelical radio host (*Line of Fire*), author, and founder and president of FIRE School of Ministry in Concord, North Carolina. "First, it is difficult to know who, exactly, is being targeted," Brown wrote of Eichenwald's essay. "Is it some evangelical politicians? A few street preachers? Evangelicals in general? Second, *Newsweek* appears to be attacking the Bible itself—although claiming not to—and it does so in a slipshod, methodologically flawed way at that. . . . While no translation (evangelical Christian or otherwise) is perfect or without bias, that is not because of evil intent. It is because no human being is perfect or without bias, and that's one of the reasons that the vast majority of translations are produced by teams of scholars who review and critique each other's work." [168]

Newsweek has run lengthy Bible stories on a number of occasions since its founding in 1933, as have *TIME* and other newsweeklies, whose numbers, incidentally, have shrunk dramatically in the digital age. In the December 27, 1982 edition of *Newsweek*, the magazine ran a cover package titled "How the Bible Made America." The in-depth story, including sidebars, was reported by staff writers Kenneth L. Woodward and David Gates, and focused on the Bible's influence in America and in public debates over the Vietnam War, the Civil Rights Movement, and other social issues dealing with morality and matters of conscience.

The Woodward and Gates package, more evenhanded than the 2014 Eichenwald piece and published in a pre-social media era, offered a mini-history lesson complete with Pilgrims, Puritans, the 1560 Geneva Bible, the King James Bible, the American Bible Society, and other historical religious touchstones. Moral Majority Founder and Baptist Preacher Jerry Falwell, whose political power was at its peak, is also mentioned. "No other country is as obsessed with the Bible as the United States," the authors wrote. "Now historians are discovering that the Bible, perhaps even more than the Constitution, is our founding document: the source of the powerful myth of the United States as a special, sacred nation, a people called by God to establish a model society, a beacon to the world." [169]

This lofty rhetoric is not surprising when placed in the context of the Ronald Reagan presidency (1980–1988), an administration practiced in lofty rhetoric and mythical image making, and steeped in religiously patriotic language. *Newsweek* quotes Reagan: "I have always believed that this anointed land was set apart in an uncommon way, that a divine plan placed this great continent here, between the oceans to be found by people from every corner of the Earth who had a special love of faith and freedom."[170] This notion of American exceptionalism buttressed by scripture endures—and thrives—in the twenthy-first century.

More relevant to the translation theme of this chapter, Woodward and Gates noted that, "Only in America do Christians still fight so bitterly over versions of the Bible and national legislators declare 1983 'The Year of the Bible.'"[171] One of the brief sidebars by Gates and writer Holly Morris is of particular interest. "Of Profits and Prophecies" profiles Thomas Nelson Publishers, then a standalone company with sales of $33 million. Thomas Nelson was spending a million dollars—the most ever up to that time—"to promote a single Bible, and Nelson's New King James Version, published last August at a cost of $4.5 million, is the product of the most expensive Bible project in history."[172]

The essay details how Nelson's chief competitor at the time, Zondervan, spent $2.25 million a few years earlier in 1978 to create the New International Version. Zondervan's NIV employed 115 scholars on its translation team, while Nelson's NKJV had 130. "Though God and gain have always gone together," the authors stated, "the jargon of advertising and marketing would be incomprehensible to the old-time Bible salesmen who spent weeks memorizing sales pitches that ran as long as 10 pages. Christian bookstores—and Christian M.B.A.'s—put most of the old-timers out of business in the 1960s, but one thing hasn't changed since door-to-door peddling days: the Good Book is still America's best seller."[173]

The Christian bookstores themselves faced an unlikely competitor in a bid to sell Bible goods to the public on a large scale. In her book, *To Serve God and Wal-Mart: The Making of Christian Free Enterprise* (2009), historian and women's studies scholar Bethany Moreton details how discount retailer Wal-Mart became associated with middle class evangelical Christian values. The association was not a foregone conclusion, as Wal-Mart founder Sam Walton and his wife, Helen Robson Walton, were liberal Presbyterians. Mrs. Walton was not only the first woman on the national governing board of the Presbyterian Church (U.S.A.), but "a public proponent of legal access to abortion and a donor to Planned Parenthood."[174] Pro-choice, activist women in positions of church authority are antithetical to conservative evangelical orthodoxy. Of Sam Walton's religiosity, his pastor declared, "When it's not bird hunting season and he's in south Texas, every Sunday Sam Walton is in church."[175]

Yet, Christian Coalition Executive Director Ralph Reed declared in the mid-1990s, "If you want to reach [the Christian population] on Saturday, you do it in Wal-Mart."[176] How did the largely secular Wal-Mart chain become identified as a champion of the Religious Right? Moreton writes:

With conservative religion an increasingly commonplace feature of American life, Christian consumer demand drove Wal-Mart's conversion to some extent. In the early 1990s, the Christian publishing and media conglomerate Thomas Nelson, Inc., took a close look at the Wal-Mart base and began pushing the mass retailer to carry more than just the company's Bibles. It was "the whole family values thing," the publisher explained. Wal-Mart tested the potential market with Christian children's books and souvenir Bibles themed to weddings and births, and then added Christian pop music and novelty items. "They understand our business," a Wal-Mart executive explained of the Nashville-based publisher. "They've brought us a lot of winners." Sales were impressive, and in many stores customers asked for even more, leading to expanded Christian product lines in about three hundred stores by the mid-1990s. Within ten years, Wal-Mart had become the country's largest merchandiser of Christian items, with over a billion dollars in annual sales.[177]

Wal-Mart's massive presence and retail dominance hurt the hundreds of smaller independent stores that had helped to create the demand for Christian merchandise. "From 2000 to 2002, the market in Christian merchandise grew by $200 million, but business at Christian stores contracted by $100 million," according to Moreton. Many smaller Christian retailers closed, while others tried to fight back by warning of "the possible polluting effects of non-Christian products alongside appropriately orthodox ones." But Wal-Mart was seen by this time as providing a "morally sanitized" place to shop, creating a safe, small-town type of environment to buy Bibles and Christian CDs alongside household products.[178]

Another major American retailer was behind the 430,000-square-foot Museum of the Bible, located near the Capitol Building in Washington, D.C. The museum is a project sponsored by conservative evangelical Christian billionaire Steve Green and his family, who own the Hobby Lobby chain of crafts stores. Placing the nonprofit Bible museum close to the nation's center of political power was intentional. Many evangelicals believe (Christian) prayer should be allowed in public schools, and that the nation was founded on Christian principles, including many evangelical lawmakers.

Prior to the museum's debut on November 17, 2017, its website promoted the uniqueness of its antiquities collection, combined with the latest digital technology. "Museum of the Bible will be an unparalleled experience, using cutting-edge technology to bring the Bible to life. It will span time, space, and cultures, inviting everyone to engage with the Bible. With three permanent sections and space for temporary exhibits, there will always be something new to explore."[179]

Using customizable technology, "Museum of the Bible's digital guide is groundbreaking and unlike any personal touring system used by any museum in the world. This system promises to become the new standard for museum navigation by equipping museumgoers with a device that personalizes, navigates and engages."[180]

Naturally, there is a gift shop to help visitors continue the experience. "Discover hundreds of unique Museum of the Bible gift products. We offer a wide variety of lifestyle apparel and accessories. There are gifts from around the world, including reproductions, sculptures, jewelry, books, stationery and exhibition catalogues. These distinctive offerings are an opportunity to continue the story and experience of the Museum of the Bible and allows our guests to take home a lasting memory that inspires them to continually engage with the Bible."[181]

Archaeological and archival concerns over the provenance of some of the Greens' artifacts were the subject of news accounts leading up to the grand opening. In 2010, the family paid $1.6 million for what turned out to be more than 5,500 artifacts looted from historical sites in Iraq. In a deal with federal prosecutors, the Greens forfeited the items and paid $3 million to settle a civil action.[182] The museum website has a separate section addressing "Provenance," and details its acquisition policy.[183]

Another concern expressed by scholars and other observers was the possibility of narrowly evangelical interpretations of scripture within the Museum of the Bible.[184] Biblical interpretation via museum exhibition, they maintain, should be as carefully considered as Biblical translation. "[T]he responsibility of the translator is clear," William A. Irwin wrote in *An Introduction to the Revised Standard Version of the Old Testament* when the RSV appeared in 1952. "Representing the best extant understanding of the language with which he deals, he is charged to tell as accurately as he can in his own language precisely what the original says."[185]

Irwin goes on to stress accuracy over partisan interpretation:

> A recent speaker has told of a project to issue "a theologically conservative translation of the Bible." Doubtless this is an appealing undertaking in the eyes of many. But the fact must be stressed that *there is no place for theology in Bible translation* [emphasis added], whether conservative or radical or whatever else. A "theological translation" is not a translation at all, but merely a dogmatic perversion of the Bible.[186]

Most Bible translations, as indicated in this chapter, have been produced by committee. Solo translation ventures have also met with mixed results. Clarence Jordan, a New Testament Greek Scholar and Georgia farmer, published a partial version of the New Testament in the late 1960s and early 1970s set in the South. *The Cotton Patch Gospel* relocated the Gospels to Georgia, and recast familiar characters, such as "Governor Herod and all his Atlanta cronies," while narrating the story of Jesus, born in Gainesville, Georgia. Jordan, who founded Koinonia Farm near Americus, Georgia in the 1940s as an interracial farming utopia, followed the lead of other modern translators, seeking to make the Bible more relatable to modern audiences.[187]

Theologian, scholar, and cultural commentator David Bentley Hart, author of *Atheist Delusions* (2009) and *The Story of Christianity* (2015) published his New Testament translation in 2017.[188] Hart admits that "yet another translation of the New Testament is probably something of a foolish venture. No matter what one produces—recklessly liberal, timidly conservative, or something poised equilibriously in between—it will provoke consternation (and probably indignation) in countless breasts."[189] Hart's translation, as *The Atlantic* contributing editor James Parker phrased it, is a "mind-bending translation" that Hart himself refers to as "almost pitilessly literal. . . . Where an author has written bad Greek. . . . I have written bad English."[190]

"One lesson I quickly learned," writes Bruce Feiler of his physical and literary journey through the land of the Bible, "was that one's view of the Bible often depends on which Bible one reads. Christian Bibles, for instance, arrange later books in the Hebrew Scriptures in a different order than Jewish Bibles. Catholic Bibles, in both their translations and their content, differ from Protestant Bibles, which differ from Anglican Bibles, which differ from Greek Orthodox Bibles."[191]

Harvard's Peter J. Gomes warned against Bibliolatry, or idolatry of the Bible and/or a particular version of it. Bible worship is to be avoided, and can lead to the bludgeoning of others with it rather than using it for its intended purpose. "The Bible is not God, nor is it a substitute for God, and to treat it as if it were God or a surrogate of God is to treat it in the very way that it itself condemns over and over again."[192]

The notion of a word-for-word translation, as the NIV and ESV proponents and many other translators had in mind, is not really an achievable goal. As Sloyan explained:

> One should not adopt a magisterial stance in presuming to name the "best" translations. . . . It would be folly. If one were to name a version for pleasurable reading, it would be *RNEB*, occasional British turns of phrase and all. But it has no apparatus aside from footnotes or textual alternatives, as does *NRSV*. For help in understanding an ancient literature in its languages, *NAB* (as revised) is clearly the best. Its translation is as dependable as the better modern ones. Unlike most others *(NJB* is an exception, but not its "study edition") it provides enlightening footnotes, splendid introductions to each book, and cross references within books and across Testaments. Often the notes are superior to those in publishers' study editions with commentary. *NAB* is especially valuable for the Bible study groups that are happily proliferating throughout the U.S. and Canada. Too often the first reflection offered is on "What this passage means to me." The initial inquiry, of course, should be what it meant to the inspired authors and editors, most of them anonymous,

who gave it to the church in the first place. Once explored, it often renders the second question needless. [193]

Contradictorily, the Bible is personal, yet is meant to be shared with others, so it is also public. The Bible is considered to be the Word of God, and that Word has been translated many times into many languages, and into many versions of the same language. What is inside is considered by believers to be a gift from God, but the message often gets lost in translation.

NOTES

1. Barna Group and American Bible Society, "State of the Bible 2016," http://www.americanbible.org/features/state-of-the-bible. This nationwide study commissioned by the American Bible Society and conducted by Barna Research Group.

2. Barna Group and American Bible Society, "State of the Bible 2015," https://www.scribd.com/document/261505121/State-of-the-Bible-2015-Report

3. Daniel Silliman, "The Most Popular Bible of the Year Is Probably Not What You Think It Is," the *Washington Post*, August 28, 2015, accessed June 27, 2016, https://www.washingtonpost.com/news/acts-of-faith/wp/2015/08/28/the-most-popular-bible-of-the-year-is-probably-not-what-you-think-it-is/.

4. Daniel Radosh, "The Good Book Business: Why Publishers Love the Bible," *The New Yorker*, December 18, 2006, 54.

5. Barna Group and American Bible Society, "State of the Bible 2015."

6. Ibid. "Elders" is the term Barna uses to identify senior or older readers, as opposed to Elders as officials of a church.

7. Barna Group and American Bible Society, "State of the Bible 2016."

8. "The Bible in America: 6-Year Trends," Barna Group Research Release, June 15, 2016, accessed June 26, 2016, https://barna.org/research/faith-christianity/research-release/the-bible-in-america-6-year-trends#.V3B831ekVqo.

9. Bruce M. Metzger, *The Bible in Translation: Ancient and English Versions* (Ada, MI: Baker Academic, 2001), 8. Metzger was a Princeton theologian who served on the board of both the American Bible Society and the United Bible Societies, and he chaired the New Revised Standard Version (NRSV) translation committee.

10. "The Bible Store," Amazon.com, accessed December 7, 2017.

11. "Bibles," Christianbook.com, accessed December 7, 2017.

12. Anne L. Borden, "Making Money, Saving Souls: Christian Bookstores and the Commodification of Christianity," in *Religion, Media, and the Marketplace*, ed. Lynn Schofield Clark (New Brunswick, NJ: Rutgers, 2007), 68. Various sources estimate the Christian retail market between $4 billion and $7 billion. See Wendy Hirdes, Robert Woods, and Diane M. Badzinski, "A Content Analysis of Jesus Merchandise," *Journal of Media and Religion* 8, no. 3 (2009): 141–157, accessed July 19, 2016, http://academic.csuohio.edu/kneuendorf/c63311/Hirdesetal09.pdf; Heather Hendershot, *Shaking the World for Jesus: Media and Conservative Evangelical Culture* (Chicago: The University of Chicago Press, 2004), 21; "Online Extra: The Fashion of the Christ," Bloomberg, May 23, 2005, http://www.bloomberg.com/news/articles/2005-05-22/online-extra-the-fashion-of-the-christ; Jay Reeves, "Some $4.6B Christian Industry Copy Designs, Logos," *USA Today*, December 18, 2009, http://usatoday30.usatoday.com/news/religion/2009-12-18-christian-copyright_N.htm. Borden cited a figure of $4.2 billion at the time her piece was written.

13. Ibid., 73.

14. Ibid. Borden is quoting an advertisement from *Bookstore Journal* (June 1973), 43.

15. Ibid., 80–81.

16. Jerry B. Jenkins, *Twenty-Five Years of Sterling Rewards in God's Service: The Story of the Christian Booksellers Association* (Nashville: Thomas Nelson, 1974), 10.

17. Carol Flake, *Redemptorama: Culture, Politics, and the New Evangelicalism.* (Garden City, NY: Doubleday, Anchor Press, 1984),18; quoted in R. Laurence Moore, *Selling God: American Religion in the Marketplace of Culture* (New York: Oxford University Press, 1994), 255.

18. R. Laurence Moore, *Selling God: American Religion in the Marketplace of Culture* (New York: Oxford UP, 1994), 253.

19. Ibid., 254.

20. Aviyah Kushner, "Seven Surprises While Reading the Torah in English Translation," The Jewish Book Council, The Prose n People blog, September 10, 2015, https://www.jewishbookcouncil.org/_blog/The_ProsenPeople/post/seven-surprises-while-reading-the-torah-in-english-translation/; Aviyah Kushner, *The Grammar of God: A Journey into the Words and Worlds of the Bible* (New York: Spiegel & Grau, 2015).

21. Radosh, "The Good Book Business," 56. Language is often a complaint about the King James Version among modern readers. For example, Luke 12:15–16 reads: "And he said unto them, Take heed, and beware of covetousness: for a man's life consisteth not in the abundance of the things which he possesseth. And he spake a parable unto them, saying, The ground of a certain rich man brought forth plentifully . . ."

22. Silliman, "The Most Popular Bible of the Year."

23. Radosh, "The Good Book Business," 56.

24. Moore, *Selling God*, 253.

25. "Winners Announcedfor 2016's *Christian Retailing's* Best Awards," *Christian Retailing* press release, June 27, 2016, accessed July 19, 2016, http://christianretailingsbest.com/winners.html.

26. English Translations of the Bible, Theopedia.com, accessed July 14, 2016, http://www.theopedia.com/english-translations-of-the-bible. Additional versions not appearing on the Theopedia list were added by the author.

27. "Top Ten Bible Translations, 2014," posted on the Thom S. Rainer website, December 10, 2014, accessed June 27, 2016, http://thomrainer.com/2014/12/top-ten-bible-translations-2014/.

28. CBA Bestsellers, June 2016, accessed June 27, 2016, http://cbanews.org/wp-content/uploads/sites/3/2016/06/BiblesDevotionals201606.pdf.

29. Nicola Menzie, "NIV More Popular Than KJV, NLT Bibles; 11 Million Copies Sold Worldwide," *Christian Post*, March 26, 2013, accessed July 21, 2016, http://www.christianpost.com/news/niv-more-popular-than-kjv-nlt-bibles-11-million-copies-sold-worldwide-92671/#axD5K8UZSXkPqHmu.99.

30. Barna Group and American Bible Society, "State of the Bible 2015."

31. As an example, missionary and independent translator Michael Johnson has created the World English Bible (WEB), a 2000 modern translation that has been trademarked but may be freely copied, as long as no punctuation or other significant changes are made. Of Bible copyrights, Johnson has said, "The problem of copyright protection of Modern English translations of the Holy Bible is not just significant on the Internet and various electronic information services. It also affects people who want to quote significant portions of Scripture in books, audio tapes, and other media. This drives up the price of preaching the Gospel. Basic economics tells us that this is not a good thing when our goal is to fulfill the Great Commission (Matthew 28:18–20). For example, the 'free' Bibles that the Gideons place cost them more if they use a modern version, like Thomas-Nelson's New King James Version, than if they use the (more difficult to read) King James Version." See http://ebible.org/web/web-faq.htm#WhyCreate.

32. Roger Syn, "Copyright God: Enforcement of Copyright in the Bible and Religious Works," *Regent University Law Review* 14, no. 1 (2001–2002): 32.

33. Ibid.

34. Ibid. "And they were judged, each one according to his works." *Revelations* 20:13 (New King James); *see also 2 Corinthians* 5:10; *Revelations* 20:12.

35. Ibid., 10.

36. Ibid., 12.

37. Bruce M. Metzger, "To the Reader," *The New Revised Standard Version Bible*, copyright © 1989, Division of Christian Education of the National Council of Churches of Christ in the U.S.A., New York. This explanatory address to the reader appears in NSRV Bibles, regardless of publisher.

38. For further historical context on translating the King James Bible, see Adam Nicholson, *God's Secretaries: The Making of the King James Bible* (New York: Perennial, 2004).

39. Gerard S. Sloyan, "Some Thoughts on Bible Translations," *Worship* 75, no. 3, May 2001, 229.

40. Preface, *The Holy Bible Containing the Old and New Testaments*, Revised Standard Version (New York: Thomas Nelson & Sons, 1952), v. The New Testament was translated into the RSV in 1946, and 1952 is the year both the Old and New Testament sections appeared together in one Bible.

41. Ibid., 235.

42. Martyn Lyons, *Books: A Living History* (Los Angeles: The J. Paul Getty Museum, 2011), 65.

43. Karen Armstrong, *The Bible: The Biography* (London: Atlantic Books, 2007), 153–154.

44. Sloyan, "Some Thoughts on Bible Translations," 232–233. The Second Vatican Council that permitted alterations in the liturgy and music, among other changes, took place from 1962–1965.

45. Donna Butler and David F. Lloyd, "John Wycliffe: Setting the Stage for Reform," *Vision* website, *Religion and Spirituality*, Winter 2004, http://www.vision.org/visionmedia/biography-john-wycliffe/613.aspx. There are many scholarly sources on Wycliffe's authorship. For example, see G. R. Evans, *John Wyclif: Myth and Reality* (Downers Grove, IL: Intervarsity Press Academic, 2005).

46. Steven M. Wise, *An American Trilogy: Death, Slavery, & Dominion on the Banks of the Cape Fear River* (Philadelphia: Da Capo Press, 2009), 21–22. See also, David Daniell, *The Bible in English: Its History and Influence* (New Haven: Yale University Press, 2003).

47. "William Tyndale," *Christian History*, accessed June 24, 2016, http://www.christianitytoday.com/history/people/scholarsandscientists/william-tyndale.html.

48. "Myles Coverdale," Greatsite.com website, accessed June 26, 2016. http://www.greatsite.com/timeline-english-bible-history/myles-coverdale.html; Adam Nicholson, *God's Secretaries: The Making of the King James Bible* (New York: Perennial, 2004), 248–249.

49. As Martyn Lyons and many others have noted, Gutenberg was not the first to create moveable type. Wood and metal characters had been used in China and Korea by the eleventh century and the thirteenth century, respectively.

50. Simon Garfield, *Just My Type* (New York: Gotham Books, 2011), 29.

51. Sarah Eekhoff Zylstra, "Why Your Bible Was Made in China," *Christianity Today*, October 23, 2014, accessed June 26, 2016, http://www.christianitytoday.com/ct/2014/october/bible-made-in-china.html.

52. Ibid.

53. "Understanding Amity," Amity website, accessed June 26, 2016, http://amityprinting.com/about-us/understanding-amity.

54. Quoted in Zylstra.

55. Ibid.

56. Cang Wei, "Spreading the Word: China's Bible Industry," *China Daily*, April 21, 2015, reprinted in *The Telegraph*, http://www.telegraph.co.uk/news/world/china-watch/culture/bible-production-in-china/.

57. Multiple sources list the media holdings of these companies. See, for example, "Who Owns What," *Columbia Journalism Review*, cjr.org [Includes searchable database of each company's holdings], https://www.cjr.org/resources/; Chris Zook, "Media Conglomerates: The Big 6," WebPage FX Data, 2017 [Includes infographic], https://www.webpagefx.com/data/the-6-companies-that-own-almost-all-media/; Theodora Moldovan, "The Six Companies That Own (Almost) All Media," *Affinity*, n.d., http://affinitymagazine.us/2016/12/07/the-six-companies-that-own-almost-all-media/.

58. "About Oxford University Press," OUP website, accessed July 14, 2016, https://global.oup.com/academic/aboutus/?lang=en&cc=us.

59. "Released on March 9, 2011, the New American Bible, Revised Edition (NABRE) is the culmination of nearly 20 years of work by a group of nearly 100 scholars and theologians, including bishops, revisers and editors. The NABRE includes a newly revised translation of the entire Old Testament (including the Book of Psalms) along with the 1986 edition of the New Testament." See "The New American Bible, Revised Edition (NABRE)," http://www.usccb.org/bible/. The Apocrypha is a title given to books and works that were part of the Septuagint from pre-Christian times that are typically excluded from Protestant Bibles.

60. According to the HarperCollins website, the New York-based company "has publishing operations in 18 countries . . . two hundred years of history and more than 120 branded imprints around the world." Although the company website declares that it's the world's second-largest consumer book publisher, *Publisher's Weekly* ranked it number 13 overall, based on revenue. See Jim Milliott, "The World's 52 Largest Book Publishers 2016," *Publisher's Weekly*, August 26, 2016, https://www.publishersweekly.com/pw/by-topic/international/international-book-news/article/71268-the-world-s-52-largest-book-publishers-2016.html.

61. "Company Information," HarperCollins Christian Publishing website, http://www.harpercollinschristian.com/info/, accessed June 16, 2016.

62. Lynn Garrett, "Stunned Reaction To HarperCollins's Acquisition of Thomas Nelson," *Publisher's Weekly*, November 4, 2011, https://www.publishersweekly.com/pw/by-topic/industry-news/religion/article/49399-stunned-reaction-to-harpercollins-s-acquisition-of-thomas-nelson.html.

63. News Corp Annual Income Statement, AmigoBulls.com, December 1, 2017, https://amigobulls.com/stocks/NWSA/income-statement/annual.

64. "Global Publishing Leaders 2016: HarperCollins," *Publishers Weekly*, August 26, 2016, https://www.publishersweekly.com/pw/by-topic/industry-news/publisher-news/article/71290-global-publishing-leaders-2016-harpercollins.html.

65. Radosh, "The Good Book Business," 54.

66. The full story of the NIV translation is on the Biblica website, http://www.biblica.com/en-us/the-niv-bible/niv-story/.

67. Ibid.

68. Ibid.

69. Ibid.

70. See HarperCollins Christian Publishing website, http://www.harpercollinschristian.com/company-news/, accessed June 16, 2016.

71. Ibid.

72. Steve Young, "Four Hundred Years Later: The Bible Isn't What It Used to Be," *Choice* 49:4, 623–633, December 2011, accessed August 12, 2016, http://search.proquest.com.ezproxy.elon.edu/pqrl/docview/1016745186/fulltextPDF/19E6850AE64B4199PQ/2?accountid=10730.

73. Marty King, "LifeWay to Continue Selling NIV; Trustees Select New Leadership," lifeway.com website, February 15, 2012, accessed June 24, 2016, http://www.lifeway.com/Article/News-LifeWay-to-continue-selling-NIV-Trustees-select-new-leadership.

74. "NIV Rainbow Study Bible, Saddle Brown LeatherTouch Indexed," bhpublishinggroup.com website, accessed June 24, 2016, http://www.bhpublishinggroup.com/products/niv-rainbow-study-bible-saddle-brown-leathertouch-indexed.

75. "History: Celebrating God's Faithfulness and Glory," Crossway website, https://www.crossway.org/about/history/, accessed June 16, 2016.

76. Ibid.

77. "About Tyndale: Kenneth N. Taylor, Tyndale.com website, accessed June 24, 2016, https://www.tyndale.com/kenneth-n-taylor.

78. Radosh, "The Good Book Business," 55.

79. "About the Navigators," NavPress website, accessed July 14, 2016, https://www.navpress.com/about-the-navigators.

80. Ibid.

81. *The Message* Permissions Information, NavPress website, accessed July 14, 2016, https://www.navpress.com/permissions.

82. Eugene H. Peterson, "Introduction to the New Testament," *The Message: The New Testament in Contemporary Language* (Colorado Springs: NavPress Publishing Group, 2003), 8.

83. Ibid.

84. Ibid., 12. Scripture quotation from *The Message*. Copyright © by Eugene H. Peterson 1993, 1994, 1995, 1996, 2000, 2001, 2002. Used by permission of NavPress. All rights reserved. Represented by Tyndale House Publishers, Inc.

85. Michael J. Cusick, "A Conversation with Eugene Peterson," *Mars Hill Review* 3, no. 3 (Fall 1995): 73–90, accessed July 14, 2016, http://www.leaderu.com/marshill/mhr03/peter1.html.

86. Cathleen Falsani, "Lost in Translation: Eugene Peterson and His 'Message,'" *Sojourners*, March 1, 2012, accessed July 14, 2016, https://sojo.net/articles/lost-translation-eugene-peterson-and-his-message.

87. Michael Marlowe, "The Message," *Bible Research*, n.d., accessed July 14, 2016, http://www.bible-researcher.com/themessage.html.

88. Justin Peters, "Why is *The Message* (Bible) Not Safe?" *For the Love of His Truth: A Christian Blog about Fundamental Biblical Facts*, October 7, 2011, accessed July 14, 2016, https://fortheloveofhistruth.com/2011/10/07/why-is-the-message-bible-not-safe/.

89. John R. Kohlenberger III, "The Message Bible," *Christian Research Journal* 17, no. 1 (1994), accessed July 14, 2016, http://www.equip.org/article/the-message-bible/.

90. Falsani, "Lost in Translation."

91. "Excision and Revision Make 'The Short Bible,'" *The Literary Digest*, November 11, 1933, 19.

92. Ibid.

93. "A Little About ABS," American Bible Society website, accessed July 22, 2016, http://www.americanbible.org/about.

94. Ibid.

95. Radosh, "The Good Book Business."

96. Dr. Robert G. Bratcher, Obituary, *News & Observer*, Raleigh, North Carolina, July 14, 2010, accessed June 24, 2016, http://www.legacy.com/obituaries/newsobserver/obituary.aspx?pid=144069874.

97. Warren Cole Smith, "Going Public," *World* 29, no. 1 (January 11, 2014), accessed August 8, 2016, https://world.wng.org/2013/12/going_public.

98. Ibid. See also, Adelle M. Banks, "Priced out of New York, American Bible Society Decamps to Philadelphia," Religion News Service, January 28, 2015, accessed August 8, 2016, http://religionnews.com/2015/01/28/priced-new-york-american-bible-society-decamps-philadelphia/; Adelle M. Banks, "American Bible Society Marks 200th Birthday," Religion News Service, May 11, 2016, http://religionnews.com/2016/05/11/american-bible-society-marks-200th-birthday/.

99. John Fea, "A Bible Translation for Everyone?" *The Christian Century*, December 13, 2016, accessed December 30, 2016, https://www.christiancentury.org/article/bible-translation-everyone. For an in-depth look at Bible Societies, Fea's book is a richly detailed look at their history and formation. See *The Bible Cause: A History of the American Bible Society* (New York: Oxford University Press, 2016).

100. Preface, *Good News for Modern Man: The New Testament in Today's English Version* (New York: American Bible Society, 1971), V-VI.

101. Luke 11: 2–4, TEV.

102. Fea, "A Bible Translation for Everyone?"

103. Ibid.

104. "The Contemporary English Version," *Extreme Faith Bible: God's Word Knows No Bounds* (New York: American Bible Society, 1995), introductory pages. For adult literacy statistics, see Irwin S. Kirsch, Ann Jungeblut, Lynn Jenkins, and Andrew Kolstad, "Adult Literacy in America: A First Look at the Findings of the National Adult Literacy Survey,"

National Center for Education Statistics, U.S. Department of Education Office of Educational Research and Improvement, April 2002, https://nces.ed.gov/pubs93/93275.pdf.

105. "About Us," United Bible Societies webpage, accessed July 22, 2016, https://www.unitedbiblesocieties.org/about-us/.

106. Ibid.

107. See *The Bible Translator*, http://tbt.sagepub.com.

108. "1,000th Language Translation Added to the Digital Bible Library," United Bible Societies website, accessed August 8, 2016, https://www.unitedbiblesocieties.org/1000th-language-translation-added-digital-bible-library/.

109. "History of Biblica," Biblica website, accessed July 22, 2016, http://www.biblica.com/en-us/about-us/our-history/.

110. Ibid.

111. "The NIV Story," Biblica website, accessed July 22, 2016, http://www.biblica.com/en-us/the-niv-bible/niv-story/.

112. "Our History," Bible Society website, accessed August 9, 2016, https://www.biblesociety.org.uk/about-us/our-history/.

113. Colleen McDannell, *Material Christianity: Religion and Popular Culture in America* (New Haven: Yale University Press, 1995), 87.

114. Radosh, "The Good Book Business," 56–57.

115. Ibid.

116. Ibid.; Donald Colbert, *What Would Jesus Eat?* (Grand Rapids: Thomas Nelson, 2005).

117. Ann Rodgers, "iPod Bibles, BibleZines? You Name It, They've Got It," *Pittsburgh Post-Gazette*, April 8, 2007, http://www.post-gazette.com/life/lifestyle/2007/04/08/iPod-Bibles-BibleZines-You-name-it-they-ve-got-it/stories/200704080350.

118. Moore, *Selling God*, 254.

119. *Extreme Faith Bible: God's Word Knows No Bounds* CEV (New York: American Bible Society, 1995), 325. Retail cost of the paperback Bible was $4.59.

120. *Teen Study Bible* NIV (Grand Rapids: Zondervan, 2008). The retail cost of the hardcover edition of this book in 2008 was $27.99.

121. The Apostle's Creed is an early and universal statement of Christian belief. One English translation of the text reads: I believe in God, the Father almighty,

creator of heaven and earth.
I believe in Jesus Christ, God's only Son, our Lord,
who was conceived by the Holy Spirit,
born of the Virgin Mary,
suffered under Pontius Pilate,
was crucified, died, and was buried;
he descended to the dead.
On the third day he rose again;
he ascended into heaven,
he is seated at the right hand of the Father,
and he will come to judge the living and the dead.
I believe in the Holy Spirit,
the holy catholic and apostolic Church,
the communion of saints,
the forgiveness of sins,
the resurrection of the body,
and the life everlasting. Amen.

122. *Operation Worship Holy Bible*, 2nd Edition, NLT (Carol Stream, IL: Tyndale House Publishers, Inc., 2008). Retail cost in 2008 was $4.99. Operation Worship website accessed July 15, 2016, http://www.operationworship.com.

123. *The One Year Bible* NIV (Carol Stream, IL: Tyndale House Publishers, Inc., 2004). Retail cost in 2004 was $12.99.

124. *Fellowship of Christian Athletes Coach's Devotional Bible: Daily Game Plans for Coaches* CSB (Nashville, TN: Holman Bible Publishers, 2006). Retail cost in 2016 for this edition was $29.99.

125. Jeremiah 10:12, NIV. *The Green Bible* NRSV (New York: HarperCollins, 2008), 747.

126. *The Green Bible* NRSV (New York: HarperCollins, 2008), copyright page. Retail cost for the 2008 edition was $24.99.

127. Luke 5:18 NRSV, *The Poverty and Justice Bible: Catholic Edition* NRSV (Swindon, England: Bible Society Resources Ltd., 2013), 1237–1238.

128. *The Poverty and Justice Bible: Catholic Edition* NRSV (Swindon, England: Bible Society Resources Ltd., 2013), 2–6. Original retail price in 2013 was $19.99.

129. *Inspired By The Bible Experience: The Complete Bible* (Zondervan, 2008), MP3 CD.

130. Rodgers, "iPod Bibles, BibleZines?"

131. Definition of "bibliotheca," Merriam-Webster, accessed June 14, 2016, http://www.merriam-webster.com/dictionary/bibliotheca. In the interest of disclosure, the author pledged $75 for a four-volume set, plus Apocrypha, backer number 9,277. The five hardcover volumes arrived in a cardboard slipcase more than two years later in December 2016.

132. Bibliotheca Kickstarter website, June 27, 2014, accessed June 14, 2016, https://www.kickstarter.com/projects/530877925/bibliotheca/updates.

133. Ibid.

134. As numerous sources on the composition of the Bible have recorded, chapters were added in England in the thirteenth century and individual verses within chapters were added in Geneva in the sixteenth century.

135. Peter J. Gomes, *The Good Book: Reading the Bible with Mind and Heart* (New York: William Morrow and Company, Inc., 1996), 15.

136. Ibid., 15–16.

137. Bruce Feiler, *Walking the Bible: A Journey by Land Through the Five Books of Moses* (New York: Harper Perennial, 2001), 95.

138. Ibid.

139. David Rosenberg, *A Literary Bible* (Berkeley: Counterpoint, 2009), 637. Rosenberg's own translations of the Bible seek "to restore the original experience of reading them." A sample from his translation of Genesis: "Yahweh shaped an earthling from clay of this earth, blew into its nostrils the wind of life. Now look: man becomes a creature of flesh."

140. There have been other Bibles that removed the verse numbers from the text and taken the story approach without including the entire Bible canon, notably *The Story*, an abridged 31-chapter chronological NIV Bible published by Zondervan. The Foreword is by bestselling Christian authors and Texas-based preachers Max Lucado and Randy Frazee. *The Story* (Grand Rapids, MI: Zondervan, 2011). See also, Rosenberg, *A Literary Bible.*

141. Bibliotheca Kickstarter website, June 27, 2014.

142. Ibid.

143. Bibliotheca Kickstarter website, June 28, 2014, accessed June 14, 2016.

144. Bibliotheca Kickstarter website, June 30, 2014, accessed June 14, 2016.

145. Bibliotheca Kickstarter website, July 27, 2014, accessed June 14, 2016.

146. Sarah Eekhoff Zylstra, "Introducing the Bible! Now with Less!" *Christianity Today*, July 25, 2014, accessed July 15, 2016, http://www.christianitytoday.com/ct/2014/july-web-only/bibliotheca-readers-bible.html.

147. John Brownlee, "Redesigning The Bible With Readability In Mind," *Fast Company*, July 17, 2014, accessed July 15, 2016, http://www.fastcodesign.com/3033067/redesigning-the-bible-with-readability-in-mind.

148. Yasmine Hafiz, "'Bibliotheca' Bible Project Blows Up On Kickstarter With Chapterless Bible," *Huffington Post*, July 24, 2014, accessed July 15, 2016, http://www.huffingtonpost.com/2014/07/24/bibliotheca-bible_n_5615243.html?utm_hp_ref=tw.

149. David deSilva, "Update #48: A Update, and a Scholar's Thoughts," Bibliotheca Kickstarter website, May 1, 2016, accessed July 14, 2016.

150. Ibid.

151. Jeremy Lagerman, Comment, Bibliotheca Kickstarter website, June 20, 2016, accessed July 14, 2016.

152. Adam Greene, "Notes on the Typography," Bibliotheca Kickstarter website, July 12, 2014 accessed July 15, 2016.

153. Aaron Souppouris, "The Bible's a Mess, but a Designer is Fixing It," *The Verge*, July 22, 2014, accessed July 15, 2016, http://www.theverge.com/2014/7/22/5922855/bibliotheca-bible-kickstarter-campaign-adam-greene-interview.

154. *The Cambridge History of the Bible: The West from the Reformation to the Present Day* Ed. S.L. Greenslade (Cambridge: Cambridge University Press, 1963), 374.

155. See: Bruce M. Metzger, *The Bible in Translation: Ancient and English Versions* (Ada, MI: Baker Academic, 2001); Jehovah's Witnesses website, https://www.jw.org/en/publications/bible/american-standard-version/books/#?insight percent5Bsearch_id percent5D=70756a4a-ffe5–4b29-a2b6–1ca8bc658f08&insight percent5Bsearch_result_index percent5D=0; Theopedia.com, http://www.theopedia.com/american-standard-version; Bible Research, http://www.bible-researcher.com/asv.html; Barry Hoberman, "Translating the Bible," *The Atlantic*, February 1985, accessed July 13, 2016, http://www.theatlantic.com/past/docs/issues/85feb/transbib.htm;

156. Adam Greene, "The Translation," Bibliotheca Kickstarter website, July 12, 2014, accessed July 15, 2016.

157. J. Mark Bertrand, "Bibliotheca, the ESV Reader's Bible, and the Future of Printed Bibles," *Bible Design Blog*, July 7, 2014, accessed July 14, 2016, http://www.bibledesignblog.com/2014/07/bibliotheca-esv-readers-bible-future-printed-bibles.html.

158. Ibid.

159. John Brownlee, "Redesigning The Bible with Readability In Mind." The link Brownlee supplied to an *Arrested Development* episode clip shows a satirical campaign commercial with dreamy ocean images, akin to Greene's video, which was produced by two of his friends.

160. J. Mark Bertrand, "Interview with Bibliotheca's Adam Lewis Greene: Part 2," *Bible Design Blog*, July 5, 2014, accessed July 15, 2016, http://www.bibledesignblog.com/2014/07/interview-bibliothecas-adam-lewis-greene-part-2.html.

161. Bibliotheca Kickstarter website, September 30, 2016, accessed November 21, 2016.

162. Ibid.

163. Ibid.

164. Email correspondence from Adam Greene, December 17, 2016.

165. Kurt Eichenwald, "The Bible: So Misunderstood It's a Sin," *Newsweek*, January 9, 2015, 27.

166. Dr. R. Albert Mohler Jr., "*Newsweek* on the Bible—So Misrepresented It's a Sin," *Albertmohler.com*, December 29, 2014, accessed July 18, 2016, http://www.albertmohler.com/2014/12/29/newsweek-on-the-bible-so-misrepresented-its-a-sin/.

167. Ben Witherington, "News Weak—The Problems with Mr. Eichenwald's Article," Patheos.com website, January 6, 2015, accessed July 18, 2016, http://www.patheos.com/blogs/bibleandculture/2015/01/06/news-weak-the-problems-with-mr-eichenwalds-article/.

168. Michael L. Brown, "A Response to *Newsweek* on the Bible," Newsweek.com website, January 15, 2015, accessed July 18, 2016, http://www.newsweek.com/response-newsweek-bible-299440. *Newsweek's* note accompanying Brown's piece read: "*Newsweek 's* recent cover story on the Bible, as we expected, proved quite controversial, particularly among the evangelical community. Some agreed with our point, others expressed anger and still others came back with substantive replies. Our hope from the beginning was to inspire debate, and so we invited one our evangelical critics, Dr. Michael Brown, to continue the discussion. While we stand by our story and disagree with some of Dr. Brown's points, we do not think it is appropriate to publish a reply here. However, Dr. Brown has generously invited the author of the piece to appear on his national radio show next week to resume this important dialogue."

169. Kenneth L. Woodward and David Gates, "How the Bible Made America," *Newsweek*, December 27, 1982, 44.

170. Ibid. The Reagan quote is dated November 25, 1982, during the Thanksgiving holiday period.

171. Ibid., 45.

172. David Gates and Holly Morris, "Of Profits and Prophecies," *Newsweek*, December 27, 1982, 48.

173. Ibid.

174. Bethany Moreton, *To Serve God and Wal-Mart: The Making of Christian Free Enterprise* (Cambridge: Harvard University Press, 2009), 90.

175. Ibid.; Gordon Garlington III, pastor of Bentonville, Arkansas First Presbyterian Church, was originally quoted in Patricia May, "Walton, Wal-Mart Leave Their Mark on Northwest Arkansas," *DR Special Commemorative Edition*, April 5, 1992, 3.

176. Quoted in Dan McGraw, "The Christian Capitalists," *U.S. News & World Report*, March 13, 1995, 52–56; reprinted in Moreton, 90.

177. Moreton, *To Serve God and Wal-Mart*, 90–91; "Fundamentalism Sells," *The Wall Street Journal*, February 6, 1995, A1, A4; Jeff Sellers, "Deliver Us from Wal-Mart," *Christianity Today*, May 2005, 40. Little wonder that Rupert Murdoch wanted the lucrative religious publishers Nelson and Zondervan, both with proven track records as savvy marketers, as part of News Corp.

178. Moreton, *To Serve God and Wal-Mart*, 91.

179. Museumofthebible.org, accessed July 19, 2016, https://www.museumofthebible.org/museum.

180. Ibid., "How it Works," accessed December 7, 2017, https://www.museumofthebible.org/museum/technology.

181. Ibid., "Gift Shop."

182. Alan Feuer, "Hobby Lobby Agrees to Forfeit 5,500 Artifacts Smuggled Out of Iraq," *New York Times*, July 5, 2017, https://www.nytimes.com/2017/07/05/nyregion/hobby-lobby-artifacts-smuggle-iraq.html?_r=1.

183. "Acquisition Policy," Museum of the Bible, https://www.museumofthebible.org/acquisitions-policy.

184. For critiques of the museum's Biblical interpretations, see, for example, Nina Burleigh, "God Bless America, Or Else," *Newsweek*, April 15, 2016, 32–41.

185. W.A. Irwin, *An Introduction to the Revised Standard Version of the Old Testament* (New York: Thomas Nelson & Sons, 1952), 12–14, in *A Documentary History of Religion in America Since 1865*, 2nd ed., ed. Edwin S. Gaustad (Grand Rapids: William B. Eerdmans, 1993), 384.

186. Ibid.

187. *The Cotton Patch Gospel* was originally published in four volumes from 1968–1973, beginning with Paul's Epistles, followed by Luke and Acts; Matthew and John; Hebrews and general Epistles. See Clarence Jordan, *The Cotton Patch Gospel* (Macon, GA: Smyth & Helwys Publishing, 2004). *The Cotton Patch Gospel* was also turned into a stage musical with lyrics by Harry Chapin. For a review of the musical version, see Mel Gussow, "Stage: 'Cotton Patch Gospel,'" *New York Times*, October 22, 1981, http://www.nytimes.com/1981/10/22/theater/stage-cotton-patch-gospel.html. From the review: "Drawing its inspiration from Clarence Jordan's book 'The Cotton Patch Version of Matthew and John,' the evening is as cute as calico and as sweet as sorghum. A little of it goes a very long way."

188. See David Bentley Hart, *The New Testament: A Translation* (New Haven: Yale University Press, 2017); *The Story of Christianity: A History of 2,000 Years of the Christian Faith* (New York: Quercus, 2015); *Atheist Delusions: The Christian Revolution and Its Fashionable Enemies* (Ann Arbor: Sheridan Books, 2009).

189. David Bentley Hart, "Introduction," *The New Testament: A Translation* (New Haven: Yale University Press, 2017), xiii.

190. James Parker, "The New New Testament," *The Atlantic*, January/February 2018, 32. Parker quotes Hart's Introduction in his book review.

191. Feiler, *Walking the Bible*, 95–96.

192. Gomes, *The Good Book*, 40.

193. "Some Thoughts on Bible Translations," 249.

Chapter Six

Jesus Laughed

The Uses and Abuses of Religious Satire

A time to break down, and a time to build up; A time to weep, and a time to laugh.

—————Ecclesiastes 3:3–4, KJV

INTRODUCTION

Making fun of religion is risky. It can lead to public disdain and get you sued. It can also get you killed.

On January 7, 2015, brothers Saïd and Chérif Kouachi forced their way into the Paris offices of the French satirical weekly *Charlie Hebdo* and shot to death 11 staffers, many of them cartoonists for the publication. The siblings, members of Al-Qaeda's branch in Yemen, also killed a French police officer and wounded 11 others. The pair was gunned down two days later by authorities. The Kouachi brothers were apparently motivated to perpetrate such murderous violence after *Charlie Hebdo* repeatedly published buffoonish cartoon images depicting the Islamic Prophet Muhammad.[1]

Secularist to the point of being anti-religious, *Charlie Hebdo* has published numerous articles and cartoons parodying religion since its founding in 1970, taking on Islam, Catholicism, Judaism, Protestantism, and other traditions. *Charlie Hebdo* journalist Laurent Leger told France's BFM-TV in 2012 that, "The aim is to laugh. We want to laugh at the extremists—every extremist. They can be Muslim, Jewish, Catholic. Everyone can be religious, but extremist thoughts and acts we cannot accept.

"In France, we always have the right to write and draw. And if some people are not happy with this, they can sue us and we can defend ourselves.

That's democracy. You don't throw bombs, you discuss, you debate. But you don't act violently. We have to stand and resist pressure from extremism."[2] The magazine's senior editor, George Biard, was quoted as saying, "Attacking all religions is the basis of our identity."[3]

According to a poll by the Pew Research Center done a few weeks after the *Charlie Hebdo* massacre, 60 percent of Americans who heard about the attack said it was fine to have published cartoons that depict the Prophet Muhammad, but 28 percent disagreed.[4] One respondent said he believed in "free speech, but I also have a strong respect for people's religious ideas. It's a matter of respect—things you just don't do."[5]

If editor Biard is to be taken at his word, a central goal of *Charlie Hebdo* is to insult religious belief for the sake of a joke. Numerous secular media have done the same, including the parody news website *The Onion;* British comedy troupe Monty Python; and Comedy Central's foul-mouthed animated series *South Park*, whose creators Trey Parker and Matt Stone were behind the hit Broadway musical *The Book of Mormon*. In *The Book of Mormon*, Parker and Stone parodied a religion with 15 million adherents globally, garnering nine Tony Awards in the process. The Mormon Church's cheeky, nonviolent response to the musical's vulgar humor capitalized on the show's fame with targeted advertising on midtown Manhattan billboards, taxicabs, and even in the musical's *Playbill* program, resulting in heightened public awareness of actual Church teachings.[6]

The rituals and wrongdoings of world religions are ripe for satire. Funny hats, incense burnings, witch hangings—mocking religion without compunction is easy for the irreligious. But is it ethical for believers in a Christian God to practice religious satire? What would be the motivation for doing so?

This chapter explores historical and contemporary instances of Christians and non-Christians utilizing humor in an attempt to highlight malfeasance and effect positive change among God's people. Multiple examples will be discussed, but examined in detail will be two religious satire magazines, *The Wittenburg Door* and *Ship of Fools*, one American and one British; and two comedians, Stephen Colbert and John Oliver, one American and one British.

The Wittenburg Door and *Ship of Fools* were humor magazines founded in the 1970s by unconventional Christian figures on opposite sides of the Atlantic who shared the common mission of tweaking the conscience of fellow believers. The two publications satirized believers who they viewed as falling short of the Glory of God through intentional deceit, misinterpretation of scripture, or hypocrisy for personal gain. Examining the actions of those professing to be faithful through a comic lens, these magazines published pieces that got under the skin of their subjects primarily because the insider humor was so well informed. The writers of each publication were devout Christians who knew the Bible as well as their targets did, and employed that knowledge to throw stones, while acknowledging they themselves were not without sin.

Stephen Colbert is a liberal Catholic who periodically featured priests and other religious figures on his Comedy Central television show *The Colbert Report* (2005–2014), and continued to do so on his CBS television talk show, *The Late Show with Stephen Colbert* (premiere 2015). Englishman John Oliver is a comedian living in the United States who created a show on HBO called *Last Week Tonight with John Oliver* (premiere 2014). Although Oliver has not publicly identified with Christianity or any other religion as Colbert has, he created an actual short-lived television ministry to prove a point about church tax exemptions. In a similar vein, Colbert once created a real political action committee, a Super PAC, to illustrate weak government oversight of campaign donations.[7] Oliver and Colbert share the experience of having worked with Jon Stewart on Comedy Central's *The Daily Show*. As the show's host, Stewart poked fun at religious controversies such as the alleged "War on Christmas," in which retailers supposedly wished people "Happy Holidays" instead of "Merry Christmas."[8]

SATIRE FROM RELIGIOUS SOURCES

Much mockery of religion could be found in mid-twentieth century popular literature, television, stand-up comedy, and movies. Religious humor from a religious standpoint was rarer for the period, although examples beyond *The Wittenburg Door* and *Ship of Fools* do exist. For example, the daily cartoon strip *Peanuts* by Charles M. Schulz, which has many religious allusions, was used by seminarian, and later Christian minister, Robert L. Short for lectures. In 1965, Short published a theological study of the comic titled, *The Gospel According to Peanuts*.

Creator and artist Schulz's incorporation of religion into his work began prior to the strip's debut in October 1950. Single-panel cartoons that originally appeared in the religious magazines *Youth* and *Reach* were collected in a 1972 book called, *I Take My Religion Seriously*. These earlier drawings dealt with wholesome teenagers and their encounters with church, parents, and each other. One illustration shows a male teen outstretched on the floor reading the Bible. A female stands over him with a puzzled look. The young man tells her, "DON'T BOTHER ME . . . I'm looking for a verse of scripture to back up one of my preconceived notions!"[9]

The Gospel According to Peanuts begat a popular culture publishing phenomenon over the next several decades with numerous titles beginning, *"The Gospel According to . . ."*[10] The series included The Simpsons, The Beatles, Walt Disney, Harry Potter, J. R. R. Tolkien, and Oprah Winfrey. In a review of seven books in the series, Francis Bridger of Fuller Theological Seminary, wrote:

> The advantage of this reformulation is that it neither claims too much nor too little. Spirituality and religion are not forced into a reductionist or functionalist paradigm and neither are they patronized. *The Gospel According To* series is allowed to speak more powerfully precisely because it can be seen to claim only to point to the possibility of transcendence. Consequently, the agnostic and believing reader alike may appreciate its contribution to understanding more of the contours and dynamic of religion in Western popular culture in a way that opens up, rather than closes down, the range of interpretative possibilities. And for this we should be grateful. [11]

HUMOR AND SATIRE IN RELIGION

A common definition across many scholarly studies of *satire* is the use of irony and ridicule to expose behavior the satirist believes to be negative or antithetical to a societal standard; to highlight faults, injustice, and hypocrisy; to reveal wrongdoing. The study of religion and humor—a strategic method often employed by satiric practitioners as a behavioral corrective for targets of the humor—has been undertaken by many scholars, including Reinhold Niebuhr and John Morreall, both of whom explore the Incongruity Theory of comedy. "In its most general form, this theory says that laughing at something is enjoying some incongruity in it," [12] Morreall writes. "[C]omedy concentrates on the incongruities in human beings, especially their shortcomings." [13]

Niebuhr considers it inappropriate to allow humor to *define* faith. Instead, "Humour is, in fact, a prelude to faith; and laughter is the beginning of prayer. Laughter must be heard in the outer courts of religion; and the echoes of it should resound in the sanctuary; but there is no laughter in the holy of holies. There laughter is swallowed up in prayer and humour is fulfilled by faith." [14] Some situations do not lend themselves to humor, Niebuhr maintains, such as Christ on the cross, and laughter is powerless in the face of real evil. "Laughter against real evil is bitter. Such bitter laughter of derision has its uses as an instrument of condemnation. But there is no power in it to deter the evil against which it is directed." [15]

"Humor brings God closer to humankind," writes Hershey H. Friedman. [16] "For instance, God seems more understandable and less aloof when he is sarcastic. . . . Humorous stories and exaggerations make the moral lessons of the Hebrew Bible more memorable, and the irony behind punishments that are 'measure for measure' hints at a world in which justice does truly prevail. . . . A major purpose of the satire and sarcasm was to ridicule the evildoer and the idolator." [17]

"In Jesus, both humor and irony come from love," Father Henri Cormier of the Canada-based Congregation of Jesus and Mary wrote in his 1977 meditation on Christian humor, simply titled *The Humor of Jesus*. "In Jesus, there is no trace of mockery, for mockery is born of hate and triumphant pride." The chief priests, scribes, and elders mocked Jesus with cruel humor. Conversely, "Jesus's humor and irony are something light," Cormier maintains.[18]

Cormier recounted the New Testament story in John 8, in which the Pharisees tell Jesus a woman has been caught in the act of adultery in order to test him. "Now Moses in the law commanded us, that such should be stoned: but what sayest thou? This they said, tempting him, that they might have to accuse him. But Jesus stooped down, and with his finger wrote on the ground, as though he heard them not. So when they continued asking him, he lifted up himself, and said unto them, He that is without sin among you, let him first cast a stone at her."[19]

"With a few well-chosen words," Cormier writes, "Jesus has forced each person to recognize, deep within his own conscience, the presence of him in whose name they meant to perpetuate this atrocious deed, him whose presence they have conveniently forgotten: God."[20] Jesus uses irony and his quiet sense of humor to dispel the crowd and to expose their hypocrisy.

Yet, "There is not a single mention to be found in the Bible of Jesus laughing,"[21] as Belgian theologian Hans Geybels points out. "Theologians from ancient and medieval times were right: nowhere is it written that Jesus ever laughed. But it is also not written that he never did. . . . Humour is a key concept in the actions of Jesus. It is his way to put the restrictive culture He grew up in, in perspective. It is the ideal method of delivering his message without moralising. Many of his parables illustrate this."[22]

Friedman disagrees that Godly laughter is missing from scripture. "The idea that God laughs is mentioned several times in Psalms," he writes.

> In Psalms (2:4) the Psalmist says: "He who sits in heaven will laugh, the Lord will mock them." In Psalms (37:13): "My Lord laughs at him for He sees that his day is coming." In Psalms (59:9): But as for You, God, You laugh at them; You mock all nations." These verses all indicate that one day the Lord will laugh at evildoers. Of course, the type of laughter described here is not a happy, fun-loving laugh, but a sarcastic, derisive one. The Psalmist is describing a contemptuous, sardonic laugh aimed at the wicked who do not realize the futility of their plots if God does not approve.[23]

Friedman also contrasts God's mocking with Cormier's description of Jesus as having "no trace of mockery, for mockery is born of hate and triumphant pride." Is the God of the Hebrew Bible hateful and prideful? These polar views, as well as the choice of language, reveal the difficulty inherent in scholarly efforts to parse the humor of God and Jesus.

Frederick Buechner, Conrad Hyers, Hans Geybels, Elton Trueblood, and numerous others have focused on the story of Abraham and Sarah becoming parents late in life as evidence of holy laughter. The Bible records that Sarah laughed at the angel who brought them the news that she, at age 90, would bear a son.[24] "According to Genesis," Buechner writes, "God intervened then and asked about Sarah's laughter, and Sarah was scared stiff and denied the whole thing."

> Then God said, "No, but you did laugh," and, of course, he was right. Maybe the most interesting part of it all is that far from getting angry at them for laughing, God told them that when the baby was born he wanted them to name him Isaac, which in Hebrew means laughter. So you can say that God not only tolerated their laughter but blessed it and in a sense joined in it himself, which makes it a very special laughter indeed—God and man laughing together, sharing a glorious joke in which both of them are involved.[25]

"The history of Israel begins—if it does not sound too impious—with a joke, a divine joke . . . it was a laughter that became the laughter of faith," Hyers adds.[26]

Earl F. Palmer, focusing on the Gospels, says, "Jesus of Nazareth is the greatest humorist of all time," citing Jesus's gift for universal knowledge and wisdom among the reasons his humor works so well.[27] From that wisdom came ironic and surprising statements that caught authorities off guard and kept his disciples guessing his meaning. Jesus related parables about sinners and prostitutes and wayward children, not about flawless holy people. "If Jesus had told stories about perfect families and perfect dinner parties, we would despair at the families we have and never dare to entertain at dinner; but in the humor of his parables, we are able to find hope in our own imperfect families and invite others over to eat with us," according to Christianity scholar Douglas Adams. Adams also notes that humor and irony are often missed by modern audiences when Biblical passages are taken out of context.[28]

Palmer, Adams, and Trueblood highlight the satire to be found in the parables of Jesus. In his study of Christ's sense of humor, Trueblood cites George Meredith's definition of the "Comic Spirit" when he suggests that, "God's laughter comes only with an underlying interest in our welfare. The laughter is directed at our frailties, but its purpose is to heal," he writes.[29] "There are, of course, persons who are opposed to laughter, especially in religion, where they think of it as inappropriate or even sacrilegious," Trueblood acknowledges in *The Humor of Christ*, one of the earliest works of its type, published in 1964. "They would be shocked at the idea that there is any connection between God and the Comic Spirit."[30]

As religion scholar and filmmaker Terry Lindvall writes in his 2015 book, *God Mocks: A History of Religious Satire from the Hebrew Prophets to Stephen Colbert*,

> Humor in the Hebrew Bible expresses itself primarily in the malicious scoffing, gloating, finger-pointing sort, the kind that comedian Lenny Bruce would later practice. . . . For the prophets, humor is secondary to proclaiming the word of the Lord. They want to shame their audiences into repentance.[31]

Shame was the tactic of *The Wittenburg Door* and *Ship of Fools*, as will become evident in the following sections.

THE WITTENBURG DOOR

The Wittenburg Door (published 1971–2008) began in the United States at the height of the "Hippies for Christ" Jesus Movement, about the same time as *Charlie Hebdo* in France.[32] In 1969, a four-page mimeographed newsletter that sold for a dollar a year was distributed to Southern California Christian youth workers and others interested in youth field ministry. In June 1971, a West Coast company called Youth Specialties, owned by Mike Yaconelli, assumed the newsletter's debts and expanded it into a sixteen-page magazine highlighting evangelical youth work.[33] What the magazine was intended to be and what it became are two vastly different things. Originally an organ for inspiring Christian youth in the mission field, the magazine evolved into the only publication in America devoted to exposing religious excess and fakery with insider satire.

The magazine's title, *The Wittenburg Door*, came from the Castle Church door in Wittenberg, Germany where 500 years ago in 1517, the monk Martin Luther nailed 95 theses criticizing practices of the Catholic Church, particularly the selling of indulgences, leading up to the Protestant Reformation. After three issues, then-publisher Yaconelli noticed the spelling of the City of Wittenberg was incorrect on the cover. "We decided that the misspelling was a kind of divine statement of the satirical nature of the magazine," he later wrote.[34] Also known as simply *The Door*, one of the magazine's slogans was "Still Nailing It to the Church," referring to the catholic church in the universal sense, not a single denomination. Another was, "Pretty Much the World's Only Religious Satire Magazine," which was close to being the case.

The blurred lines of religious criticism and Godly praise were present in *The Wittenburg Door* from the beginning. In one of *The Door*'s first issues in 1972, writer and Youth Movement worker Craig Wilson is pictured in front of the mid-nineteenth-century Castle Church door that now stands in Wittenberg, near the original site where Luther is said to have nailed his protests centuries earlier. Wilson's essay set the parodic tone for future *The Door* pieces by picturing the same event occurring in the twentieth century: "Many will say that we are heading for a second reformation. I am afraid, though, that the Martin Luther of the 1970s would have trouble finding a church that wouldn't call a special meeting of the board of trustees to bring action against the vandal who put a nail in the $5,000.00 sanctuary door, instead of concerning themselves with his thesis."[35]

Attacking the institutional church's bureaucracy and materialism was characteristic of many *The Door* pieces. This early selection is pro-Christian and anti-religion; its dual purpose is to urge readers to focus on Christ while "reforming" the church. Wilson sees a dead church in 1970s United States, one too preoccupied with materiality to hear the Gospel. "The hypocrite is always vulnerable to ridicule," according to Trueblood. "This is why it is easy for us to understand the meaning of Christ's wit when He directs his barbs at the religious. He is talking to us! But the purpose of the Gospel, even of its jokes, is redemption."[36] He adds that, "Though Christ employed several types of humor, the most common type which he used is *irony*, that is a holding up to public view of either vice or folly, but without a note of bitterness or the attempt to harm."[37]

William J. Leonard, former dean of The Divinity School at Wake Forest University, agrees that laughing at religious people and institutions, and even the Bible itself, is a healthy and very human thing. He echoes Niebuhr when he says, "Faith always has that other side. I've sometimes said we take faith very seriously, but we never take ourselves, as people of faith, all that seriously, because we're always stumbling and fumbling our way."[38]

After 25 years of publishing *The Wittenburg Door*, Yaconelli, who was also a lay pastor in a Christian church, tired of producing satire and donated the entire magazine enterprise to Ole Anthony and his Texas-based Trinity Foundation in 1996. Trinity, founded by Anthony in 1972 in a poor neighborhood in East Dallas, is a nonprofit 501(C)(3) organization that houses, counsels, and feeds homeless people in a series of row houses in east Dallas. The foundation is also an investigative watchdog of unscrupulous television ministries who defraud the faithful, housing hundreds of hours of televangelism video, and maintaining an extensive record of complaints from those who contact Trinity to look into suspicious practices.

Longtime *The Door* editor Robert Darden, a gospel music historian and Baylor University journalism professor, recounted the transfer in 2000:

> The original publisher, Youth Specialties, Inc. is filthy rich. It is the world's largest purveyor of youth-oriented products and seminars. Founder Mike Yaconelli . . . against the advice of all of Y.S.'s high-priced accounting staff, heroically labored to continue the magazine into the nineties.

Once the nineties rolled around, and staff cut-backs became the norm in America's corporations, Y.S. deeded *The Door* over to the Trinity Foundation, a not-so-for-profit-that-you-could-tell organization in the ghetto of Southeast Dallas. The Trinity Foundation's twin goals are:

1. To follow the biblical mandate to take care of the homeless.
2. To follow the biblical mandate to bust idols.[39]

Before he took ownership, Anthony had previously been featured for his dual occupations as homeless caretaker and ministerial investigator in a 1994 interview by the magazine, and he had written a piece for *The Door* about televangelist and faith healer Benny Hinn.[40] During that *The Door* interview, Anthony recalled the names of televangelists he had investigated over the years had saddled him with, including "instrument of the devil." Trinity, he said, had been called a "lunatic, supposed-Christian organization," run by "slime who periodically crawl out from under a rock." *The Door* interviewer had replied, "Hmmmm. You sound like our kind of person."[41]

Anthony and his handful of staff members make poverty wages of around $80 per week, $30 of which is paid back into the foundation for room and board. Trinity also has volunteers, some of whom are homeless themselves. The foundation's annual budget is $500,000, "a sum that some of the nation's most popular televangelists routinely raise in a single day," according to religion journalist William Lobdell of the *Los Angeles Times*, who profiled Anthony in 2002.[42] Anthony has said that he promotes "First Century Christianity," illustrated by his willingness to own nothing personally and spend his life caring for the less fortunate.[43] In addition to the homeless ministry Anthony has established in Dallas, Trinity has purchased or built housing for the poor in Dayton, Ohio, and in Oklahoma City.

The Door was a mixed financial blessing for the struggling Trinity Foundation. The magazine never turned a profit for Yaconelli's Youth Specialties until 1994, more than twenty years after it debuted, and it began spilling red ink again the following year. According to Anthony, *The Door* lost between $30,000 and $50,000 a year between 1995 and 1999.[44] After a readership high of 15,000 in the late 1970s, paid circulation shrank to roughly 6,500 subscribers in 1998, and declined thereafter. The magazine was never heavily marketed, and it was available on a limited number of newsstands and in only a handful of religious bookstores. It was later banned from many religious outlets for being too risqué.

THE WITTENBURG DOOR'S SATIRE UNDER THE TRINITY FOUNDATION

After making the move from California to religion-soaked Dallas, *The Wittenburg Door* continued to mock the failings of the devout, or those pretending to be devout. Under Trinity's ownership, however, the magazine's humor became more biting. The foundation's website stated that, "Trinity has broadened the magazine's mission to deflate pompous individuals, movements and institutions from ANY religious persuasion that take themselves too seriously. . . . The basis for The Door's mission is a scriptural injunction to mock idolatry. . . . The rabbinic teachers said Israel was forbidden to mock or jeer anyone or anything except idolatry."[45]

Its writers and cartoonists parodied religious figures, particularly avaricious televangelists, but took God seriously. The magazine appealed primarily to zealous Christian youth and seminarians who preferred an edgier tone to their religious messages than mainstream fodder, such as *Christianity Today*. Jewish culture magazine *Heeb* and the hip Christian magazine *Relevant* are more recent publications that fill that gap, but neither pushes the taste envelope the way *The Door* did under Anthony's leadership.

As a 1998 newspaper profile put it, "This group of slightly wacky Christians uses laughter, sarcasm and irony to ridicule religion's sacred cows, deflate pious egos and expose religious charlatans. . . . 'The purpose of *The Door* is to satirize and make fun of anyone who takes themselves seriously in the name of God,' said publisher Ole Anthony. 'I'd like to smash the idolatry that is so common in the American church.'"[46]

Assorted religious groups suffered their share of mockery, from the Amish to Baptists to Scientologists.[47] Mother Teresa, heralded during her lifetime for her work in the slums of Calcutta with orphans and lepers, earned the designation of "Loser of the Decade" by *The Door* in 1996. She was canonized by the Catholic Church as Saint Teresa of Calcutta in 2016, but *The Door* staffers declared two decades earlier that, "she's no more a saint than you or me."[48] The first issue published under Trinity's ownership took the then 85-year-old nun, founder of the Order of the Missionaries of Charity, to task for a variety of sins. Among Mother Teresa's offenses was the acceptance of the Haitian Legion d'honneur from "the murderous Duvaliers" who "had been terrorizing, murdering, and stealing from the Haitian people since 'Papa Doc' Duvalier rose to power in 1957."[49] The essay criticizes her for accepting $1.4 million from Charles Keating, implicated in the Savings and Loan scandals of the 1980s and 1990s.[50]

After berating the future saint, the writer acknowledges his own sinful shortcomings, and places Mother Teresa on a level with the rest of humanity:

I suppose we'll never know if you're merely operating in a holy daze or if you're running the world's biggest Catholic Charity Bazaar. Most likely you're just a normal everyday loser, like the rest of us. And that's the whole point.

But you're our Loser . . . the Loser of the Decade. [51]

Ole Anthony's faith is reflected in this harsh assessment. Holding Mother Teresa up as a saint during her lifetime was seen as vanity from *The Door's* theological viewpoint. Vanity is also what Anthony sees in the millionaire televangelists he ridicules. As Burkhard Bilger wrote in a *New Yorker* profile of Anthony, "he found religion at the pinnacle of his career and has grown steadily poorer since. God's purpose, he believes, is . . . to reveal the hollowness of our existence so that we might sacrifice our lives for others, as Christ did." [52] While it can be argued that Mother Teresa did just that—sacrifice her life for others—she was not perfect, and *The Door* did not hesitate to point out her imperfections.

Ninety percent of *The Wittenburg Door's* articles came from freelance writers, with editor Robert Darden and a small core staff from Trinity sifting through the submissions. Darden has said that editorial meetings were occasions for laughter and fellowship, and for arguing and positioning and daring. Conceptualizing the concept for the cover was the most difficult decision, he said.

With the committee, there's a brainstorming. And the whole time we're throwing out ideas, I'm watching Harry [Guetzlaff]. I never take my eyes off Harry, because Harry is our promotions manager and our circulation manager and that stuff, and if all the blood drains out of his face, and he looks at me after he hears an idea, and he says, "dear Jesus, no, no," then I think we're on to something. [53]

In an interview with CNN, Darden said, "At its best, religious satire fulfills the Old Testament mandate to break down idols. . . . As a culture, we're idol-makin' fools—wealth, glory, prestige, power, personalities. If fallible, wounded People of God resist that [mandate]—be it [idols such as] a Golden Calf or a golden-throat TV evangelist—then they're doing themselves a grave disservice." [54]

A 1997 issue of *The Wittenburg Door* featured an interview with *National Lampoon* magazine's former editor Henry Beard. *The Door's* cover sported a parody of the *Lampoon's* infamous January 1973 cover of a gun pointed at the head of a nervous looking dog, with the headline: "If You Don't Buy This Magazine, We'll Kill This Dog." *The Wittenburg Door* cover showed a gun pointing at evangelist Billy Graham with the headline: "Buy this magazine, or Billy gets it." [55]

The late National Rifle Association chairman and actor Charlton Heston was on the September/October 1998 cover, dressed as Moses holding a machine gun instead of tablets bearing the Ten Commandments. Heston, a favorite of evangelical conservatives and star of the 1956 epic *The Ten Commandments*, was a longtime spokesman for the NRA. In the NRA version of the Commandments envisioned by *The Door*, Number Ten was "Thou shalt not covet thy neighbor's Uzi, nor his Glock, nor his Browning, nor his Colt, nor his Weatherby, nor any other instrument by which thy neighbor exercises his right to keep and bear arms."[56]

The cover story combining religion and the NRA was prescient. Seventeen years later in December 2015, 14 people were killed and 22 injured in San Bernardino, California by a heavily armed married couple, both Muslims of Pakistani descent. Sayed Rizwan Farook was a U.S.-born American citizen, and his wife Tashfeen Malik was a legal permanent resident.[57] In response to the attack, Jerry Falwell, Jr., president of Liberty University, a Christian institution in Lynchburg, Virginia, told students at a convocation service four days later that, "If more good people had concealed-carry permits, then we could end those Muslims before they walked in and killed them."[58]

In contrast to Falwell's stance, at a Religion Newswriters Association multi-faith gun control panel in Georgia a year earlier, panelist David Gushee, a Christian ethicist at Mercer University, said, "It's hard to articulate a strong Biblical case for a heavily armed society. . . . That's not Biblical reasoning; that's cultural reasoning."[59]

Trinity vice-president John Rutledge, who created *The Door's* first web-page in 1997, said the magazine's content generated scores of angry letters and emails from both sides of the religious fence, conservative and liberal. Readers occasionally canceled subscriptions after taking offense at an article or a cover illustration, but Rutledge has seen some people become more open to Christianity after corresponding with the magazine via email. "We had so many agnostics, and all kinds of people would write us, or taking objection at something. I must have talked to more unbelievers . . . either by e-mail or just talked to them," he said.[60] In some cases at least, the magazine's unusual way of witnessing was effective.

SATIRIC MISSION FIELD: EXPOSING TELEVANGELISTS

"Vanity is a great weakness of mankind in general," Trueblood observed, "but it seems especially ludicrous when it appears among the professionally religious. The contradiction between man's humility before God and his strutting before men is a perfect opening for ridicule."[61] The Trinity Foundation's investigations of televangelists alleged to have defrauded the public are serious affairs—they wound up not only as fodder for humor in the pages of *The Wittenburg Door*, but also on television news shows such as ABC's *Primetime Live, Dateline NBC*, and the syndicated *Inside Edition*, and as part of a congressional inquiry.

Senator Charles Grassley of Iowa, the ranking Republican on the Senate Finance Committee, investigated six prominent televangelists in 2007 for possible financial misconduct: Paula White, Joyce Meyer, Creflo Dollar, Eddie Long, Kenneth Copeland, and Benny Hinn. He did so in response to letters from Ole Anthony. According to a CBS News story:

> Because they have tax status as churches, the ministries do not have to file IRS 990 forms like other non-profit organizations—leaving much financial information largely behind closed doors.
>
> The letters sent Monday were the culmination of a long investigation fueled in part by complaints from Ole Anthony, a crusader against religious fraud who operates the Dallas-based Trinity Foundation, which describes itself as a watchdog monitoring religious media, fraud and abuse. "We've been working with them for two years," Anthony told *CBS News*. "We have furnished them with enough information to fill a small Volkswagen."
>
> Anthony said after twenty years of working with media organizations to expose televangelists, he saw little reform. He says that's why he turned to another tactic, going straight to Grassley. He is confident that Grassley's inquiry will be different, "What we hope is that this will lead to reform in religious nonprofits."[62]

To Anthony's dismay, no charges were ever filed against any of the televangelists featured in the report.

The late circulation manager for *The Door*, Harry Guetzlaff, a former Coca-Cola executive, originally came to the Trinity Foundation seeking help after he had been turned down for assistance from televangelist Robert Tilton's church when Guetzlaff found himself on hard times. He had been a longtime donor to Tilton's ministry and had donated his last $5,000 prior to being turned away by Tilton. Anthony hired Guetzlaff and offered him a home. Guetzlaff became archivist and editor of the thousands of hours of television ministry video recordings in Trinity's archive. Working with ABC News, journalist Diane Sawyer, and the show *Primetime Live* in 1991, Trinity investigated Tilton and found prayer requests for healing in a dumpster that Tilton had claimed to pray over. Checks to Tilton's ministry had been removed and the requests discarded, Anthony told Sawyer.

Tilton was at his peak in 1991, with his ministry bringing in some $80 million per year. The resulting televised reports on Tilton cost him many viewers and followers, as well as his first marriage. He was sued by multiple plaintiffs for fraud, and lost much of his wealth and reputation. Tilton was unsuccessful in his own libel suit against Trinity and ABC News.[63] Trinity's reports have landed Anthony in court many times, but thus far no televangelist has sued him successfully.

Tilton later appeared on *The Door*'s cover as the Dr. Seuss character the Grinch in the November/December 2000 issue. "Brother Bob Tilton: The Grinch Who Stole Christmas" was the headline, and inside there was a purported interview with Tilton as Grinch, using fictional questions paired with Tilton's actual words from a 1991 broadcast transcript from his former show *Success-N-Life*. [64] The effect was to make Tilton look avaricious and foolish, which *The Door* considered him to be.

In his back of the book column in the same issue, Anthony, with assistance from a staffer known only as Skippy R., highlighted Tilton's legal troubles, but ended on a redemptive note:

> When Tilton reviled me, I reviled him right back. I called him a snake oil salesman, a joke, a fraud, dumber than a box of rocks and someone who "has nothing to do with the God I believe in." But on reflection, I was wrong. He does have something to do with God.
>
> The church needs people like Tilton, just as I personally do. Let me explain.
>
> Sure, I could justify judging Tilton, but only if I've never lied, never tried to manipulate someone, never had an illicit sexual thought, never ignored the needs of people around me, never tried to numb the grind of daily existence by seeking escape. Jesus was very clear about this. These are all just variations on the theme of self-seeking. . . . How can God expect us to meet that kind of standard? He doesn't. He knows we can't. . . . But God has provided a way for us to repent. . . . The church needs to take a glance in the mirror. Until we see Tilton's face in the reflection, we'll continue to wander in the deception of self-righteousness, never realizing we've left the narrow way.
>
> Repentance. Even Tilton can do that. Even you can.
>
> And even me. [65]

The Wittenburg Door sought to discuss topical religious issues in both serious and comic ways, and while it often resembled *MAD* magazine more than Holy Scripture, the staff maintained its Christian identity. Writing in the *Washington Post* in 1997, reporter Peter Carlson observed that, "sometimes it's hard to tell whether *The Door* is a funny religious magazine or a funny anti-religious magazine. And the editors seem to enjoy sowing that confusion." [66]

SHIP OF FOOLS

Sebastian Brandt, a conservative religious scholar and humanist, wrote *Das Narrenschiff*, or *The Ship of Fools*, a moralistic poem that describes 110 assorted follies and vices, in 1494. Originally published in German with descriptive woodcuts typically attributed to famed artist Albrecht Dürer of Nuremberg, the various chapters are devoted to such offenses as "Arrogance Toward God" and "Marrying for Money," and satirize religious corruption. According to scholar Terry Lindvall:

> Brandt's floating community of fools personifies the compelling place of laughter and satire in religious life. If satire is to be defined as the ridiculing of human vanity, folly, and hypocrisy, one finds no better metaphor than a boat-load of stupid people obliviously drifting toward the edge of the world. To recognize the church as a similar tub of rogues and village idiots is to recognize a fundamental truth about human nature, within or without the Christian community—namely that none are righteous or wise, but all have fallen into the folly of sin.[67]

Ship of Fools: The Magazine of Christian Unrest is the British counterpart to *The Wittenburg Door*. The two magazines were unrelated in business terms, but share satiric sensibilities and same mission of religious parody, though *Ship of Fools* humor is on the gentler side. The magazine folded as a print publication after ten issues when its readership dropped to 450 subscribers.[68] Developed by a group of professional writers who put out the magazine in their spare time, *Ship of Fools*, or *SOF*, attacked such sacred cows as the cult of C.S. Lewis, the Papal souvenir trade, and born-again celebrities who make public testimonials. Founding editor and designer Simon Jenkins revived the magazine as a website on April Fool's Day 1998, a year after *The Door* went online. The web incarnation is updated weekly with articles and features resembling the earlier print version. Ship-of-fools.com records 150,000 unique visitors each month.[69] "We're here for people who prefer their religion disorganized," according to Jenkins. "Our aim is to help Christians be self-critical and honest about the failings of Christianity, as we believe honesty can only strengthen faith."[70]

Jenkins and co-editor Stephen Goddard both have backgrounds in religion. Jenkins earned a master's degree in theology and education from King's College London and is the author of several religious books. In addition, he is a Lay Reader in the Church of England. Goddard, also a theology graduate, edited *Buzz*, a leading Christian monthly in Britain, for seven years. In a 2000 interview with *The Door*, Jenkins said, "*Ship of Fools* doesn't do much satire, actually, but because our humor is critical of church leaders and church life, people think of us as satirical."

> Real satire has a lot of cruelty in it, I think, whether it's the satire of Hogarth and Swift in the eighteenth century, which was fueled by moral indignation at the evils happening at the time, or the TV satire of today, which doesn't seem to come from a moral center, but from a love of pulling things down. Our humor tends to be less cruel and more playful than satire, although I think there's room for sharpening ourselves up.[71]

On the website, Goddard states, "As committed Christians ourselves, we can't help laughing at the crazy things that go wrong with the church, and we're also drawn to those questions which take us beyond easy believing. In the end, we want to make sense of the Christian faith in today's complex world."[72] In place of a mission statement, Jenkins posted a long poem he wrote at the magazine's founding, which ends with this verse:

> a ship of fools
> but there are fools and
> those who only appear to be
>
> —*Simon Jenkins, 1977*[73]

Jenkins's verse summarizes the bold notion of being a "fool for Christ" by citing the flawed faith of the frightened and wondering apostles who followed "a small sleeping carpenter."[74] *Ship of Fools* adopted as its patron saint "the coolest saint in all Christendom—St. Simeon the Holy Fool, whose feast day we celebrate every 21st July."[75] After living in a cave near the Dead Sea for 29 years during the sixth century, Simeon arrived at the gate of Edessa in Syria one day dragging a dead dog from a rope tied around his waist. He exhibited other erratic behaviors, such as blowing out the candles during church and passing gas in public. "Simeon had decided to play the fool in order to mock the idiocy of the world and also to conceal his own identity as a saint," according to *SOF.*[76]

Sociologist Peter L. Berger has written about holy fools, which "have been both real madmen (what today would be called cases of mental illness or retardation) and individuals feigning madness. . . . There are important elements of religiously privileged folly in Taoism and Zen Buddhism, among the wandering *sanyasin* of India, and in primal regions in Africa and the Americas."[77] Berger also notes that holy fools have appeared in Judaism, Christianity, and Islam. Quoting the Bible, he writes:

> The prophetic literature has a number of cases that can properly be described as holy folly. In the Book of Isaiah, the prophet is reported to have walked naked and barefoot for three years (Is. 20). The prophet Jeremiah put on a wooden yoke around his neck (Jer. 27). And Ezekiel was commanded to eat excrement (Ezek. 4).[78]

Berger identifies, as many scholars do, the apostle Paul's letters to the Corinthians in the New Testament concerning being a fool for Christ:

> We are fools for Christ, but you are so wise in Christ! We are weak, but you are strong! You are honored, we are dishonored! . . .
> But God chose the foolish things of the world to shame the wise; God chose the weak things of the world to shame the strong. God chose the lowly

things of this world and the despised things—and the things that are not—to nullify the things that are, so that no one may boast before him. [79]

Berger also cites more modern examples of holy folly. "Dietrich Bonhoeffer, the Protestant theologian executed by the Nazis for his involvement in the attempt to assassinate Hitler, wrote from prison how humor sustains Christian faith in adversity. Alfred Delp, a Catholic priest who was another victim of Nazism, joked in the best tradition of Christian martyrdom when he was actually walking toward his execution. He asked the chaplain accompanying him about the latest news from the front, then said, 'In a half hour I will know more than you!'"[80]

"We think Christians should be restless about the state of church today, and stirring up unrest in the wider world as well," Jenkins told *The Door*. "We want to ask: isn't there a better way to do Christianity than this?"[81]

The *SOF* website has various departments, including "The Fruitcake Zone," harboring weird religious news; "Gadgets for God," showcasing strange religious merchandise (similar to *The Door*'s "Truth is Stranger than Fiction" and "Loser" features); and "The Mystery Worshipper," made up of hundreds of volunteers around the world who attend church services, take notes on the experience based on a questionnaire, and report their findings on the *SOF* site. "We want to help churches see what they look like to someone who comes to them as a stranger," Jenkins told *The Door*. "It's like holding up a mirror to churches and saying, 'Is this how you expected to look? Are you happy looking like this?' But it's also a tongue-in-cheek sort of project. . . . If the communion wafers are soggy, or the pastor's jokes aren't funny, we'll say so. We're offering a snapshot of how church really is experienced around the world today."[82]

The website for *Ship of Fools* offers visitors explanations of its many components:

> Regular features include the Mystery Worshipper, the Caption Competition, and Gadgets for God. Ship of Fools has also run a number of projects, including The Ark, an online gameshow, and Church of Fools, an early experiment in online 3D church. The Laugh Judgment, our investigation into funny and offensive religious jokes, prompted journalist Julie Burchill to say of us: "If one must choose a modern symbol of what is so good about Britain, I would choose Ship of Fools."
>
> Alongside these is a thriving online community, including the famed Heaven, Hell and Purgatory bulletin boards, where shipmates debate everything from "Religion and Buffy the Vampire Slayer" and "The status of Mormonism" to "Hitchcock and Catholic Guilt." Over 13,500 people joined the boards in its first ten years online. [83]

"When we started, we thought we were just launching a magazine—but we've found that we actually launched a community, too," Simon said.[84]

Ship of Fools had many things in common with its late American cousin, *The Wittenburg Door.* Each was a religious satire magazine run by a religious publisher; each had the mission of evangelizing by exposing vanity and tearing down idols and sacred cows in the church; and each urged a return to the core teachings of the Bible, highlighting humor and humanity. One last thing the magazines shared in common was poor financial health. "We don't have a shortage of ideas," Jenkins opined to *The Door* in 2000, "just a shortage of money."[85]

RELIGIOUS SATIRE MOVES TO LATE NIGHT TELEVISION

Two of the twenty-first century's sharpest wits are Stephen Colbert and John Oliver, one American and one British, like *The Wittenburg Door* and *Ship of Fools.* Colbert's fame grew on two of cable channel Comedy Central's shows, *The Daily Show* (from 1997–2005) and *The Colbert Report* (from 2005–2014). Colbert was always in character as a conservative blowhard on *The Colbert Report*, allowing him to satirize right wing pundits such as former FOX News host Bill O'Reilly. Viewers wondered if O'Reilly was in on the joke, as he and Colbert were occasional guests on each other's shows. Colbert eventually moved to late night broadcast television. Taking over the 11:35 p.m. slot on CBS from the retiring David Letterman, Colbert began hosting *The Late Show with Stephen Colbert*, as himself, in September 2015.

Oliver, another *Daily Show* alumnus (from 2006–2014), moved to premium cable channel HBO as the host of *Last Week Tonight with John Oliver* in April 2014. Oliver is a standup comedian and writer, and took over as temporary host of The Daily Show when Jon Stewart took a leave of absence in the summer of 2013 to direct the film *Rosewater.* The Oliver show's format is closer to an extended comic monologue. He spends much of the show solo, behind a desk, as an anchorman/commentator. He and his writing staff do extensive research on a single topic, intersperse jokes among a flurry of facts, and turn out detailed social commentary that has been praised for raising awareness of important topics that often fly under the radar of most Americans' news feeds.

Neither Colbert nor Oliver has religion as the sole focus of his comedy material, but both have indulged in elaborate parodies that showcase hypocrisy and deceit in the name of faith.

STEPHEN COLBERT, THEOLOGIAN

There was some historical overlap between *The Wittenburg Door* and *The Daily Show.* From its earliest incarnation with host Craig Kilborn, *The Daily Show* had a segment called "Godstuff" featuring clips of histrionics and antics from religious television shows, including those of Benny Hinn and Robert Tilton, as well as a number of televangelists asking for money. The clips were supplied by the Trinity Foundation, and were introduced by John Bloom, whose alias Joe Bob Briggs is a B-movie reviewer and comic writer. Bloom reported on televangelists and wrote parodies for *The Door*, and served as president of Trinity for a time. "Godstuff" was eventually dropped from *The Daily Show*, but after Jon Stewart became host in 1999, a similar skit called "This Week in God" was created by Stephen Colbert, a Catholic actor and comedian who regularly attends mass and can recite Bible verses from memory.

Colbert told Terry Gross of NPR's *Fresh Air* that he wasn't "a particularly religious person," but he goes to church, "which makes me kind of odd for my profession. You know, most people can't understand why I do, other comedians. And I have to walk that thin line because I don't want to criticize anyone's religion for the fact that it is a religion, and what's funny to me is what people do in the name of religion."[86] Walking a thin like to mock "what people do in the name of religion" rather than religion itself is the same impulse behind the humor of *The Wittenburg Door* and *Ship of Fools.*

In a YouTube video from March 2015 prior to the debut of his eponymous CBS show, Colbert submitted to an interview with Jesuit Priest James Martin, editor-at-large for *America* magazine, author of *Between Heaven and Mirth: Why Joy, Humor, and Laughter Are at the Heart of the Spiritual Life*, and a frequent guest on *The Colbert Report*. So frequent, in fact, that Colbert typically introduced him as *"The Colbert Report* chaplain." An excerpt from their conversation:

> *Martin:* "Who's your favorite saint?"
> *Colbert:* "I like St. Peter, 'cause he's so flawed. . . . I always liked Peter because he's the rock, but the rocks are between the ears. Because he has the insight, or the grace, to know that you are the Messiah, the Son of God. And then he denies Christ. . . . He's angry, like, he's known as like having an anger. I like him 'cause he's super-flawed. And yet he gets the big job."
> *Martin:* "He does, that's right, at the end. He gets to be pope."[87]

In this casual exchange, recorded standing amid file cabinets and desks in the offices of *America* magazine, Colbert acknowledges the humanity present in the first pope. The six-minute, unstructured conversation is by turns funny and serious, like Colbert himself. At one point, Colbert addresses humor, saying it's a commandment from God not to worry. "It's sort of autonomic that you can't laugh and be afraid at the same time."[88]

Stephen Colbert experienced tragedy early in life when his father and two brothers died in a plane crash. Colbert was 10 years old. He described to *The New York Times Magazine* how he coped afterward:

"I'm not bitter about what happened to me as a child, and my mother was instrumental in keeping me from being so." He added, in a tone so humble and sincere that his character [on *The Colbert Report*] would never have used it: "She taught me to be grateful for my life regardless of what that entailed, and that's directly related to the image of Christ on the cross and the example of sacrifice that he gave us. What she taught me is that the deliverance God offers you from pain is not no pain—it's that the pain is actually a gift. What's the option? God doesn't really give you another choice."[89]

In September 2010, Colbert testified before a U.S. Congressional Subcommittee—in character as his *Colbert Report* America-first conservative pundit—about the plight of migrant farmworkers. The real Stephen Colbert wanted to raise awareness about human rights violations of the workers, as did U.S. Democratic Representative Zoe Lofgren of California, who invited him to testify.[90] Colbert's four-minute address mingled humor with truth, which is a quality of satire.

"I don't want a tomato picked by a Mexican," Colbert said. "I want it picked by an *American*, sliced by a Guatemalan and served by a Venezuelan in a spa where a Chilean gives me a Brazilian."[91]

Dan Zak reported in the *Washington Post* that Colbert, still in character, got in a dig at lawmakers for Congressional gridlock.

"I'm a free-market guy," Colbert said when it was his turn to speak. "Normally I'd leave this to the invisible hand of the market. . . . But the invisible hand has moved farm work to Mexico" because of the lack of available labor in the United States. If Congress passes the AgJobs—intended to provide legal farm labor and secure the rights of immigrant workers—"Americans may consider taking jobs once conditions are better," Colbert continued, sarcasm creeping across his face. "I trust both sides will work on this together in the best interests of the American people—*as you always do.*"[92]

Writing in *The Huffington Post*, blogger Brad A. Greenberg highlighted Colbert's Biblical citation of Matthew 25:

The *Washington Post*'s BlogPost shared a transcript of the opening statement of Colbert's testimony. Unfortunately, that omits what I found to be the most interesting part—in fact, what made Colbert's appearance before Congress more than just a humorous moment for this blog.

It was the moment in his testimony when Colbert broke character, in responding to a question from Rep. Judy Chu, D-CA, and he quoted Matthew 25 in explaining why he cares about the plight of migrant workers:

"One of the least powerful people in the United States are migrant workers who come and do our work but don't have any rights as a result. . . . That is an interesting contradiction to me. And, you know, whatsoever you do for the least of my brothers, and these seem like the least of our brothers right now. . . . Migrant workers suffer and have no rights."[93]

Representative Lofgren explained why she brought Colbert to Congress. "His actions are a good example of how using both levity and fame, a media figure can bring attention to a critically important issue for the good of the nation," she said as she opened the hearing to discuss the bill to legalize undocumented field workers.[94] Lynn Schofield Clark wrote that "Colbert's audience arguably wasn't the members of Congress in attendance or the reporters who covered the event. The intended audience seemingly included those who saw the video once it went viral thanks to YouTube, Facebook, and blog mentions."[95] She noted that within two months, the testimony reached one million views on YouTube.[96] Social media is often the friend of satire, and the enemy of satirical targets.

Clark argues that Colbert and other comedians need to be taken seriously as social commentators on religion, not as replacements for religious authorities, but as "interpreters of how various players in our societal fabric operate in relation to one another. Those who are positioned to serve as interpreters of religion's role in society, and whose views articulate those that are consensually accepted, thus emerge as authoritative figures in contemporary culture." Clark's study of Colbert evaluated what she termed his "consensus-based interpretive authority," even as he does not speak for all citizens.[97]

Clark says comedians and others, such as conservative Mormon commentator Glenn Beck, "speak about the role of religion in relation to culture in a way that echoes our own beliefs." She continues:

> As we participate in watching their programs, purchasing their books, contributing to their fan websites, and sharing clips from their programs with others in our social circles, we are contributing to their consensus-based interpretive authority in a remix culture. We participate in a process of remixing cultural elements in a way that reinforces some perspectives and narratives and deemphasizes others. In this sense, then, it is not the media that undermine traditional or promote charismatic authority, but rather it is the collective uses of the media in a remix culture that enable a new form of authority to emerge and become reinforced.[98]

Colbert's credibility is based in part on his celebrity, but his religious credibility is derived from being a churchgoer who speaks the language. As Clark concluded, "[G]iven the importance of both consensus and interpretation in contemporary society, Colbert has come to take on an authoritative position regarding religion as he has critiqued religion from the position of a well-placed insider."[99]

In his Congressional testimony, he added, "If this is going to be a Christian nation that doesn't help the poor, either we have to pretend that Jesus was just as selfish as we are, or we've got to acknowledge that He commanded us to love the poor and serve the needy without condition and then admit that we just don't want to do it."[100] This quote circulated widely as an internet meme, and has shown up in social media posts and on posters accompanied by Colbert's image.

"Due to Colbert's indirect satire, he does not easily disclose an agenda," writes Terry Lindvall. "As with the parables of Jesus, one is not quite sure what he is really saying with his monologues, interviews, and skits, but one has a notion that it strikes deeply into the heart, while jogging the lungs with unexpected laughter."[101]

JOHN OLIVER, CRUSADING NON-THEOLOGIAN

Unlike Stephen Colbert, John Oliver does not carry with him the authority and knowledge of the religious insider, but *Last Week Tonight with John Oliver* does radiate authenticity. His work on the HBO comedy show has been likened to investigative journalism.[102] His former colleague Jon Stewart also used to be considered by some to be a journalist when he hosted *The Daily Show*, and like Stewart, Oliver brushes off the label.[103] "We are making jokes about the news and sometimes we need to research things deeply to understand them," Oliver says, "but it's always in service of a joke. If you make jokes about animals, that does not make you a zoologist. We certainly hold ourselves to a high standard and fact-check everything, but the correct term for what we do is 'comedy.'"[104]

Stewart's *Daily Show* made "heavy use of news footage, often in a documentary way that employs archival video to show contrast and contradiction, even if the purpose is satirical rather than reportorial. . . . *The Daily Show* not only assumes, but even requires, previous and significant knowledge of the news on the part of viewers if they want to get the joke."[105]

Last Week Tonight's format is similar to that of *The Daily Show*, but where Oliver's show diverges is in investigating and highlighting significant but often underreported issues, and explaining them to the audience in detail. With its deep dives into analysis and interpretations of primary research, *Last Week Tonight* utilizes journalistic techniques, enhancing credibility. Careful research and fact checking is routinely practiced, and the writing staff scours primary documents of all kinds to understand an issue. The show then offers factual reporting in a humorous vein, meaning jokes are mingled with reporting, on a variety of serious topics, including religion. As opposed to Colbert's religiosity, Oliver's tone is one of moral outrage over injustice in various sectors of society. The result is a hybrid of comedy and explanatory journalism.

The weekly show, airing at 11 p.m. Sunday nights, resembles an evening newscast. Oliver sits at a desk, and graphics appear over his shoulder as he speaks into the camera. Occasionally, he cuts to video. The centerpiece of the show is a long-form segment that reveals disturbing facts on obscure issues typically not on American viewers' radar screens. Among the complex topics Oliver has tackled:

- How American evangelical Christians preaching homophobic messages may have played a role in the harsh treatment of gay, lesbian, and transgender citizens in Uganda. As *Variety* noted, "The segment included nods to information from Al Jazeera, NPR, the Kaiser Family Foundation, CNN, MSNBC, Christian evangelical news organization World, and advocacy group Political Research Associates, not to mention an interview with Ugandan LGBT rights advocate Pepe Julian Onziema."[106]

- The questionable nutritional value of dietary supplements, including a slam against celebrity pitchmen for the products, such as television host Dr. Mehmet Oz, the surgeon/star of *The Dr. Oz Show.*

- The debate over Net Neutrality, which led to viewers apparently crashing the FCC's website with comments—twice. Oliver, arguing that the internet should be regulated like a utility as opposed to a tiered system of privileging corporations who could pay for higher speed connections, encouraged viewers to take advantage of the 120-day open commenting period on the FCC's site. More than 45,000 people responded.[107]

- A detailed account of the 2015 corruption charges surrounding officials of FIFA, the Zurich-based governing body of world soccer.[108]

- The scope of predatory lending in the payday loan industry.

Once Oliver raises awareness on a topic among his millions of viewers, both on HBO and on his YouTube channel, he urges them to take action by getting in touch with the appropriate party or government agency. He also acts as a consumer advocate, warning people to avoid certain practices that may be detrimental to their health or their pocketbook.

OUR LADY OF PERPETUAL EXEMPTION CHURCH

In August 2015, Oliver took on televangelism and the tax-exempt status of churches, an industry that he demonstrated could be both unhealthy and costly. "Churches are a cornerstone of American life," Oliver said at the top of the segment. "There are roughly 350,000 congregations in the United States and many of them do great work: feeding the hungry, clothing the poor. But, this is not a story about them. This is about the churches that exploit people's faith for monetary gain."[109]

Oliver showed clips from 1980s religious television shows, focusing on longtime Trinity Foundation nemesis Robert Tilton. "We've seen midgets grow. . . . I don't make this stuff up!" Tilton shouts in one vintage snippet. Oliver then showed a more recent clip of Tilton, who now has a much smaller audience, but is still on the air in syndication. "He never really went away," Oliver tells the audience. "Though you may not be aware of it, televangelism is still thriving in this country, and Robert Tilton is just a very small part of it."

The clips came straight from the Trinity Foundation's vault. In a post on the Blind Folly Christian humor blog, longtime Trinity associate Skippy R. wrote:

> Nowhere in the program does it mention the source of most of this information: Trinity Foundation, a Dallas-based, public religious non-profit charged with keeping tabs on religious fraud and helping its victims.
>
> Trinity worked for months with the program, providing video, photos and reams of documentation. The result, of course, was hilarious. But after we've all had a good laugh and the smoke clears, the televangelists will continue to ply their trade, defaming the Christian gospel and the selfless work of millions of believers around the world, many suffering fierce persecution.
>
> And that's the way it's been going for Trinity Foundation since it started monitoring religious broadcasting in 1974, before many in John Oliver's audience were born.[110]

Full networks devoted to televangelism exist, Oliver continued, citing Inspiration Ministries; Daystar; and Trinity Broadcast Network (TBN is not associated with the Trinity Foundation). Oliver showed examples of the wealthy lifestyles of televangelists who own—and demand from congregants the money to buy—multimillion dollar airplanes and lavish estates.

Oliver called out several televangelists for preaching the Prosperity Gospel, the belief that the more you give, the more likely God will bless you—especially if you give to *their* ministry. Kate Bowler, an assistant professor of the history of Christianity in North America at Duke Divinity School and the author of *Blessed: A History of the American Prosperity Gospel*, offers this definition: "Put simply, the prosperity gospel is the belief that God grants health and wealth to those with the right kind of faith."[111]

Oliver cited the case of Bonnie Parker, a woman with cancer who did not seek treatment, but "sowed money" into the church run by "healing through faith" televangelists Kenneth and Gloria Copeland.[112] Parker gave thousands of dollars to the Copelands in hopes of being healed, and eventually died, according to Oliver.

A clip of Gloria Copeland followed this story showing her in the pulpit discussing a hypothetical scenario of a doctor delivering the news to a patient about a cancer diagnosis. "The bad news is we don't know what to do about it," Copeland says. "Except give you some poison that'll make you sicker. Now, which do you want to do? You want do that, or you want to sit here on Saturday morning, hear the word of God, and let faith come into your heart and be healed? Hallelujah!"

"It's pretty clear that woman cannot hear the word of God," Oliver comments to audience applause, "because if He could, I'm pretty sure He would be shouting, 'F**k you, Gloria!' right in her ear."

After establishing the supernatural claims and opulent lifestyles of many popular televangelists, Oliver showed a portion of an IRS training video featuring Virginia Richardson, senior tax law specialist with the federal agency. Going over "Church and Religious Organizations Do's and Don'ts," Richardson declared that IRS regulations are "purposely broad, and sometimes a little vague."

"A little vague!" Oliver says with a sardonic chuckle. "They are underselling that." Oliver channeled his outrage toward this section of the IRS code:

> The IRS makes no attempt to evaluate the content of whatever doctrine a particular organization claims is religious, provided the particular beliefs of the organization are *truly and sincerely held* by those professing them and the practices and rites associated with the organization's belief or creed are not illegal or contrary to clearly defined public policy [emphasis added]. [113]

It is likely no tax-exempt televangelist has ever confessed to *not* holding "truly and sincerely held" beliefs about his or her ministry. When Oliver's staff asked the IRS how many churches had been audited in recent years for irregularities, the response was one in FY 2014, and two in FY 2013. "The odds of a church getting audited are basically the same as Gloria Copeland curing your f**king cancer," Oliver remarked.

Oliver launched a correspondence with Robert Tilton's Word of Faith Worldwide Church over the course of seven months "to try and found out what he tells people." Oliver sent $20 to Tilton in January 2015, asking to be added to his mailing list. Tilton's ministry sent a thank you letter, followed by a second letter containing a $1 bill, with the instructions to "Send it back to me with your Prove God tithes or offering." This went on for some weeks until Oliver received three small packets of colored oil, which he was to pour on letters and send them back "by specific dates, along with more money."

Back came a manila envelope containing a $5 check—*from John Oliver*—made out to Word of Faith Worldwide Church. A few weeks later Oliver received some pieces of cloth folded like small mountains. Tilton asked for the mountains back, along with more money. Tilton then sent another $1 bill with the instructions to "Put the One Dollar Gift of God Seed in your Bible." The next day, Oliver was to send the $1 back with an additional $49. Tilton was going to anoint the $1 bill and send the blessed dollar back to Oliver. An admonition accompanied the request for $49: "I must warn you not to rob God with your tithes and offerings. . . . I can't urge you enough: DO NOT LET THIS ONE DOLLAR BILL STAY IN YOUR HOUSE."

Oliver then pulled the dollar from his pocket, saying he was going to keep that one. In all, Oliver sent the ministry $319. Tilton's ministry was relentless, sending more letters (26 in all), oil, and prayer cloths, along with other items. Oliver told the audience this was all hilarious, until he thought of all the people who can't afford to send Tilton money, but feel coerced or compelled to do so. Angry, Oliver was looking for a sign of what to do, he said, so he watched "a little more Robert Tilton, and the most amazing thing happened." A clip of Tilton then played:

"There's a person watching me and you've been very frustrated with your purpose in life," Tilton says into the camera.

"That might be me, Bob!" Oliver exclaimed to thunderous audience applause.

"And that is when I realized," Oliver continued, "that the message Robert Tilton was sending me, was that I should set up my own church to test the legal and financial limits of what religious entities are able to do." After realizing that these controversial and nonprofit churches—which often bring in vast sums of money—are legal under existing Internal Revenue Service rules, Oliver was called to ministry. He actually incorporated his own television ministry called, appropriately, Our Lady of Perpetual Exemption.[114] The show hired an attorney to lead the show's staff through governmental filings and IRS paperwork, and created a televised church that was a legal nonprofit religious entity. Oliver said he found out it is "disturbingly easy" to set up Our Lady of Perpetual Exemption. Prosperity Gospel preachers and their ministries pay no taxes, simply because they meet the vague IRS requirement to be declared tax exempt.

Moving from his desk to a cozy den-like set resembling those on many evangelistic broadcasts, Oliver proceeded to solicit money from his television audience. "With a little help from Sister Wanda Jo Oliver, played by former *Saturday Night Live* star Rachel Dratch," reporter Melissa Locker wrote in *TIME* magazine, "Oliver's church will collect copious donations while encouraging congregants to silently meditate on the nature of fraudulent churches."[115] Setting up a real toll-free telephone number, 1–800–THIS-IS-LEGAL (1–800–844–7475), "Megareverend and C.E.O. of Our Lady of Perpetual Exemption Church, Pastor John Oliver," and sister Wanda Jo requested donations from viewers.

"Call the number on your screen right now," Oliver said, "Because if Robert Tilton, Kenneth Copeland, and all these bastards can get away with it and we get stopped, truly we have witnessed a f**king miracle tonight! Give us money!" Oliver, breaking character, kept repeating "And this is real," and "That is apparently something I am allowed to say," as he told viewers to touch the television screen to be cured of lupus.

The following week, Oliver told the audience that when he asked them the previous week to sow their seed, "Slightly more of you responded than we expected." The tens of thousands of dollars sent in to the fake, yet real, Our Lady of Perpetual Exemption Church were donated to the international charity Doctors Without Borders. In September 2015, Oliver shut the church down, having made his point that it is actually quite simple to defraud the public—and the government—with religion.

"If you want to send your money to a fake church," he said, "send it to Scientology."

CONCLUSION

Humor can be cutting or funny, and perception rests on the attitude of the recipient. A 2013 study found that audiences perceive ridicule of religious and other groups differently, depending upon the group being disparaged. Experiments "showed that disparagement humor fosters discrimination against groups for whom society's attitudes are ambivalent. Participants higher in anti-Muslim prejudice tolerated discrimination against a Muslim person more after reading anti-Muslim jokes than after reading anti-Muslim statements or neutral jokes." Further, "participants higher in anti-Muslim prejudice discriminated against Muslims more after reading anti-Muslim jokes than neutral jokes, while antiterrorist jokes did not promote discrimination against terrorists."[116] In this study, jokes intensified existing prejudices.

"As the process of mediatization means that collective uses of media push popularity and consensus above other criteria of cultural authority," Lynne Schofield Clark has observed, "so the authority to articulate common perspectives will continue to shift into more diverse locations and will be found in operation in perhaps increasingly brief forms. Together, audiences, taken-for-granted perspectives of certain powerful interpretive communities, and the institutional forces of the media are working together to reconstitute the field of cultural production in relation to religion and authority."[117] Humor, like any other form of communication, can be deployed and aggregated quickly by various forms of media.

There is risk involved in satire—religious, political, or otherwise. A satirist may wish to deploy humor as a behavioral corrective, but the implication can be perceived by audiences and recipients as, "I know better, I am smarter, and I am mocking your folly." Yet, as this chapter shows, satire and parody can also be useful in pointing out wrongdoing and vanity. There is a reason Hans Christian Andersen's fairy tale of "The Emperor's New Clothes" endures. Political—and religious—leaders can be duped, vain, misguided, and destructive. Satire is the child at the parade who exclaims of the pompous and naked king, "But he hasn't got anything on."[118]

Comic artist Adam Ford is the creator of the online site *The Babylon Bee* (babylonbee.com). "I'm Adam Ford, AKA Adam4d, a Christian, husband, and father who likes to draw comics and things," is how he describes himself.[119] *The Babylon Bee* offers gentle Christian satire, sporting headlines such as "'What Do I Have To Be Thankful For?' Asks Man Whose Heart Is Beating;" and "Christian Radio Station Expands Playlist To Nine Different Songs." The effect is a kinder, gentler version of *The Onion*, which is more biting and occasionally obscene.

"This is an inside-baseball brand of satire that allows *Babylon Bee* creator Adam Ford to gently explore the yins and yangs of evangelical Christianity," writes "On Religion" columnist Terry Mattingly. Mattingly describes the attraction of the site:

> Most *Babylon Bee* newcomers, however, are almost certainly be drawn there by social-media references to the site's popular items dissecting modern evangelical life. Take, for example, a "news report" about a new $90 million, 170-acre church complex with a petting zoo, seven bookstores, nine coffee shops, three restaurants, a baseball field and a monorail to the parking lots. But church leaders forgot something. Thus the headline: "Sanctuary Mistakenly Omitted From Megachurch Campus Design."
>
> Ford, who once yearned to be a pastor, stressed that he is trying to be critical and supportive at the same time.
>
> "God can and does use goofy things like lasers and smoke machines to bring people to Christ, sure, but I believe church services that are reminiscent of WWE productions have peaked and will be less and less successful and prevalent moving forward," he said.[120]

The Babylon Bee, according to Terry Lindvall, "is piercing, yet gentle. . . . It's more of a poke in the ribs, instead of a poke in the eyes."[121]

Ford has self-published a book of his comics with accompanying commentary titled, *Thy Kingdom Comics: Curiously Christian Drawings and Writings About Jesus, Tolerance, Abortion, Atheism, Homosexuality, Theology, and Lots of Other Stuff*. He is conservative in his Christian outlook, making a vivid Biblical case against abortion and homosexuality through his comics. He stresses that while he disagrees with those who support such positions, he does not hate them.

Ford has a number of comics that address taking scripture out of context, and chastises those who do so to condemn religion. "Do not believe something is biblical just because somebody else says it is," he writes in his book. "Go, look for yourself! Study! Work! Read! Learn! No matter how long it takes! Nothing is more important than knowing what the Bible really says."[122]

"The Hebrew Bible employs many sorts of humor, but its purpose is not to entertain," notes Hershey H. Friedman. "The major goal of the Hebrew Bible is to teach humanity how to live the ideal life. Much of the humor found in the Hebrew Bible has a purpose: To demonstrate that evil is wrong and even ludicrous, at times."[123]

The Wittenburg Door and *Ship of Fools* sought to entertain *and* teach people how to live according to Christian principles. As *The Door* explained, "We satirize something we love—the Church, and more generally people of faith—with the hope that our prodding might generate some course corrections while inducing a laugh or two . . . or three."[124]

"Satire is necessary. It's critical," wrote Mike Yaconelli in his farewell column as publisher of *The Wittenburg Door* seven years before his death in 2003. "The Church needs *The Door* more than ever. . . . For 25 years I have held the Church's feet to the fire. . . . For 25 years, I have focused on what the church is doing to Jesus."[125] *The Wittenburg Door* was serious in its mission to reform the church and to radically shift from traditional ways of thinking about God. It took on the follies of the church even as it embraced the teachings of Jesus Christ. The magazine, in both print and Web form, spread Christ's message of redemption and salvation by smashing the idols of religion, such as prosperity ministries; cults of personality; kitschy religious artifacts; the artificiality of man-made worship rituals; and short-lived spiritual fads. *Ship of Fools* continues the tradition.

While much religion journalism in secular media tends toward either features or the reporting of scandals, these magazines framed religion as a mission to evangelize through satire. The magazines were partly about saving souls, partly about exposing the unscrupulous masquerading as the virtuous, and partly about having a good time.

Morreall writes, "Humor, I conclude, not only fosters virtues, but is best seen as itself a virtue; and like wisdom, it is an intellectual and moral excellence of a high order. And any religion purporting to show people how to live needs to take it seriously."[126] One of Stephen Colbert's gifts to modern English usage is the word "truthiness." The Merriam-Webster dictionary made "truthiness" its "Word of the Year" in 2006, giving it two definitions: "truth that comes from the gut, not books," and "the quality of preferring concepts or facts one wishes to be true, rather than concepts of facts known to be true."[127] As CBSNews.com Editorial Director Dick Meyer wrote in a commentary:

> Truthiness actually has a long philosophic pedigree. It is called "emotivism," a term resurrected by a Scottish philosopher who lives and works in America, Alasdair MacIntyre. In 1981 he published one of the most influential works of

moral philosophy in the later part of the twentieth century, "After Virtue." MacIntyre defines it this way: "Emotivism is the doctrine that all evaluative judgments and, more specifically, all moral judgments are *nothing but* expressions of preference, expressions of attitude or feeling . . ." In this view there is no difference between saying "the death penalty is wrong" and "I don't like the death penalty."

Where emotivism prevails, MacIntyre argues, moral arguments become "interminable." There are no agreed-on, common criteria for evaluating moral truth or judgment. . . . MacIntyre's entire intellectual mission is to rescue this descent into social and moral incoherence not by arguing that there is such a thing as immutable, absolute and discoverable truth, but that within a community, within a cultural and ethical heritage, there are clear and absolute virtues. . . . The best social critics of 2006 were make-believe. Not just Stephen Colbert, the fake right-winger, but also Jon Stewart, the fake news anchor. . . . Somehow in a world of truthiness, where we select the truths we like, it has become too easy to dismiss "straight" commentary and criticism. If it's not fake, we don't believe it.[128]

Meyer and MacIntyre hold that there are clear truths and virtues in life, whether or not we choose to acknowledge them. Stephen Colbert, John Oliver, Jon Stewart, Adam Ford, Ole Anthony, and Simon Jenkins would likely agree with this assessment.

NOTES

1. Many news organizations covered the terror attack. See, for example, "Charlie Hebdo Attack: Three Days of Terror," BBC News, January 14, 2015, http://www.bbc.com/news/world-europe-30708237; Scott Bronstein, "Cherif and Said Kouachi: Their Path to Terror," CNN, January 14, 2015, accessed August 16, 2016, http://www.cnn.com/2015/01/13/world/kouachi-brothers-radicalization/.

2. Nick Thompson, "Charlie Hebdo: Satirical magazine is No Stranger to Controversy," CNN, January 7, 2015, accessed August 16, 2016, http://www.cnn.com/2015/01/07/europe/charlie-hebdo-controversy/index.html.

3. Don Murray, "France even more fractured after the Charlie Hebdo rampage," CBC News, January 8, 2015, accessed May 11, 2015, http://www.cbc.ca/news/world/france-even-more-fractured-after-the-charlie-hebdo-rampage-1.2893262.

4. Jeffrey Gottfried and Michael Barthel, "After Charlie Hebdo, Balancing Press Freedom and Respect for Religion: Majority Says Publishing Cartoons Was 'Okay,' But About Half of Non-Whites Say 'Not Okay, '" Pew Research Center, January 28, 2015.

5. Ibid.

6. For examples of Church of Latter Day Saints advertising and promotional response to *The Book of Mormon*, see: Danielle Tumminio, "Don't Judge a Book of Mormon By Its Cover: How Mormons Are Discovering the Musical as a Conversion Tool," *Huffington Post*, July 13, 2013, accessed August 10, 2016, http://www.huffingtonpost.com/danielle-tumminio/dont-judge-a-book-of-mormon-by-its-cover-how-mormons-are-discovering-the-musical-as-a-conversion-tool_b_3267252.html; David Ng, "Mormon Church Buys Ads in 'Book of Mormon' Playbill in L.A.," *Los Angeles Times*, September 6, 2012, accessed August 10, 2016, http://articles.latimes.com/2012/sep/06/entertainment/la-et-cm-mormon-church-lds-ads-book-of-mormon-playbill-20120906.

7. See website: "Stephen Colbert's Colbert Super PAC: Making a Better Tomorrow, Tomorrow," accessed August 16, 2016, http://colbertsuperpac.com/home.php.

8. Antonia Blumberg, "Jon Stewart's 10 Best Religious Moments," *Huffington Post*, February 14, 2015, accessed August 16, 2016, http://www.huffingtonpost.com/2015/02/14/jon-stewart-religion-clips_n_6673586.html. Fox News Channel and other conservative outlets often featured commentaries on the alleged "Merry Christmas" issue.

9. Charles M. Schulz, *I Take My Religion Seriously* (Anderson, IN: Warner Press, 1972), 45.

10. Over the course of 40 years, religious publisher Westminster John Knox Press (WJK) has released a series of *Gospel According to . . .* books linking popular culture icons with religious themes, beginning with *The Gospel According to Peanuts* by Robert L. Short in 1965. *Gospel According to . . .* books have been published by other presses as well. Additionally, *A Charlie Brown Christmas* debuted on CBS December 9, 1965. The animated special was notable for its recitation of Luke 2:8–14 (KJV) by the character of Linus, the blanket-toting child philosopher created by Charles Schulz.

11. Francis Bridger, "The Gospel and Popular Culture," book review, *Implicit Religion* 13, no. 2, December 2010, 218.

12. John Morreall, *Comedy, Tragedy, and Religion* (Albany: State University of New York Press, 1999), 16.

13. Ibid., 14.

14. Robert McAfee Brown, Ed. *The Essential Reinhold Niebuhr: Selected Essays and Addresses* (New Haven: Yale University Press, 1986), 49.

15. Ibid., 52.

16. Hershey H. Friedman, "Humor in the Hebrew Bible," *Humor: International Journal of Humor Research* 13.3 (2000): 257–258. See also, Thomas Jemielity, *Satire and the Hebrew Prophets* (Louisville, KY: Westminster John Knox Press, 1992.

17. Ibid.

18. Henri Cormier, *The Humor of Jesus* (New York: Alba House, 1977), 9.

19. John 8:5–7, KJV.

20. Cormier, *The Humor of Jesus*, 52–53.

21. Hans Geybels, *Humour and Religion: Challenges and Ambiguities* (London: Bloomsbury, 2011), 14.

22. Ibid., 16. Original European spellings are maintained in the quotes.

23. Friedman, "Humor in the Hebrew Bible," 258.

24. Genesis 10–19.

25. Frederick Buechner, *Telling the Truth: The Gospel as Tragedy, Comedy & Fairy Tale* (New York: HarperCollins, 1977), 53.

26. Conrad Hyers, *And God Created Laughter: The Bible As Divine Comedy* (Atlanta: John Knox Press, 1987), 10.

27. Earl F. Palmer, *The Humor of Jesus: Sources of Laughter in the Bible* (Vancouver, BC: Regent College Publishing, 2001), 25.

28. Douglas Adams, *The Prostitute in the Family Tree: Discovering Humor and Irony in the Bible* (Louisville, KY: Westminster John Knox Press, 1997), 3, 12.

29. Elton Trueblood, *The Humor of Christ* (New York: Harper & Row, 1964), 55. Trueblood was citing *Comedy*, being *An Essay on Comedy* by George Meredith and *Laughter* by Henri Bergson, Introduction and Appendix by Wylie Sypher (Garden City: Doubleday Anchor Books, 1956), 48.

30. Ibid.

31. Terry Lindvall, *God Mocks: A History of Religious Satire from the Hebrew Prophets to Stephen Colbert* (New York: New York University Press, 2015), 14.

32. Many scholarly sources and assorted websites cite the origins of the Jesus People, but the Christian music group All Saved Freak Band has one of the more concise definitions of the movement: "By most accounts, the Jesus People Movement began in 1967 with the opening of a small storefront evangelical mission called the Living Room in San Francisco's Haight Ashbury district. Though other missionary type organizations had preceded them in the area, this was the first one run solely by street Christians." Website accessed August 16, 2016, http://www.allsavedfreakband.com/jesus_movement.htm.

33. Mike Yaconelli, Wayne Rice, and Denny Rydberg, "Interview: The Keepers of *The Door*," *The Wittenburg Door*, June/July 1976, 6.

34. Mike Yaconelli, "I Had No Idea How Difficult It Is To Give Up Something That Matters To You," *The Door*, March/April 1996, 14.

35. Craig Wilson, "Remember the Burning Bush," *The Wittenburg Door*, February/March 1972, 7.

36. Trueblood, *The Humor of Christ*, 40.

37. Ibid., 55.

38. William Leonard, telephone interview with author, March 10, 1999.

39. Robert Darden, Introduction, *On the 8th Day God Laughed*, ed. Robert Darden (North Richland Hills, Texas: Bibal Press, 2000), 1.

40. See Ole Anthony, "Has Benny Hinn Been Born Again . . . Again?" *The Door*, September/October 1993, 24–26, 33.

41. "*The Door* Interview: Ole Anthony," *The Door*, November/December 1994.

42. William Lobdell, "Onward Christian Soldier: Ole Anthony Has Devoted His Life–and His Ministry–to Exposing Corrupt Televangelists. But Not Everyone Agrees He's Doing God's Work." *Los Angeles Times*, 8 December 2002, at www.WittenburgDoor.com, accessed March 1, 2005.

43. Ole Anthony, interview with author, Dallas, Texas, February 27, 1999.

44. Ibid.

45. The Trinity Foundation Website, accessed March 5, 2005, http://trinityfi.org.

46. Steve Gushee, "Magazine Skewers Religion's Sacred Cows," *The Palm Beach Post*, August 22, 1998, accessed December 21, 2015, http://articles.orlandosentinel.com/1998–08–22/lifestyle/9808210481_1_magazine-door-anthony.

47. For example, "Top Ten Signs Your Amish Teen is in Trouble" lists such warnings as "Sometimes stays in bed until after 6 a.m.," and "His name is Jebediah, but he goes by 'Jeb Daddy,'" *The Door*, July/August 1999, back cover. A satiric piece on fundamentalist Baptists appeared in *The Door*: "Fundy School: How to Make the Most of Being Right," *The Wittenburg Door*, July/August 2004, 20–21. A critical story in the July/August 2002 issue, "Scientology Unplugged," featured cover photos of adherents John Travolta and Tom Cruise, as well as Scientology founder L. Ron Hubbard.

48. "Who Does She Think She Is . . . Mother Teresa?" *The Door*, March/April 1996, 11. Mother Teresa was born to Albanian parents in Macedonia in 1910 and traveled to India in 1929. She set up the Missionaries of Charity in 1950 and dedicated her life to the poor. She was awarded the Nobel Prize for Peace in 1979 and died in 1997. She was beatified, the first step towards sainthood, by Pope John Paul II in 2003. On December 18, 2015, Pope Francis declared that Mother Teresa had met the Catholic Church's threshold for sainthood through recognition of two miracles.

49. Ibid., 12.

50. Ibid.

51. Ibid., 13.

52. Burkhard Bilger, "The Antichrist of East Dallas: God Doesn't Need Ole Anthony," *The New Yorker*, 6 December 2004, at www.WittenburgDoor.com, accessed March 1, 2005.

53. Robert Darden, interview with author, Fort Worth, Texas, February 26, 1999. Harry Guetzlaff, who died in 2008, was variously listed in the masthead as Marketing-Production Director, the Senior Editor's Editor, Editor Editor, and so on. Titles often change with each issue. Such jokes ran throughout the magazine, including the margins, much like *MAD* magazine's marginal gags.

54. Robert Darden, "Is 'religious humor' an oxymoron?" email interview by Todd Leopold, *CNN.com*, November 19, 2002.

55. Becky Garrison, "Henry Beard: International Man of Mystery," *The Door*, September/October 1997, 8.

56. Paul Somerville, "The Ten Commandments of NRA President Charlton Heston," *The Door*, September/October 1998, 3. The cover of this issue had *The Door* logo in the upper left corner, with the primary title reading, *Christian Soldier of Fortune*.

57. For background on the San Bernardino attack, see, for example: "San Bernardino Shooting Updates," *Los Angeles Times*, December 9, 2015, http://www.latimes.com/local/lanow/la-me-ln-san-bernardino-shooting-live-updates-htmlstory.html.

58. Jonathan Merritt, "Jerry Falwell Jr's Troubling Remarks on Guns," *The Atlantic*, December 6, 2015, https://www.theatlantic.com/politics/archive/2015/12/jerry-falwell-jrs-troubling-remarks-on-guns/419019/.

59. Brian Anderson, "Religious Gun Control Group: 'Jesus Was Not A Member of the NRA,'" Downtrend.com, September 20, 2014, accessed August 16, 2016, http://downtrend.com/71superb/religious-gun-control-group-jesus-was-not-a-member-of-the-nra. In 2016, Jerry Falwell Jr., president of Liberty University, encouraged students of legal age to exercise their Second Amendment right to purchase a handgun to keep on the Christian university's campus to protect themselves.

60. John Rutledge, interview with author, Dallas, Texas, February 27, 1999.

61. Trueblood, *The Humor of Christ*, 35–36.

62. Laura Strickler, "Senate Panel Probes 6 Top Televangelists," *CBS News*, November 6, 2007, accessed August 16, 2016, http://www.cbsnews.com/news/senate-panel-probes-6-top-televangelists/.

63. "The Apple of God's Eye," prod. Robbie Gordon, *Primetime Live*, November 21, 1991. For a summary of details concerning Tilton's ministry and the *Primetime Live* report, see "Robert Tilton–biography," FAMPeople.com, n.d., accessed August 16, 2016, http://www.fampeople.com/cat-robert-tilton. See also, Scott Hough, "Robert Tilton Inspires John Oliver to Found Our Lady of Perpetual Exemption," Inquisitr, August 18, 2015, accessed August 16, 2016, http://www.inquisitr.com/2345157/robert-tilton-inspires-john-oliver-to-found-our-lady-of-perpetual-exemption/. Part of Trinity's core ministry is to investigate claims of fraud perpetrated by unscrupulous ministers, particularly televangelists who solicit donations. Many news organizations have interviewed Anthony on camera, and pay the ministry for use of its archival footage.

64. Doug Duncan, "An Interview with the Grinch Who Stole Christmas: Bro. Robert Tilton," *The Door Magazine*, November/December 2000, 2–5, 22.

65. Ole Anthony with Skippy R., "The Last Word: Why We Need Robert Tilton," *The Door Magazine*, November/December 2000, 39.

66. Peter Carlson, "An Odd Door at Heaven's Gate," *Washington Post*, January 14, 1997, C07.

67. Terry Lindvall, *God Mocks: A History of Religious Satire from the Hebrew Prophets to Stephen Colbert* (New York: New York University Press, 2015), 1.

68. The magazine ran 1977–1983 in print, and was resurrected in 1998 as a webzine and online community, http://shipoffools.com/shipstuff/index.html.

69. See *Ship of Fools* at http://www.ship-of-fools.com, cited December 21, 2015.

70. Ibid.

71. Becky Garrison, "*The Door Interview:* Simon Jenkins," *The Door*, September/October 2000, 3.

72. *Ship of Fools* website, cited December 21, 2015.

73. Ibid., cited August 16, 2016.

74. Jenkins is referencing Mark 4:35–41: 35 That day when evening came, he said to his disciples, "Let us go over to the other side." 36 Leaving the crowd behind, they took him along, just as he was, in the boat. There were also other boats with him. 37 A furious squall came up, and the waves broke over the boat, so that it was nearly swamped. 38 Jesus was in the stern, sleeping on a cushion. The disciples woke him and said to him, "Teacher, don't you care if we drown?" 39 He got up, rebuked the wind and said to the waves, "Quiet! Be still!" Then the wind died down and it was completely calm. 40 He said to his disciples, "Why are you so afraid? Do you still have no faith?" 41 They were terrified and asked each other, "Who is this? Even the wind and the waves obey him!" NIV.

75. *Ship of Fools* website, cited August 2, 1999.

76. Ibid.

77. Peter L. Berger, *Redeeming Laughter: The Comic Dimension of Human Experience* (Berlin: Walter de Gruyter & Co., 1997), 187.

78. Ibid., 188.

79. 1 Corinthians 4:10; 1:27–29, NIV.

80. Berger, 200, quoting Werner Thiede, *Das Verheissende Lachen: Humor in Theologischer Perspektive* (Goettingen: Vandenhoek & Ruprecht, 1966, 127.

81. Garrison, 4.

82. Ibid., 5.

83. *Ship of Fools* website, cited December 21, 2015.

84. Garrison, 5.

85. Ibid., 30.

86. Stephen Colbert quoted in Terry Gross, "A Fake Newsman's Fake Newsman: Stephen Colbert," January 24, 2005, http://www.npr.org/templates/story/story.php?storyId=4464017; excerpt quoted in Terry Lindvall, *God Mocks: A History of Religious Satire from the Hebrew Prophets to Stephen Colbert* (New York: New York University Press, 2015), 264–265.

87. "Colbert Catechism: Stephen Colbert Professes His Faith to Fr. James Martin," YouTube, *America* Media, March 2, 2015, accessed August 10, 2016, https://www.youtube.com/watch?v=o-zxn-YGUI4.

88. Ibid.

89. Charles McGrath, "How Many Stephen Colberts Are There?" *The New York Times Magazine*, January 4, 2012, accessed August 10, 2016, http://www.nytimes.com/2012/01/08/magazine/stephen-colbert.html?pagewanted=1&_r=1.

90. Dan Zak, "Stephen Colbert, in GOP Pundit Character, Testifies on Immigration in D.C.," the *Washington Post*, September 25, 2010, accessed August 17, 2016, http://www.washingtonpost.com/wp-dyn/content/article/2010/09/24/AR2010092402734.html.

91. Ibid.

92. Ibid.

93. Brad A. Greenberg, "Colbert Quoting Jesus in Congressional Testimony," *The God Blog, The Jewish Journal*, September 27, 2010, accessed August 17, 2016, http://www.jewishjournal.com/thegodblog/item/colbert_quoting_jesus_in_congressional_testimony_20100926. Matthew 25:40: "The King will reply, 'Truly I tell you, whatever you did for one of the least of these brothers and sisters of mine, you did for me.'" (NIV)

94. Ibid.

95. Lynn Schofield Clark, "Religion and Authority in a Remix Culture: How a Late Night TV Host Became an Authority on Religion," in *Religion, Media and Culture: A Reader* Eds. Gordon Lynch and Jolyon Mitchell with Anna Strhan (London: Routledge, 2012), 111.

96. Ibid.

97. Ibid., 113.

98. Ibid., 119.

99. Ibid., 120.

100. Lindvall, *God Mocks*, 263.

101. Ibid., 264.

102. James Poniewozik, "Unfortunately, John Oliver, You Are a Journalist," *TIME*, November 17, 2014, accessed August 17, 2016, http://time.com/3589285/unfortunately-john-oliver-you-are-a-jouresernalist/.

103. "Journalism, Satire or Just Laughs? 'The Daily Show with Jon Stewart,' Examined," Pew Research Center, May 8, 2008, accessed August 19, 2016, http://www.journalism.org/2008/05/08/journalism-satire-or-just-laughs-the-daily-show-with-jon-stewart-examined/. "In 2007, when the public was asked about their most admired journalist, Stewart appeared in the mix with other journalists who work for more traditional outlets. While no individual journalist was named by more than 5 percent, Stewart was still volunteered by 2 percent of the American public. Stewart also rises to the top among younger Americans, being named by 6 percent of those younger than 30 years old," according to Pew.

104. Ibid.

105. Ibid.

106. Brian Steinberg, "How John Oliver and HBO Shattered TV's Comedy-News Format," *Variety*, July 2, 2014, accessed August 19, 2016, http://variety.com/2014/tv/news/how-john-oliver-and-hbo-shattered-tvs-comedy-news-format-1201257084/. For background on American

evangelicals in Uganda, see, for example: Jeffrey Gettleman, "Americans' Role Seen in Uganda Anti-Gay Push," January 3, 2010, accessed August 20, 2016, http://www.nytimes.com/2010/01/04/world/africa/04uganda.html?_r=0.

107. See: Amanda Holpuch, "John Oliver's Cheeky Net Neutrality Plea Crashes FCC Website," June 3, 2014, accessed August 19, 2016, https://www.theguardian.com/technology/2014/jun/03/john-oliver-fcc-website-net-neutrality; Kevin Slane, "John Oliver May Have Crashed the FCC Website (Again) with Segment on Net Neutrality," *The Boston Globe*, May 8, 2017, accessed June 1, 2017, https://www.boston.com/culture/entertainment/2017/05/08/john-oliver-may-have-crashed-the-fcc-website-again-with-segment-on-net-neutrality. The U.S. Court of Appeals for the District of Columbia Circuit ruled June 14, 2016 to uphold the F.C.C. proposal to declare broadband a utility. See Cecilia Kang, "Court Backs Rules Treating Internet as Utility, Not Luxury," *New York Times*, June 14, 2016, accessed August 19, 2016, http://www.nytimes.com/2016/06/15/technology/net-neutrality-fcc-appeals-court-ruling.html?_r=0. The court's judgment is at https://www.cadc.uscourts.gov/internet/opinions.nsf/3F95E49183E6F8AF85257FD200505A3A/percent24file/15-1063-1619173.pdf.

108. There are many news stories about FIFA corruption. See, for example, "Fifa Corruption Crisis: Key Questions Answered," BBC News, December 21, 2015, accessed August 19, 2016, http://www.bbc.com/news/world-europe-32897066.

109. All quotes are taken from the televised segment: "Televangelists: Last Week Tonight with John Oliver," HBO, YouTube, August, 16, 2015, accessed August 19, 2016, https://www.youtube.com/watch?v=7y1xJAVZxXg.

110. Skippy R., "John Oliver Takes Down the Televangelists, Thanks to Small Investigative Non-profit Trinity Foundation," *Blind Folly* website, August 18, 2015, http://blindfolly.org/blindfolly/news/john-oliver-takes-down-the-televangelists-thanks-to-small-investigative-non-profit-trinity-foundation/.

111. Kate Bowler, "Death, the Prosperity Gospel and Me," *New York Times*, National Edition, February 14, 2016, SR1.

112. Kenneth Copeland Ministries, http://www.kcm.org.

113. "Tax Guide for Churches and Religious Organizations," Internal Revenue Service, IRS.gov, Revised August 2015, accessed August 17, 2016, https://www.irs.gov/pub/irs-pdf/p1828.pdf.

114. See Church website: http://www.ourladyofperpetualexemption.com.

115. Melissa Locker, "John Oliver Becomes a Televangelist and Finally Starts His Own Church," *TIME*, August 17, 2015, accessed August 19, 2016, http://time.com/3999933/john-oliver-televangelist-church-alst-week-tonight/.

116. Thomas E. Ford, Julie A. Woodzicka, Shane R. Triplett, Annie O. Kochersberger, and Christopher J. Holden, "Not All Groups Are Equal: Differential Vulnerability of Social Groups to the Prejudice-Releasing Effects of Disparagement Humor," *Group Processes and Intergroup Relations* 17, no. 2, March 1, 2014, http://journals.sagepub.com/doi/abs/10.1177/1368430213502558.

117. Lynne Schofield Clark, "Religion and Authority in a Remix Culture," 120.

118. "The Emperor's New Clothes," Translation of "Keiserens Nye Klæder" by Jean Hersholt, The Hans Christian Andersen Centre, accessed August 16, 2016, http://andersen.sdu.dk/vaerk/hersholt/TheEmperorsNewClothes_e.html.

119. "Adam Ford is Creating A Curiously Christian Webcomic," Patreon website, n.d., accessed November 27, 2016, https://www.patreon.com/Adam4d.

120. Terry Mattingly, "The Gentle, Evangelical Insider Religious Satire of *The Babylon Bee*," "On Religion" website, September 29, 2016, accessed November 27, 2016, http://www.tmatt.net/columns/2016/9/13/the-gentle-insider-satire-of-the-babylon-bee.

121. Terry Lindvall, quoted by Terry Mattingly.

122. Adam Ford, *Thy Kingdom Comics: Curiously Christian Drawings and Writings About Jesus, Tolerance, Abortion, Atheism, Homosexuality, Theology, and Lots of Other Stuff* (Canton, MI: Adam4d, LLC., 2016), 128.

123. Friedman, 258–259.

124. About *The Door*, www.TheWittenburgDoor.com, accessed March 17, 2005.

125. Mike Yaconelli, "Closing the Back Door," *The Door*, May/June 1996, 40.

126. Morreall, 154.

127. "Merriam-Webster Announces 'Truthiness' As 2006 Word of the Year," Press Release, accessed August 16, 2016, http://www.merriam-webster.com/press-release/2006-word-of-the-year.

128. Dick Meyer, "The Truth of Truthiness," CBS News, December 12, 2006, accessed August 17, 2016, http://www.cbsnews.com/news/the-truth-of-truthiness/.

Conclusion

Religion and Media in the Digital Age presents six distinct studies showing the myriad ways religion, Christianity in particular, has been woven into American popular and civic culture. Each chapter is an examination of the adaptation of media forms by various Christian actors, some of whom are literally actors doing stage, television, and film work. The book explores and explains religious interactions with a range of cultural phenomena such as pilgrimage, publishing, protest, politics, production, and parody. While the three sections—*civil religion, religion and entertainment*, and *sacred and profane media*—and six chapters may appear unrelated at first, they all present narratives of religious and spiritual negotiations with culture.

CIVIL RELIGION

The *Moral Monday* movement thrived in part thanks to heavy news coverage and social media sharing, attracting praise and condemnation, both of which raised the movement's profile. The Rev. William Barber's progressive politics and religious social justice rhetoric united ethnically and religiously diverse populations, as well as a sizeable nonreligious contingent. Moral Mondays were based on the politically diverse fusion movements of the nineteenth and early twentieth centuries, as well the civil rights career of Martin Luther King, Jr. William Barber frequently referenced King, going so far as to declare, "This is our Selma." Reporting on Moral Mondays appeared in traditional media such as newspapers and television news, and on digital media such as websites designed specifically to promote or mock the movement's actions. Despite coverage on a national scale, the immediate political effectiveness of the movement was modest. Most of the same forces Barber targeted in the North Carolina General Assembly remained in place after a

midterm election, but two years later voters replaced the Republican govern-
or with a moderate Democrat, and there were court victories against gerrymandering of legislative districts that heavily favored GOP candidates. The
chapter on Moral Mondays is the first comprehensive history of this movement outside of Barber's own books.

The Pledge of Allegiance to the Flag was co-opted during the Cold War
by religious and secular media forces seeking to add the name of God to a
civic oath. The Catholic Knights of Columbus and the Hearst newspaper
chain were ultimately successful in reaching the ears of President Eisenhower and the Congress, with only token opposition from moderate and progressive religious voices. The original pledge was written in 1892 by The Rev.
Francis Bellamy, a socialist minister, as a marketing ploy for a magazine. It
originally read: "I pledge allegiance to my flag and the Republic for which it
stands: one nation indivisible, with liberty and justice for all." Subsequent
alterations and the final addition of "under God" made the pledge a religious,
though not mandatory, oath for a pluralistic nation. During the same Cold
War era of the 1950s, the phrase "In God We Trust" was added to paper
currency. It also became the official motto of the United States, replacing the
unofficial motto "E pluribus unum" ("Out of many, one"), which had been
adopted in 1782 for the Great Seal of the United States. Religiosity has gone
hand-in-hand with patriotism ever since, a reality amplified in politically
divisive times.

RELIGION AND ENTERTAINMENT

Actors, Models, & Talent for Christ (AMTC) seeks to instill Christian morals
in entertainers, with a goal of planting believers in the entertainment industry, which AMTC views as a mission field. Some performers who have had
an association with AMTC have moved on to television appearances and
roles in mainstream and Christian films. Hundreds more regularly vie for the
opportunity, and pay the fees, to audition before agents, scouts, producers,
and directors at AMTC's SHINE conferences. Evolving from a for-profit
modeling agency to a nonprofit Christian-focused training ground for artists,
AMTC's emphasis on values and ethical behavior seems particularly relevant
with the advent of the "Me Too" and "Time's Up" movements to counter
sexual harassment within the industry.

Independent film *The Way* uses pilgrimage, personal loss, community
bonds, and liberal Catholicism to communicate a vulnerable, imperfect, ultimately relatable version of Christianity. *The Way*, despite being nearly invisible at the box office, stands as a realistic counterpoint to Hollywood Bible
blockbusters and the Christian film industry's sentimental offerings. The
chapter on *The Way* presents an overview of Christian filmmakers and their

motives, and discusses the excesses of Hollywood epics that incorporate religion primarily for commercial purposes. The Bible and various religious traditions have provided cinematic source material since the beginning of the silent era (roughly 1895–1927). Many of the earliest films portrayed Jesus, God, and religious people in reverential ways. The motion picture considered to be the breakthrough film that first introduced sound, *The Jazz Singer* (1927), presented Jewish life in a deferential, worshipful light. Many Jewish filmmakers have created numerous movies for Christian audiences over the years. By its very nature, film has the ability to evoke strong emotion, and remains a potent force in an age of distracting digital devices. Indeed, most of those devices, such as smartphones and tablets, are capable of displaying movies on-demand for personal viewing.

SACRED AND PROFANE MEDIA

Many companies and religious organizations translate, market, and sell *the Bible*. The Bible is a sacred (for many) bestselling product from which profits can be made, although many Bibles are provided for free by nonprofit groups such as the Gideons. The Hebrew Bible and Christian Old Testament are published as standalone editions, and multiple translations and formats of The New Testament are produced for Christian audiences. Copyrighting an exclusive version of Scripture can be both profitable and culturally influential. There is disagreement among churches, charities, and religious readers over which translation constitutes the "real" Bible, helping to push sales of assorted versions. Biblica's *New International Version*, or NIV, is one of the top selling Bibles in the world. Zondervan has exclusive publishing rights to the NIV in the United States; Zondervan is owned by HarperCollins, a subsidiary of News Corp; most Bibles are assembled at plants in China that specialize in the thin paper preferred by publishers such as Zondervan. The exploration of corporate Bible publishing in this chapter reveals that it can be as consumer oriented and competitive as any other industry. The tale of Adam Lewis Greene's Kickstarter Bible project is an illustration of the successful use of new media to sell an old product—Holy Scripture in a bound book on high quality paper. Yet, the Good Book doesn't come in just book form. Research shows that generational differences appear to affect Bible readership, but with products such as glossy magazine formats, online texts, smartphone applications, and Bible podcasts, this may change in the future. The growing number of "nones," people who do not identify with a particular faith, is another factor in how much, or how little, the Bible is actually read.

Religious satire, like religious film, can come from secular or religious sources, and can be used for critical or constructive purposes. Like their secular counterparts, religious producers of such material tend to lean liberal, but not always, as evidenced by *The Babylon Bee*. This chapter discussed the situational appropriateness of satirizing religion and religious people, but illustrated the dangers of doing so by detailing the murders of staff cartoonists at *Charlie Hebdo* in Paris. In the United States and Great Britain, *The Wittenburg Door, Ship of Fools*, and comedian John Oliver all picked the same easy targets: televangelists and other preachers who prey on unsuspecting and often desperate people. Are these humorists criticizing religion, or shedding light on con artists pretending to be religious? One could argue that the mission and end result was the same—exposing corruption—but Oliver's tone and foul language differed significantly from the devoutly religious staffs of the two magazines. The origins and precedents of religious satire, as well as previous scholarship on the subject, are laid out in this chapter. There is even Biblical precedent for Holy Laughter. "In Hebrew, the word for *laughter* is fairly inclusive. Its variations cover everything from merriment and joy to mockery and derision," notes religious humor scholar Terry Lindvall. "Notice that when God had first told Abraham that he and Sarah would bear a son, Abraham fell down laughing," and God knew that the old man was laughing because of his delight and surprise. "Why did Sarah laugh? The Book of Genesis seems to make it clear that Sarah was not laughing at God. . . . Sarah was laughing with God. . . . This geriatric couple was going to be spending a lot of time in the pediatric ward. What's not funny about that?"[1] Religious satirists laugh with God. Nonreligious satirists may have other ideas.

THE FOCUS ON CHRISTIANITY IN THIS BOOK

The top religion story of 2017 in the Religion News Association's (RNA) annual Top 10 Religion Stories of the Year Poll was conservative evangelicals' support of, and strong representation in, President Donald Trump's administration. "Conservative evangelicals gain strong representation in the Trump administration, notably with Vice President Mike Pence, and on the president's informal religious advisory body," reads an RNA news release listing the story as number one. "Trump maintains strong grassroots support among white evangelicals, polls show."[2] The top RNA religion story for 2016 was "Donald Trump gets strong support from white Christians, especially evangelicals, in an upset presidential election."[3] Note the generic use of "evangelicals."

These stories are especially notable because of Trump's harsh, often foul language during his campaign and in tweets and public appearances after his election. While Trump is not historically known for piety, Pence is an evangelical, and Christian-focused Bible studies were often held among members of Trump's cabinet, usually conducted by Ralph Drollinger of Washington,

D.C.-based Capitol Ministries. One source called it "the most evangelical Cabinet in history."[4] As noted elsewhere in this book, the composition of the U.S. Congress is far more Christian than the general public. Christians are not a monolithic group, its adherents as diverse in their points of view as Muslims, Jews, and other faiths, as well as those of no faith. Politically, American Christians may lean liberal, conservative or in between. Nuance among positions on individual issues is often overlooked.

Despite declining mainline church attendance and an increasing diversity of faiths, Christianity remains an influence on American politics, journalism, media, entertainment, and popular culture. Pew Research and others have established that even non-Christians typically view religion in the United States through a Christian lens, partly due to sheer numbers (70 percent of the population), as well as historical precedent.[5] If conservative and fundamentalist Christians have their way, this perspective will become even more ubiquitous. Two well-funded examples of this evangelical effort are Kentucky's Creation Museum and the Museum of the Bible, which opened in Washington, D.C. in late 2017.

The Creation Museum displays dinosaurs coexisting with Adam and Eve bathing in a stream, maintaining that the Book of Genesis provides a documentary basis for the assertion that the world is thousands of years old instead of billions. The Museum of the Bible "is a safe space for Christian nationalists," according to liberal journalist Katherine Stewart, "and that is the key to understanding its political mission. The aim isn't anything so crude as the immediate conversion of tourists to a particular variety of evangelical Christianity. Its subtler task is to embed a certain set of assumptions in the landscape of the capital. . . . Given the theologico-political goals of its founders and patrons, it isn't hard to see that the location of this museum was an act of symbolic and practical genius. If you're going to build a Christian nation, this is where you start."[6]

Writer Caroline D'Agati, a Christian herself, sees the Museum of the Bible differently. On the conservative/libertarian website *The Federalist*, D'Agati described her emotional response to the media on display: "As you look at first editions of the Gutenberg Bible or scraps of the Dead Sea Scrolls, you encounter the billions of people God has spoken to in the past. Just as he made sure he was known to them, he has made sure his word has come to you. For those who believe, we know that we are just as priceless a part of this story as any of the treasured artifacts under the glass. For us, it is not a history museum. It is the first few chapters in the story of a God who endures and keeps his promises. He is not distant. We are characters in his story."[7] For D'Agati, the original books, scrolls, and cuneiforms testify to a living God. The museum also has digital technology to tell the old, old story, as well as a gift shop for buying tchotchkes and materials for ongoing fellowship and learning. The Creation Museum also has a gift shop with similar items, including toy dinosaurs.

Lynn Schofield Clark has written of evangelical Christians as targets for marketing with specialty products aimed to appeal directly to their consumerist impulse. "There are three reasons why evangelicalism has been the largest 'new market' segment for mediated, marketed religion: the size, or the number of people who claim to be evangelical (somewhere between 30 and 40 percent of the population), the emphasis in that tradition on expression, and the disposable income of the group. . . . Once conservative Christian religion was identified as capable of producing and selling goods and services as part of what marketers would call a hot lifestyle brand, companies serving other religions have followed suit in the United States, such as in the case of Jewish 'kewlju' and 'Hot4Hebrew' T-shirts, the Celtic tarot card and handbook set, or the chakra kit that 'shows you how to locate the seven energy centers and achieve balance.'"[8]

Richard Flory has researched Christian megachurches and how they affect culture. In the mid-twentieth century, megachurches became a phenomenon, Flory writes, and California has more than any other state, "over 200 Protestant, theologically conservative churches with at least 2,000 weekly attenders."[9] In Flory's view, "the most important characteristic of megachurches is their ability to 'appropriate' elements from the larger culture, be it popular music, performances or even dress styles. . . . While they are found in major cities across the U.S. and globally, it is in California that megachurches led the way in merging larger cultural trends into people's religious lives."[10]

Flory cites the Crystal Cathedral, founded in 1955 by Robert Schuller, and its *Hour of Power* Sunday morning service as a prime example. Its televised services, particularly theatrical at Christmas and Easter, "both extended the reach of the church and allowed people to enjoy Sunday worship service from the comfort of their living rooms." Crystal Cathedral had its origins in Schuller's conversion of a drive-in theater into an outdoor church. The post-World War II boom meant people depended more and more on automobiles, and people going to church didn't have to dress up or even leave the comfort of their car. "Motivated at least in part by the lack of availability of other venues, Schuller turned the necessity of meeting in a drive-in theater into a cultural adaptation," according to Flory.[11]

"Current iterations of California megachurches . . . follow a similar script and arguably build on elements of California culture: the promise of a comfortable experience in church, the opportunity to feel good about oneself, and participation in a community of like-minded people that doesn't require any deeper commitments unless one so desires." Flory cites examples across the country, including Seattle's City Church, "which caters to young Christian hipsters," and Chicago's family-oriented Willow Creek Church.[12]

SPIRITUAL, BUT NOT RELIGIOUS

Many who do not follow a particular religion call themselves "spiritual, but not religious," receiving sustenance from nature, yoga, music, or as noted in the Introduction, sunsets. The definitions of spirituality from religion scholars reveal a vagueness in the terminology, a description of "feeling" that does not necessarily extend to commitment or belief in a deity, much less a savior.

In 2017, Pew Research data revealed for the first time that a majority of Americans, 56 percent, say it is possible to be a good person without religious belief. Religion News Service reported that "God is not a prerequisite for good values and morality," according to Greg Smith, Pew's associate director of research. "[T]he public's increased rejection of the idea that belief in God is necessary for morality is due, in large part, to the spike in the share of Americans who are religious 'nones.'" Some 23 percent of Americans now fall into the category of "none," meaning they follow no faith. More surprising in the survey was that 45 percent of Protestants and Catholics agreed that nonreligious people can be personally moral without God in their lives.[13]

RELIGION, MEDIA, AND CULTURE

Prior research has demonstrated that "religion and media" is a redundant phrase. The same can be said for "religion and popular culture." In chapter 4 on Actors, Models, & Talent for Christ, Daniel A. Stout is quoted as saying, "Religious groups are often at odds with popular culture, but they also help create and sustain it. . . . It is insufficient to examine religious groups only as critics; they must also be studied as creators of and participants in popular culture. In some ways, *religion is popular culture* and can never be completely detached from it"[14]

William James in 1902 published the now-classic *Varieties of Religious Experience: A Study in Human Nature.* An empirical psychologist, James believed in facts, and he held individual religious experience in higher regard than organized and denominational religion. While not approaching the depth of James's philosophical and psychological observations, *Religion and Media in the Digital Age* has offered a critical assessment of a variety of Christian engagements and interactions with American media and popular culture. As noted throughout this book, whether conservative, moderate, or liberal, religious people utilize and appropriate media and culture to varying degrees for messaging, outreach, accommodation, comfort, and consumption.

Many of the topics covered in this book arose from class discussions in a Religion and Media class the author has taught at Elon University every year since 2003. The upper level course draws students from different majors and a variety of backgrounds, both religious and nonreligious. The central theme of the class was explained in a previously published essay:

> The core course assignment requires students to visit a house of worship outside their personal faith and report on the experience. They must also interview church leaders and congregation members, research the tradition or denomination and report on media use during services ...
>
> Today's college students ... have come of age in a time of ISIS, religious assaults on abortion providers, moral protests concerning gay marriage and stories of Catholic priests and pedophilia ...
>
> Despite many being raised in religious families and some even attending faith-based schools for a dozen years prior to starting college, the millennial generation often views religious people with suspicion and as inherently intolerant.
>
> Millennials typically distrust institutions, and church is just one more institution.
>
> Students in the class attended services of their choosing at 33 different Christian churches, Islamic mosques, Jewish synagogues and Hindu and Buddhist temples over the course of several weeks ...
>
> The assignment forced them to interact with people they feared, avoided or just never thought much about. Faith communities throughout central North Carolina hosted the students, who were warmly welcomed, hugged, fed and always invited to return.
>
> Some of the sermons and worship styles threw students off balance, and there were language barriers—even when the language being spoken was English. Let's just say areas of theological disagreement arose.
>
> Despite these issues, or perhaps because of them, results were highly encouraging. The ... entire class expressed enthusiasm for the opportunity to get out of their religious comfort zones. Once they met the "other" face-to-face, fear and prejudice vanished. [15]

As outlined in the assignment, students take stock of the wide range of media use among the churches, synagogues, mosques, and temples they visit during the semester: A megachurch features ushers, a praise band, a movie screen, and a sound system. A tiny brick church has one small room with a piano and a microphone. A mosque has one large room with only a microphone. A biker church meeting in a high school classroom features readings from paperback Bibles and the roar of motorcycle engines arriving and departing. Hindu and Buddhist temples, and Catholic and Greek Orthodox churches, display iconography. A Jehovah's Witness Kingdom Hall is plain, and welcomes visitors with multiple publications such as *New World Translation* Bibles and copies of *Watchtower* magazine. Most of these congregations will have a website. Some are not updated for months.

As noted throughout this book, religious people, particularly Christians, have a tradition of being early adopters of media technology. Rapidly evolving media tools are used by religions and individually religious people to worship, evangelize, teach, and transmit culture. Media formats and their usage affect how audiences perceive religions and their messages, along with journalistic and popular culture depictions of religion. Understanding this can lead to increased media literacy, as well as religious literacy.

Media do not replace religion, but can be religiously and spiritually significant.

NOTES

1. Terry Lindvall, *The Mother of All Laughter: Sarah & the Genesis of Comedy* (Nashville: Broadman & Holman Publishers, 2003), 34–36.

2. "Evangelical Presence in Trump Administration Voted No. 1 Religion Story; Trump Selected Newsmaker," Religion News Association press release, December 14, 2017, http://www.rna.org/news/378691/Evangelical-presence-in-Trump-administration-voted-No.-1-religion-story-Trump-selected-newsmake.htm.

3. "Trump's Election Voted No. 1 Religion Story of 2016; Khizr & Ghazala Khan Selected As Top Newsmakers," Religion News Association press release, December 14, 2016, http://www.rna.org/news/321947/Trumps-election-voted-No.-1-religion-story-of-2016-Khizr-Ghazala-Khan-selected-as-top-newsmakers.htm.

4. See: Leah Marieann Klett, "Bible Studies Held at the White House for First Time in 100 Years: 'These are Godly Individuals,'" The Gospel Herald Society, August 4, 2017, http://www.gospelherald.com/articles/71211/20170804/bible-studies-held-white-house-first-time-100-years-godly.htm; Valerie Strauss, "Top Trump Administration Officials Flock To Weekly Bible Study Classes at White House," the *Washington Post*, August 1, 2017, https://www.washingtonpost.com/news/answer-sheet/wp/2017/08/01/top-trump-administration-officials-flock-to-weekly-bible-study-classes-at-white-house/?utm_term=.032ee5a463e2. Capitol Ministries website (https://capmin.org/about/)states, "Since our founding in 1996 our vision has not changed: to evangelize elected officials and lead them toward maturity in Christ. We stay away from politics and concentrate on the hearts of leaders." Bible studies were held among officials during the George W. Bush administration as well. Bush was a born again Christian. There are no rules against Bible or religious study in a federal building, as long as there is no coercion to participate.

5. Pew Research Center, Religious Landscape Study, http://www.pewforum.org/religious-landscape-study/.

6. Kathrine Stewart, "The Museum of the Bible is a Safe Space for Christian Nationalists," *New York Times*, January 6, 2018, https://www.nytimes.com/2018/01/06/opinion/sunday/the-museum-of-the-bible-is-a-safe-space-for-christian-nationalists.html. See Kathrine Stewart, *The Good News Club: The Religious Right's Stealth Assault on America's Children* (New York: PublicAffairs, 2012).

7. Caroline D'Agati, "Why You Should Visit the Museum of the Bible Even If You're Not Religious," *The Federalist*, December 18, 2017, http://thefederalist.com/2017/12/18/visit-museum-bible-even-youre-not-religious/.

8. Lynn Schofield Clark, ed., *Religion, Media, and the Marketplace* (New Brunswick, NJ: Rutgers University Press, 2007), 25.

9. Richard Flory, "How California's Megachurches Changed Christian Culture," USC Dornsife, January 11, 2018, http://dornsifecms.usc.edu/news/stories/2736/how-californias-megachurches-changed-christian-culture/.

10. Ibid.

11. Ibid.

12. Ibid.

13. Kimberly Winston, "Good Without God? More Americans Say Amen To That," Religion News Service, October 17, 2017, http://religionnews.com/2017/10/17/good-without-god-

more-americans-say-amen-to-that/; for original Pew data, see Gregory A. Smith, "A Growing Share of Americans Say It's Not Necessary To Believe In God To Be Moral," Pew Research Center, October 16, 2017, http://www.pewresearch.org/fact-tank/2017/10/16/a-growing-share-of-americans-say-its-not-necessary-to-believe-in-god-to-be-moral/.

14. Daniel A. Stout, "Beyond Culture Wars: An Introduction to the Study of Religion and Popular Culture," *Religion and Popular Culture: Studies on the Interaction of Worldviews* (Ames, IA: Iowa State University Press, 2001), 8.

15. Anthony Hatcher, "They're Just Like Us," *Huffington Post*, June 9, 2016, http://www.huffingtonpost.com/anthony-hatcher/theyre-just-like-us_b_10336092.html. There are 33 students in each section of the class.

Bibliography

"1.5 Million Homeschooled Students in the United States in 2007," U.S. Department of Education, December 2008, https://nces.ed.gov/pubs2009/2009030.pdf.

"A BILL TO BE ENTITLED AN ACT TO PROVIDE FOR SINGLE-SEX MULTIPLE OCCUPANCY BATHROOM AND CHANGING FACILITIES IN SCHOOLS AND PUBLIC AGENCIES AND TO CREATE STATEWIDE CONSISTENCY IN REGULATION OF EMPLOYMENT AND PUBLIC ACCOMMODATIONS," NC House Bill 2, March 23, 2016.

"A New Poor People's Campaign for Today," accessed June 14, 2017, https://poorpeoplescampaign.org/new-poor-peoples-campaign/.

Abrams, Amanda. "Love Thy Neighbor: Jonathan Wilson-Hartgrove on Race, Faith, and Resistance," *The Sun*, September 2017.

Adams, Douglas. *The Prostitute in the Family Tree: Discovering Humor and Irony in the Bible.* Louisville, KY: Westminster John Knox Press, 1997.

Adler, Jerry. "In Search of the Spiritual," *Newsweek* (August 29/September 5, 2005): 46–65.

Albanese, Catherine L. "Religion and American Popular Culture: An Introductory Essay," *Journal of the American Academy of Religion* 59, no. 4 (Fall 1996): 736.

Allen, Bob. "Southern Baptists Have Lost A Million Members in 10 Years," *Baptist News Global*, June 9, 2017, https://baptistnews.com/article/southern-baptists-lost-million-members-10-years/#.WT__7Mb1lDX.

Alper, Becka A. "Millennials Are Less Religious Than Older Americans, But Just As Spiritual," Pew Research Center, November 23, 2015, http://www.pewresearch.org/fact-tank/2015/11/23/millennials-are-less-religious-than-older-americans-but-just-as-spiritual/.

Alvarez, Angelica. "Website Mocks Moral Monday Protests," *ABC 11 Eyewitness News*, June 19, 2013, accessed March 9, 2016, http://abc11.com/archive/9145248/. The site has since been removed from https://www.nccivitas.org/moralmonday/.

Ambrosino, Brandon. "Why Are Christian Movies So Painfully Bad?" *Vox*, April 1, 2016. https://www.vox.com/2015/2/15/8038283/christian-movies-bad-old-fashioned-fifty-shades.

"America's Changing Religious Landscape," Pew Research Center, May 12, 2015, http://www.pewforum.org/2015/05/12/americas-changing-religious-landscape/.

"(AMTC) Actors, Models, and Talent for Christ," *Ndepedia*, Taylor Bear Publication, November 30, 2013, accessed May 26, 2016, https://ndiepediablog.wordpress.com/2013/11/30/amtc-actors-models-and-talent-for-christ/.

Anderson, Milton. *The Modern Goliath: A Study of Talking Pictures with a Treatment of Non-Theatrical Talking Pictures Especially Talking Pictures for Schools and Churches and Some Chapters on Character Education and Values.* Los Angeles: David Press, 1935.

Anthony, Ole. Interview with author. Dallas, Texas, February 27, 1999.

"The Apple of God's Eye," prod. Robbie Gordon, Primetime Live, November 21, 1991.

Arban, Carey Lewis. "The Business of Branding," *Backstage.com*, February 23, 2016, accessed May 23, 2016.

Armstrong, Karen. *The Bible: The Biography*. London: Atlantic Books, 2007.

Ashley, Kathleen and Marilyn Deegan. *Being a Pilgrim: Art and Ritual on the Medieval Routes to Santiago*. London: Lund Humphries, 2009.

Baer, John W. Email interview by author, October 20, 1996.

Baer, John W. *The Pledge of Allegiance: A Centennial History, 1892–1992*. Annapolis, MD: J.W. Baer, 1992.

Bailey, Sarah Pulliam. "How Donald Trump is Bringing Billy Graham's Complicated Family Back into White House Circles," *Washington Post*, January 12, 2017, https://www.washingtonpost.com/news/acts-of-faith/wp/2017/01/12/how-donald-trump-is-bringing-billy-grahams-complicated-family-back-into-white-house-circles/?utm_term=.0485709baed8.

Banov, Jessica. "Movie Filming in Triangle Inspired by Cary's Corral Riding Academy," *News & Observer*, February 25, 2016, http://www.newsobserver.com/news/local/news-columns-blogs/article62274017.html.

Barber II, William J. "It's Not About Trump. Our Political Culture is Corrupt," *The Nation*, March 12, 2016, accessed March 12, 2016, http://www.thenation.com/article/north-carolinas-new-moral-majority-goes-to-the-polls/.

Barber II, William J. "We Are In a Crisis—A Moral Crisis," *Sojourners*, May 13, 2014.

Barber II, William J. with Barbara Zelter. *Forward Together: A Moral Message for the Nation*. St. Louis, MO: Chalice Press, 2014.

Barber II, William J. and Jonathan Wilson-Hartgrove. "Holding Candidates Morally Accountable," *News & Observer*, February 21, 2016, 15A.

Barber II, William J. with Jonathan Wilson-Hartgrove. *The Third Reconstruction: Moral Mondays, Fusion Politics, and the Rise of a New Justice Movement*. Boston: Beacon Press, 2016.

Barclay, William. *Jesus of Nazareth*. New York: Ballantine Books, 1977.

Barna Group, "Spiritual Profile of Homosexual Adults Provides Surprising Insights," June 20, 2009, accessed July 10, 2015, https://www.barna.org/barna-update/article/13-culture/282-spiritual-profile-of-homosexual-adults-provides-surprising-insights#.VZ_7zXhNV6N.

Barna Group and American Bible Society. "State of the Bible 2015." https://www.scribd.com/document/261505121/State-of-the-Bible-2015-Report.

————. "State of the Bible 2016." http://www.americanbible.org/features/state-of-the-bible.

Barrett, David. "Barack Obama Prayed with Bear Grylls in Alaskan Wilderness," *The Telegraph*, December 13, 2015, http://www.telegraph.co.uk/news/worldnews/barackobama/12048108/Barack-Obama-prayed-with-Bear-Grylls-in-Alaskan-wilderness.html.

Baugh, Lloyd. "The African Face of Jesus in Film: Two Texts, a New Tradition." In *Son of Man: An African Jesus Film*, edited by Richard Walsh, Jeffrey L. Staley, and Adele Reinhartz. Sheffield, UK: Sheffield Phoenix Press, 2013.

Bawer, Bruce. *Stealing Jesus: How Fundamentalism Betrays Christianity*. New York: Three Rivers Press, 1997.

Bebbington, David W. *Evangelicalism in Modern Britain: A History from the 1730s to the 1980s*. New York: Taylor & Francis, 1989.

Bellah, Robert "Civil Religion in America," *Daedalus* 96, no. 1 (Winter 1967): 1–21. Reprinted with commentary and rejoinder in Donald R. Cutler, ed., *The Religious Situation 1968*, Boston: Beacon Press, 1968: 388–393.

Bellamy, Francis. *Effective Magazine Advertising: 508 Essays About 111 Advertisements*. New York: Mitchell Kennerley, 1909.

Berger, Peter L. *Redeeming Laughter: The Comic Dimension of Human Experience*. Berlin: Walter de Gruyter & Co., 1997.

Berger, Peter L. *The Sacred Canopy: Elements of a Sociological Theory of Religion*. Garden City, NY: Anchor Books, 1969.

Bergman, Jerry. "The Modern Religious Objection to Mandatory Flag Salute in America: A History and Evaluation," *Journal of Church and State* 39 (1997): 215–236.

Bertrand, J. Mark. "Bibliotheca, the ESV Reader's Bible, and the Future of Printed Bibles," *Bible Design Blog*, July 7, 2014, accessed July 14, 2016, http://www.bibledesignblog.com/2014/07/bibliotheca-esv-readers-bible-future-printed-bibles.html.

Bertrand, J. Mark. "Interview with Bibliotheca's Adam Lewis Greene: Part 2," *Bible Design Blog*. July 5, 2014, accessed July 15, 2016, http://www.bibledesignblog.com/2014/07/interview-bibliothecas-adam-lewis-greene-part-2.html.

Beyerlein, Kraig, Sarah A. Soule, and Nancy Martin, "Prayers, Protest, and Police: How Religion Influences Police Presence at Collective Action Events in the United States, 1960 to 1995," *American Sociological Review* 80, no. 6 (2015).

Bible on the Table. *Family Films*, 1951.

Bibliotheca Kickstarter website, June 27, 2014, accessed June 14, 2016, https://www.kickstarter.com/projects/530877925/bibliotheca/updates.

Bilger, Burkhard. "The Antichrist of East Dallas: God Doesn't Need Ole Anthony," *The New Yorker*, December 6, 2004, at www.WittenburgDoor.com, accessed March 1, 2005.

Binker, Mark. "Republicans decry harsh rhetoric at 'Moral Monday' events," *WRAL.com* September 17, 2013, accessed June 29, 2015, http://www.wral.com/republicans-decry-harsh-rhetoric-at-moral-monday-events/12896893/#p1AwQMjXhA32gwsW.99.

Binker, Mark, "Researchers Find 'Moral Monday' Crowd Mostly from North Carolina," *WRAL*, June 18, 2013, accessed March 9, 2016, http://www.wral.com/researchers-find-moral-monday-crowd-mostly-from-north-carolina/12562184/.

Bishop, Ronald. "That is Good to Think of These Days: The Campaign by Hearst Newspapers to Promote Addition of 'Under God' to the Pledge of Allegiance," *American Journalism* 24, no. 2 (2007): 81.

Bivins, Jason C. *Spirits Rejoice! Jazz and American Religion*. New York: Oxford University Press, 2015.

Black, Merle and Earl Black. *The Rise of Southern Republicans*. Cambridge, MA: Harvard University Press, 2003.

Blythe, Anne. "Moral Monday Rally Against HB2 Brings 11 Arrests," *News & Observer*, May 16, 2016, accessed January 5, 2017, http://www.newsobserver.com/news/politics-government/article77988752.html.

Bonhoeffer, Dietrich. *The Cost of Discipleship*. London: SCM Press, 1959.

Borden, Anne L. "Making Money, Saving Souls: Christian Bookstores and the Commodification of Christianity." In *Religion, Media, and the Marketplace*, edited by Lynn Schofield Clark. New Brunswick, NJ: Rutgers, 2007.

Bridger, Francis. "The Gospel and Popular Culture." Book review, *Implicit Religion* 13, no. 2 (December 2010): 218.

Brown, Robert McAfee, Ed. *The Essential Reinhold Niebuhr: Selected Essays and Addresses*. New Haven, CT: Yale University Press, 1986.

Browne, Ray B. "Popular Culture: Notes Toward a Definition," *Popular Culture and Curricula*. Bowling Green, OH: Bowling Green University Popular Press, 1970.

Brownlee, John. "Redesigning the Bible with Readability in Mind," *Fast Company*, July 17, 2014, accessed July 15, 2016, http://www.fastcodesign.com/3033067/redesigning-the-bible-with-readability-in-mind.

Buddenbaum, Judith M. "Religious Journalism," *History of the Mass Media in the United States*, edited by Margaret A. Blanchard. Chicago: Fitzroy Dearborn Publishers.

Buddenbaum, Judith M. and Debra L. Mason. *Readings on Religion as News*. Ames, IA: Iowa State University Press, 2000.

Buddenbaum, Judith M. and Daniel A. Stout. *Religion and Mass Media: Audiences and Adaptations*. Thousand Oaks, CA: Sage, 1996.

————. *Religion and Popular Culture: Studies on the Interaction of Worldviews*. Ames, IA: Iowa State University Press, 2001.

Buechner, Frederick. *Telling the Truth: The Gospel as Tragedy, Comedy & Fairy Tale*. New York: HarperCollins, 1977.

Burleigh, Nina. "God Bless America, Or Else," *Newsweek* (April 15, 2016): 32–41.

Butler, Donna and David F. Lloyd. "John Wycliffe: Setting the Stage for Reform." Vision website, *Religion and Spirituality*, Winter 2004. http://www.vision.org/visionmedia/biography-john-wycliffe/613.aspx.

The Cambridge History of the Bible: The West from the Reformation to the Present Day, edited by S. L. Greenslade. Cambridge, UK: Cambridge University Press, 1963.

Campbell, Colleen Carroll. "The Enduring Costs of John F. Kennedy's Compromise," *The Catholic Word Report*. San Francisco: Ignatius Press, February 2007.

Campbell, Heidi. *Digital Religion: Understanding Religious Practice in New Media Worlds*. London: Routledge, 2013.

Campbell, Heidi. *When Religion Meets New Media*. London: Routledge, 2010.

Carty, Thomas J. *A Catholic in the White House? Religion, Politics, and John F. Kennedy's Presidential Campaign*. New York: Palgrave Macmillan, 2004.

"The Catholic Way of Death & Burial," Catholic Cemeteries, Archdiocese of Washington website, accessed August 3, 2015, http://www.ccaw.org/wayofdeath_cremation.html.

Chaney, Lindsay and Michael Cieply. *The Hearsts: Family and Empire: The Later Years*. New York: Simon and Schuster, 1981.

Christensen, Rob, "N.C. Has New Diversity," *News & Observer*, July 1, 2015, 2A.

Christensen, Rob, "State GOP Rolls Back Era of Democratic Laws," *The Courier-Tribune*, June 18, 2013, accessed June 9, 2015, http://courier-tribune.com/sections/news/north-carolina/state-gop-rolls-back-era-democratic-laws.html.

Clark, Lynn Schofield. "Overview: The 'Protestantization' of Research into Media, Religion, and Culture," In *Practicing Religion in the Age of Media,* edited by Stewart M. Hoover and Lynn Schofield Clark. New York: Columbia University Press, 2002.

————. "Religion and Authority in a Remix Culture: How a Late Night TV Host Became an Authority on Religion." In *Religion, Media and Culture: A Reader*, edited by Gordon Lynch and Jolyon Mitchell with Anna Strhan. London: Routledge, 2012.

Cobb, Jerry. "Marketing 'The Passion of the Christ.'" *CNBC*, February 25, 2004, accessed July 30, 2015, http://www.nbcnews.com/id/4374411/ns/business-cnbc_tv/t/marketing-passion-christ/#.VbpsfXhNV6M.

"Colbert Catechism: Stephen Colbert Professes His Faith to Fr. James Martin." YouTube, *America Media*, March 2, 2015, accessed August 10, 2016, https://www.youtube.com/watch?v=o-zxn-YGUI4.

Colbert, Donald. *What Would Jesus Eat?* Grand Rapids, MI: Thomas Nelson, 2005.

Cone, James H. *A Black Theology of Liberation*. Philadelphia: J.B. Lippincott, 1970.

Cormier, Henri. *The Humor of Jesus*. New York: Alba House, 1977.

"The Court and its Procedures," U.S. Supreme Court website, accessed January 16, 2016, https://www.supremecourt.gov/about/procedures.aspx

Covington v. North Carolina. 161 (M.D.N.C. Aug. 11, 2016).

Crawford, Amy. "Anatomy of an Oath: How a PR Gimmick Became a Patriotic Vow," *Smithsonian Magazine*, September 2015, 9.

Cress, Daniel M. and David A. Snow, "Mobilization at the Margins: Resources, Benefactors, and the Viability of Homeless Social Movement Organizations," *American Sociological Review* 61, no. 6 (1996): 1089–1109.

Crosby, Donald. *God, Church, and Flag: Senator Joseph R. McCarthy and the Catholic Church 1950–1957*. Chapel Hill: UNC Press, 1978.

Curtis, Mary C., "Is North Carolina Moving Backward on Civil Rights?" S*he the People, Washington Post Blogs*, washingtonpost.com, October 3, 2013, accessed July 13, 2015.

Cusick, Michael J. "A Conversation with Eugene Peterson," *Mars Hill Review* 3, no. 3 (Fall 1995): 73–90. Accessed July 14, 2016, http://www.leaderu.com/marshill/mhr03/peter1.html.

Daniel, Lillian. "Spiritual But Not Religious? Please Stop Boring Me," *Huffington Post*, September 13, 2011, http://www.huffingtonpost.com/lillian-daniel/spiritual-but-not-religio_b_959216.html

————. *When "Spiritual But Not Religious" Is Not Enough: Seeing God in Surprising Places, Even the Church*. New York: Jericho Books, 2013.

Daniell, David. *The Bible in English: Its History and Influence.* New Haven, CT: Yale University Press, 2003.

Darden, Robert. Interview with author. Fort Worth, Texas, February 26, 1999.

—————. "Is 'Religious Humor' an Oxymoron?" Email interview by Todd Leopold, *CNN.com*, November 19, 2002.

—————. *On the 8th Day God Laughed.* North Richland Hills, TX: Bibal Press, 2000.

Davis, Joshua Clark. "The March on Washington, Moral Mondays, and the Media," *Huffington Post Blog*, August 27, 2013, updated October 27, 2013, accessed June 29, 2015, http://www.huffingtonpost.com/joshua-clark-davis/the-march-on-washington-m_b_3818222.html.

Deacy, Christopher. "Redemption," *The Routledge Companion to Religion and Film*, edited by John Lyden. London: Routledge, 2011, pbk.

Demerath III, N. Jay, "Cultural Victory and Organizational Defeat in the Paradoxical Decline of Liberal Protestantism," *Journal for the Scientific Study of Religion* 34, no. 4 (1995): 458–469.

Detweiler, Craig. "Christianity: The Subtle and the Spectacular." In *The Routledge Companion to Religion and Film*. Abingdon, UK: Routledge, 2011.

Dorrien, Gary. "Recovering the Black Social Gospel," *Harvard Divinity Bulletin*, Summer/Autumn 2015.

Drake, Tim. "Emilio Estevez and Martin Sheen Talk About 'The Way,'" *The National Catholic Register*, September 14, 2011, accessed September 29, 2015, http://www.ncregister.com/daily-news/martin-sheen-and-emilio-estevez-talk-about-the-way.

Ebert, Roger. "The Way," *Rogerebert.com*, October 5, 2011, accessed October 20, 2015.

Elk Grove Unified School Dist. v. Newdow, 542 US 1 (2004).

Ellis, Richard J. *To the Flag: The Unlikely History of the Pledge of Allegiance.* Lawrence: University Press of Kansas, 2005.

Engel v. Vitale, 370 U.S. 421 (1962).

Evans, G. R. *John Wyclif: Myth and Reality.* Downers Grove, IL: Intervarsity Press Academic, 2005.

Extreme Faith Bible: God's Word Knows No Bounds. CEV. New York: American Bible Society, 1995.

Fea, John. *The Bible Cause: A History of the American Bible Society.* New York: Oxford University Press, 2016.

Feiler, Bruce. *Walking the Bible: A Journey by Land through the Five Books of Moses.* New York: Harper Perennial, 2001.

Feinberg, Scott. "Bill Clinton Attends Premiere of 'The Way,' Cheers Film and Related Foundation," *Hollywood Reporter*, October 7, 2011, https://www.hollywoodreporter.com/race/bill-clinton-attends-premiere-way-245255.

Fellowship of Christian Athletes Coach's Devotional Bible: Daily Game Plans for Coaches, CSB. Nashville, TN: Holman Bible Publishers, 2006.

Feuer, Alan. "Hobby Lobby Agrees to Forfeit 5,500 Artifacts Smuggled Out of Iraq," *New York Times*, July 5, 2017, https://www.nytimes.com/2017/07/05/nyregion/hobby-lobby-artifacts-smuggle-iraq.html?_r=1.

FitzGerald, Frances. *The Evangelicals: The Struggle to Shape America.* New York: Simon & Schuster, 2017.

Flake, Carol. *Redemptorama: Culture, Politics, and the New Evangelicalism.* Garden City, NY: Doubleday, Anchor Press, 1984.

Ford, Adam. *Thy Kingdom Comics: Curiously Christian Drawings and Writings About Jesus, Tolerance, Abortion, Atheism, Homosexuality, Theology, and Lots of Other Stuff.* Canton, MI: Adam4d, LLC., 2016.

Ford, Thomas E., Julie A. Woodzicka, Shane R. Triplett, Annie O. Kochersberger, and Christopher J. Holden. "Not All Groups Are Equal: Differential Vulnerability of Social Groups to the Prejudice-Releasing Effects of Disparagement Humor," *Group Processes and Intergroup Relations* 17, no. 2, March 1, 2014, http://journals.sagepub.com/doi/abs/10.1177/1368430213502558.

Fore, William F. "The Church and Communication in the Technological Era," *The Christian Century*, September 24, 1986, 811.

Frank, John. "NC NAACP president, 16 other protestors arrested outside NC Senate," *News & Observer*, April 29, 2013, accessed June 9, 2015. http://beavercountyblue.org/2013/05/04/ naacp-president-arrested-at-nc-protest-of-medicaid-cuts/.

Frey, Carol. "The Quietly Positive Way," *News & Observer*, November 30, 2014, 19A.

Friedman, Hershey H. "Humor in the Hebrew Bible," *Humor: International Journal of Humor Research* 13, no. 3 (2000).

Frost, Michael, "Colin Kaepernick vs. Tim Tebow: A Tale Of Two Christians On Their Knees," *Washington Post*, September 24, 2017, https://www.washingtonpost.com/amphtml/ news/acts-of-faith/wp/2017/09/24/colin-kaepernick-vs-tim-tebow-a-tale-of-two-christian-ities-on-its-knees/.

Garfield, Simon. *Just My Type*. New York: Gotham Books, 2011.

Garrett, Greg. *The Gospel According to Hollywood*. Louisville, KY: Westminster John Knox Press, 2007.

Gates, David and Holly Morris, "Of Profits and Prophecies," *Newsweek,* December 27, 1982.

Gaustad, Edwin S. *A Documentary History of Religion in America Since 1865*, 2nd ed. Grand Rapids, MI: Eerdmans, 1993.

Gautney, Heather, "What is Occupy Wall Street? The History of Leaderless Movements," *Washington Post*, October 10, 2011, accessed July 10, 2015, http://www.washingtonpost. com/national/on-leadership/what-is-occupy-wall-street-the-history-of-leaderless-movements/2011/10/10/gIQAwkFjaL_story.html.

Geertz, Clifford. *The Interpretation of Cultures*. New York: Basic Books, 1977.

Genzlinger, Neil. "A Trek From Loss and Grief to a Life Given Greater Meaning," *New York Times*, October 6, 2011, http://www.nytimes.com/2011/10/07/movies/the-way-directed-by-emilio-estevez-review.html.

Gervais, Will M. and Maxine B. Najle, "How Many Atheists Are There?" *University of Kentucky Psychology*, PsyArXiv, May 31, 2017, https://psyarxiv.com/edzda/ DOI 10.17605/ OSF.IO/EDZDA.

Geybels, Hans. *Humour and Religion: Challenges and Ambiguities*. London: Bloomsbury, 2011.

Gilbert, Kathleen. "Catholic Actor Martin Sheen: 'The Church is not God' on Gay 'Marriage' Issue," *Life Site News*, April 3, 2012, accessed August 9, 2015, https:// www.lifesitenews.com/news/catholic-actor-martin-sheen-the-church-is-not-god-on-gay-marriage-issue, quoted in Phillips.

Gjelten, Tom. "Evangelical Pastors Gather To Learn Another Calling: Politics," *NPR*, July 10, 2015, accessed July 10, 2015, http://www.npr.org/2015/07/10/421684410/evangelical-pas-tors-gather-to-learn-another-calling-politics?utm_source=npr_newsletter& utm_medium=email&utm_content=20150710&utm_campaign=npr_email_a_friend& utm_term=storyshare.

Gledhill, Ruth. "Bear Grylls: My Christian Faith is My Backbone," *Christian Today* website, September 8, 2015, https://www.christiantoday.com/article/bear.grylls.my.christian.faith.is. my.backbone/64197.htm.

Gloege, Timothy. "#Itsnotus: Being Evangelical Means Never Having To Say You're Sorry," *Religion Dispatches*, January 3, 2018, http://religiondispatches.org/itsnotus-being-evangeli-cal-means-never-having-to-say-youre-sorry/.

Gomes, Peter J. *The Good Book: Reading the Bible with Mind and Heart.* New York: William Morrow and Company, Inc., 1996.

Good News for Modern Man: The New Testament in Today's English Version. TEV. New York: American Bible Society, 1971.

Goodstein, Laurie, "Religious Liberals Sat Out of Politics for 40 Years. Now They Want in the Game," *New York Times*, June 11, 2017, A22.

Goodwyn, Hannah. "Emilio Estevez and Martin Sheen on Faith and Filming *The Way*," *CBN.com*, n.d., accessed August 11, 2015, http://www.cbn.com/entertainment/screen/emi-lio-estevez-martin-sheen-faith-the-way-goodwyn.aspx.

Goolsby, Thom. "Moron Monday Shows Radical Left Just Doesn't Get It," *The Chatham Journal*, June 7, 2013, accessed June 26, 2015, http://www.chathamjournal.com/weekly/ opinion/myopinion/moron-monday-shows-radical-left-just-does-not-get-it-130607.shtml.

Gottfried, Jeffrey and Michael Barthel. "After Charlie Hebdo, Balancing Press Freedom and Respect for Religion: Majority Says Publishing Cartoons Was 'Okay,' But About Half of Non-Whites Say 'Not Okay.'" Pew Research Center, January 28, 2015.

Gotzon, Jenn. Telephone interview by author. February 11, 2016.

Greeley, Andrew M. *God in Popular Culture*. Chicago: The Thomas More Press, 1988.

The Green Bible. NRSV. New York: HarperCollins, 2008.

Green, Emma. "Franklin Graham Is the Evangelical Id," *The Atlantic*, May 21, 2017, https://www.theatlantic.com/politics/archive/2017/05/franklin-graham/527013/;

Greenberg, Brad A. "Colbert Quoting Jesus in Congressional Testimony," *The God Blog, The Jewish Journal*, September 27, 2010, accessed August 17, 2016, http://www.jewishjournal.com/thegodblog/item/colbert_quoting_jesus_in_congressional_testimony_20100926.

Greenwalt, Kyle. "Here's How Homeschooling is Changing America," *The Conversation*, September 11, 2016, http://theconversation.com/heres-how-homeschooling-is-changing-in-america-63175

Greydanus, Steven D. "Martin Sheen and Emilio Estevez Travel the Ancient Pilgrimage Route Together and Finish their Journey of Faith with a Flourish," *National Catholic Register*, October 7, 2011, accessed August 9, 2015, http://www.ncregister.com/daily-news/sdg-reviews-the-way.

Gritten, David. "*The Way*, Review," *The Telegraph*, May 12, 2011, accessed October 20, 2015, http://www.telegraph.co.uk/culture/film/filmreviews/8510077/The-Way-review.html.

Grylls, Edward Michael. "Glad This Was the Only Bear I Met in the Park," *The Sunday Times*, December 13, 2015, Accessed May 3, 2016, http://www.thesundaytimes.co.uk/sto/Magazine/article1640800.ece.

Guba, Egon G. and Yvonna S. Lincoln. "Paradigmatic Controversies, Contradictions, and Emerging Confluences." In *The Landscape of Qualitative Research: Theories and Issues* 2nd ed., edited by Norman K. Denzin and Yvonna S. Lincoln. Thousand Oaks, CA: Sage, 2003.

Hafiz, Yasmine. "'Bibliotheca' Bible Project Blows Up On Kickstarter With Chapterless Bible," *Huffington Post*, July 24, 2014, accessed July 15, 2016, http://www.huffingtonpost.com/2014/07/24/bibliotheca-bible_n_5615243.html?utm_hp_ref=tw.

Hart, David Bentley. *Atheist Delusions: The Christian Revolution and Its Fashionable Enemies*. Ann Arbor, MI: Sheridan Books, 2009.

————. *The New Testament: A Translation*. New Haven, CT: Yale University Press, 2017.

————. *The Story of Christianity: A History of 2,000 Years of the Christian Faith*. New York: Quercus, 2015.

HB 589, July 26, 2013, http://www.ncga.state.nc.us/Sessions/2013/Bills/House/PDF/H589v8.pdf.

Hendershot, Heather. *Shaking the World for Jesus: Media and Conservative Evangelical Culture*. Chicago: The University of Chicago Press, 2004.

Herberg, Will. *Protestant, Catholic, Jew*. Garden City, NY: Anchor Books, 1955, rpt. 1960.

Herbert, Steve. *Policing Space*. Minneapolis: University of Minnesota Press, 1996.

Hillman, Os. *Change Agent: Engaging Your Passion To Be the One Who Makes a Difference*. Lake Mary, FL: Charisma House, 2011.

Hirdes, Wendy, Robert Woods, and Diane M. Badzinski. "A Content Analysis of Jesus Merchandise," *Journal of Media and Religion* 8, no. 3 (2009).

Hitt, Jack. *Off the Road: A Modern-Day Walk Down the Pilgrim's Route into Spain*. New York: Simon & Schuster Paperbacks, 2005.

Hjarvard, Stig. "The Mediatization of Society: A Theory of Media as Agents of Social and Cultural Change," *Nordicom Review* 29, no. 2 (2008): 105.

Hoberman, Barry. "Translating the Bible," *The Atlantic*, February 1985, accessed July 13, 2016, http://www.theatlantic.com/past/docs/issues/85feb/transbib.htm.

Hollywood, Amy. "Spiritual but Not Religious," *Harvard Divinity Bulletin* (Winter/Spring 2010): 19–20.

The Holy Bible Containing the Old and New Testaments, Revised Standard Version. New York: Thomas Nelson & Sons, 1952.

Hoover, Stewart M. and Lynn Schofield Clark. *Practicing Religion in the Age of the Media: Explorations in Media, Religion, and Culture*. New York: Columbia University Press, 2002.

Hoover, Stewart M. *Religion in the Media Age*. London: Routledge, 2006.

————. *Religion in the News: Faith and Journalism in American Public Discourse*. Thousand Oaks, CA: Sage, 1998.

Horton, Ciera. "*The Record* Meets with Acclaimed Academic Mark Noll," *The Wheaton Record*, December 28, 2017, http://www.wheatonrecord.com/news/record-meets-acclaimed-academic-mark-noll/.

Huntsberry, Will. "The Rev. William Barber Leads a New Era of Progressive Politics in North Carolina," *Indy Week*, July 24, 2013, accessed July 13, 2015, http://www.indyweek.com/indyweek/the-rev-william-barber-leads-a-new-era-of-progressive-politics-in-north-carolina/Content?oid=3681510.

Hyers, Conrad. *And God Created Laughter: The Bible As Divine Comedy*. Atlanta, GA: John Knox Press, 1987.

Inspired By The Bible Experience: The Complete Bible. Zondervan, 2008, MP3 CD.

Irwin, W.A. *An Introduction to the Revised Standard Version of the Old Testament*. New York: Thomas Nelson & Sons, 1952.

"It's Time to Laugh at the Marxist Monday Crowd!" The Voter Integrity Project of North Carolina, July 8, 2013, accessed March 9, 2016, http://voterintegrityproject.com/its-time-to-laugh/#more-673.

Jarvis, Craig, Colin Campbell, and Lynn Bonner. "HB2 Off The Books As Gov. Roy Cooper Signs Compromise Into Law," *News & Observer*, March 30, 2017, http://www.newsobserver.com/news/politics-government/politics-columns-blogs/under-the-dome/article141716579.html; Text of HB 142: http://media2.newsobserver.com/content/media/2017/3/29/H142v1-HB2changes.pdf.

Jemielity, Thomas. *Satire and the Hebrew Prophets*. Louisville, KY: Westminster John Knox Press, 1992.

Jenkins, Jack. "Nobody is Laughing at the Religious Left in 2017," *Think Progress*, December 13, 2017, https://thinkprogress.org/2017-is-the-year-trump-and-the-religious-right-made-the-religious-left-unavoidable-3e89528104b6/.

Jenkins, Jerry B. *Twenty-Five Years of Sterling Rewards in God's Service: The Story of the Christian Booksellers Association*. Nashville, TN: Thomas Nelson, 1974.

Johnston, Robert K. "Theological Approaches," *The Routledge Companion to Religion and Film*, edited by John Lyden. London: Routledge, 2011, pbk.

Jones, Jeffrey Owen. "The Man Who Wrote the Pledge of Allegiance," *Smithsonian Magazine*, November 2003, Smithsonian.com.

Jones, Robert P. *The End of White Christian America*. New York: Simon & Schuster, 2016.

————. "The Great Trump Hope," *New York Times*, July 11, 2016, A23.

Jordan, Clarence. *The Cotton Patch Gospel*. Macon, GA: Smyth & Helwys Publishing, 2004.

"Journalism, Satire or Just Laughs? 'The Daily Show with Jon Stewart,' Examined," Pew Research Center. May 8, 2008, accessed August 19, 2016, http://www.journalism.org/2008/05/08/journalism-satire-or-just-laughs-the-daily-show-with-jon-stewart-examined/.

Kardish, Chris. "NC Protests Split on Bible's Message to Help Poor," Associated Press, *Yahoo! News*, June 12, 2013, accessed June 30, 2015, http://news.yahoo.com/nc-protests-split-bibles-message-help-poor-161430742.html.

King, Jr., Martin Luther. "Letter from Birmingham Jail," *Why We Can't Wait*. New York: Mentor, 1964.

Knoll, Mark A. *The Scandal of the Evangelical Mind*. Grand Rapids, MI: Eerdmans, 1994.

Kohlenberger III, John R. "The Message Bible," *Christian Research Journal* 17, no.1 (1994). Accessed July 14, 2016, http://www.equip.org/article/the-message-bible/.

Kohn, Eric. "Emilio Estevez's 'The Way' Is A Lot Better Than It Looks," *IndieWire*, October 7, 2011, http://www.indiewire.com/2011/10/review-emilio-estevezs-the-way-is-a-lot-better-than-it-looks-51769/.

Kruse, Kevin M. *One Nation Under God: How Corporate America Invented Christian America*. New York: Basic Books, 2015.

Labaton, Stephen. "Constitution Based in Christian Principles, McCain Says," *New York Times*, September 29, 2007, http://www.nytimes.com/2007/09/29/us/politics/29cnd-mccain.html.

Lachman, Samantha. "Moral Monday Returns With Public Opinion, If Not The North Carolina Legislature, On Its Side," January 28, 2015, accessed January 16, 2017, http://www.huffingtonpost.com/2015/01/28/moral-monday-north-carolina_n_6564352.html.

Lacour, Greg. "Opinion: The N.C. 'Bathroom Bill,' In Sum," *Charlotte Magazine*, March 23, 2016, accessed January 5, 2017, http://www.charlottemagazine.com/Charlotte-Magazine/March-2016/Opinion-the-NC-Bathroom-Bill-In-Sum/.

Lawton, Kim. "Church Movies Keep Coming," *Christianity Today*, April 20, 2011, accessed August 11, 2015. http://www.christianitytoday.com/ct/2011/aprilweb-only/churchmovies-coming.html.

————. "Fed Up with Hollywood, Churches Make their Own Films," *The Christian Century*, March 11, 2011, accessed January 6, 2017, https://www.christiancentury.org/article/2011-03/fed-hollywood-churches-make-their-own-films.

Lenski, Gerhard. *The Religious Factor: A Sociologist's Inquiry*, Rev. ed. New York: Anchor Books, 1963.

Leonard, William. Telephone interview with author. March 10, 1999.

Leslie, Laura. "Cancellations over HB2 Make Headlines but Barely Dent NC Economy," *WRAL.com*, September 21, 2016, accessed January 5, 2017, http://www.wral.com/cancellations-over-hb2-make-headlines-but-barely-dent-nc-economy/16035660/.

Leuchtenburg, William E. *The Perils of Prosperity, 1914–1932*. Chicago: University of Chicago Press, 1958.

Lindlof, Thomas R. "Interpretive Community: An Approach to Media and Religion," *Journal of Media and Religion* 1, no. 1 (2002): 62.

Lindvall, Terry. *God Mocks: A History of Religious Satire from the Hebrew Prophets to Stephen Colbert*. New York: New York University Press, 2015.

Lindvall, Terry and Andrew Quicke. *Celluloid Sermons: The Emergence of the Christian Film Industry, 1930–1986*. New York: New York University Press, 2011.

Lipka, Michael. "Key Findings About American Catholics," Pew Research Center, September 2, 2015, http://www.pewresearch.org/fact-tank/2015/09/02/key-findings-about-american-catholics/.

Lobdell, William. "Onward Christian Soldier: Ole Anthony Has Devoted His Life—and His Ministry—to Exposing Corrupt Televangelists. But Not Everyone Agrees He's Doing God's Work," *Los Angeles Times*, December 8, 2002.

Lofton, Kathryn. *Oprah: The Gospel of an Icon*. Berkeley, CA: University of California Press, 2011.

Long, Charles H. "Popular Religion," *The Encyclopedia of Religion*, edited by Mircea Eliade, et al. New York: Macmillan, 1987.

Lyden, John C. and Eric Michael Mazur, eds. *The Routledge Companion to Religion and Popular Culture*. London: Routledge, 2015.

Lynch, Gordon. *Understanding Theology and Popular Culture*. Oxford, UK: Blackwell, 2005.

Lyons, Martyn. *Books: A Living History*. Los Angeles: The J. Paul Getty Museum, 2011.

Mahan, Jeffrey H. *Media, Religion, and Culture: An Introduction*. New York: Routledge, 2014.

Malone, Peter. "The Roman Catholic Church and Cinema (1967 to the Present)." In *The Routledge Companion to Religion and Film*, edited by John Lyden. London: Routledge, 2011, pbk.

Manning, Peter K. *Policing Contingencies*. Chicago: University of Chicago Press, 2003.

"Many Americans Mix Multiple Faiths," Pew Research Center, December 9, 2009, http://www.pewforum.org/2009/12/09/many-americans-mix-multiple-faiths/

Masci, David. "5 Questions About the Contraception Mandate," Pew Research Center, August 5, 2015, http://www.pewresearch.org/fact-tank/2015/08/05/contraception-mandate-questions/.

May, John. *New Images of Religious Film*. Kansas City, KS: Sheed & Ward, 1997.

Mazza, Ed. "Jerry Falwell Jr. Calls Donald Trump The 'Dream President' For Evangelicals," *Huffington Post*, April 30, 2017, http://www.huffingtonpost.com/entry/jerry-falwell-jr-dream-president-trump_us_5906950fe4b05c3976807a08;

McCarthy, John P. "The State of the Catholic Church in Contemporary Ireland," *The Catholic World Report*, March 16, 2017, http://www.catholicworldreport.com/Item/5500/the_state_of_the_catholic_church_in_contemporary_ireland.aspx.

McCombs, Brady and Rachel Zoll. "Episcopal Church Elects Michael Curry, Its First Black Presiding Bishop," *Associated Press, Huffington Post Religion*, June 27, 2015, accessed June 29, 2015. http://www.huffingtonpost.com/2015/06/27/episcopal-church-michael-curry-black_n_7679264.html.

McCombs, Maxwell E. and Donald L. Shaw. "The Agenda-Setting Function of Mass Media," *Public Opinion Quarterly* 36, no. 2 (January 1972): 176–187.

McDannell, Colleen. *Material Christianity: Religion and Popular Culture in America*. New Haven, CT: Yale University Press, 1995.

McKenna, John. "Bear Grylls Prayed with Barack Obama . . . and Gave Me My New Year's Resolution," *Catholic Charismatic Renewal*, n.d., http://www.ccr.org.uk/articles/bear-grylls-prayed-with-barack-obamaand-gave-me-my-new-years-resolution/#sthash.7bqJXhWO.dpuf.

Meacham, Jon. *American Gospel: God, the Founding Fathers, and the Making of a Nation*. New York: Random House, 2006.

Meacham, John. "A Nation of Christians Is Not a Christian Nation," *New York Times*, October 7, 2007, http://www.nytimes.com/2007/10/07/opinion/07meacham.html.

"Media and the Movement: Journalism, Civil Rights, and Black Power in the American South," accessed June 29, 2015, http://mediaandthemovement.unc.edu.

Medved, Michael. "Reconciliation Should Follow Mel's Malibu Meltdown," *USA Today*, August 2, 2006, accessed August 5, 2015, http://usatoday30.usatoday.com/news/opinion/editorials/2006-08-02-gibson-edit_x.htm.

Meredith, George, Henri Bergson, and Wylie Sypher. *Comedy*. Garden City, NY: Doubleday Anchor Books, 1956.

Merritt, Jonathan. "Jerry Falwell Jr's Troubling Remarks on Guns," *The Atlantic*, December 6, 2015, https://www.theatlantic.com/politics/archive/2015/12/jerry-falwell-jrs-troubling-remarks-on-guns/419019/.

Metzger, Bruce M. *The Bible in Translation: Ancient and English Versions*. Ada, MI: Baker Academic, 2001.

Miller, Daniel. "Selling Stardom: A Christian Pathway to Hollywood," *Los Angeles Times*, December 30, 2015, accessed June 8, 2016, http://www.latimes.com/entertainment/la-et-ct-selling-stardom-christian-talent-seminar-20151230-story.html.

Miller, Emily McFarlan. "Survey: White Evangelicals Say US No Longer a Christian Nation," *Religion News Service*, June 23, 2016, accessed January 18, 2017, http://religionnews.com/2016/06/23/survey-evangelicals-say-us-no-longer-a-christian-nation/.

Miller, Eric C. "The Origin Story of the Evangelical Mindset: A Conversation with Frances FitzGerald," *Religion Dispatches*, May 31, 2017, http://religiondispatches.org/the-origin-story-of-the-evangelical-mindset-a-conversation-with-frances-fitzgerald/?utm_source=Religion+Dispatches+Newsletter&utm_campaign=dd7c19e658-RD_Weekly_Newsletter&utm_medium=email&utm_term=0_742d86f519-dd7c19e658–84559769.

Minersville School District v. Gobitis. 310 U.S. 586 (1940).

Miracles from Heaven. Directed by Patricia Riggen. Columbia Pictures, 2016.

Moore, R. Laurence. *Selling God: American Religion in the Marketplace of Culture*. New York: Oxford University Press, 1994.

Moore, R. Laurence. *Touchdown Jesus: The Mixing of Sacred and Secular in American History*. Louisville, KY: Westminster John Knox Press, 2003.

Morefield, Kenneth R. "The Way: A Poignant Drama about the Journey Toward Healing, Wholeness, and the Help We Find Along The Way," *Christianity Today*, October 7, 2011, accessed October 20, 2015, http://www.christianitytoday.com/ct/2011/octoberweb-only/way.html.

Moreton, Bethany. *To Serve God and Wal-Mart: The Making of Christian Free Enterprise.* Cambridge, MA: Harvard University Press, 2009.

Morgan, K. "Asheville Supporters Demonstrate in Favor of HB2 Bathroom Bill," *The Tribune Papers*, April 6, 2016, accessed January 5, 2017, http://www.thetribunepapers.com/2016/04/06/asheville-supporters-demonstrate-in-favor-of-hb2-bathroom-bill/.

Morreall, John. *Comedy, Tragedy, and Religion.* Albany, NY: State University of New York Press, 1999.

"The Movement of #MeToo," *The Atlantic*, October 16, 2017, https://www.theatlantic.com/entertainment/archive/2017/10/the-movement-of-metoo/542979/.

Myers, Kenneth A. *All God's Children and Blue Suede Shoes: Christians & Popular Culture.* Westchester, IL: Crossway Books, 1989.

Myers v. Loudoun County Public Schools. No. 03–1364 (August 10, 2005).

Newdow v. U.S. Congress. 292 F.3d 597 (9th Cir. 2002)

Newdow v. U.S. Congress. 328 F.3d 466 (9th Cir. 2002).

The New Revised Standard Version Bible. Copyright © 1989, Division of Christian Education of the National Council of Churches of Christ in the U.S.A., New York.

"News Coverage of the 2016 Presidential Primaries: Horse Race Reporting Has Consequences," Shorenstein Center on Media, Politics, and Public Policy, July 11, 2016, https://shorensteincenter.org/news-coverage-2016-presidential-primaries/.

Nicholson, Adam. *God's Secretaries: The Making of the King James Bible.* New York: Perennial, 2004.

"'Nones' on the Rise," Pew Research Center, Religion and Public Life, October 9, 2012. http://www.pewforum.org/2012/10/09/nones-on-the-rise/.

Nord, David Paul. "The Evangelical Origins Of Mass Media in America, 1815–1835," *Journalism Monographs* 88 (1984): 1–30.

Norris, Kathleen. "Prayer as a Mystery," *Amazing Grace: A Vocabulary of Faith.* New York: Riverhead Books, 1998.

"North Carolina's Moral Monday Movement," *Progresivo* blog, accessed July 5, 2015, https://progresivoblog.wordpress.com/north-carolinas-moral-monday-movement/.

"North Carolinians on Perdue, Rivalries," Public Policy Polling, June 15, 2012, accessed June 26, 2015, http://www.publicpolicypolling.com/main/2012/06/north-carolinians-on-perdue-rivalries.html.

Obergefell v. Hodges, 576 U. S. ____ (2015).

Ofulue, Nneka Ifeoma, "President Clinton and the White House Prayer Breakfast," *Journal of Communication and Religion* 25, no. 1 (March 2002): 49–63.

O'Hare, Kate. "'The Passion of the Christ,' Mel Gibson and Hugging the Cactus," *Catholic-Vote*, March 11, 2014, accessed August 3, 2015, https://www.catholicvote.org/the-passion-of-the-christ-mel-gibson-and-hugging-the-cactus/.

The One Year Bible. NIV. Carol Stream, IL: Tyndale House Publishers, Inc., 2004.

Operation Worship Holy Bible. 2nd Edition. NLT. Carol Stream, IL: Tyndale House Publishers, Inc., 2008.

Orsi, Robert A. *Between Heaven and Earth: The Religious Worlds People Make and the Scholars Who Study Them.* Princeton, NJ: Princeton University Press, 2006.

"Our Mission & Vision," AMTC website. https://www.shine.us.

Pacatte, Rose. *Martin Sheen: Pilgrim on The Way.* Collegeville, MN: Liturgical Press, 2015.

———. "On 'The Way' with Martin Sheen, *National Catholic Reporter*, October 7, 2011, accessed September 8, 2015, http://ncronline.org/news/spirituality/way-martin-sheen.

———. "The Way," *AmericanCatholic.org*, n.d., http://www.americancatholic.org/Entertainment/entertainment.aspx?id=13045.

Palmer, Earl F. *The Humor of Jesus: Sources of Laughter in the Bible.* Vancouver, BC: Regent College Publishing, 2001.

Parker, James. "The New New Testament," *The Atlantic* (January/February 2018): 32.

Parramore, Lynn Stuart, "The Man Behind Moral Mondays," *The American Prospect*, June 17, 2013, accessed June 26, 2015, http://prospect.org/article/man-behind-moral-mondays.

Peters, Shawn Francis. *Judging Jehovah's Witnesses: Religious Persecution and the Dawn of the Rights Revolution.* Lawrence, KS: University Press of Kansas, 2000.

Peterson, Eugene H. *The Message: The New Testament in Contemporary Language*. Colorado Springs, CO: NavPress Publishing Group, 2003.

Phillips, Francis. "Martin Sheen is a Better Actor than Theologian: The Actor, Like So Many Liberal Catholics, Seems to have Lost His Way," *Catholic Herald*, April 9, 2012, accessed August 9, 2015, http://www.catholicherald.co.uk/commentandblogs/2012/04/09/martin-sheen-is-a-better-actor-than-theologian/#.VcGD7XnMDoE.mailto.

"Poor People's Campaign," *King Encyclopedia*, The Martin Luther King, Jr. Research and Education Institute, Stanford University, http://kingencyclopedia.stanford.edu/encyclopedia/encyclopedia/enc_poor_peoples_campaign/.

Pope Francis, "Evangelii Gaudium: Apostolic Exhortation on the Proclamation of the Gospel in Today's World" (November 24, 2013), accessed June 29, 2015. http://w2.vatican.va/content/francesco/en/apost_exhortations/documents/papa-francesco_esortazione-ap_20131124_evangelii-gaudium.html.

The Poverty and Justice Bible: Catholic Edition. NRSV. Swindon, UK: Bible Society Resources Ltd., 2013.

Primiano, Leonard Norman. "Oprah, Geraldo, Barbara, and Things That Go Bump in the Night: Negotiating the Supernatural on American Television." In *God in the Details: American Religion in Popular Culture*, eds. Eric Michael Mazur and Kate McCarthy. New York: Routledge, 2001.

Public Law 396, 83rd Cong., 2nd sess., Cong. Rec. 249. Joint resolution to codify and emphasize existing rules and customs pertaining to the display and use of the flag of the United States of America, amendment of sec. 7, H.J.R. 243 (1954) (enacted).

"Public Policy in North Carolina," Ballotpedia, accessed March 15, 2016, https://ballotpedia.org/Redistricting_in_North_Carolina.

Putnam, Robert and David E. Campbell. *American Grace*. New York: Simon & Schuster, 2010.

Raboteau, Albert J. *American Prophets: Seven Religious Radicals & Their Struggle for Social and Political Justice*. Princeton, NJ: Princeton University Press, 2016.

Radosh, Daniel. "The Good Book Business: Why Publishers Love the Bible," *The New Yorker*, December 18, 2006.

Ramis, Sergi. *Camino de Santiago*. Trans. Peter Barraclough. London: Aurum Press, 2014.

Rapoport, Abby. "Moral Mondays and the South's New Liberal Gospel," *The American Prospect*, July 29, 2013, accessed June 9, 2015, http://prospect.org/article/moral-mondays-and-south's-new-liberal-gospel.

Rawls, Kristin. "The Liberal Protest that Would Shock the Right: Moral Monday," *Salon*, July 23, 2013, accessed June 30, 2015, http://www.salon.com/2013/07/23/moral_mondays_the_liberal_protest_that_would_shock_the_right/.

Reader, Ian. *Pilgrimage: A Very Short Introduction*. Oxford, UK: Oxford University Press, 2015.

Religion and Popular Culture, eds. Daniel A. Stout and Judith M. Buddenbaum. Ames, IA: Iowa State University Press, 2001.

"Religion and the Unaffiliated," Pew Research Center, October 9, 2012, accessed August 3, 2015, http://www.pewforum.org/2012/10/09/nones-on-the-rise-religion/.

"The Religious Affiliation of U.S. Immigrants: Majority Christian, Rising Share of Other Faiths," Pew Research Center, May 17, 2013, http://www.pewforum.org/2013/05/17/the-religious-affiliation-of-us-immigrants/.

"Religious Landscape Study," Pew Forum, 2017. http://www.pewforum.org/religious-landscape-study/.

"Repairers of the Breach," website accessed June 14, 2017, http://www.breachrepairers.org.

Roark, David. "The Way," *Paste*, October 10, 2011, http://www.pastemagazine.com/articles/2011/10/the-way.html.

Rockett, Will. "Crossing Wire Borders: Concepts of Popular Culture in Film & Television Studies." In *Continuities in Popular Culture: The Present in the Past & The Past in the Present and Future*, edited by Ray B. Browne and Ronald J. Ambrosetti. Bowling Green, KY: Bowling Green State University Popular Press, 1993.

Romanowski, William D. *Eyes Wide Open: Looking for God in Popular Culture*. Grand Rapids, MI: Brazos Press, 2001.

Roof, Wade Clark. *A Generation of Seekers: The Spiritual Journeys of the Baby Boom Genera-tion*. San Francisco: Harper San Francisco, 1993.

———. *Spiritual Marketplace: Baby Boomers and the Remaking of American Religion*. Princeton, NJ: Princeton University Press, 1999.

Rosenberg, David. *A Literary Bible*. Berkeley, CA: Counterpoint, 2009.

Ross, Janell. "The Rev. William Barber Dropped the Mic," *Washington Post*, July 28, 2016, accessed January 5, 2017, https://www.washingtonpost.com/news/the-fix/wp/2016/07/28/the-rev-william-barber-dropped-the-mic/?utm_term=.187a19ad21e7.

Rutledge, John. Interview with author. Dallas, Texas, February 27, 1999.

Sandstrom, Aleksandra. "Faith on the Hill," Pew Research Center, January 3, 2017. http://www.pewforum.org/2017/01/03/faith-on-the-hill-115/.

Santiago de Compostela, Spain, Organization of World Heritage Cities, http://www.ovpm.org/en/spain/santiago_de_compostela.

Schlanger, Zoe. "North Carolina's Moral Mondays are Back with Massive March," *Newsweek*, February 10, 2014, http://www.newsweek.com/n-carolina-progressive-group-kicks-2014-massive-march-228585.

Schrader, Paul. *Transcendental Style in Film*. Boston: Da Capo Press. Reprint Edition, 1988.

Schrader, Paul. Interview. Transcendental Style in Film. TIFF Originals. YouTube, April 26, 2017, https://www.youtube.com/watch?v=mFcCs8c2n6I.

Schuck, Peter H. "The Pledge on the Edge," *American Lawyer* 24, September 2002.

Schultze, Quentin J. *Christianity and the Mass Media in America: Toward a Democratic Accommodation*. East Lansing, MI: Michigan State University Press, 2003.

Schultze, Quentin J. "Touched by Angels and Demons: Religion's Love-Hate Relationship with Popular Culture." In *Religion and Popular Culture*, edited by Daniel A. Stout and Judith M. Buddenbaum. Ames, IA: Iowa State University Press, 2001.

Schulz, Charles M. *I Take My Religion Seriously*. Anderson, IN: Warner Press, 1972.

Schulz, Winfried. "Reconstructing Mediatization as an Analytical Concept," *European Journal of Communication* 19, no. 1 (2004): 87–101.

Semonche, John E. "The Flag as Religious Symbol Versus the First Amendment as Holy Writ: A Battle Among the Faithful," *North Carolina Humanities* 1, no. 1 (Fall 1992).

Severson, Kim. "G.O.P.'s Full Control in Long-Moderate North Carolina May Leave Lasting Stamp," *New York Times*, December 11, 2012, accessed January 16, 2017, http://www.nytimes.com/2012/12/12/us/politics/gop-to-take-control-in-long-moderate-north-car-olina.html.

The Shack. Directed by Stuart Hazeldine. Summit Entertainment, 2017.

She, Adam. Email interview by author. February 18, 2016.

Sheen, Martin, and Emilio Estevez with Hope Edelman. *Along the Way: The Journey of a Father and Son*. New York: Free Press, 2012.

Shimron, Yonat. "NAACP's William Barber Emerges as Leader of Moral Monday Protests," June 24, 2013, accessed July 13, 2015, http://www.religionnews.com/2013/06/24/naacps-william-barber-emerges-as-leader-of-moral-monday-protests/.

Ship of Fools. Website, http://www.ship-of-fools.com.

Siedlecka, Jo. "A Father and Son Project: Martin Sheen, Emilio Estevez Discuss *The Way*," *Independent Catholic News*, February 24, 2011, https://www.indcatholicnews.com/news.php?viewStory=17731.

Sikkema, Debbie. "Is AMTC a Scam?" *YourYoungActor.com*, September 10, 2009, accessed June 9, 2016, http://www.youryoungactor.com/2009/09/10/is-amtc-a-scam/.

Silk, Mark. "The Civil Religion Goes to War," *Religion in the News* 4, no. 5 (Fall 2001).

Silk, Mark. *Unsecular Media: Making News of Religion in America*. Urbana, IL: University of Illinois Press, 1995.

Skelton, Red. "Commentary on the Pledge of Allegiance," transcript, American Rhetoric On-line Speech Bank, http://www.americanrhetoric.com/speeches/redskeltonpledgeofalle-giance.htm.

Skelton, Red. "The Pledge of Allegiance As Reviewed By Red Skelton On The Red Skelton Hour, Jan. 14, 1969," *CBS Television Network*. 7-inch vinyl record, Columbia 4-44798, February 25, 1969.

Sloan, David. *Media and Religion in American History*. Northport, AL: Vision Press, 2000.

Sloyan, Gerard S. "Some Thoughts on Bible Translations," *Worship 75*, no. 3, May 2001.

Smietana, Bob. "Latest Survey: Most Evangelicals Are Not Voting Trump," *Christianity Today*, October 14, 2016, http://www.christianitytoday.com/news/2016/october/most-evangel-icals-not-voting-trump-beliefs-identity-lifeway.html.

Smith, Christian. "On 'Moralistic Therapeutic Deism' as U.S. Teenagers' Actual, Tacit, De-Facto Religious Faith," *Religion and Youth* (2010): 41–46.

Smith, Gregory A. and Jessica Martinez. "How the Faithful Voted: A Preliminary 2016 Analysis," Pew Research Center, November 9, 2016, http://www.pewresearch.org/fact-tank/2016/11/09/how-the-faithful-voted-a-preliminary-2016-analysis/.

Smith, Warren Cole. "Going Public," *World* 29, no. 1 (January 11, 2014), accessed August 8, 2016, https://world.wng.org/2013/12/going_public.

Souppouris, Aaron. "The Bible's a Mess, but a Designer is Fixing It," *The Verge*, July 22, 2014, accessed July 15, 2016, http://www.theverge.com/2014/7/22/5922855/bibliotheca-bible-kickstarter-campaign-adam-greene-interview.

Stancato, Abbie. "The Truth, the Myths, and the Facts About Actors, Models & Talent for Christ (AMTC)," *Rockin' God's House* (March 31, 2013), accessed June 8, 2016, http://rockingodshouse.com/the-truth-the-myths-and-the-facts-about-actors-models-talent-for-christ-amtc/.

Stern, Marlow. "Sheen Family's Epic Journey," *The Daily Beast* (October 6, 2011), accessed September 9, 2015, http://www.thedailybeast.com/articles/2011/10/06/the-way-martin-sheen-emilio-estevez-on-charlie-sheen-occupy-wall-street.html.

The Story. Grand Rapids, MI: Zondervan, 2011.

Stout, Daniel A. "Beyond Culture Wars: An Introduction to the Study of Religion and Popular Culture," *Religion and Popular Culture: Studies on the Interaction of Worldviews*. Ames, IA: Iowa State University Press, 2001.

Stout, Harry. *The New England Soul: Preaching and Religious Culture in Colonial New England* Oxford: Oxford University Press, 1986.

Strickler, Laura. "Senate Panel Probes 6 Top Televangelists," *CBS News*, November 6, 2007, accessed August 16, 2016, http://www.cbsnews.com/news/senate-panel-probes-6-top-tele-vangelists/.

Sturgis, Sue. "A Year In, Moral Monday Movement Plans New Protests, More Organizing," *The Institute for Southern Studies* (April 29, 2014), accessed March 10, 2016. http://www.southernstudies.org/2014/04/a-year-in-moral-monday-movement-plans-new-pro-tests.html.

Sturgis, Sue. "Tea Party Group Responds to NC Protest Movement with 'Marxist Mondays' Song," *The Institute for Southern Studies* (July 8, 2013), accessed March 9, 2016, http://www.southernstudies.org/2013/07/tea-party-group-responds-to-nc-protest-movement-wi.html.

Syn, Roger. "Copyright God: Enforcement of Copyright in the Bible and Religious Works," *Regent University Law Review* 14, no. 1 (2001–2002).

"Taking a Christian Path to Hollywood," *AJC.com* (January 8, 2016), accessed May 25, 2016, http://www.ajc.com/news/lifestyles/religion/taking-a-christian-path-to-hollywood/npymx/.

Tarrow, Sidney. "Modular Collective Action and the Rise of the Social Movement: Why the French Revolution Was Not Enough," *Politics and Society* 21 (1993): 69–90.

"Tax Guide for Churches and Religious Organizations," Internal Revenue Service, IRS.gov (Revised August 2015), accessed August 17, 2016, https://www.irs.gov/pub/irs-pdf/p1828.pdf.

"T.C. Stallings: An AMTC Story," Actors Models & Talent for Christ, 2014 Annual Report.

Teen Study Bible. NIV. Grand Rapids, MI: Zondervan, 2008.

Thiede, Werner. *Das Verheissende Lachen: Humor in Theologischer Perspektive*. Goettingen, Germany: Vandenhoek & Ruprecht, 1966.

Thomason, Andy. "3 Things You Should Know About Jerry Falwell Jr.," *The Chronicle of Higher Education*, January 31, 2017, http://www.chronicle.com/article/3-Things-You-Should-Know-About/239065;

Tilley, Charles. *Popular Contention in Great Britain, 1758–1834.* Cambridge, MA: Harvard University Press, 1995.

Tippett, Krista. "Spirituality of Imagination," *On Being,* December 17, 2015, https://onbeing.org/programs/martin-sheen-spirituality-of-imagination/8257/.

Tomlinson, Tommy. "Reverend Resistance," *Esquire* (April 25, 2017), http://www.esquire.com/news-politics/a54573/reverend-william-barber-progressive-christianity/.

"Top 100 Pro-Catholic Movies," *National Catholic Register,* accessed July 30, 2015, http://www.ncregister.com/info/top_100_pro_catholic_movies/.

ToshaSilver.com, accessed December 20, 2017, https://toshasilver.com.

Trinity Foundation. Website, http://trinityfi.org.

Trueblood, Elton. *The Humor of Christ.* New York: Harper & Row, 1964.

Unbridled. Directed by John David Ware. Moving Visions Entertainment, 2017.

Underwood, Doug. *From Yahweh to Yahoo! The Religious Roots of the Secular Press.* Urbana, IL: University of Illinois Press, 2002.

van der Horst, Charles. "Civil Disobedience and Physicians—Protesting the Blockade of Medicaid," *The New England Journal of Medicine* 371, no. 21 (November 20, 2014): 1958–1959.

Vanvalin, Eric. "Marc Maron: Peeling Back the Layers of Comedy's Most Spiritually Minded Skeptic," *Relevant,* (May–June 2015): 62.

Voas, David, and Mark Chaves. "Is the United States a Counterexample to the Secularization Thesis?," *American Journal of Sociology* 121, no. 5 (March 2016): 1517–1556.

Vock, Daniel C. "With Hundreds of Arrests, North Carolina Preacher Ups the Stakes in Showdown With Republicans," The Pew Charitable Trusts (July 9, 2013), accessed June 30, 2015, http://www.twincities.com/politics-national/?third_party=north-carolina-preacher-raises-the-stakes-in-legislative-showdown.

Voskuil, Dennis N. "Reaching Out: Mainline Protestantism and the Media." In *Between the Times: The Travail of the Protestant Establishment in America 1900–1960,* edited by William R. Hutchinson. Cambridge, MA: Cambridge University Press, 1989.

Wallace-Wells, Benjamin. "The Limits of Protest in Charlotte," *The New Yorker,* September 23, 2016, https://www.newyorker.com/news/benjamin-wallace-wells/the-limits-of-protest-in-charlotte.

Walters, David. "Why Audiences Flock to Faith-Based Films," *Bloomberg Businessweek,* March 30, 2016, https://www.bloomberg.com/news/articles/2016-03-30/why-audiences-flock-to-faith-based-films.

War Room. Directed by Alex Kendrick. TriStar Pictures, 2015.

Warshow, Robert. *The Immediate Experience: Movies, Comics, Theatre and Other Aspects of Popular Culture.* Garden City, NY: Anchor Books, 1964.

Waters, David, Holly Meyer, and Amy McRary. "How Trump is Highlighting Divisions Among Southern Baptists," *USA Today Network,* June 10, 2017, https://www.usatoday.com/story/news/nation-now/2017/06/10/how-trump-highlighting-divisions-among-southern-baptists/386329001/?utm_source=Pew+Research+Center&utm_campaign=2b3cd8e83b-EMAIL_CAMPAIGN_2017_06_13&utm_medium=email&utm_term=0_3e953b9b70-2b3cd8e83b-399903629.

The Way. Directed by Emilio Estevez. ARC Entertainment, 2010.

West Virginia State Board of Education et al. v. Barnette et al. 319 U.S. 624, 1943.

Whisenant, David. "Former NC Gov. Mike Easley enters felony plea agreement," *WBTV.com,* December 23, 2010, accessed June 26, 2015, http://www.wbtv.com/story/13554761/former-governor-easley-expected-to-pla.

Whitt, Chrystal. "Actors, Models, and Talent for Christ?" December 22, 2010, accessed June 9, 2010. https://slaughteringthesheep.wordpress.com/2010/12/22/actors-models-and-talent-for-christ/.

Wilkinson, Alissa. "Why Christian Artists Don't Want to be 'Christian Artists,'" *IndieWire,* November 11, 2013. http://www.indiewire.com/2013/11/why-christian-artists-dont-want-to-be-christian-artists-127322/.

"William Barber II, Legendary Civil Rights Leader, Steps Down From NC NAACP Leadership Role," *The Root*, May 11, 2017, http://www.theroot.com/rev-william-barber-ii-legendary-civil-rights-leader-1795137036.

Wilson-Hartgrove, Jonathan. Telephone interview with author, January 12, 2017.

Winston, Diane. "'There is Sin and Evil in the World': Reagan, Trump, and the News Media," *Los Angeles Review of Books*, September 30, 2016, https://lareviewofbooks.org/article/sin-evil-world-reagan-trump-news-media/#.

Wise, Steven M. *An American Trilogy: Death, Slavery, & Dominion on the Banks of the Cape Fear River*. Philadelphia: Da Capo Press, 2009.

Woodward, Kenneth L. *Getting Religion: Faith, Culture, and Politics from the Age of Eisenhower to the Era of Obama*. New York: Convergent Books, 2016.

Woodward, Kenneth L. and David Gates, "How the Bible Made America," *Newsweek*, December 27, 1982.

Wynn, Mike and Chris Kenning. "Timeline of a Kentucky Clerk's Gay-Marriage Defiance," (Louisville, KY) *Courier-Journal*, September 3, 2015, accessed March 15, 2016, http://www.usatoday.com/story/news/politics/2015/09/03/ky-clerk-gay-marriage-timeline/71670068/

Yeoman, Barry. "The End of Moderation?" *Duke Magazine*, November 14, 2013, accessed July 13, 2015, http://dukemagazine.duke.edu/article/end-moderation.

Young, Michael P. "Confessional Protest: The Religious Birth of U.S. National Social Movements," *American Sociological Review* 67, October 2002.

Zarembo, Alan. "With Pope Francis, Catholicism has a New Brand—an Everyman's Pope," *Los Angeles Times*, September 28, 2015, accessed September 29, 2015, http://www.latimes.com/nation/la-na-pope-visit-assess-20150928-story.html.

Zauzmer, Julie and Michelle Boorstein. "Evangelicals Fear Muslims; Atheists Fear Christians: New Poll Show[s] How Americans Mistrust One Another," *Washington Post*, September 7, 2017, https://www.washingtonpost.com/news/acts-of-faith/wp/2017/09/07/evangelicals-fear-muslims-atheists-fear-christians-how-americans-mistrust-each-other/?utm_term=.c3e632c6408c. For original poll data, see Baylor Religion Survey, September 2017, https://www.baylor.edu/baylorreligionsurvey/doc.php/292546.pdf.

Zucchino, David. "N.C. Legislature Draws Protests; Clergy, Others Welcome Arrest at 'Moral Monday' Demonstrations Against GOP Policies," *Los Angeles Times*, June 13, 2013, accessed July 13, 2015, A14.

Zylstra, Sarah Eekhoff. "Introducing the Bible! Now with Less!" *Christianity Today*, July 25, 2014, accessed July 15, 2016, http://www.christianitytoday.com/ct/2014/july-web-only/bibliotheca-readers-bible.html.

Index

About the Author

Anthony Hatcher is associate professor of communications at Elon University, where he created a religion and media class in 2003 and has taught it every year since. Hatcher also teaches journalism, writing, and communications research. He is coeditor of a media textbook, *Mass Communication in the Global Age*. A former newspaper reporter, Hatcher worked at the *Winston-Salem Journal*, the *Thomasville Times*, the (Jacksonville, NC) *Daily News*, and was a Faith & Values correspondent for *The Charlotte Observer* and the (Durham, NC) *Herald-Sun*. He earned his BA in English and MEd in speech communications at the University of North Carolina at Greensboro, and his PhD in mass communications research at the University of North Carolina at Chapel Hill.